Mastering PowerCLI

Master PowerCLI to automate all aspects of VMware environments

Sajal Debnath

[PACKT] PUBLISHING

enterprise
professional expertise distilled

BIRMINGHAM - MUMBAI

Mastering PowerCLI

First published: October 2015

Production reference: 1131015

Published by Packt Publishing Ltd.
Livery Place
35 Livery Street
Birmingham B3 2PB, UK.

ISBN 978-1-78528-685-8

www.packtpub.com

Credits

Author
Sajal Debnath

Reviewers
Amit Agarwal
Jason Gaudreau
Kyle Ruddy
Brian Wuchner

Commissioning Editor
Ashwin Nair

Acquisition Editor
Kevin Colaco

Content Development Editor
Arun Nadar

Technical Editors
Saurabh Malhotra
Mitali Somaiya

Copy Editors
Roshni Banerjee
Rashmi Sawant

Project Coordinator
Nikhil Nair

Proofreader
Safis Editing

Indexer
Priya Sane

Production Coordinator
Shantanu N. Zagade

Cover Work
Shantanu N. Zagade

Foreword

In the last nine years that I've been with VMware India, I have had the privilege of hearing from several CIOs and heads of infrastructure that VMware is an industry innovator and leader, creating amazing products that are disrupting and evolving businesses and the personal lives of many of us. I consider myself extremely lucky to be leading one of the best technical teams in the IT infrastructure space today.

When one of these technical brains in my team, Sajal Debnath, who comes from a small village in West Bengal, told me that he is writing a book on *Mastering PowerCLI*, the first question I asked him was "Why scripting?". I asked this question because scripting is a popular and great way to make up for a product's shortcomings or missing features, and it can be a real-time saver for administrators. But, to the best of my knowledge, every new release of VMware's products tends to have several features or enhancements that have been requested by our customers.

Sajal told me that the reason he has been successful in meeting the demanding needs of his customers is his expertise in scripting. PowerCLI is a very powerful command-line tool that allows you to automate all aspects of vSphere management, including network, storage, VM, guest OS, and more. There are unimaginable things that you can do in a VMware environment, and it is impossible for any product to include all of these features. I've heard from some of my customers too that tasks, such as automatically controlling the growth of snapshots, reporting on thin provisioned disks and their over allocation, and so on, are areas where scripting comes to their rescue.

The second question that I asked was, why the need to write a book on this topic when there was plenty of documentation available in VMware itself and the PowerCLI community? This is when I realized that most of the documentation available is predominantly written for software developers who are from a scripting background. Having known Sajal for the last four years, I know that he is very much customer-driven. Having interacted with several system administrators in his career, he wanted to write this book purely for VMware administrators who spend every single day managing a virtual environment.

This book starts off with an introduction to PowerShell and PowerCLI. If you are new to it, then it walks you through the process of how to configure and manage hosts, VMs, and networks and storage in detail. But the chapters that I liked the most were *Chapter 8, Managing vSphere Security, SRM, vCloud Air, and vROps* and *Chapter 10, Using REST APIs. Chapter 8, Managing vSphere Security, SRM, vCloud Air, and vROps,* goes beyond normal vSphere management and deals with one of the most ignored aspects today, security. I have seen very few customers in India who give importance to security hardening of their VMware environments. With the increasing threat perception these days, it is absolutely imperative for you to pay attention to how you can keep environments secure. *Chapter 10, Using REST APIs,* discusses how you can use REST APIs to manage other VMware products beyond vSphere that may not have native PowerCLI cmdlets. Toward the end, it also gives you some sample scripts that you can use straightaway in your environments.

I believe that VMware is a very exciting technology company that allows us to deeply influence and rapidly evolve technology and business for our customers, and I want to thank Sajal for writing this book.

If this isn't enough to spark interest in reading further, I don't know what is! I highly recommend that you read this book.

B. S. Nagarajan
Senior Director, Systems Engineering, VMware India

About the Author

Sajal Debnath is a highly certified Cloud computing technocrat with more than 12 years of experience in virtualized data center design, Cloud computing, and BC/DR solutions. He is an EMCISA, VCAP-DCD/DCA, VCAP-CID/CIA, RHCE 4/5/6, RHCVA, Openstack, and ITIL certified person. He is presently associated with VMware Software India Pvt. Ltd. as a senior system engineer. Previously, he worked with France Telecom, Hewlett Packard, and many more in multiple roles. He is involved in prestigious Indian government projects, such as National Cloud, Digital Locker, and so on.

Acknowledgment

First and foremost, I would like to thank my wife, Ananya, for standing beside me throughout my career and writing this book. She has been my inspiration and motivation for continuing to improve my knowledge and move my career forward. During the writing of this book, I spent nearly every waking hour of my day either in the office or writing this book, including weekends. Whenever I felt low and lacked enthusiasm, she guided me through this phase; sometimes with me complaining and kicking. She had to bear with the grumpy me. She is my rock and I would like to dedicate this book to her.

I would like to thank my parents for giving me the freedom to choose my career path and always believing in me, and my elder brother, Ujjwal, for being my best friend.

Thank you Niladri Chakraborty for being there and supporting me. Without you, I wouldn't be where I am today.

Thank you Kalyan Guin and Suprovat Sinha for supporting me through thick and thin.

I must thank B S Nagarajan for supporting me throughout my career in VMware and helping whenever I required it. I hope that someday I can be more like you.

I want to specially thank Naresh Purohit for always believing in me and being the guiding star for me both professionally and personally.

Prashant Dwivedi, without you this book wouldn't have happened in the first place. Thank you for encouraging me so much.

I want to thank Alan Renouf for taking time out of his busy schedule, supporting me, and providing me with access to the required materials and information.

Thank you Brian Graf, Massimo Re Ferre, Dr. Tobias Weltner, and Jason Wasser for providing me with the material and support for this book.

I would like to thank my reviewers, especially Kyle Ruddy, Jason Gaudreau, Amit Agarwal, and Brian Wuchner, for not only reviewing the book but also for giving me suggestions to improve it as well. I would also like to thank Arun Nadar for following up with me and arranging everything for me.

Last but not least, thank you Packt Publishing for giving me the opportunity to write this book. I'd also like to thank every team member who contributed to this project, the external reviewers, and the other guys whom I didn't meet — your contributions were invaluable and this book wouldn't be what it is without you.

About the Reviewers

Amit Agarwal is a senior software engineer working with Great Software Laboratory (GS Lab), Pune, in its Cloud and infrastructure practice.

He is a VMware Certified Professional 5 – Data Center Virtualization, VMware Certified Associate – Data Center Virtualization, and a VMware Certified Associate – Cloud. He is also a frequent contributor to the VMware Technology Network (VMTN).

He has more than three years' experience working with PowerShell and VMware vSphere PowerCLI for building test automation frameworks and scripts, contributing to quality assurance for complex virtualization and network security products.

GS Lab is a product development partner for software product companies with customers that include world-leading technology vendors, as well as start-ups. Our customer engagements span the entire product journey right from prototyping, to development, support, DevOps, and professional services.

I would like to thank my colleagues from Calsoft — Amar, Archana, and Madhumita — for their help during my learning process. I also would like to thank my family and friends for their continuous support.

Jason Gaudreau has over 24 years of industry experience. He is currently working as a senior product marketing engineer at VMware, a leading information technology provider of enterprise application solutions.

He focuses on virtualization solutions and aligning infrastructure technologies to meet strategic business objectives. He has been concentrating on data center virtualization, desktop virtualization, and building internal private clouds in a variety of technical roles the past 10 years and more. He has been an active blogger on virtualization since 2012 at www.jasongaudreau.com and can be found on Twitter at @JAGaudreau. He is honored to have been designated as a vExpert by VMware in 2013-2015 and an EMC Elect in 2014.

Before VMware, he was an IT architect for AdvizeX Technologies and in IT leadership at Unum Group, where he helped to develop the organization's IT strategy.

When not talking shop, he enjoys spending time with his wife, Christine, and his two kids, Dylan and Tyler.

Kyle Ruddy is a senior technical consultant. He has over 10 years of experience in the IT field. He has obtained multiple certifications, including VCAP-DCD and DCA, held the VCP since Version 3, GCWN (GIAC Certified Windows Security Administrator), and MCITP: SA, MCSE, among others. He has also been a VMware vExpert since 2012, a Cisco Champion since 2014, and a leader for the Indy VMUG since 2011.

You can contact him on LinkedIn at www.linkedin.com/in/kmruddy, Twitter at @kmruddy, or through his blog at www.thatcouldbeaproblem.com.

Brian Wuchner is a deputy IT director of a government agency. He has over 15 years of industry experience in infrastructure automation, directory services, server hosting, storage, and data center virtualization. He holds the EMC proven professional cloud architect and VMware VCP5-DCV certifications. He was awarded the VMware vExpert title from VMware in 2011-2015. He can be contacted on LinkedIn at http://www.linkedin.com/in/bwuch, Twitter at @bwuch, or through his blog at http://enterpriseadmins.org.

www.PacktPub.com

Support files, eBooks, discount offers, and more

For support files and downloads related to your book, please visit www.PacktPub.com.

Did you know that Packt offers eBook versions of every book published, with PDF and ePub files available? You can upgrade to the eBook version at www.PacktPub.com and as a print book customer, you are entitled to a discount on the eBook copy. Get in touch with us at service@packtpub.com for more details.

At www.PacktPub.com, you can also read a collection of free technical articles, sign up for a range of free newsletters and receive exclusive discounts and offers on Packt books and eBooks.

https://www2.packtpub.com/books/subscription/packtlib

Do you need instant solutions to your IT questions? PacktLib is Packt's online digital book library. Here, you can search, access, and read Packt's entire library of books.

Why subscribe?

- Fully searchable across every book published by Packt
- Copy and paste, print, and bookmark content
- On demand and accessible via a web browser

Free access for Packt account holders

If you have an account with Packt at www.PacktPub.com, you can use this to access PacktLib today and view 9 entirely free books. Simply use your login credentials for immediate access.

Instant updates on new Packt books

Get notified! Find out when new books are published by following @PacktEnterprise on Twitter or the *Packt Enterprise* Facebook page.

Table of Contents

Preface

If you are a system administrator who manages a considerable-sized environment, then I do not need to elaborate on the importance of scripting to you. Scripting was and always will be one of the most important arsenals in a system administrator's weaponry. With the term scripting, till very recently typically bash or other such shell scripts used to come to mind and more advanced ones, such as Perl, PHP, or Ruby. I love this scripting language for the sheer beauty and power that it presents. If you are coming from a *NIX environment, PowerShell will completely change your perception about scripting. If you are managing a vSphere environment, then besides vRealize Orchestrator, PowerCLI is the most powerful tool available to help you automate the different aspects of a vSphere environment. Probably, if I need to get something done really quickly, I will still rely on PowerCLI scripting.

In all my years of experience as a working professional and before that as a student and teacher, I have seen primarily two methods of explanation: the first approach, and the most widely used one, is to take an example problem and solve it while explaining the solution to the student. This way, the student learns how to solve a particular type of problem. The second approach is the one in which a teacher explains the basic logic and principles of a solution behind the problem, and then asks the students to solve the problem all by themselves. As a student, I always found myself struggling with the first approach. Though the first approach was easier to understand, it tends to limit my knowledge to solving only similar problems. Because of the lack of the understanding of the underlying logic, faced with a new problem, I could not solve it most of the time. This happened especially in mathematical problems. It was like showing me a program written in C to implement Dijkstra's algorithm and explaining how this program was written. Knowing this, will I be able to implement any other algorithm in C or utilize Dijkstra's algorithm for my advantage? Probably not. Instead, if someone teaches me the different aspects of C language and how to write programs using C, then I can utilize this knowledge to write any programs.

You may disagree or agree with me, but I always preferred the second approach as it worked for me and gave me a better understanding and hold on the topic.

So, throughout this book, I tried to explain all the building blocks of advanced PowerShell and PowerCLI scripting and then provided examples to showcase what I am trying to say. I tried this approach with the hope that it will give you a better understanding and clarity of the underlying constructs so that you can build on top of this.

What this book covers

Chapter 1, PowerShell and PowerCLI Refresher, refreshes the basics of PowerShell and introduces you to concepts that are necessary to develop, run, and test PowerShell scripts using PowerCLI cmdlets.

Chapter 2, Reusable Advanced Functions and Scripts, covers how to create reusable advanced functions and scripts. Advanced functions can be used like cmdlets in PowerShell and give much more power over normal functions.

Chapter 3, Deploying vSphere Hosts, covers how to automatically deploy and configure ESXi hosts using different tools, such as Image Builder, Auto Deploy, and Host Profiles.

Chapter 4, Managing Networks, discusses how to configure and manage vSphere networking through standard and distributed switches using PowerCLI.

Chapter 5, Managing Storage, discusses how to create and manage storage in a vSphere environment, including SAN, NAS, iSCSI, and VSAN.

Chapter 6, Managing Clusters and Other Constructs, covers how to manage logical constructs in a vCenter environment, including but not limited to HA and DRS clusters.

Chapter 7, Managing Virtual Machines, covers how to configure the different aspects of virtual machines and guest operating systems using PowerCLI.

Chapter 8, Managing vSphere Security, SRM, vCloud Air, and vROps, covers security hardening and patching vSphere environments along with other VMware solutions, such as SRM, vCloud Air, and vRealize Operations Manager.

Chapter 9, Managing the vSphere API, discusses how to use the vSphere API in PowerCLI and how we can manage advanced aspects of a vSphere environment using APIs.

Chapter 10, Using REST APIs, discusses Representational state transfer (REST) APIs and how PowerCLI can be used to manage the VMware vRealize Automation environment using REST APIs.

Chapter 11, Creating Windows GUI, discusses how to create a Windows graphical user interface (GUI) using PowerShell and other tools.

Chapter 12, Best Practices and Sample Scripts, describes PowerShell scripting best practices. This chapter also covers two sample scripts, one to get a security report and another to find the capacity of a vSphere environment.

What you need for this book

To test the examples provided in Chapters 1 to 7 and to practice further, you need to have access to a vSphere environment with vCenter and ESXi servers. For *Chapter 8, Managing vSphere Security, SRM, vCloud Air, and vROps*, you need to have access to the vCloud Air and vRealize Operations Manager environment. For *Chapter 10, Using REST APIs*, you need to have access to the vRealize Automation environment. I have used the following versions of different software to write this book:

- PowerShell Version 5.0.10532.0
- For most part PowerCLI 6.0 R1, and for *Chapter 8, Managing vSphere Security, SRM, vCloud Air, and vROps* PowerCLI 6.0 R2
- ESXi 6.0
- vCenter 6.0
- vRealize Automation 6.2
- vRealize Operations 6.2

If you do not have access to physical server-grade systems, you can build your test setup in a lab environment as well. For most of the book, I used a Whitebox desktop with 32 GB RAM in it. To build a vSphere environment, I have used VMware Workstation Version 12 and nested VMs for ESXi hosts. For vRealize Operations Manager, SRM, and vCloud Air, I had to rely on traditional resources.

So, before you start reading the chapters, I suggest that you get ready to build a vSphere lab. Also, as the chapters progress, we will build the lab step by step because different chapters cover different areas of a vSphere environment, starting from the ground up.

Who this book is for

This book is aimed at anyone who has a working knowledge of PowerShell and PowerCLI and who wants to script a vSphere environment like a pro with PowerCLI and PowerShell. This book is written from a system admin's perspective, so you do not need to be a development wizard. You just need to know the basics of programming and programming logic so that you can utilize the knowledge gained in this book to your advantage.

Conventions

In this book, you will find a number of styles of text that distinguish between different kinds of information. Here are some examples of these styles, and an explanation of their meaning.

Code words in text, database table names, folder names, filenames, file extensions, pathnames, dummy URLs, user input, and Twitter handles are shown as follows: "I strongly suggest that you type Get-Help in PowerShell and read the output."

A block of code is set as follows:

```
Switch (value) {
Pattern 1 {Script Block}
Pattern 2 {Script Block}
Pattern n {Script Block}
Default   {Script Block}
}
```

When we wish to draw your attention to a particular part of a code block, the relevant lines or items are set in bold:

```
{
  "firstName": "Sajal",
  "lastName": "Debnath",
  "isWorking": true,
  "age": 35,
  "address": {
    "streetAddress": "2435 A.B.C Road",
    "city": "New Delhi",
    "state": "Karnataka",
    "postalCode": "123456"
  },
  "contactNumbers": [
    {
      "type": "home",
```

```
      "number": "1234567897"
    },
    {
      "type": "office",
      "number": "123456789876"
    }
  ],
  "children": [],
  "spouse": null
}
```

Any command-line input or output is written as follows:

```
PS C:\> Connect-CIServer -Server <server name> -User <user name>-Password
<Password>
```

New terms and **important words** are shown in bold. Words that you see on the screen, in menus or dialog boxes for example, appear in the text like this: "To unblock it, right-click on the file, and select **Properties**. From the **Properties** menu, select **unblock**."

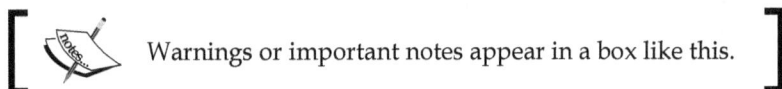

> Warnings or important notes appear in a box like this.

> Tips and tricks appear like this.

Reader feedback

Feedback from our readers is always welcome. Let us know what you think about this book—what you liked or may have disliked. Reader feedback is important for us to develop titles that you really get the most out of.

To send us general feedback, simply send an e-mail to feedback@packtpub.com, and mention the book title via the subject of your message.

If there is a topic that you have expertise in and you are interested in either writing or contributing to a book, see our author guide on www.packtpub.com/authors.

Customer support

Now that you are the proud owner of a Packt book, we have a number of things to help you to get the most from your purchase.

Downloading the example code

You can download the example code files for all Packt books you have purchased from your account at http://www.packtpub.com. If you purchased this book elsewhere, you can visit http://www.packtpub.com/support and register to have the files e-mailed directly to you.

Errata

Although we have taken every care to ensure the accuracy of our content, mistakes do happen. If you find a mistake in one of our books—maybe a mistake in the text or the code—we would be grateful if you would report this to us. By doing so, you can save other readers from frustration and help us improve subsequent versions of this book. If you find any errata, please report them by visiting http://www.packtpub.com/submit-errata, selecting your book, clicking on the **errata submission form** link, and entering the details of your errata. Once your errata are verified, your submission will be accepted and the errata will be uploaded on our website, or added to any list of existing errata, under the Errata section of that title. Any existing errata can be viewed by selecting your title from http://www.packtpub.com/support.

Piracy

Piracy of copyright material on the Internet is an ongoing problem across all media. At Packt, we take the protection of our copyright and licenses very seriously. If you come across any illegal copies of our works, in any form, on the Internet, please provide us with the location address or website name immediately so that we can pursue a remedy.

Please contact us at copyright@packtpub.com with a link to the suspected pirated material.

We appreciate your help in protecting our authors, and our ability to bring you valuable content.

Questions

You can contact us at questions@packtpub.com if you are having a problem with any aspect of the book, and we will do our best to address it.

1
PowerShell and PowerCLI Refresher

Well, you have taken up this book that means you already know about PowerShell and PowerCLI and in all probability use it in your day to day routine and now you want to learn more in-depths about them. You want to master the art of writing production-grade scripts for your environment or for others, and in the process, master the mysteries of this technology.

In all my years of experience, I have seen that the difference between a normal technical person and the coveted one is the advanced knowledge. To become a master of your technology, you need to know the background of the technology, how it works, how it behaves, and so on. Any person working with a tool knows how to run the tool, knowing the logic behind the tool, knowing how the tool exactly works at the back-end makes you different, it makes you the master of the tool. So, if you want to master PowerCLI, then you need to expand your horizons beyond the normal cmdlets, and you need to go deeper and get to know the intricacies of PowerShell because it is based on it.

My work experience varies widely, but it has all been related to the data center environment. In all my years of work, my programming has been related to writing scripts for automating daily tasks in the data center environment or writing small tools for the DC environment. At the time of learning advanced topics of PowerShell and PowerCLI, most of the books that I read were written more from a developer's perspective, making them 'developer-ish' in nature (sounds familiar?). I also had to look into many different books to find different topics; there was not a single place where I could get all the topics (which covers both PowerShell and PowerCLI), which covered the advanced topics.

This book tries to cover all or most of the advanced topics of PowerShell and PowerCLI to enable you to master the subject and become a master scripter/tool maker, but at the same time, this book is written from the perspective of a system admin. To achieve this, I would try to avoid the developer jargons and replace them with normal, simple examples. Note that this is a 'mastering PowerCLI' book, not a mastering PowerShell book, so the examples given in this book are from the PowerCLI perspective. You can say that I am looking at PowerShell through the eyes of PowerCLI, and we will cover those topics of PowerShell that will enable us to write production-grade scripts for managing VMware environments.

In this chapter, we will cover the following topics:

- The essence of PowerShell and PowerCLI
- Programming constructs and ways in which they are implemented in PowerShell
- Automation through PowerShell scripts
- How to run scripts from Command Prompt and as scheduled tasks
- Using GitHub
- Testing your scripts using Pester
- How to connect to a vCenter environment and other VMware environments using PowerCLI cmdlets

The essence of PowerShell and PowerCLI

In the following sections, we are going to cover a brief background of PowerShell and PowerCLI and the latest changes in both of them. First, I am going to talk about PowerShell and then PowerCLI.

The history of scripting

The need for computers came into existence for two purposes: the first purpose was to do number crunching fast and accurately, and the second and most important purpose was to automate tasks. In this age of cloud computing, automation is the most used word and one of the basic characteristics of cloud. From the beginning of the data center age, system administrators started automating their daily repetitive tasks so that they would not have to do the same tedious tasks again and again. Also, the purpose of automation was to avoid human errors that may creep in while writing long instructions or repetitive commands.

Now, the question that comes to mind is how can we automate? There are so many ways in which we can automate a task (ask any developer). For a general system administrator, who is not a developer, there are some basic weapons from which they can choose. But the most basic and widely used method for any system administrator is to use Shell scripts. For any operating system, a Shell is the interface through which you can interact with the operating system. Traditionally, we have used **Shell scripts** to automate mundane work of daily life and tasks that do not require very extensive programming. Unix and Linux operating systems provide many Shells, such as Bash Shell, C Shell, KORN Shell, and so on. For the Windows environment, we have command.com (in MS-DOS-based installations) and cmd.exe (in Windows NT-based installations). Before we start talking about more advanced ones, let's take a look at scripting and its history.

In general, a scripting language is a high-level programming language that is interpreted by another program at runtime rather than being compiled by the computer's processor as other programming languages are. The first interactive shells were developed in the 1960s and these used Shell Scripts that controlled the running of computer programs in a computer program, the shell. It started with **Job Control Language** (JCL), moving to Unix shells, REXX, Perl, Tcl, Visual Basic, Python, JavaScript, and so on. For more details, refer to https://en.wikipedia.org/wiki/Scripting_language.

PowerShell

Traditional shell commands and scripts are best suited for command-line-based tasks or console-based environments, but with the advent of more GUI-based servers and operating systems, there is a greater need for a tool that can work with the more sophisticated GUI environment. This particular requirement has become more prominent for the Windows environment since Windows shifted its core from MS-DOS implementations to the NT-based core. Also, traditionally, Windows provided batch scripts in terms of basic scripting functionality, which was not enough for its GUI-based environment.

To solve the situation and comply with the updated environment, Microsoft came up with a novel solution in the form of PowerShell. It is more of a natural progression of the traditional shell in the advanced operating system environment. It is the one of the best and most powerful shell environments I have worked with. Now, more and more serious development is going on in this tool. Today, this has become so important and mainstream that all the major virtualized environments support their general operations being automated through this environment.

The major difference between the traditional Shell and PowerShell is that traditional Shells are inherently text-based; that is, they work on texts (inputs/outputs), but PowerShell works inherently on objects. So, PowerShell is far more modern and powerful than other Shells. Since it also supports and works on objects rather than texts, let's perform tasks, which were not possible with the earlier Shell Scripts.

Windows PowerShell supports running four types of commands:

- Cmdlets that are native commands in PowerShell (basically, .NET programs designed to interact with PowerShell)
- PowerShell functions
- PowerShell scripts
- Other standalone executable programs

At the time of writing this book, the latest stable version of PowerShell is 4.0 and Microsoft released a preview version of PowerShell 5.0 (Windows Management Framework 5.0 Preview November 2014). A few of the new features in this preview version are as follows:

- The most important addition from the programming perspective is the added support for classes. Like any other object-oriented programming language, you can now use typical keywords, such as `Classes`, `Enum`, and so on.
- A new `ConvertFrom-String` cmdlet has been added that extracts and parses the structured objects from the content of text strings.
- A new `Microsoft.PowerShell.Archive` module has been added that will allow you to work on the ZIP files from the command line.
- A new OneGet module has been added that will allow you to discover and install software packages from the Internet.

> For details of a list of the enhancements, you can check the documentation from Microsoft at `https://technet.microsoft.com/en-us/library/hh857339.aspx`.

PowerCLI

VMware PowerCLI is a tool from VMware that is used to automate and manage vSphere, vCloud Director, vCloud Air, and Site Recovery Manager environments. It is based on PowerShell and provides modules and snap-ins of cmdlets for PowerShell.

Since it is based on PowerShell, it provides all the benefits of PowerShell scripting, along with the capability to manage and automate the entire VMware environment. It also provides C# and PowerShell interfaces to VMware vSphere, vCloud, and vCenter Site Recovery Manager APIs.

Generally, PowerCLI has the following features:

- It is aimed toward system administrators.
- It is installed on a Windows machine (client or server) as PowerShell snap-ins and modules.
- It is supported at a low level (1:1 mappings of API) and high level (API abstracted) cmdlets.
- No licenses are required to use it. It comes free.

At the time of writing of this book, VMware released PowerCLI 6.0 R1. The major new features of this release, among others, are as follows:

- PowerCLI 6.0 R1 is backward compatible with vSphere 5.0 and the versions are up to 6.0.
- Now, in this version, support for vCloud Air has been added. We can now manage the vCloud Air environment from the same single console.
- User guides and 'getting started' PDFs are included as part of the PowerCLI installation.
- PowerShell V3 and V4 are supported.
- The VSAN support has been added.
- The vCloud Suite SDK access has been added.
- IO Filter Management can be done.
- Hardware Version 11 management has been added.

Traditionally, PowerCLI provided two different components: One for managing the vSphere environment and another for the vCloud Director environment. With this release, there is no separate module for tenants. Now, a single installation package is provided, and at the time of installation, you have the option to install both the components (vSphere PowerCLI and vCloud PowerCLI) and only vSphere PowerCLI (vCloud PowerCLI is an optional component).

Earlier, PowerCLI had two main snap-ins to provide major functionalities, namely, `VMware.VimAutomation.Core` and `VMware.VimAutomation.Cloud`. These two will provide the core cmdlets to manage the vSphere environment and vCloud Director environment. In this release, to keep up with the best practices of PowerShell, most of the cmdlets are available as "modules" instead of "snap-ins". So, now in order to use the cmdlets, you need to import the modules into your script or into the Shell. For example, run the following code:

```
Import-Module 'C:\Program Files(x86)\VMware\Infrastructure\vSphere
PowerCLI\Modules\VMware.VimAutomation.Cloud'
```

This code will import the module into the current running scope and these cmdlets will be available for you to use.

Another big change, especially if you are working with both the vCloud Director and vSphere environment is the `RelatedObject` parameter of vSphere PowerCLI cmdlets. With this, now you can directly retrieve vSphere inventory objects from cloud resources. This interoperability between the vSphere PowerCLI and vCloud Director PowerCLI components makes life easier for system admins. Since any VM created in vCloud Director will have an UUID attached to the name of their respective VMs in the vCenter server, so extra steps are necessary to correlate a VM in the vCenter environment to its equivalent vApp—VM in vCloud Director. With this parameter, these extra steps are no longer required.

The vSphere PowerCLI package

Here is a list of snap-ins and modules that are part of the vSphere PowerCLI package:

Module/Snap-in	Type	Details of the module/snap-in
VMware.VimAutomation.Core	Snap-in/Module	This provides cmdlets for the automated administration of the vSphere environment
VMware.VimAutomation.Vds	Module	This provides cmdlets for managing vSphere distributed switches and distributed port groups
VMware.VimAutomation.Cis.Core	Module	This provides cmdlets for managing the vCloud Suite SDK servers
VMware.VimAutomation.Storage	Module	This provides cmdlets for managing the vSphere policy-based storage

Module/Snap-in	Type	Details of the module/snap-in
`VMware.VimAutomation.HA`	Module	This provides one cmdlet for managing the High Availability functionality
`VMware.VimAutomation.License`	Snap-in	This provides the `Get- LicenseDataManager` cmdlet for managing VMware license components
`VMware.ImageBuilder`	Snap-in	This provides cmdlets for managing depots, image profiles, and VIBs
`VMware.DeployAutomation`	Snap-in	This provides cmdlets that provide an interface for VMware to auto-deploy for provisioning physical hosts to the ESXi software

The vCloud PowerCLI package

Here is a list of modules available in the vCloud PowerCLI package. Note that all the components in the vCloud package are available as "modules", so there are no snap-ins in this package:

Module/Snap-in	Type	Details of the module/snap-in
`VMware.VimAutomation.Cloud`	Module	This provides cmdlets for automating vCloud Director features
`VMware.VimAutomation.PCloud`	Module	This provides cmdlets for automating vCloud Air features

Implementing programming constructs in PowerShell

Since this is a book on mastering PowerCLI, I will assume that you already know the basics of the language. For example, how variables are declared in PowerShell and various restrictions on them. So, in this section, I am going to provide a short refresher on the different programming constructs and how they are implemented in PowerShell. I will deliberately not go into much detail. For details, check out `https://technet.microsoft.com/en-us/magazine/2007.03.powershell.aspx`.

In any programming language, the first thing that you need to learn about is the variables. Declaring a variable in PowerShell is pretty easy and straightforward; simply, start the variable name with a $ sign. For example, run the following code:

```
PS C:\> $newVariable = 10
PS C:\> $dirList = Dir | Select Name
```

Note that at the time of variable creation, there is no need to mention the variable type.

You can also use the following cmdlets to create different types of variable:

- `New-Variable`
- `Get-Variable`
- `Set-Variable`
- `Clear-Variable`
- `Remove-Variable`

Best practice for variables is to initialize them properly. If they are not initialized properly, you can have unexpected results at unexpected places, leading to many errors. So, you can use `Set-Strictmode` in your script so that it can catch any uninitialized variables and thus remove any errors creeping in due to this. For details, check out `https://technet.microsoft.com/en-us/library/hh849692.aspx`.

When we started programming, we started with flowcharts, then moved on to pseudo code, and then, finally, implemented the pseudo code in any programming language of our choice. But in all this, the basic building blocks were the same. Actually, when we write any code in any programming language, the basic logic always remains the same; only the implementation of those basic building blocks in that particular language differs. For example, when we greet someone in English, we say "Hello" but the same in Hindi is "Namaste". So, the purpose of greeting remains the same and the effect is also the same. The only difference is that depending on the language and understanding, the words change.

Similarly, the building blocks of any logic can be categorized as follows:

- Conditional logic
- Conditional logic using loops

Now, let's take a look at how these two logics are implemented in PowerShell.

Conditional logic

In PowerShell, we have `if, elseif, else` and `switch` to use as conditional logic. Also, to use these logics properly, we need some comparison or logical operators. The comparison and logical operators available in PowerShell are as follows:

Comparison operators:

Operator	Description
-eq	Equal to
-ne	Not equal to
-lt	Less than
-gt	Greater than
-le	Less than or equal to
-gt	Greater than or equal to

Logical operators:

Operator	Description
-not	Logical Not or negate
!	Logical Not
-and	Logical AND
-or	Logical OR

The syntax for the `if` statement is as follows:

```
If (condition) { Script Block}
Elseif (condition) { Script Block}
Else { Script Block}
```

In the preceding statement, both `elseif` and `else` are optional. The "condition" is the logic that decides whether the "script block" will be executed or not. If the condition is true, then the script block is executed; otherwise, it is not. A simple example is as follows:

```
if ($a-gt$b) { Write-Host "$a is bigger than $b"}
elseif ($a-lt$b) { Write-Host "$a is less than $b"}
else { Write-Host " Both $a and $b are equal"}
```

The preceding example compares the two variables $a and $b and depending on their respective values, decides whether $a is greater than, less than, or equal to $b.

The syntax for the Switch statement in PowerShell is as follows:

```
Switch (value) {
Pattern 1 {Script Block}
Pattern 2 {Script Block}
Pattern n {Script Block}
Default   {Script Block}
}
```

If any one of the patterns matches the value, then the respective Script Block is executed. If none of them matches, then the Script Block respective for Default is executed.

The Switch statement is very useful for replacing long if {}, elseif {}, elseif {} or else {} blocks. Also, it is very useful for providing a selection of menu items.

One important point to note is that even if a match is found, the remaining patterns are still checked, and if any other pattern matches, then that script block is also executed. For examples of the Switch case and more details, check out https://technet.microsoft.com/en-us/library/ff730937.aspx.

Conditional logic using loops

In PowerShell, you have the following conditional logic loops:

- do while
- while
- do until
- for
- Foreach
- Foreach-Object

The syntax for do while is as follows:

```
do {
Script Block
}while (condition)
```

The syntax for the while loop is as follows:

```
While (condition) { Script Block}
```

The following example shows the preceding `while` loop. Say, we want to add the numbers 1 through 10.

The `do while` implementation is as follows:

```
$sum = 0
$i = 1
do {
$sum = $sum + $i
$i++
}while( $i -le 10)

$sum
```

The `while` implementation is as follows

```
$sum = 0
$i = 1

while($i -le 10)
{
    $sum = $sum + $i
    $i++
}
$sum
```

In both the preceding cases, the script block is executed until the condition is `true`. The main difference is that, in the case of `do while`, the script block is executed at least once whether the condition is `true` or `false`, as the script block is executed first and then the condition is checked. In the case of the `while` loop, the condition is checked first and then the script block is executed only if the condition is `true`.

The syntax for the `do until` loop is as follows:

```
do {
Script Block
}until (condition)
```

The main difference between `do until` and the preceding two statements is that, logically, `do until` is the opposite of `do while`. This is the script block is that is run until the time the condition is `false`. The moment it becomes `true`, the loop is terminated.

The syntax for the `for` loop is as follows:

```
for (initialization; condition; repeat)
{code block}
```

The typical use case of a `for` loop is when you want to run a loop a specified number of times. To write the preceding example in a `for` loop, we will write it in the following manner:

```
For($i=0, $sum=0; $i -le 10; $i++)
{
$sum = $sum + $i
}
$sum
```

The syntax for the `foreach` loop is as follows:

```
foreach ($<item> in $<collection>)
{code block}
```

The purpose of the `foreach` statement is to step through (iterate) a series of values in a collection of items. Note the following example. Here, we are adding each number from 1 to 10 using the `foreach` loop:

```
# Initialize the variable $sum
$sum = 0
# foreach statement starts
foreach ($i in 1..10)
{
# Adding value of variable $i to the total $sum
    $sum = $sum + $i
} # foreach loop ends
# showing the value of variable $sum
$sum
```

Logically, `foreach` and `Foreach-Object` do similar tasks, and sometimes this can create confusion between the two. Both of them are used to iterate through collections and perform an action against each item in the collection. In fact, `foreach` is an alias for `Foreach-Object`.

```
PS C:\> Get-Alias -Definition ForEach-Object

CommandType     Name                              Version    Source
-----------     ----                              -------    ------
Alias           % -> ForEach-Object
Alias           foreach -> ForEach-Object


PS C:\> Get-Alias foreach

CommandType     Name                              Version    Source
-----------     ----                              -------    ------
Alias           foreach -> ForEach-Object
```

The difference between Foreach and Foreach-object

When we use Foreach in the middle of a pipeline, that is, when we pipe into Foreach, it is used as an alias for Foreach-Object, but when used at the beginning of the line, it is used as a PowerShell statement.

Also, the main difference between foreach and Foreach-Object is that when Foreach-Object is used, it executes the statement body as soon as the object is created, but when foreach is used, all the objects are collected first and then the statement body is executed.

So, when we are using foreach, we need to make sure that there is enough memory space available to hold all the objects.

Having said that due to optimizations in foreach, foreach will run much faster than the Foreach-Object statement, so the decision again boils down to that age-old question of performance versus space.

So, depending on the program that you are writing, you need to choose wisely between these two.

Automation through PowerShell scripts

From a programming perspective, there is not much difference between a scripting language and a more traditional programming language. You can make pretty complex programs with a scripting language.

The main difference between any traditional programming language and scripts is that in programming language, you can build compiled binary code, which can run as a standalone. In scripting, it cannot run as a standalone. A script depends on another program to execute it at runtime, or you can say that it requires another program to interpret it. Also, the code for the script is normally available for you to read. It is there in plain text form and at run time, it is executed line by line. In the case of a traditional programming language, you get a binary code which cannot be easily converted to the source code.

To summarize, if the runtime can see the code, then it is scripting language. If it is not then it was generated through a more traditional language.

Another more generic difference is that in typical scripting languages such as shell and PowerShell scripts, we use commands, which can be run directly from the command line and can give you the same result. So, in a script, we use those full high-level commands and bind them using basic programming structures (conditional logic, loops, and so on) to get a more sophisticated and complex result, whereas in traditional programming you use basic constructs and create your own program to solve a problem.

In PowerShell, the commands are called cmdlets, and we use these cmdlets and the basic constructs to get what we want to achieve. PowerShell cmdlets typically follow a verb-noun naming convention, where each cmdlet starts with a standard verb, hyphenated with a specific noun. For example, `Get-Service`, `Stop-Service`, and so on.

To write a PowerShell script, you can use any text editor, write the required code, and then save the file with a `.ps1` extension. Next, from the PowerShell command line, run the script to get the desired result.

Running and scheduling scripts

There are many ways in which you can run a PowerShell script. Most of the time the PowerShell console or ISE is used to run the scripts. There will be instances (and in the daily life of a system administrator, these instances occur frequently) when you would like to schedule the script so that it runs at a particular time on a daily basis or at one time. These processes are described as follows:

Let's see how we use the PowerShell console/ISE.

In the PowerShell console, you get only a command-line console, such as the CMD shell, and the ISE provides a more graphical interface with multiple views. As can be seen from the following screenshot, the PowerShell ISE provides three main views. On the left-hand side of the screen you have an editor and a console, and on the right-hand side you have the command window. Using the editor, you can write your scripts quickly and then run them from this window itself. The output is shown on the console given below the editor. Also, from the command selector window, you can search for the command that you are looking for and simply choose to run the `insert` or `copy` command. It also gives you multiple options to run the different aspects of the command.

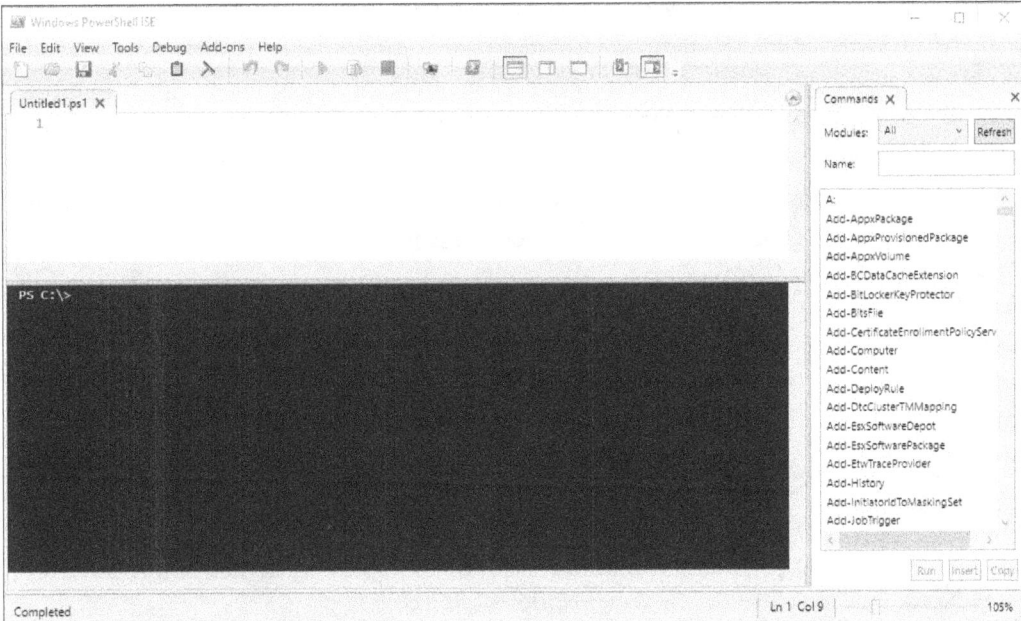

Due to the flexibility of the ISE and ease with which we can work with it, it is my preferred way of working here, and for the rest of the book, it will be used for examples. Although there are many specific editors available for PowerShell, I am not going to cover them in this chapter. In the last chapter, I will cover this topic a bit and talk about my favorite editor.

So, we've started the ISE. Now let's write our first script that consists of a single line:

```
Write-Host "Welcome $args !!! Congratulations, you have run your first
script!!!"
```

Now, let's save the preceding line in a file named `Welcome.ps1`. From the ISE command line, go to the location where the file is saved and run the file with the following command line:

```
PS C:\Scripts\Welcome.ps1
```

What happened? Were you able to run the command? In all probability, you will get an error message, as shown in the following code snippet (in case you are running the script for the first time):

```
PS C:\Scripts> .\Welcome.ps1 Sajal Debnath

.\Welcome.ps1 : File C:\Scripts\Welcome.ps1 cannot be loaded because
running scripts is disabled on this system. For more
```

information, see about_Execution_Policies at http://go.microsoft.com/fwlink/?LinkID=135170.

At line:1 char:1

+ .\Welcome.ps1 Sajal Debnath

+ ~~~~~~~~~~~~~

    + CategoryInfo   : SecurityError: (:) [], PSSecurityException

    + FullyQualifiedErrorId : UnauthorizedAccess

So, what does it say and what does it mean? It says that running scripts is disabled on the system.

Whether you are allowed to run a script or not is determined by the ExecutionPolicy set in the system. You can check the policy by running the following command:

```
PS C:\Scripts> Get-ExecutionPolicy
Restricted
```

So, you can see that the execution policy is set to Restricted (which is the default one). Now, let's check what the other options available are:

```
PS C:\Scripts>Get-Help ExecutionPolicy
```

```
Name                            Category  Module
Synopsis

----                            --------  ------                         ---
-----

Get-ExecutionPolicy             Cmdlet    Microsoft.PowerShell.S...
Gets the execution policies for the current session.
Set-ExecutionPolicy             Cmdlet    Microsoft.PowerShell.S...
Changes the user preference for the Windows PowerSh...
```

Note that we have Set-ExecutionPolicy as well, so we can set the policy using this cmdlet. Now, let's check the different policies that can be set:

```
PS C:\Scripts> Get-Help Set-ExecutionPolicy -Detailed
```

> Perhaps the most useful friend in the PowerShell cmdlet is the Get-Help cmdlet. As the name suggests, it provides help for the cmdlet in question. To find help for a cmdlet, just type Get-Help <cmdlet>. There are many useful parameters with this cmdlet, especially -Full and -Examples. I strongly suggest that you type Get-Help in PowerShell and read the output.

Part of the output shown is as follows:

```
Specifies the new execution policy. Valid values are:

        -- Restricted: Does not load configuration files or run
scripts. "Restricted" is the default execution policy.

        -- AllSigned: Requires that all scripts and configuration
files be signed by a trusted publisher, including scripts that you
write on the local computer.

        -- RemoteSigned: Requires that all scripts and configuration
files downloaded from the Internet be signed by a trusted publisher.

        -- Unrestricted: Loads all configuration files and runs all
scripts. If you run an unsigned script that was downloaded from the
Internet, you are prompted for permission before it runs.

        -- Bypass: Nothing is blocked and there are no warnings or
prompts.

        -- Undefined: Removes the currently assigned execution policy
from the current scope. This parameter will not remove an execution
policy that is set in a Group Policy scope
```

For the purpose of running our script and for the rest of the examples, we will set the policy to Unrestricted. We can do this by running the following command:

```
PS C:\ Set-ExecutionPolicy Unrestricted
```

> Although I have set the policy as Unrestricted, it is not at all secure. From the security perspective, and for all other practical purposes, I suggest that you set the policy to RemoteSigned.

Now, if we try to run the earlier script, it runs successfully and gives the desired result:

```
PS C:\Scripts> .\Welcome.ps1 Sajal Debnath
Welcome Sajal Debnath !!! Congratulations you have run your first
script!!!
```

So, we are all set to run our scripts.

Now, let's take a look at how we can schedule a PowerShell script using Windows Task Scheduler.

Before we go ahead and schedule a task, we need to finalize the command which, when run from the task scheduler, will run the script and give you the desired result. The best way to check this is to run the same command from **Start → Run**.

For example, if I have a script in `C:\` by the name `Report.ps1`, I can run the script from the command line by running the following command:

```
powershell -file "C:\Report.ps1"
```

Another point to note here is that once the preceding command is run, the PowerShell window will close. So, if you want the PowerShell window to be opened so that you can see any error messages, then add the `-NoExit` switch. So, the command becomes:

```
Powershell-NoExit -file "C:\Report.ps1"
```

Depending on the version of Windows installed, Windows Task Scheduler is generally found in either **Control Panel → System and Security → Administrative Tools → Task Scheduler** or **Control Panel → Administrative Tools → Task Scheduler**, or you can go to **Task Scheduler** from the **Start** menu, as shown in the following screenshot:

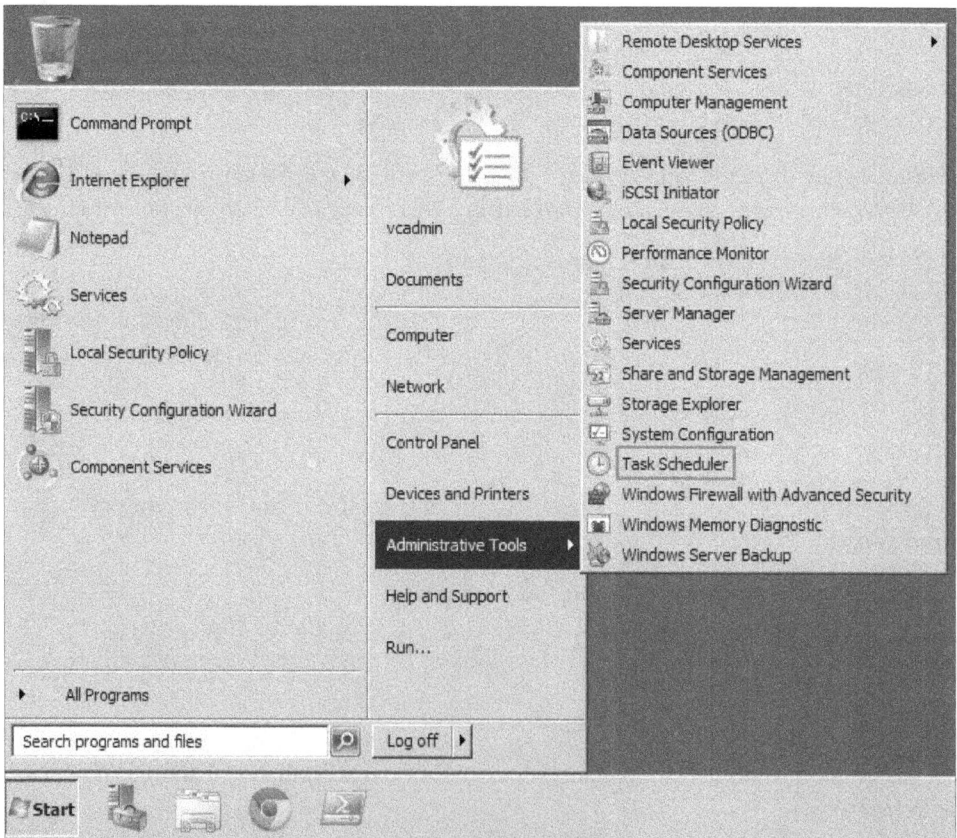

On the right-hand side pane, under **Actions,** click on **Create Basic Task.** A new window opens. In this window, provide a task name and description:

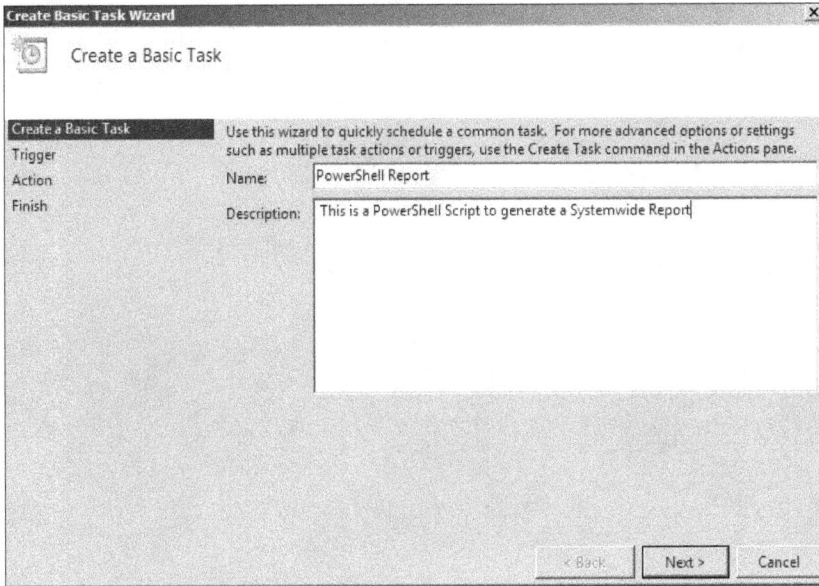

The next window provides you with the trigger details, which will trigger the action. Select the trigger according to your requirements (how frequently you want to run the script).

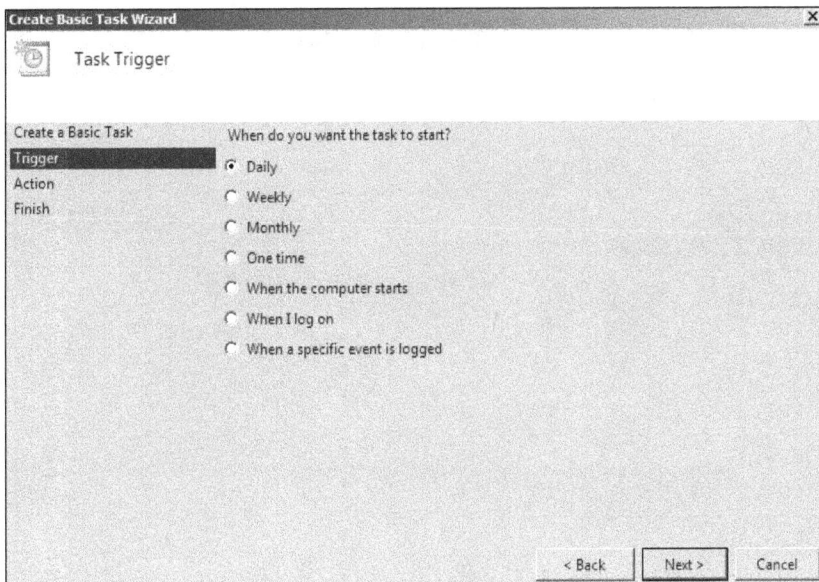

Select a type of action that you want to perform. For our purpose, we will choose **Start a program**.

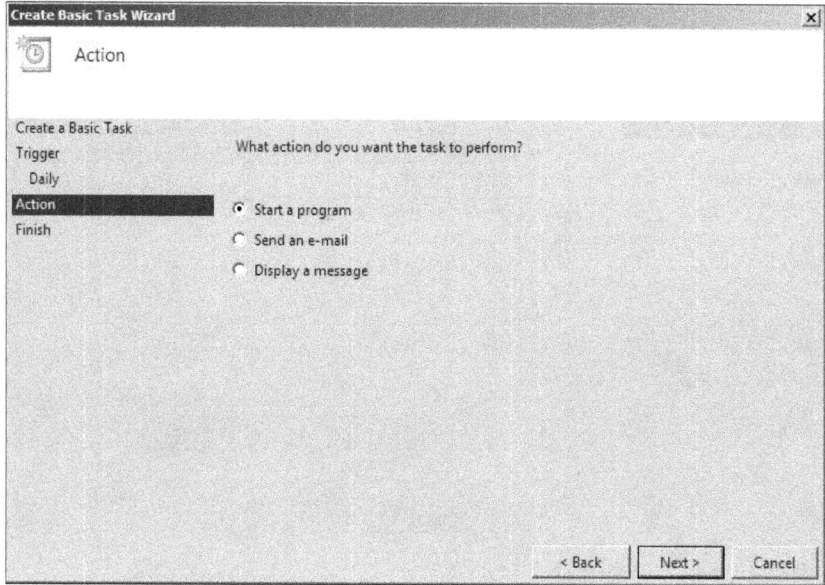

In the next window, provide the command that you want to execute (the command that we checked by running it in **Start → Run**). In our example, it is as follows:

```
Powershell -file "C:\Report.ps1"
```

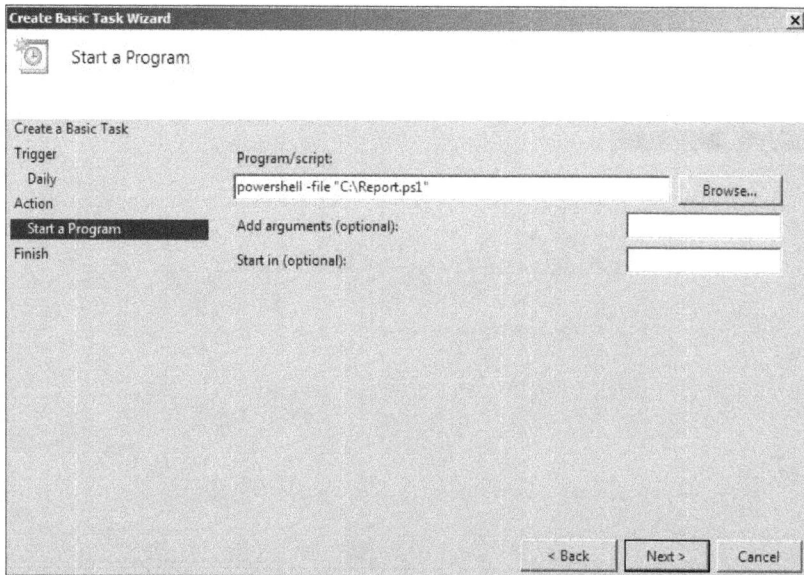

In the next confirmatory window, select **Yes**.

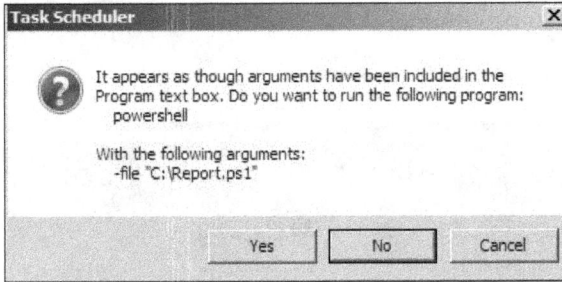

Task Scheduler

It appears as though arguments have been included in the Program text box. Do you want to run the following program:
powershell

With the following arguments:
-file "C:\Report.ps1"

Yes No Cancel

The last window will provide you an overview of all the options. Select **Finish** to complete the creation of the scheduled task. Now, the script will run automatically at your predefined time and interval.

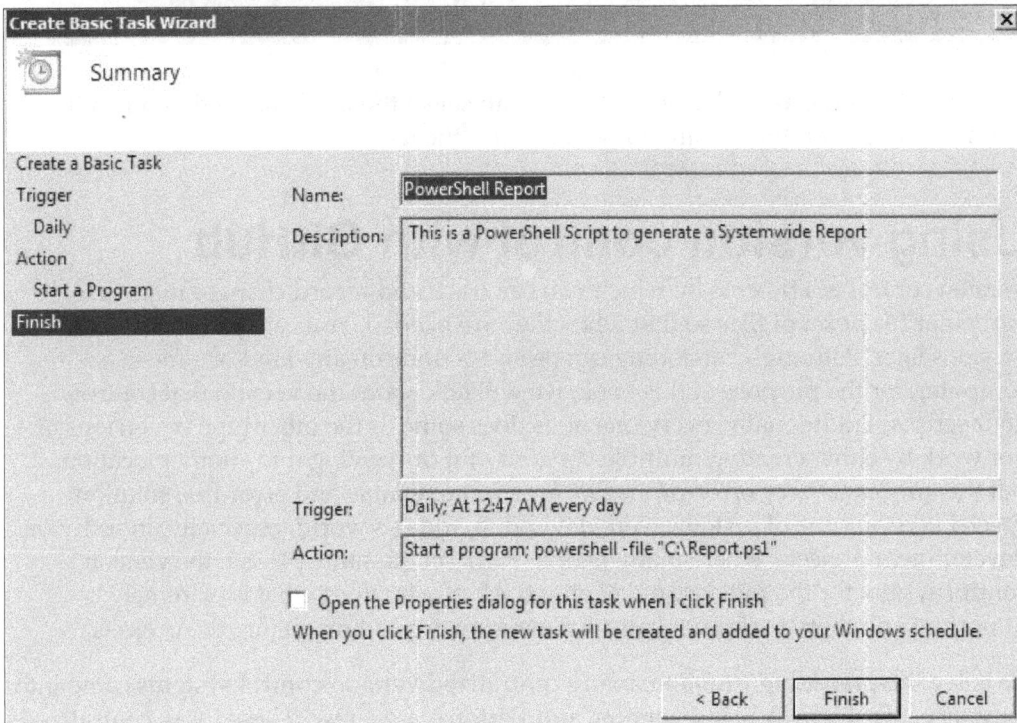

Create Basic Task Wizard

Summary

Create a Basic Task
Trigger
  Daily
Action
  Start a Program
Finish

Name: PowerShell Report

Description: This is a PowerShell Script to generate a Systemwide Report

Trigger: Daily; At 12:47 AM every day

Action: Start a program; powershell -file "C:\Report.ps1"

☐ Open the Properties dialog for this task when I click Finish

When you click Finish, the new task will be created and added to your Windows schedule.

< Back   Finish   Cancel

Instead of using the GUI interface, you can create, modify, and control scheduled tasks from the PowerShell command line as well. For a detailed list of the commands, you can run the following command:

```
PS C:\> Get-Command *ScheduledTask
```

```
PS C:\Windows\System32\WindowsPowerShell\v1.0> Get-Command *ScheduledTask

CommandType     Name                                     Version      Source
-----------     ----                                     -------      ------
Function        Disable-ScheduledTask                    1.0.0.0      ScheduledTasks
Function        Enable-ScheduledTask                     1.0.0.0      ScheduledTasks
Function        Export-ScheduledTask                     1.0.0.0      ScheduledTasks
Function        Get-ClusteredScheduledTask               1.0.0.0      ScheduledTasks
Function        Get-ScheduledTask                        1.0.0.0      ScheduledTasks
Function        New-ScheduledTask                        1.0.0.0      ScheduledTasks
Function        Register-ClusteredScheduledTask          1.0.0.0      ScheduledTasks
Function        Register-ScheduledTask                   1.0.0.0      ScheduledTasks
Function        Set-ClusteredScheduledTask               1.0.0.0      ScheduledTasks
Function        Set-ScheduledTask                        1.0.0.0      ScheduledTasks
Function        Start-ScheduledTask                      1.0.0.0      ScheduledTasks
Function        Stop-ScheduledTask                       1.0.0.0      ScheduledTasks
Function        Unregister-ClusteredScheduledTask        1.0.0.0      ScheduledTasks
Function        Unregister-ScheduledTask                 1.0.0.0      ScheduledTasks
```

From the list of the available cmdlets, you can select the one you need and run it. For more details on the command, you can use the Get-Help cmdlet.

Using version control with GitHub

Version control is a process by which you can track and record changes made to a particular file or set of files so that when they are needed, you can get back specific versions later. Although versioning can be and is done on any kind of a file in a computer, for the purpose of this book, we will talk about the version that controls your scripts. Traditionally, every one of us does some or the other type of versions of our work by either creating multiple versions of it or copying it to another location. But this process is very error-prone. So, for a more reliable and error-free solution, special version control systems were devised. In today's world, especially, in software development projects, where many people work on the same project, the version control system for the purpose of keeping track of who does what is extremely important and these tools are a must for maintaining and managing the projects.

To solve the preceding problem, many centralized version control systems came into existence, of which CVS, Subversion, and Perforce are a few. These local, centralized version control systems were easy to maintain but they had the serious issue of putting every egg in a single basket. If for some reason, the centralized version control server breaks down during that time frame, no one would be able to collaborate and work. Also, if due to some problem, the hard disk crashes or data gets corrupted, then all the data is lost.

Due to the preceding problem, distributed version control systems came into existence. In a distributed version control system, the clients can not only check the snapshots of the files kept in the centralized server, but they can also maintain a full replica of those files in their local system. So, if something happens to the main server, a local copy is always maintained and the server is restored by simply copying the data from any of the local systems. Thus, in a distributed version control system, all the local clients act as a full backup system of the central data of the server. A few such tools are Git, Mercurial, Darcs, and so on.

Among all the distributed version control systems, Git is the most widely used because of the following advantages:

- The speed at which it functions
- It supports thousands of parallel branches of the same project
- It is a fully distributed architecture
- It can handle very large projects very efficiently
- It has a simplistic design

The following are a few of the differences between Git and other version control systems:

- In a traditional version control system, the difference between the files is saved as the difference between the two versions. Only the deltas are saved, whereas in Git, the versions are saved as snapshots. So, when the traditional tools treat the data as files and changes are made to the files over time, Git treats the data as a series of snapshots.

- Most of the operations in Git are local. You can make changes to the files, or if you want to check something in the history or want to get an old version, you no longer need to be connected to a remote server. Also, you don't need to be connected to make changes to the files; they will be locally saved, and you can push the changes back to the remote server at a later stage. This gives Git the speed to work.

- Whatever is saved in Git is saved with a checksum. So, making changes to the saved information in Git and expecting that Git will not know about it is nearly impossible.

- In Git, we generally always add data. So, it is very difficult to lose data in Git. In most cases, as the data is pushed to other repositories as well, we can always recover from any unexpected corruption.

This was a very short discussion on Git because GitHub is based entirely on Git. In this book, we will talk about GitHub and check how it is used because of the following reasons:

- Git is a command line tool and can be intimidating for a not-so-daily programmer. For a scripter, GitHub is a far better solution.
- Bringing your scripts to GitHub connects you to the social network of collaboration, and you can work with others in a more collaborative way.

So, without further ado, let's dive into GitHub. GitHub is the largest host for Git repositories. Millions of developers work on thousands of projects in GitHub. To use GitHub, the first thing you need to do is create an account in GitHub. We can create an account in GitHub by simply visiting `https://github.com/` and signing up in the section provided for sign up. Note the e-mail ID that you used to create the account, as you will use the same e-mail ID to connect to this account from the local repository at a later stage.

One point to note is that once you log in to GitHub, you can create an SSH key pair to work with your local account and the GitHub repository. For security reasons, you should create a two-factor authentication for your account. To do so, perform the following steps:

1. Log in to your account and go to **Settings** (top-right hand corner).
2. On the left-hand side, under the **Personal settings** category, choose **Security**.
3. Next, click on **Set up two-factor authentication**.
4. Then, you can use an app or send an SMS.

So, you have created an account and set up two-factor authentication. Now, since we want to work on our local systems as well, we need to install it on the local system. So, go ahead and download the respective version for your system from `http://git-scm.com/downloads`.

Now, we can configure it two ways. Git is either included or can be installed as part of it in GitHub for Windows/Mac/Linux. GitHub uses a GUI tool. First, let's start with the command-line tool. For my examples I have used GitHub Desktop, which can be downloaded from `https://desktop.github.com/`.

Open the command-line tool and run the following commands to configure the environment:

```
git config --global user.name "Your Name"
git config --global user.email "email@email.com"
```

You need to replace `Your Name` with your name and `email@email.com` with the e-mail with which you created your account in GitHub.

You can set the same using the GitHub tool as well. Once you install GitHub, go to **Preferences** and then **Accounts**. Log in with your account that you created on the GitHub site. This will connect you to your account in GitHub.

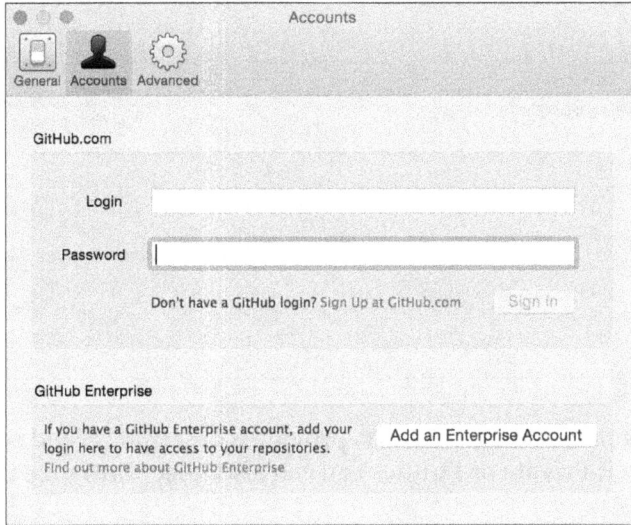

Next, go to the **Advanced** tab and fill in the details that you provided in the previous configuration under the **Git Config** section. Also, under the **Command Line** section, click on **Install Command Line Tools**. This will install the GitHub command-line utility on the system.

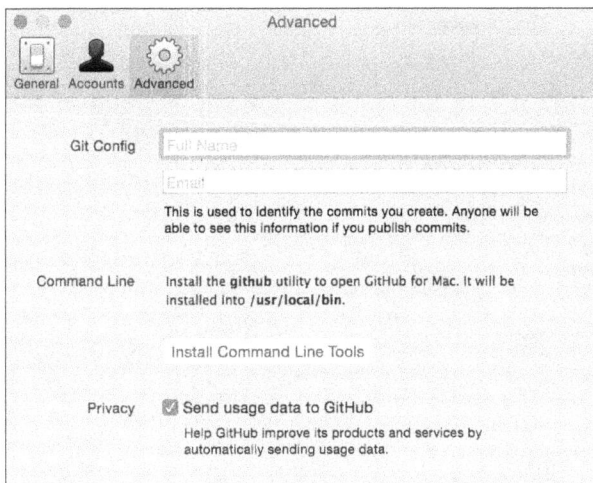

Okay, so now we have installed everything that we require, so let's go ahead and create our first repository.

To create a repository, log in to your account in GitHub, and then click on the **+New Repository** tab:

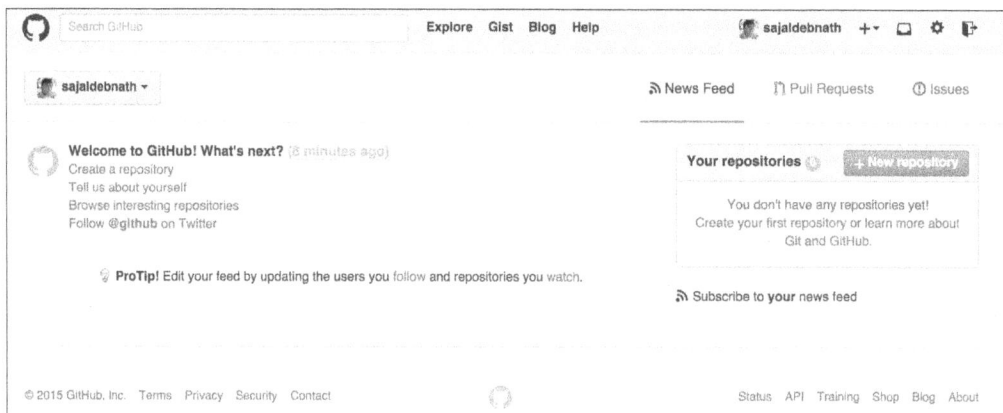

Next, provide a name for the repository, provide a description, and select whether you want to make it **Private** or **Public**. You can also select **Initialize this repository with a README**.

Once the preceding information is provided, click on **Create Repository**. This will create a new repository under your name and you would be the owner of the repository.

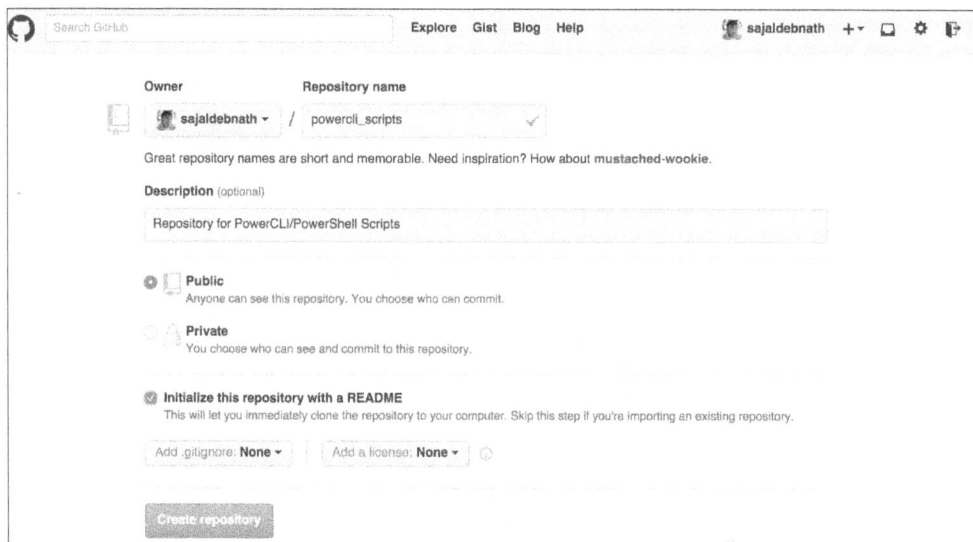

Before we go ahead and talk more about using GitHub, let's talk about a few concepts and how they work in GitHub.

There are two collaborative models in which GitHub works.

The fork & pull model

In this model, anyone can fork an existing repository and push changes to their personal fork. To do this, they do not need to have permissions granted to access the source repository. When the changes made to the personal repository are ready to be pushed to the original repository, the changes must be pulled back by the project owner. This reduces the initial collaboration required between team members and collaborators, who can work more independently. This is a popular model between open source collaborators.

> Traditionally, fork is used to mean a deviation from the original project. But in the GitHub environment, a fork is simply a copy of the existing project that you can work and then merge back into the original project.

The shared repository model

In the shared repository model, everyone working on the project is granted push access to the original repository, and thus, anyone working on this project can update the original project. This is mainly used in small teams or private projects where organizations collaborate to work on a project.

Pull requests are more useful in the fork & pull model as they notify the project maintainer about the changes that have been made. They also initiate the code review and discussions on the changes made before they can be pushed back to the original project.

Branch

When you create a repository, it is, by default, the `master` repository. So, how does another person work on the same project? They create a branch for themselves. A branch is a replica of the main repository. You can make all the changes to the branch, and when you are ready, you can merge your changes to the `main` repository.

To summarize, a typical GitHub workflow is as follows:

1. Create a branch of the `master` repository.
2. Make some changes of your own.
3. Push this branch to your GitHub project.
4. Open a pull request in GitHub.
5. Discuss the changes, and if required, continue working on the changes.
6. The project owner merges or closes the pull request.

Now, we can work on the preceding workflow from the command line using Git or use GUI from GitHub. The commands are as provided below (for those who prefer CLI to GUI):

- `git init`: This command initializes a directory as a new Git repository in your local system. Until this is done, there's no difference between a normal directory and a Git repository.

- `git help`: This command will show you a list of commands available with Git.

- `git status`: This command checks the status of the repository.

- `git add`: This command adds files to the Git index.

- `git commit`: This command asks Git to mark changes made to a repository. It will take a snapshot of the repository.

- `git branch`: This command allows you to make a branch of an existing repository.

- `git checkout`: This command allows you check the contents of the repository without going inside the repository.

- `git merge`: As the name suggests, this command allows you to merge the changes that you made to the master.

- `git push`: This particular command allows you to push the changes you made on your local computer back to the GitHub online repository so that other collaborators are able to see them.

- `git pull`: If you are working on your local computer and want to bring the latest changes from the GitHub repository to your local computer, you can use this command to pull down the changes back to the local system.

Since we have already created an online repository named `powercli_scripts`, let's create a local repository and sync them.

To create a local repository, all you need to do is create a local directory, and then from inside the directory, run the `git init` command:

```
sdebnath:~ sdebnath$ mkdir git
sdebnath:~ sdebnath$ cd git
sdebnath\git$ git init
Initialized empty Git repository in /Users/sdebnath/git/.git/.
```

To use the GUI tool open the GitHub application, and then from the **File** menu, select **Add Local Repository**.

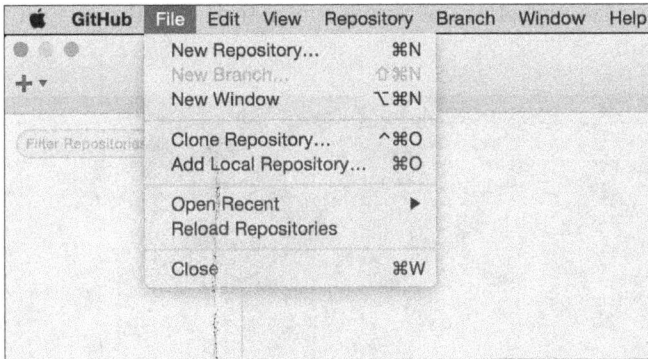

This will bring up a pop-up window saying that **This folder is not a repository** and asking if you want to create and add the repository. Click on **Create and Add**. This will create a local repository for you.

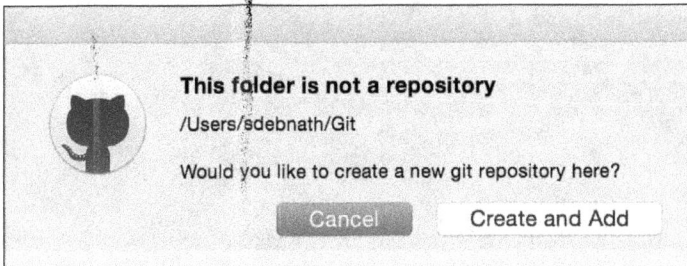

Now, let's go to the directory and create a file and put some text into it. Once the file is created, we will check the status of the repository that will tell us that there are untracked files in the repository. Once done, we will notify Git that there is a file that has changed. Then, we will commit the change to Git so that Git can take its snapshot. Here is a list of commands:

```
$ cd Git
$ touch README.txt
$ echo "Hello there, first document in the repository" > README.txt
$ git status
$ git add README.txt
$ git commit -m "README.txt added"
```

The following is a screenshot of the above commands and the output that we get for a successful run.

```
del-sdebnath:Git sdebnath$ touch README.txt
del-sdebnath:Git sdebnath$ echo "Hello there, first document in the repository" > README.txt
del-sdebnath:Git sdebnath$ git status
On branch master

Initial commit

Untracked files:
  (use "git add <file>..." to include in what will be committed)

        README.txt

nothing added to commit but untracked files present (use "git add" to track)
del-sdebnath:Git sdebnath$ git add README.txt
del-sdebnath:Git sdebnath$ git commit -m "README.txt added"
[master (root-commit) 09945e3] README.txt added
 Committer: sajal debnath <sdebnath@del-sdebnath.local>
Your name and email address were configured automatically based
on your username and hostname. Please check that they are accurate.
You can suppress this message by setting them explicitly:

    git config --global user.name "Your Name"
    git config --global user.email you@example.com

After doing this, you may fix the identity used for this commit with:

    git commit --amend --reset-author

 1 file changed, 1 insertion(+)
 create mode 100644 README.txt
```

Now, we need to add the remote repository. We do this by running the following command:

```
$ git remote add origin https://github.com/yourname/repository.git
```

Replace `yourname` with your username and `repository` with your repository name.

You can do the same work through the GitHub's GUI application as well. Once you open the application, go to **Preferences**, and then under **Accounts**, log in to your GitHub account with your account details. Once done, you can create a branch of the repository.

Let's create a `my-changes` branch from `master`. Click on the Branch icon next to `master` (as shown in the following screenshot):

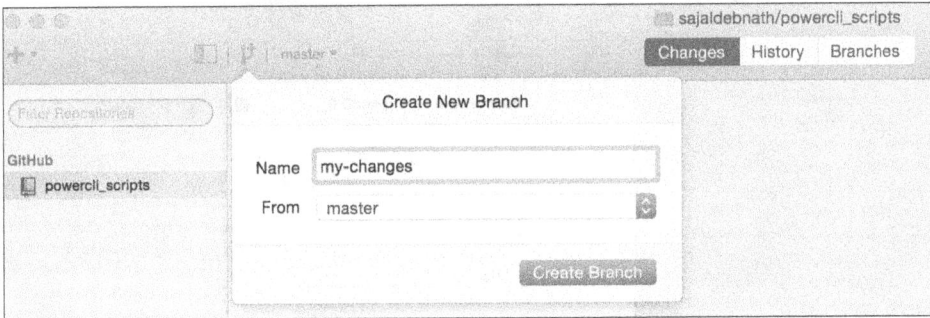

Once you do this, your working branch changes to `my-changes`. Now, add a file to your local repository, say, `changes.txt`, and add some text to it:

```
$ touch changes.txt
$ echo "Changes I made" > changes.txt
```

The changes that you made will immediately be visible in the GitHub application. You commit the changes made to the `my-changes` repository.

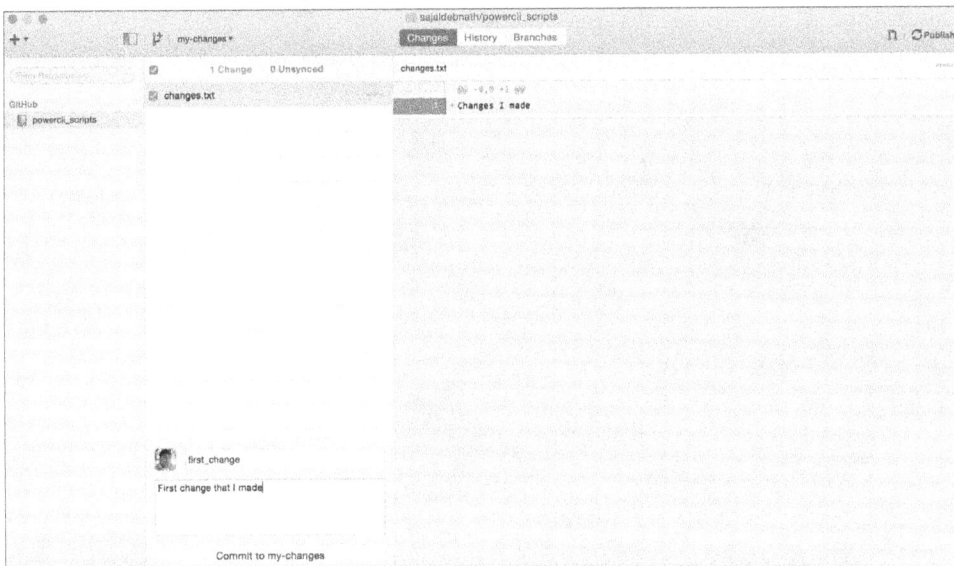

In the **Repository** option, select the **Push** option to push the changes to GitHub.

Next, I have added another file and again committed to `my-changes`.

This will keep the status of the local and remote repositories as **Unsynced**. Click on the right-hand side **Sync** button to sync the repositories.

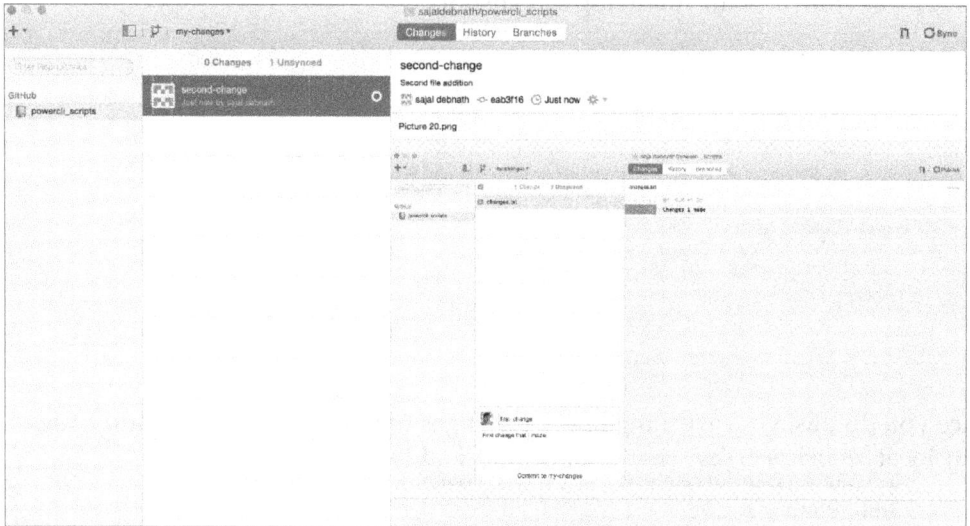

Now, if I go back to the GitHub site, I can see the changes that I made to the `my-changes` branch.

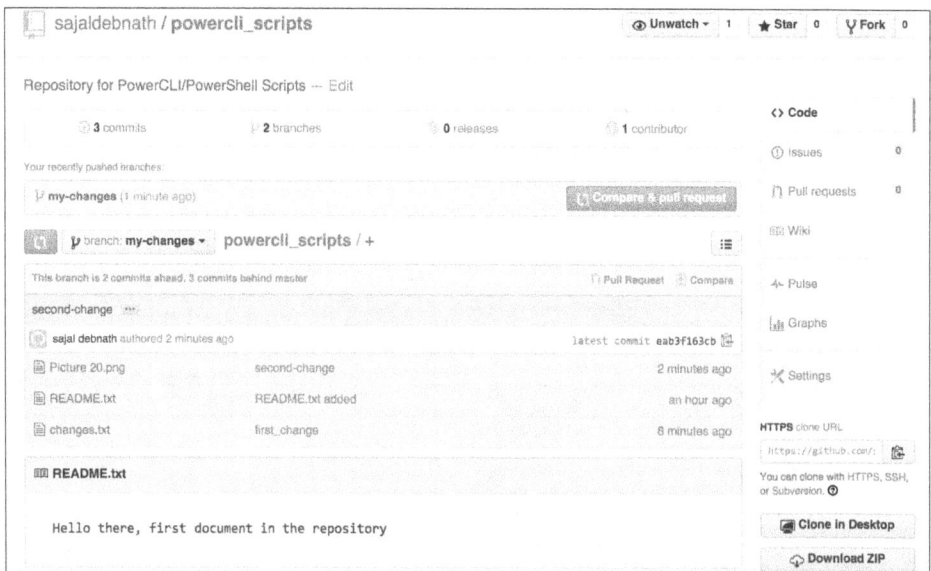

Next, I want to merge the branch into the main branch. I create a pull request. I can do this directly from the GitHub online page or from the GitHub application. In the GitHub application on the local system, go to **Repository**, and then click on **Create Pull Request**. Provide it a name and description, and click on **Create**. This will create a pull request in the main branch.

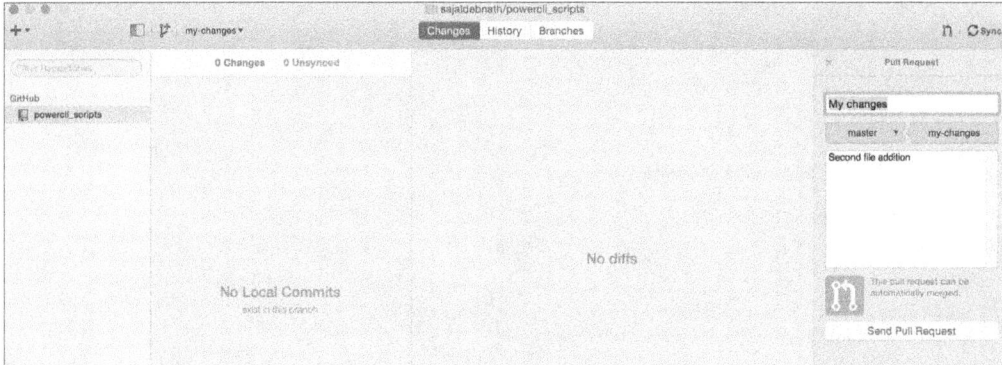

Now, go back to the GitHub page, and you will be able to see the details of the pull request.

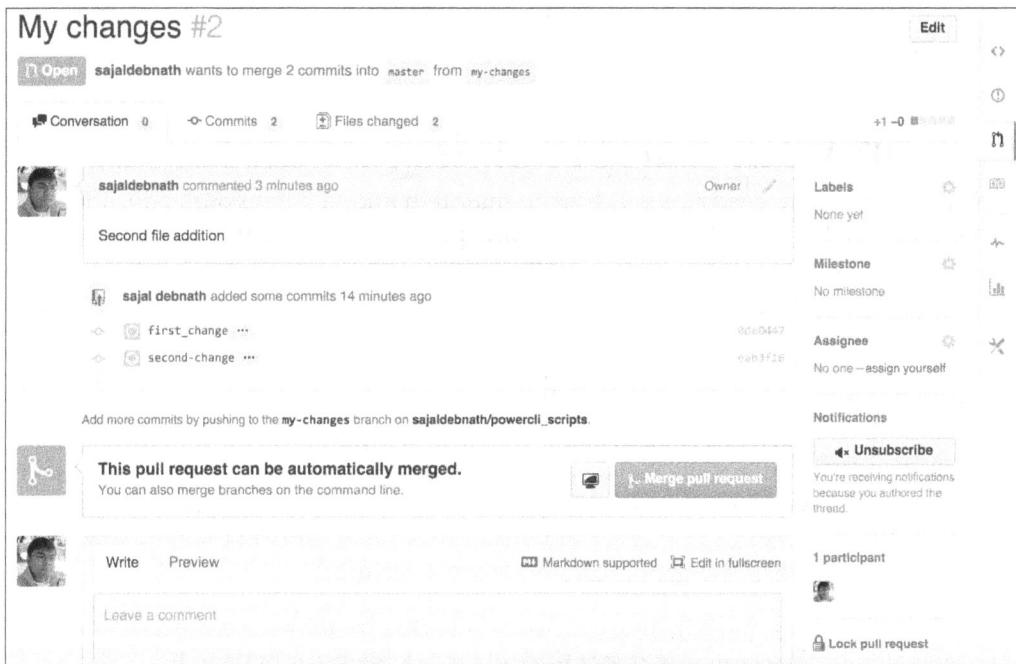

Click on **Merge pull request**, provide your comment, and click on **Confirm merge** to merge the change. Now, you can click on **Delete the branch**.

Also, if you go back to your main branch (which is `powercli_scripts` in my case), you will be able to see the changes in the main branch.

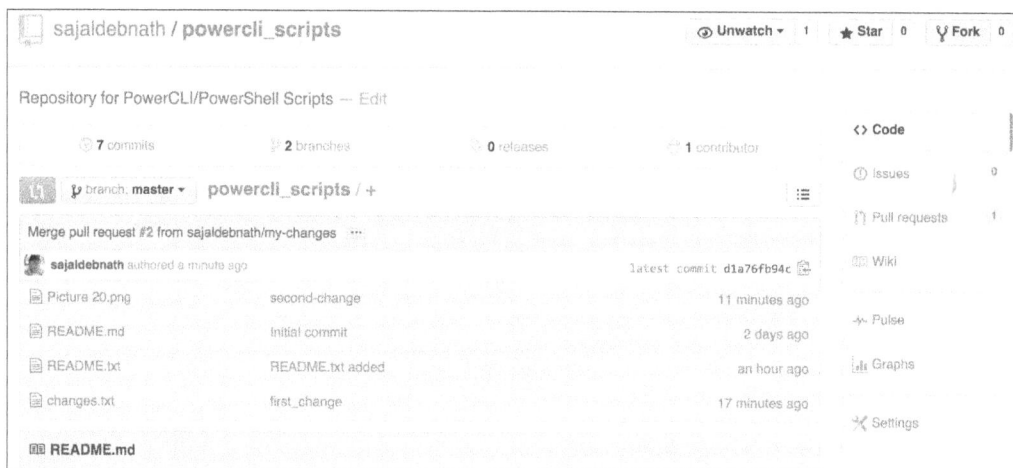

This concludes this section. Now, you should be able to create your own project or fork and work on existing projects.

Testing your scripts using Pester

In the previous topic, we discussed how to maintain and version your code, and how to collaborate with others to work on the same project using GitHub. In this topic, we will discuss how to test your code with Pester. But before we go ahead and jump into the topic, let me ask you some questions: How do you code? How long are those scripts? You might think "testing my code, but I am not a developer, I am a system administrator, and whenever I have a task at hand, I write some lines of code (well to be honest, it can be few hundred as well), do some testing, and then leave it as it is". Well, since the beginning of this book, I have been using the word "code" more and more, so we should accept the fact and start writing amazing new programs to make our lives easier. If you have started reading this book, then you are definitely going to write complex pieces of programs, and you should definitely know how to test them in order to perfect them. So, what is software testing?

Software testing is an investigative process conducted on the written code to find out the quality of the code. It may not find all the problems or bugs in the code, but it guarantees the working of the code under certain conditions.

Pester is an unit testing framework for PowerShell, which works great for both white box and black box testing.

> White box testing (also known as clear box testing, glass box testing, transparent box testing, and structural testing) is a method of testing software that tests the internal structures or workings of an application, as opposed to its functionality (that is, black box testing). In white box testing, an internal perspective of the system, as well as programming skills, are used to design test cases. The tester chooses inputs to exercise paths through the code and determine the appropriate outputs. This is analogous to testing nodes in a circuit, for example, **in-circuit testing (ICT)**.
>
> Black box testing is a method of software testing that examines the functionality of an application without peering into its internal structures or workings. This method of testing can be applied to virtually every level of software testing: unit, integration, system, and acceptance. It typically comprises of mostly all higher level testing, but also dominates unit testing as well.
>
> You can refer to https://en.wikipedia.org/wiki/White-box_testing and https://en.wikipedia.org/wiki/Black-box_testing.

Pester is a framework based on **behavior-driven development (BDD)**, which is again based on the **test-driven development (TDD)** methodology. Well, I have used a lot of development jargons. Let me clarify them one by one.

Earlier, we used to write the entire code, define the test cases, and run the tests based on those definitions. In recent times, with the development of philosophies, such as "Extreme Programming", came a new concept of testing. Instead of writing some code to solve some problems, we first define what we want to achieve in the form of test cases. We run the tests and make sure that all the tests fail. Then, we write the minimum amount of code to remove the errors and iterate through the process to make sure that all the tests pass. Once this is done, we refactor the code to an acceptable level and get the final code. It's just the opposite of a traditional way of development. This is called test-driven development or TDD for short.

Behavior-driven development is a software development process, which is based on TDD, and is based on the behavioral specification of the software units. TDD, by default, is very nonspecific in nature; it can allow tests in the form of a high-level requirement or a low-level technical requirement. BDD brings more structure and makes more specific choices than TDD.

Well, now that you understand what testing is and the methodologies used, let's dive into Pester.

Pester is a PowerShell module developed by Scott Muc and is improved by the community. It is available for free on GitHub. So, all that you need to do is download it, extract it, put it into the `Modules` folder, and then import it to the PowerShell session to use it (since it is a module, you need to import it just like any other module).

To download it, go to `https://github.com/pester/Pester`.

In the lower right-hand corner, click on **Download Zip**.

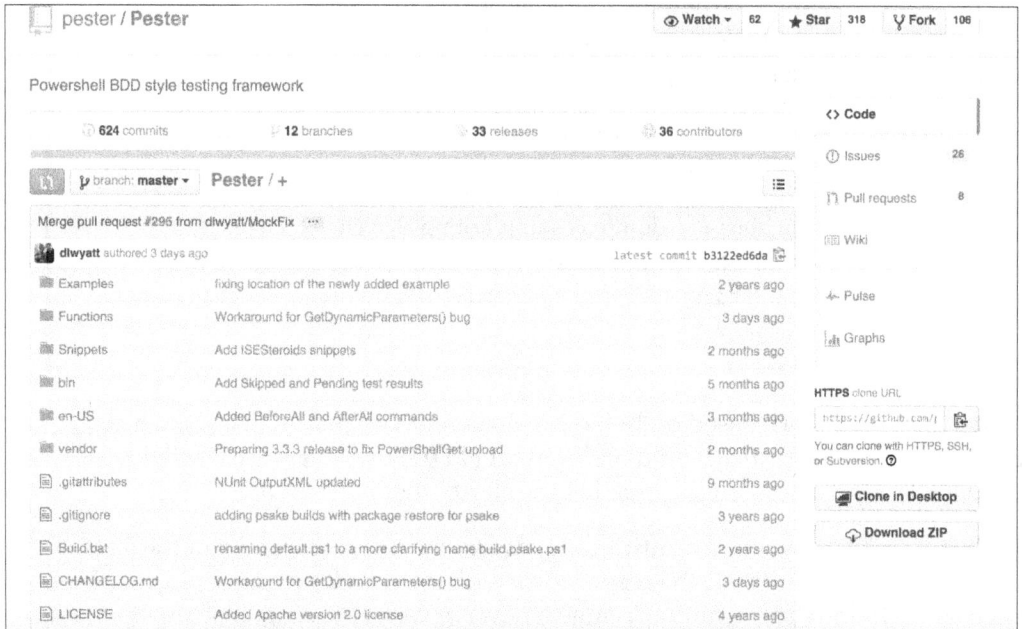

Once you download the ZIP file, you need to unblock it. To unblock it, right-click on the file and select **Properties**. From the **Properties** menu, select **Unblock**.

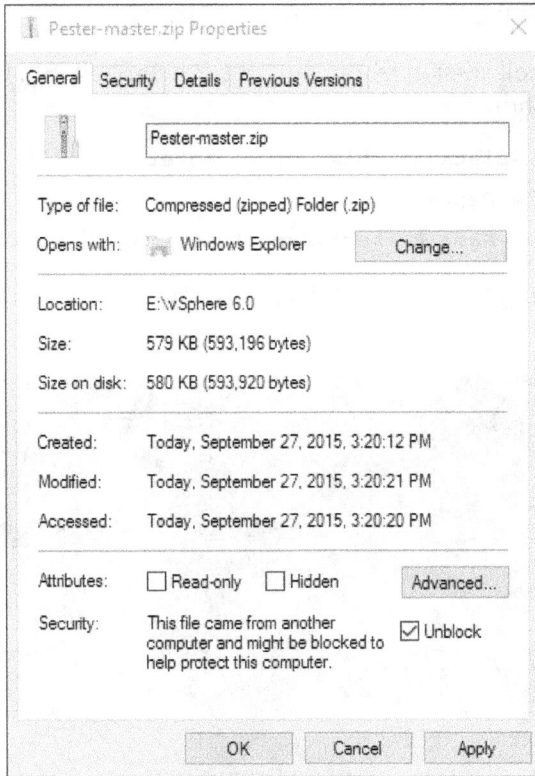

You can unblock the file from the PowerShell command line as well. Since I have downloaded the file into the `C:\PowerShell Scripts` folder, I will run the command as follows. Change the location according to your download location:

```
PS C:\> Unblock-File -Path 'C:\PowerShell Scripts\Pester-master.zip'
-Verbose
```

```
VERBOSE: Performing the operation "Unblock-File" on target "C:\PowerShell
Scripts\Pester-master.zip".
```

Now, copy the unzipped folder `Pester-master` to `C:\Program Files\WindowsPowerShell\Modules` or `C:\Windows\System32\WindowsPowerShell\v1.0\Modules`.

For simplicity, rename the folder to Pester from Pester-master.

Now open a PowerShell session by opening the PowerShell ISE. In the console, run the following commands:

```
PS C:\> Get-Module -ListAvailable -Name Pester
PS C:\>Import-Module Pester
PS C:\> (Get-Module -Name Pester).ExportedCommands
```

The last command will give you a list of all the commands imported from the Pester module.

```
PS C:\> Get-Module -ListAvailable Pester


    Directory: C:\Program Files\WindowsPowerShell\Modules


ModuleType Version    Name                        ExportedCommands
---------- -------    ----                        ----------------
Script     3.3.5      Pester                      {Describe, Context, It, Should...}


PS C:\> Import-Module Pester

PS C:\> Get-Command -Module Pester

CommandType     Name                              Version    Source
-----------     ----                              -------    ------
Function        AfterAll                          3.3.5      Pester
Function        AfterEach                         3.3.5      Pester
Function        Assert-MockCalled                 3.3.5      Pester
Function        Assert-VerifiableMocks            3.3.5      Pester
Function        BeforeAll                         3.3.5      Pester
Function        BeforeEach                        3.3.5      Pester
Function        Context                           3.3.5      Pester
Function        Describe                          3.3.5      Pester
Function        Get-MockDynamicParameters         3.3.5      Pester
Function        Get-TestDriveItem                 3.3.5      Pester
Function        In                                3.3.5      Pester
Function        InModuleScope                     3.3.5      Pester
Function        Invoke-Mock                       3.3.5      Pester
Function        Invoke-Pester                     3.3.5      Pester
Function        It                                3.3.5      Pester
Function        Mock                              3.3.5      Pester
Function        New-Fixture                       3.3.5      Pester
Function        Set-DynamicParameterVariables     3.3.5      Pester
Function        Setup                             3.3.5      Pester
Function        Should                            3.3.5      Pester
```

You can get a list of cmdlets available in the module by running the following command as well:

```
PS C:\>Get-Command -Module Pester
```

Now let's start writing our code and test it. Let's first decide what we want to achieve. We want to create a small script that will access any name as the command-line parameter and generate as output a greeting to the name. So, let's first create a `New-Fixture`:

```
PS C:\PowerShell Scripts> New-Fixture -Path .\HelloExample -Name Say-
Hello
Directory: C:\PowerShell Scripts\HelloExample
Mode                LastWriteTime          Length Name
----                -------------          ------ ----
-a----        3/23/2015   12:39 AM             30 Say-Hello.ps1
-a----        3/23/2015   12:39 AM            252 Say-Hello.Tests.ps1
```

Notice that one folder named `HelloExample`, and two files are created in this folder. The `Say-Hello.ps1` file is the file for the actual code, and the second file, `Say-Hello.Tests.ps1`, is the test file.

Now go to the directory and set the location as the current location:

```
PS C:\PowerShell Scripts> cd .\HelloExample
PS C:\PowerShell Scripts\HelloExample> Set-Location -Path 'C:\PowerShell
Scripts\HelloExample'
```

Now, let's examine the contents of these two files.

We can see that `Say-Hello.ps1` is a file with the following lines:

```
function Say-Hello {

}
```

The contents of the file `Say-Hello.Tests.ps1` are far more informative, as shown here:

```
$here = Split-Path -Parent $MyInvocation.MyCommand.Path
$sut = (Split-Path -Leaf $MyInvocation.MyCommand.Path).Replace(".
Tests.", ".")
. "$here\$sut"

Describe "Say-Hello" {
    It "does something useful" {
        $true | Should Be $false
    }
}
```

The first three lines extract the filename of the main script file, and then the dot sources it to the current running environment so that the functions defined in the script will be available in the current scope.

Now, we need to define what the test should do. So, we define our test cases. I have made the necessary modifications:

```
$here = Split-Path -Parent $MyInvocation.MyCommand.Path
$sut = (Split-Path -Leaf $MyInvocation.MyCommand.Path).Replace(".
Tests.", ".")
. "$here\$sut"

Describe "Say-Hello" {
    It "Outputs Hello Sajal, Welcome to Pester" {
Say-Hello -name Sajal | Should Be 'Hello Sajal, Welcome to Pester'
    }
}
```

What I am expecting here is that when `Say-Hello.ps1` is run from the command line with a name as a parameter, it should return `Hello <name>, Welcome to Pester`.

Let's run the first test. As expected, we get a failed test.

```
PS C:\PowerShell Scripts\HelloExample> Invoke-Pester
Describing Say-Hello
  [-] Outputs Hello Sajal, Welcome to Pester 595ms
    Expected: {Hello Sajal, Welcome to Pester}
    But was:  {}
    at line: 7 in C:\PowerShell Scripts\HelloExample\Say-Hello.Tests.ps1
    7:        Say-Hello -name Sajal | Should Be 'Hello Sajal, Welcome to Pester'
Tests completed in 595ms
Passed: 0 Failed: 1 Skipped: 0 Pending: 0
```

Now, let's correct the code with the following code snippet:

```
function Say-Hello {

    param (
        [Parameter(Mandatory)]
        $name
    )
    "Hello $name, Welcome to Pester"
}
```

Let's run the same test again. Now, it passes the test successfully.

```
PS C:\PowerShell Scripts\HelloExample> Invoke-Pester
Describing Say-Hello
  [+] Outputs Hello Sajal, Welcome to Pester 245ms
Tests completed in 245ms
Passed: 1 Failed: 0 Skipped: 0 Pending: 0
```

Since Pester is based on BDD, which is again modeled around a domain-specific language (support natural language), Pester uses a set of defined words to specify the test cases.

We first start by using a `Describe` block to define what we are testing. Then, `Context` is used to define the context in which the test block is being run. We take the help of `It` and `Should` to define the test:

```
Describe "<function name>" {
    Context "<context in which it is run>" {
        It "<what the function does>" {
            <function> | Should <do what>
        }
    }
    Context "<context in which it is run>" {
        It "<what the function does>" {
            <function> | Should <do what>
        }
    }
}
```

Remember one point that though we call `Describe`, `Context`, and It as keywords, they are basically functions. So, when we use script blocks to call them, we need to use them in a specific way. So, the following is incorrect:

```
Context "defines script block incorrectly"
{
    #some tests
}
```

The checkpoints or assertions are as follows:

- Should Be
- Should BeExactly
- Should BeNullOrEmpty
- Should Match
- Should MatchExactly
- Should Exist
- Should Contain
- Should ContainExactly
- Should Throw

Also, all the assertions have an opposite, negative meaning, which we get by adding a 'Not' in between. For example, Should Not Be, Should Not Match, and so on.

Now, you should be able to go ahead and start testing your scripts with Pester. For more details, check out the Pester Wiki at `https://github.com/pester/Pester/wiki/Pester`.

Connecting to a vCenter and other VMware environments using PowerCLI cmdlets

The last topic of this chapter is how to connect to vCenter and other VMware environments using PowerCLI cmdlets.

To use the PowerCLI cmdlets, you need to add the snap-ins and import the modules accordingly. As mentioned previously in the sections *The vSphere PowerCLI package* and *The vCloud PowerCLI package*, to connect to a vCenter environment, you first need to add the Snap-in `VMware.VimAutomation.Core`, and to connect to a vCloud Director environment you need to import the `VMware.VimAutomation.Cloud` module. If you install the package in its default location and your system is a 64-bit OS, then the location of the module is given in the following folder:

```
PS C:\>Add-PSSnapin VMware.VimAutomation.Core
```

```
PS C:\>Import-Module 'C:\Program Files (x86)\VMware\Infrastructure\
vSphere PowerCLI\Modules\VMware.VimAutomation.Cloud'
```

Once the snap-in is added and the module is imported, you will have access to all the PowerCLI commands from the PowerShell ISE console.

Now, let's connect to the vCenter environment by running the following command:

```
PS C:\>Connect-VIServer -Server <server name> -User <user name>-Password
<Password>
```

Similarly, to connect to the vCloud Director server, run the following command:

```
PS C:\> Connect-CIServer -Server <server name> -User <user name>-Password
<Password>
```

There are many other options. You can see the details using the `Get-help` cmdlet or the online help for these commands.

Summary

In this chapter, we touched on the basics of PowerShell, covering the main added advantages of the PowerShell 5.0 preview and basic programming constructs, and how they are implemented in PowerShell. We also discussed PowerCLI, what's new in Version 6.0, and how to run PowerCLI scripts from Command Prompt or as a scheduled task. Next, we discussed version control and how to use GitHub to fully utilize the concepts. At the end of this chapter, we saw how to use Pester to test PowerShell scripts and how to connect to vCenter and vCloud Director environments.

In the next chapter, we are going to cover advanced functions and parameters in PowerShell. We will also cover how to write your own help files and error handling in PowerShell.

2

Reusable Advanced Functions and Scripts

In the first chapter, we revisited PowerShell and PowerCLI basics. Then, we discussed how we could use the GitHub version to control our work and collaborate with others to work on the same project. We also learned how to use Pester to do unit testing on our work. In this chapter, we are going to cover advanced functions and their implementations in PowerShell. Specifically, we are going to talk about the following topics:

- Specifying function attributes
- Specifying parameter attributes
- Using parameter validation attributes
- Using dynamic parameters
- PowerShell help files
- Creating comment-based help
- Error handling in PowerShell

Before we start discussing advanced functions, let's take a look at normal functions. If you type `Get-Help About_Functions` in PowerShell, you can get the details of functions. The description says a function is a list of Windows PowerShell statements that has a name that you can assign. When you run a function, you type the function name. The statements in the list run as if you had typed them at the Command Prompt. Typically, we will use a function to write a portion of code that we will reuse multiple times in a script or external to the script. A sample of a typical function is as follows:

```
Function Get-VC( $vcname,$username){
    Write-Host "vCenter Server is $vcname"
    Write-Host "User name is $username"
}
```

When the preceding function is called, we get the required result:

```
PS C:\> Get-VC vcenter.lab.com vcadmin@lab.com
vCenter Server is vcenter.lab.com
User name is vcadmin@lab.com
```

Since this is a mastering book, I will assume that you already know about functions and will not go into details of a simple function.

> For more details, I suggest that you go through the following two links, which will provide you a very good explanation of the same:
>
> http://blogs.technet.com/b/heyscriptingguy/
> archive/2015/07/08/fun-with-powershell-functions.aspx
>
> http://blogs.technet.com/b/heyscriptingguy/
> archive/2013/04/09/using-powershell-functions-best-
> practices.aspx

Before we go ahead and start talking about the details of an advanced function, let's find out what exactly is an advanced function, how are they different from the normal functions, and where we can or should use them.

Cmdlet in PowerShell is like a function written in C# and provides a lot more functionalities than a standard function. An advanced function in PowerShell is a function that lets you define and write a function but with all the added benefits of cmdlets. So, an advanced function is more like a cmdlet, but it is written in a normal PowerShell way rather than in C#.

The main difference between normal functions and advanced ones is the capabilities that advanced functions provide. With advanced functions, you can have native support for pipeline input, use common parameters that you use with cmdlets, such as -Verbose and -WhatIf, parameter validation, and you can use dynamic parameters to name a few.

So, where should we use normal functions and advanced functions? Well, by all means advanced functions are much better than normal functions, but they are complex as well. So, it depends on the purpose and the personal choice. But in general, if you are writing a function that is very small (consisting of few lines at most) or if you are going to use it as a helper function for another function, probably a normal function would be more appropriate for this. But if you want to write a function that is a major one or if you want to share the function with others, probably you are better off with an advanced function. By all means, if you are sharing it with others and treating it like a module, then you should use an advanced function instead of a simple normal function.

Since we have spoken about advanced functions, what they are, and their main uses, let's take a look at the structure of one advanced function.

In general, an advanced function will look like the following code:

```
<#
        Comment Based Help
#>
Function <function_name> {
[CmdletBinding()]
[OutputType()]
Param(
<Parameters>
)
BEGIN{<# some script> }
PROCESS{<#some script>}
END{<#some script>}
}
```

> It is not mandatory to place Help before the function. We can place it inside the function as well. We will talk more about help in the upcoming sections.

Before we go ahead and talk about the other topics, let's discuss the general structure of an advanced function. In the structure provided earlier, I started with the comment-based help. Then comes the function declaration with the function name.

In the preceding format, the [CmdletBinding()] line is very important and denotes that the function is an advanced function. A function must have the CmdletBinding attribute, the Parameters attribute, or both in order to mark the function as an advanced function. The other lines and formats are optional and can be used with normal functions as well. Advanced functions are more or less used to make the functions more structured and compact and to provide advanced capabilities.

The [OutputType()] line denotes the type of the output variable of the function.

Next comes the Param() definition. Here, we need to define all the parameters and their attributes that we are going to use in the function.

Next come the three very interesting declarations:

```
BEGIN{<# some script> }
PROCESS{<#some script>}
END{<#some script>}
```

The script block defined in the BEGIN portion will be executed only once and can be used as a preprocessing section. So, if you want to execute/do some tasks, such as initializing certain parameters or checking some prerequisites, then write this portion here.

The PROCESS section is the portion that will be processed every time for each of the objects. So, your actual script should go here.

The END portion will be executed only once, at the end of the script execution. So, you should put your house keeping/clearing portion of the script here. Also, if you want to do something that needs to be executed only once and at the end of the script, then it should go into this section.

Specifying function attributes

In case of advanced functions, we use Cmdlet bindings to control the feature or function of the function itself. With this, we define how the function works or behaves.

Addition of the [CmdletBinding()] line allows you to define these controls in an advanced function. Note that with the use of CmdletBinding(), we get the $PSCmdlet automatic variable, but the $Args variable is not available in these functions.

In advanced functions, with the CmdletBinding attribute, unknown parameters and positional arguments that do not have any matching positional parameters results in parameter binding to fail.

Let's examine the available options with the CmdletBinding() attribute and their meaning:

```
<#
     Comment Based Help
#>
function <function_name> {

[CmdletBinding(ConfirmImpact=<String>,
                    DefaultParameterSetName=<String>,
                    HelpURI=<URI>,
                    SupportsPaging=<Boolean>,
                    SupportsShouldProcess=<Boolean>,
                    PositionalBinding=<Boolean>)]
```

```
[OutputType()]
Param(
<Parameters>
)
BEGIN{<# some script> }
PROCESS{<#some script>}
END{<#some script>}
}
```

So, the options available with `CmdletBinding()` are as follows:

- `ConfirmImpact=<String>`: By specifying this argument, we can control when the action of the function can be confirmed by calling the `ShouldProcess` method. We need to specify this argument along with the `SupportsShouldProcess` argument.

- `DefaultParameterSetName=<String>`:As the name suggests, this argument specifies which parameter is set to be used as the default value if PowerShell cannot find other parameters.

- `HelpURI=<URI>`: This argument specifies the Internet address of the external online location of the function's help. It should start with http or https, thus specifying the address.

- `SupportsPaging=<Boolean>`: This argument adds the `First`, `Skip`, and `IncludeTotalCount` parameters to the functions. This argument is generally used when there is a large set of input parameters and you need to select these input parameters. The parameters allow you to define the following:
    - `First`: It returns the first n objects from all the input objects.
    - `Skip`: Using this parameter, you can skip the first n objects and get the remaining objects.
    - `IncludeTotalCount`: This parameter reports the number of total objects in the dataset. This is an integer.

- `SupportsShouldProcess=<Boolean>`: Using this argument, you can use the `Confirm` and `WhatIf` parameters of the function. The `Confirm` parameter will `Confirm` before the command is run on the objects, and the `WhatIf` parameter will list the changes that the commands will make. By specifying the `WhatIf` parameter, we will know what will happen and we can ensure that no unnecessary changes will be made.

- `PositionalBinding=<Boolean>`: Using this argument, you can check whether the parameters in the function are positional in nature. By default, this is taken as `$true`, making the parameters positional in nature; thus, if you want to make it otherwise, you need to specify `$false` as the value to this argument.

The parameters in the PowerShell function are of two types: static and dynamic. For now, we will talk about static parameters, and later in this chapter, we will cover the dynamic parameters.

Static parameters are the ones that are always available in the function scope. Most of the cmdlets and scripts in PowerShell belong to this category.

Parameter attributes are used in order to control and manage the behaviors of the parameters. They define the characteristics of the parameter. The general format to define parameter attributes is as follows:

```
Param(
    [parameter(attribute=value, attribute=value)]
    [<variable type>]
    $variable
)
```

If we use the `param` attribute to define an advanced function, then we need to write it in the following format:

```
Param (
  [parameter()]
  [<variable type>] $variable
)
```

Notice that, though we did not provide any attributes to the parameter, we still need to mention it in the opening and closing brackets. This is what will indicate that the function is an advanced function. The attributes that we specify for a parameter can be divided into the following two categories:

- The `parameter` attribute
- The `parameter` and variable validation attributes

Let's discuss these categories and the different attributes available under them in detail.

Specifying parameter attributes

In this section, we will discuss the `parameter` attributes and how to set them. The attributes falling under this category define the different attributes of the parameter itself. Let's take a closer look at the most useful and common options available to define parameter attributes and their uses:

- `Mandatory` argument: This argument indicates that this particular parameter is compulsory, otherwise it is optional. For example, if I am writing a function to connect to a vCenter server and doing some work and I want the vCenter name to be provided at runtime, then the following code makes sure that the cmdlet call will fail without the `$VCName` parameter:

```
Param (
   [parameter(Mandatory=$true)]
   [String] $VCName
)
```

- `Position` argument: We define the positional argument to specify which value will be assigned to which parameter by the position of the values at runtime, without the need to specify the parameter name. PowerShell will understand which parameter the value needs to be assigned to by the order they are provided at runtime. If the position parameter is not specified, then the parameter name must precede the value so that it can be assigned properly. By default, in PowerShell, all the function parameters are positional in nature. At the time of calling the function, if we do not provide the parameter names ahead of the values, then they will be assigned by the position of the parameters. For example, notice the following function, which simply takes the vCenter name and username as input parameters to the function and prints them out. Here, though the `$UName` parameter is mentioned first, because its position is 1 the second value is assigned to it:

```
Function Get-VC{
    [cmdletbinding()]

    Param(
    [Parameter(Position=1)]
    [String[]]
    $UName,
```

```
[Parameter(Position=0)]
[String[]]
$VCName
)

Write-Host "vCenter Name: $VCName"
Write-Host "User Name: $UName"

}
```

```
PS C:\> Function Get-VC{
    [cmdletbinding()]

    Param(
    [Parameter(Position=1)]
    [string[]]
    $UName,

    [Parameter(Position=0)]
    [string[]]
    $VCName
    )

    Write-Host "vCenter Name: $VCName"
    Write-Host "User Name: $UName"

}

PS C:\> Get-VC vcenter.lab.com administrator
vCenter Name: vcenter.lab.com
User Name: administrator
```

- `ValueFromPipeline`: This particular argument specifies the parameters the function can take as values from the pipeline. Note that this will enable the function to take the entire object not just a property of the object. To enable this, check and use the `ValueFromPipelineByPropertyName` argument. Check the following examples. When the `ValueFromPipeline` argument is not provided, the function does not accept the object value from the pipeline. For example, run the following code:

```
Function Get-VC{
    [cmdletbinding()]

    Param(
    [Parameter()]
    [String[]]
    $VCName
    )
```

```
        Write-Host "vCenter Name: $VCName"


    }
```

```
PS C:\> Function Get-VC{
    [cmdletbinding()]

    Param(
    [Parameter()]
    [string[]]
    $VCName
    )

    Write-Host "vCenter Name: $VCName"

}


PS C:\> 'vcenter.lab.com' | Get-VC
The input object cannot be bound to any parameters for the command either becaus
e the command does not take pipeline input or the input and its properties do no
t match any of the parameters that take pipeline input. (raised by: Get-VC)
vCenter Name:
```

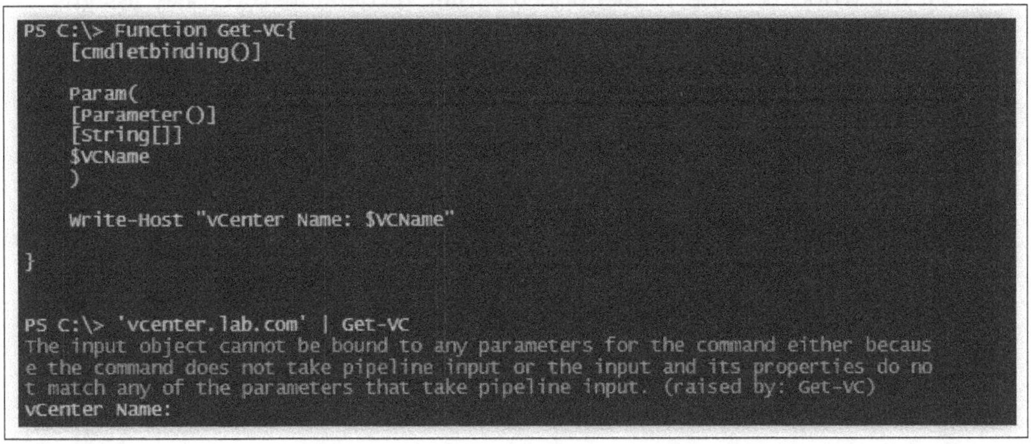

When we provide the ValueFromPipeline parameter, it now works
as expected:

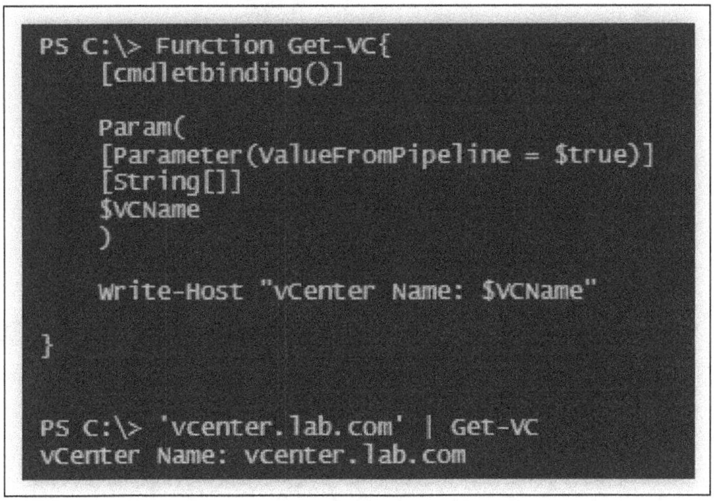

```
PS C:\> Function Get-VC{
    [cmdletbinding()]

    Param(
    [Parameter(ValueFromPipeline = $true)]
    [string[]]
    $VCName
    )

    Write-Host "vCenter Name: $VCName"

}


PS C:\> 'vcenter.lab.com' | Get-VC
vCenter Name: vcenter.lab.com
```

- `Alias`: This attribute provides alternate names for the parameters. It is possible to use as many aliases as needed for the parameters. Check the following example; also note that if we do not mention any parameter name, it still works because, as mentioned earlier, by default PowerShell assigns the value to the parameter that matches the position. For example, let's take a look at the following example where we have mentioned multiple aliases for the `$VCName` parameter:

```
Function Get-VC{
    [cmdletbinding()]

    Param(
    [Parameter(Mandatory = $true)]
    [alias('VC','vcenter')]
    [String[]]$VCName
    )

    Write-Host "vCenter Name: $VCName"

}
```

When we run the function, we get the required output.

```
PS C:\> Function Get-VC{
    [cmdletbinding()]

    Param(
    [Parameter(Mandatory = $true)]
    [alias('VC','vcenter')]
    [String[]]$VCName
    )

    Write-Host "vCenter Name: $VCName"

}
PS C:\> Get-VC vcenter.lab.com
vCenter Name: vcenter.lab.com

PS C:\> Get-VC -vc vcenter.lab.com
vCenter Name: vcenter.lab.com

PS C:\> Get-VC -vcenter vcenter.lab.com
vCenter Name: vcenter.lab.com

PS C:\> Get-VC -vcname vcenter.lab.com
vCenter Name: vcenter.lab.com
```

> The alias name or the parameter is not case sensitive.

Using parameter validation attributes

Attributes falling under this category define the attributes that we can use to validate the value of a parameter/variable itself. The following is a list of the most commonly used parameters:

- `AllowNull` / `AllowEmptyString`: This attribute allows a mandatory parameter to accept a NULL value or empty string. Check the following example. When this attribute is not set, the function does not allow us to give an empty string as an input to the `$VCName` parameter, as it is a mandatory input. When we comment out the `AllowEmptyString` parameter, it throws an error:

```
Function Get-VC{
    [cmdletbinding()]

    Param(
    [Parameter(Mandatory = $true)]
#    [AllowEmptyString()]
    [String]$VCName
    )
    Write-Host "vCenter Name: $VCName"
}
```

```
PowerCLI C:\> Function Get-VC{
>>>      [cmdletbinding()]
>>>
>>>      Param(
>>>      [Parameter(Mandatory = $true)]
>>> #    [AllowEmptyString()]
>>>      [String]$VCName
>>>      )
>>>
>>>      Write-Host "vCenter Name: $VCName"
>>> }
PowerCLI C:\> $name = $null
PowerCLI C:\> Get-VC $name
Connect-VIServer : Cannot validate argument on parameter 'Server'. The
argument is null or empty. Provide an argument that is not null or
empty, and then try the command again.
At line:1 char:8
+ Get-VC $name
+        ~~~~~
    + CategoryInfo          : InvalidData: (:) [Connect-VIServer], Param
   eterBindingValidationException
    + FullyQualifiedErrorId : ParameterArgumentValidationError,VMware.Vi
   mAutomation.ViCore.Cmdlets.Commands.ConnectVIServer
```

Notice that, when this attribute is set, the function allows us to give an empty string as the input to the $VCName parameter:

```
PS C:\> Function Get-VC{
    [cmdletbinding()]

    Param(
    [Parameter(Mandatory = $true)]
    [AllowEmptyString()]
    [string]$VCName
    )

    write-Host "vCenter Name: $VCName"
}

PS C:\> Get-VC $name
vCenter Name:
```

- ValidateCount: This attribute specifies the minimum and maximum number of values that a parameter accepts. PowerShell will generate an error if the number of values provided along with the command is greater or fewer than the specified ones. For example, in the following code, the minimum number of values permitted with the $VMName variable is 2 and the maximum is 10:

```
Param
    (
        [parameter(Mandatory=$true)]
        [ValidateCount(2,10)]
        [String[]]
        $VMName
    )
```

- ValidateLength: Using this attribute, we can restrict the number of characters that can be provided as values to a parameter. PowerShell will generate an error if the length of a value specified for a parameter or a variable is outside the range. In the following example, the value of the $VMName parameter must be between 1 to 10 characters:

```
Param
    (
        [parameter(Mandatory=$true)]
        [ValidateLength(1,10)]
        [String[]]
        $VMName
    )
```

- `ValidatePattern`: This attribute restricts the parameter value according to the regular expression specified by the pattern mentioned by the attribute. PowerShell will generate an error if the value does not match the regular expression pattern. In the following example, the `$VMName` variable must have a value that starts with two characters followed by any one of the special characters `@`, `#`, and `!` and followed by two digits, of which the first digit can lie between `0` to `9` and the last digit must be between `0` to `5`:

```
Param(
[parameter(Mandatory=$true)]
    [ValidatePattern("[A-Z][a-z][@,#,!][0-9][0-5]")]
    [String[]]
    $VMName
)
```

> For more details on parameter attributes, check out `https://technet.microsoft.com/en-us/library/hh847743.aspx`.

Dynamic parameters

All the earlier examples were examples of static parameters. Before the cmdlets of the function are executed, these parameters come into existence and remain available for the entire duration of the scope of the function. Dynamic parameters are those parameters that are defined in such a way that depending on certain conditions only, they come into existence. It may be designed in such a way that a dynamic parameter will come into existence only when another parameter is used in the function or a parameter has a certain value. So, late binding is applied for these types of parameters.

For example, let's discuss the following requirements:

- We want to create a VM, provided the VM name is given by a user.
- We have three different environments named Dedicated, Shared, and Cloud where the VM can be created.
- If any environment is not mentioned by a user, then by default the VM will be created in the shared environment.
- For a shared and Cloud environment, providing a VM name would be enough to create a VM in that environment as we will use a default user ID to create a VM in that environment.

- If a user wants to create a VM in a dedicated environment, then the script asks the user for `userid` with which the VM will be created.

- In a dedicated environment, users with VM creation rights have `admin` included in their `userid` or username. So, if the value entered by the user does not contain `admin` in their `userid`, then the task will fail.

We will use a dynamic parameter in the function to achieve the things mentioned in the preceding points. But before we go ahead and discuss the function, let's first take a look at the syntax and steps to create such a parameter:

- The syntax for the declaration is `DynamicParam {<Script block>}`.

- In the script block, we will use an `If` statement block to specify the condition, which in turn will check whether the parameter will come into existence in the function or not.

- In the `If` statement, we will first define the attributes of the parameter with `System.Management.Automation.ParameterAttribute`.

- Next, we need to create an attribute collection object with `System.Collections.ObjectModel.Collection[System.Attribute]`.

- Then, we need to add `ParameterAttributes` to the attribute collection.

- Next we need to define a runtime defined parameter object with `System.Management.Automation.RuntimeDefinedParameter`. We also need to provide the following details:
  - Name of the parameter
  - Type of the parameter
  - The attribute collection object that we created earlier

- We need to create a runtime defined parameter dictionary object with `System.Management.Automation.RuntimeDefinedParameterDictionary`.

- Next, we need to add `RuntimeDefinedParameter` to the `RuntimeDefinedParameterDictionary` object.

- Finally, we need to return the `RuntimeDefinedParameterDictionary` object back to the runtime.

> We can create all these attributes, which are similar to the ones used in the static type of parameter, in a dynamic parameter as well.

So, let's first analyze the function and, at the end, we will stitch everything together to get the final script.

First, we will define the function name. For the purpose of this function, I have declared a function with the function name, `Create-VM`.

Next, `CmdletBinding()` was mentioned to define that the function is an advanced function. Then, we declared two static parameters: `$vmname` and `$environment`, to store values of the VM name and the environment where the VM will be created, respectively. Note that the `$environment` parameter can have only three values: `Dedicated`, `Shared`, and `Cloud`. We enforced this check using the `ValidateSet` attribute of the parameter.

In the next section, we defined the dynamic parameter with `DynamicParam()` followed by the `IF` statement, where we check whether the `$environment` variable has been given a `Dedicated` value or not. If it has been given this value, then the next portion will be executed and the dynamic parameter will be created. If it has not, then the next portion will not get executed and the dynamic parameter will not be created:

```
Function Create-VM {
    [CmdletBinding()]
    param(
        [Parameter(
            Mandatory=$true,
            Position=1,
            HelpMessage="Enter the name of the VM to be created:"
        )]
        [string]$vmname,

        [Parameter(
            Mandatory=$false,
            Position=2,
            HelpMessage="Enter the environment where you want to
create the VM:"
        )]
        [ValidateSet("Dedicated","Shared","Cloud")]
        [string]$environment="Shared"

    )

    DynamicParam {
If ($environment -eq "Dedicated") {

            #declaring the parameter name for the user name
            $user = 'username'
            #creating a new ParameterAttribute Object and then setting
the attributes of the parameter
```

```
            $userAttribute = New-Object System.Management.Automation.
ParameterAttribute
            $userAttribute.Position = 3
            $userAttribute.Mandatory = $true
            $userAttribute.HelpMessage = "Only named users can create
a VM in this environment. Please enter your name:"

            #create an attributecollection object for the attributes
we just created
            $attributeCollection = new-object System.Collections.
ObjectModel.Collection[System.Attribute]

            #adding our defined custom attributes to the collection
            $attributeCollection.Add($userAttribute)

            #creating the new dynamic paramater with attributes
mentioned in the attribute collection
            $userParam = New-Object System.Management.Automation.
RuntimeDefinedParameter($user, [string], $attributeCollection)

            #exposing the parameter to the runspace and returning it
            $paramDictionary = New-Object System.Management.
Automation.RuntimeDefinedParameterDictionary
            $paramDictionary.Add($user, $userParam)
            return $paramDictionary
        }
    }

  Begin {
        #Checking if the dynamic parameter was created and expected
value was provided to it
        if ($PSBoundParameters.userName -and $PSBoundParameters.
userName -NotMatch "admin") {
            Write-Error "You do not have enough permission to create a
VM in this environment" -ErrorAction Stop
        }
        #Creating an easy parameter name for the Dynamic Parameter so
that we can use it easily in the function
        $username = $PSBoundParameters.userName
    }

  Process {

        # We can create input for our custom scripts
# For the purpose of checking the script we are just
```

```
#printing the name to the screen here.
if ($environment -ne "Dedicated") {
        Write-Host "You have entered VMname: $vmname Environment:
$environment"
        }
        Else{
Write-Host "You have entered VMname: $vmname Environment: $environment
UserID:$username "
        }
    }
}
```

Now, let's run the function. But before we call the function and use it from
the PowerShell Command Prompt, we need to import the function into our
environment. To do this, we will dot source the functions in the current environment.
Dot sourcing enables us to bring the variables and functions from another script into
the current scope. We dot source another script in the following way:

PS C:\> . .\Create-VM.ps1

Now, we can call the function in a normal way by calling out its name:

PS C:\> Create-VM test-vm web

First, we will provide parameters that do not have values within the permissible
range, that is, Dedicated, Shared, and Cloud. As expected, the command fails.
It shows you the reason as well.

```
PS C:\Users\sdebnath\Desktop> Create-VM test-vm web
Create-VM : Cannot validate argument on parameter 'environment'. The argument "web" does not belong to the set
"Dedicated,Shared,Cloud" specified by the ValidateSet attribute. Supply an argument that is in the set and then try the
command again.
At line:1 char:19
+ Create-VM test-vm web
+                   ~~~
    + CategoryInfo          : InvalidData: (:) [Create-VM], ParameterBindingValidationException
    + FullyQualifiedErrorId : ParameterArgumentValidationError,Create-VM
```

Next, we will provide a valid value for the environment. It shows you the
right information.

```
PS C:\Users\sdebnath\Desktop> Create-VM test-vm Shared
You have entered VMname : test-vm Environment: Shared
```

Now, we will provide the environment value as `Dedicated` but will not provide a `userid`. PowerShell will prompt us for the `userid`, so we will provide a `userid` that will not have an admin in the `userid`. Again, as expected, the command fails saying that the user does not have enough permission. This is what we wanted.

```
PS C:\Users\sdebnath\Desktop> Create-VM test-vm Dedicated
cmdlet Create-VM at command pipeline position 1
Supply values for the following parameters:
(Type !? for Help.)
userName: sajal
Create-VM : You do not have enough permission to create a VM in this environment
At line:1 char:1
+ Create-VM test-vm Dedicated
+ ~~~~~~~~~~~~~~~~~~~~~~~~~~~~
    + CategoryInfo          : NotSpecified: (:) [Write-Error], WriteErrorException
    + FullyQualifiedErrorId : Microsoft.PowerShell.Commands.WriteErrorException,Create-VM
```

Finally, let's provide all the correct values and see what the output is like.

```
PS C:\Users\sdebnath\Desktop> Create-VM test-vm Dedicated systemadmin
You have entered VMname : test-vm Environment: Dedicated UserID:systemadmin
```

Everything runs as expected.

The preceding example shows you how dynamic parameters can be used in a function to do special tasks.

These parameters are very useful, but they should be used carefully as users may find it very difficult to discover them.

Switch parameters

Switch parameters are parameters without any need to assign any value to them. As the name suggests, they act as a switch. By default, their values are `$false`. Once these parameters are mentioned in the command line, their values become `$true`. We can use this switch parameter to perform our checks and run their respective script blocks. The following example is a function that connects to a vCenter server or vCloud Director server based on the input that we provide. As parameter values, we accept `ServerName` and `UserName` to connect to the server, `Password` for the connection, and another parameter that will act as a switch. If we mention `-VCServer` in the command line, then the `Connect-VIServer` cmdlets will be executed; if `-VCDServer` is mentioned, then the `Connect-CIServer` cmdlets will be executed. So, run the following code snippet:

```
Function Connect-Server{
[CmdletBinding()]
 Param(
    [Parameter(Mandatory=$true)]
```

```
            [string] $ServerName,
            [string] $UserName,
        [String] $Pass,
            [switch] $VCServer,
        [Switch] $VCDServer
            )


    If ($VCServer) {
            # Connect-VIServer -Server $VCServer -User -$Username -
Password $Pass
            Write-Host "vCenter Server: $ServerName User: $UserName
Password: $Pass"
            }
    If ($VCDServer) {
            # Connect-CIServer -Server $VCDServer -User -$Username -
Password $Pass
            Write-Host "vCD Server: $ServerName User: $UserName Password:
$Pass"
            }
}
```

```
PS C:\> Function Connect-Server{
[CmdletBinding()]
 Param(
    [Parameter(Mandatory=$true)]
        [string]$ServerName,
        [string]$UserName,
        [String]$Pass,
        [switch]$VCServer,
        [Switch]$VCDServer
        )

    If ($VCServer) {
        # Connect-VIServer -Server $VCServer -User -$Username -Password $Pass
        Write-Host "vCenter Server: $ServerName User: $UserName Password: $Pass"
        }
    If ($VCDServer) {
        # Connect-CIServer -Server $VCDServer -User -$Username -Password $Pass
        Write-Host "vCD Server: $ServerName User: $UserName Password: $Pass"
        }
}

PS C:\> Connect-Server -ServerName vcenter.lab.com -UserName vcadmin@lab.com -Pass PasswOrd -VCServer
vCenter Server: vcenter.lab.com User: vcadmin@lab.com Password: PasswOrd

PS C:\> Connect-Server -ServerName vcenter.lab.com -UserName vcadmin@lab.com -Pass PasswOrd -VCDServer
vCD Server: vcenter.lab.com User: vcadmin@lab.com Password: PasswOrd
```

Since I do not have a vCD environment ready, I have decided to just show the values
to the console so that the way they work can be understood.

PowerShell help files

Help files are the best way to get help (pun intended) in PowerShell. They provide the most intensive details about the cmdlet and includes overviews, detailed explanations, examples, and much more. As its name suggests, you get help by running the `Get-Help` cmdlet.

For people out there who love *NIX, `Get-Help` is the equivalent of man pages in the Linux or Unix environment. Actually, an alias of man à `Get-Help` exists in PowerShell (thanks to Brian Wuchner for pointing this out).

The first thing that you notice in PowerShell 3.0 onward is that all the help files are not included as part of the package itself. In order to use the full range and the updated help files, you need to get them from the Microsoft website. If you try to use `Get-Help` for a cmdlet for which the help files are not downloaded yet, you get a short help description and then the following notification:

```
REMARKS
    Get-Help cannot find the Help files for this cmdlet on this computer. It is displaying only partial help.
    -- To download and install Help files for the module that includes this cmdlet, use Update-Help.
    -- To view the Help topic for this cmdlet online, type: "Get-Help Get-Help -Online" or
       go to http://go.microsoft.com/fwlink/?LinkID=113316.
```

So, you need to run `Update-Help` to update all the help files. What this command does is that it checks all the installed cmdlets and verify them against the online version. If it finds an updated version available online, then it downloads the updated version. So, when you run `PS C:\ Update-Help`, it updates the help files.

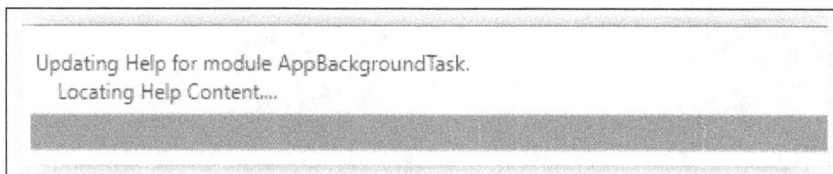

```
Updating Help for module AppBackgroundTask.
    Locating Help Content....
```

Remember that, since it will update the help files placed in the default system path, you need to have administrator rights to run this command, otherwise this command will run but will fail to put the files in the system directories. So, before you run this command, open and run the console as an administrator.

There are times when we do not have an Internet connection in a system, especially in data center environments. In such a situation, we can download the help files into a central repository and then later use that repository to update the help files. The first part can be done by running the `Save-Help` cmdlet:

```
PS C:\> Save-Help –DestinationPath  <Path where to store the files>
```

```
PS C:\Windows\system32> Save-Help -DestinationPath 'C:\Users\sdebnath\Desktop\Help Files'
```

Once the files are downloaded, you can use that location to update the help files:

```
PS C:\> Update-Help -SourcePath <Path where the help files are>
```

```
PS C:\Windows\system32> Update-Help -SourcePath 'C:\Users\sdebnath\Desktop\Help Files'
```

> Note that Update-Help and Save-Help work only with XML-based help files. It is not available for comment-based help files. In the next section, we are going to talk more about comment-based help files.

Creating comment-based help

Comment-based help is the easiest way to create help for the scripts that you write. If you write comment-based help in your function, then the Get-Help cmdlet will show you help for the function in the same way as it shows the help for any other PowerShell native cmdlet. So, whenever you are writing an advanced function, you should include comment-based help so that end users can utilize the help of the Get-help cmdlet to work with the function.

Before we go ahead and dive into comment-based help, I would like to draw your attention to the following fact.

You have just seen the preceding function where I created a dynamic variable to accept the user id, vmName, and environment where I can create VMs. Note that, in this function, I did not write any help, so what happens if I try to run Get-Help on this function? Let's see.

```
PS C:\PowerShell Files> Get-Help Create-VM

NAME
    Create-VM

SYNTAX
    Create-VM [-vmName] <string> [[-environment] <string> {Dedicated | Shared | Cloud}] [<CommonParameters>]

ALIASES
    None

REMARKS
    None
```

Wow! It gives a short description. Let's try the -Full version.

```
PS C:\PowerShell Files> Get-Help Create-VM -Full
NAME
    Create-VM

SYNTAX
    Create-VM [-vmName] <string> [[-environment] <string> {Dedicated | Shared | Cloud}] [<CommonParameters>]

PARAMETERS
    -environment <string>
        Enter the environment where you want to create the VM::

        Required?                    false
        Position?                    2
        Accept pipeline input?       false
        Parameter set name           (All)
        Aliases                      None
        Dynamic?                     false

    -vmName <string>
        Enter the name of the VM to be created::

        Required?                    true
        Position?                    1
        Accept pipeline input?       false
        Parameter set name           (All)
        Aliases                      None
        Dynamic?                     false

    <CommonParameters>
        This cmdlet supports the common parameters: Verbose, Debug,
        ErrorAction, ErrorVariable, WarningAction, WarningVariable,
        OutBuffer, PipelineVariable, and OutVariable. For more information, see
        about_CommonParameters (http://go.microsoft.com/fwlink/?LinkID=113216).

INPUTS
    None

OUTPUTS
    System.Object

ALIASES
    None

REMARKS
    None
```

Pretty amazing right? It provides help in the same format as it provides for other cmdlets without us doing anything. So, how do we fill up those empty areas and write our own help portions? Let's start doing this.

Comment-based help can be used in the following three situations:

- Functions
- Scripts
- Script modules

The syntax of comment-based help is as follows:

```
# .< help keyword>
# <help content>
```

OR:

```
<#
            .< help keyword>
< help content>
        #>
```

There are several rules for writing comment-based help. We will cover a few of them in this section. The rest will be covered in their respective sections:

- Rule 1: You can write the entire help portion with successive comment lines with # or you can simply create a comment block with <# and #>.

- Rule 2: All the lines in a comment-based help topic must be contagious. If a help topic follows a normal comment, which is not part of the topic, then there must be at least one blank line between the last nonhelp comment line and the beginning of a comment-based help line.

- Rule 3: Keywords define each section of comment-based help. Each keyword must start with a dot (.).

- Rule 4: Keywords can appear in any order and the keyword names are not case sensitive.

- Rule 5. The most important fact is that, if one of the keywords is misspelled, then the entire block may be ignored. So, take special care to properly spell each keyword.

- Rule 6: The comment block must contain at least one keyword. The help content begins one line after the keyword line and may span multiple lines.

In **functions**:

Comment-based help for a function can be inserted in any one of three locations:

- At the beginning of the function body:

```
function Get-Function
        {
<#
            .< help keyword>
< help content>
            #>

<function commands>
        }
```

- At the end of the function body:

```
function Get-Function
        {
<function commands>

<#
          .< help keyword>
< help content>
               #>
        }
```

- Just before the function keyword. Note that there cannot be more than one blank line between the last line of the function help and the function declaration:

```
<#
        .< help keyword>
< help content>
          #>
          function Get-Function { }
```

In **scripts**:

The following rules apply for the location of comment-based help in scripts:

- The comment-based help portion can be kept at the beginning of the script file. The help portion can be preceded either by comment lines or blank lines:

```
<#
        .< help keyword>
< help content>
          #>

          function Get-Function { }
```

- If the first item in the script body after the help declaration is a function, then there must be at least two blank lines between the end of the script help and the beginning of the function declaration. Otherwise, the help will be considered to be the help for the function and not for the script.

- The help script block can be put at the end of the script file. But if the script is signed, then we need to put the help block at the beginning of the script file, as the end is reserved for the signature block:

```
function Get-Function { }


<#
        .< help keyword>
< help content>
            #>
```

In **script modules**:

In script modules, we need to put comment-based help as per the syntax for functions. We cannot use comment-based help here, as we do in case of scripts, to define help for all the functions defined in the module. So, in case of modules, if we are using comment-based help, then we need to either define help for each of the functions, or if we are using external help files (XML-based help files), then we need to define them for each of the functions:

```
# .ExternalHelp <XML-file-name>
function <function-name>
{
    ...
}
```

> Here, we used an XML-based help file as a help file so that it can be updated. Also, note the position of the `.ExternalHelp` keyword declaration location.

Next, let's take a closer look at some of the most used keywords in comment-based help:

- **.SYNOPSIS**: This section provides a short description of the function or script. This keyword can be used only once in each topic.

- **.DESCRIPTION**: This section provides a detailed description of the function or script. This keyword can also be used only once in each topic.

- **.PARAMETER <Parameter Name>**: In this section, we provide a description of each parameter defined in the function. We need to use the .PARAMETER keyword for each parameter defined in the function/script and provide details of the parameter. Note that the parameter name must be on the same line as the .PARAMETER keyword.

- **.EXAMPLE**: We can use this keyword to define an example for the script. We can give a sample command that will use the function/script with option output details. We can give as many examples as we want. Typically, it should cover most of the use cases for the script.

- **.INPUTS**: Using this keyword, we can show what type of objects can be piped into the function/script with an optional description of the object.

- **.OUTPUTS**: Similar to the .INPUTS keyword, we can use this keyword to define the type of the outputs.

- **.NOTES**: The portion succeeding this keyword provides additional information of the function or script.

- **.EXTERNALHELP <XML Help File>**: This keyword specifies the XML-based help file for the script or function. This XML-based help file takes precedence over the comment-based help. If this keyword is present, then the comment based help is ignored.

> There are other keywords as well. For a detailed list and discussion, visit `https://technet.microsoft.com/en-us/library/hh847834.aspx`.

Now, let's take a look at an example. In the previous section, we created an advanced function (`Create-VM`) with dynamic parameters. Let's write a help topic for it. Since this is a single function, we will follow the procedure for writing a comment-based help for functions:

Sample Help:

```
<#
.SYNOPSIS
    Creates a VM in particular environment based on the inputs
provided by the user.
.DESCRIPTION
    Create-VM is a function that can create a VM in any of the three
given environment namely "Dedicated", "Shared" and "Cloud". The user
chooses where he wants to create the VM. If the user wants to create
a VM in the Dedicated environment then he needs to have special
administrative permission to create the VM in that environment. The
function throws an error if the user provided value does not match
the environment permissible values. Also for a user to create a vm
in Dedicated environment needs to have "admin" in his user id. Unless
his/her userid does not contain "admin" as a keyword he/she will be
denied the permission to create a VM there.
.PARAMETER vmName
```

The name of the VM which needs to be created. This is a simple string variable.
.PARAMETER environment

A normal string parameter which identifies which environment should be chosen for the VM creation. The value of this variable can be from "Dedicated", "Shared" and "Cloud" only.
.PARAMETER userName

This is a dynamic parameter defined within the script. This parameter comes into effect to store the user name when the end user choses "Dedicated" as their destination environment for VM creation.
.EXAMPLE

```
Create-VM -vmName 'test-vm' -environment Shared
Output:
You have entered VMname : test-vm Environment: Shared
```

.EXAMPLE

```
Create-VM -vmName 'test-vm' -environment Cloud
Output:
You have entered VMname : test-vm Environment: Cloud
```

.EXAMPLE

```
Create-VM -vmName 'test-vm' -environment Dedicated -userName
sysadmin
Output:
You have entered VMname : test-vm Environment: Dedicated
UserID:sysadmin
```

.INPUTS

None. This function can not take input from pipeline

.OUTPUTS

System.Object

.NOTES

Author: Sajal Debnath
#>

Now, we can get the full help using the Get-Help cmdlet.

Also, note that using the -ShowWindow switch will display the help in a separate window. An example of such a help is shown in the following example. Since I used the ShowWindow parameter, the output is given in another window:

```
PS C:\PowerShell Files> Get-Help Create-VM -ShowWindow
```

```
Synopsis
    Creates a VM in particular environment based on the inputs provided by the user.

Syntax
    Create-VM [-vmName] <String> [[-environment] <String>] [-Errrolog ] [-LogFile <String>] [<CommonParameters>]


Description
    Create-VM is a function that can create a VM in any of the three given environment namely "Dedicated", "Shared" and "Cloud".
    The user chooses where he wants to create the VM. If the user wants to create a VM in the Dedicated environment then he needs to
    have special administrative permission to create the VM in that environment. The function throws an error if the user provided
    value does not match the environment permissible values. Also for a user to create a vm in Dedicated environment needs to have
    "admin" in his user id. Unless his/her userid does not contain "admin" as a keyword he/she will be denied the permission to
    create a VM there.


Parameters
    -vmName <String>
        The name of the VM which needs to be created. This is a simple string variable

        Required?                 true
        Position?                 2
        Default value
        Accept pipeline input?    false
        Accept wildcard characters? false

    -environment <String>
        A normal string parameter which identifies which environmetn should be chosen for the VM creation. The value of this variable
        can be from "Dedicated", "Shared" and "Cloud" only.

        Required?                 false
        Position?                 3
        Default value             Shared
        Accept pipeline input?    false
        Accept wildcard characters? false

    -Errrolog <SwitchParameter>
        Switch to turn on Errrolog

        Required?                 false
        Position?                 named
        Default value             False
        Accept pipeline input?    false
        Accept wildcard characters? false
```

Since the output could not be given in a single screen, the following is the rest of the output:

```
    -LogFile <String>
        Log file Location

        Required?                false
        Position?                named
        Default value            C:\Errolog.txt
        Accept pipeline input?   false
        Accept wildcard characters?  false


Inputs
    None. This function can not take input from pipeline

Outputs
    System.Object

Notes
    Author:  Sajal Debnath

Examples
    ------------------------- EXAMPLE 1 -------------------------|
    C:\PS>Create-VM -vmName 'test-vm' -environment Shared

    Output:
You have entered VMname : test-vm Environment: Shared




    ------------------------- EXAMPLE 2 -------------------------
    C:\PS>Create-VM -vmName 'test-vm' -environment Cloud

    Output:
You have entered VMname : test-vm Environment: Cloud              I




    ------------------------- EXAMPLE 3 -------------------------
    C:\PS>Create-VM -vmName 'test-vm' -environment Dedicated -userName sysadmin

    Output:
You have entered VMname : test-vm Environment: Dedicated UserID:sysadmin
```

Note that the help file in the preceding screenshot shows the information I provided as the $Errorlog and $LogFile parameters. The function that generated the preceding help file is shown in the following screenshot. The $Errorlog and $LogFile parameters were switched in order to turn on logging and had normal comments, shown in the help file.

```
[CmdletBinding()]
param(
    [Parameter(
        Mandatory=$true,
        Position=1,
        HelpMessage="Enter the name of the VM to be created::"

        )]
    [Alias('VM')]
    [string]$vmName,

    [Parameter(
        Mandatory=$false,
        Position=2,
        HelpMessage="Enter the environment where you want to create the VM::"
    )]
    [Alias('env')]
    [ValidateSet("Dedicated","Shared","Cloud")]
    [string]$environment="Shared",

    # Switch to turn on Errrolog
    [Switch]$Errrolog,

    # Log file Location
    [String]$LogFile = 'C:\Errolog.txt'

)
```

You can now go ahead and use other keywords in the help topic to make it more informative. Remember that the more information you provide, the easier it becomes for the end users to work with the function or script that you write.

Error handling in PowerShell

Before we go ahead and talk about how to handle errors or avoid them while writing scripts in PowerShell, let's speak about a few of the inherent features of advanced functions that can help end users. These are `Write-Verbose`, `Write-Error`, `Write-Warning`, and `-Whatif`. These are not typical error handling ways in PowerShell, but by using these in advanced functions, you can provide more ways to avoid errors in scripts.

`Write-Verbose` allows you to define more information for end users when they run the script/function/cmdlet with the `-Verbose` option. The same goes for the `Write-Error` and `Write-Warning` options. Defining `-Whatif` would allow end users to know what exactly the script will do if it is run normally. The following is a sample script showing all of these:

```powershell
Function Create-VM{
    [CmdletBinding()]
    param(
        [Parameter()]
        [String[]]$VMNames,
        [Switch]$WhatIf

    )

    PROCESS{

        If($WhatIf){
            "What If: Will create a VM with the name that was provided as input"
        }
        Else{
            If($VMNames.Count -gt 2){
                Write-Verbose "Checking to see if more than 2 VM names were provided"
                Write-Warning "You have entered more than 2 VM names, it will take time to create them"
            }

            Write-Verbose "Checking to see if no value was provided"
            If($VMNames.Count -eq 0){
                Write-Error "No VM Names were provided"
            }

            Write-Verbose "Providing the VM names as output. Typically I would create a VM at this stage"
            Write-Host "The VMnames are : : $VMNames"

        }
    }
}
```

-WhatIf will only show the purpose of the script. If more than two VMnames are provided, then there will be an error message shown but not providing any VM name will result in an error. The following is a screenshot showing all of these use cases in the script:

```
PS C:\PowerShell Files> Create-VM test1
The VMnames are : : test1

PS C:\PowerShell Files> Create-VM test1 -Verbose
VERBOSE: Checking to see if no value was provided
VERBOSE: Providing the VM names as output. Typically I would create a VM at this stage
The VMnames are : : test1

PS C:\PowerShell Files> Create-VM test1 -whatIf
What If: Will create a VM with the name that was provided as input

PS C:\PowerShell Files> Create-VM test1,test2,test3
WARNING: You have entered more than 2 VM names, it will take time to create them
The VMnames are : : test1 test2 test3

PS C:\PowerShell Files> Create-VM test1,test2,test3 -Verbose
VERBOSE: Checking to see if more than 2 VM names were provided
WARNING: You have entered more than 2 VM names, it will take time to create them
VERBOSE: Checking to see if no value was provided
VERBOSE: Providing the VM names as output. Typically I would create a VM at this stage
The VMnames are : : test1 test2 test3

PS C:\PowerShell Files> Create-VM
Create-VM : No VM Names were provided
At line:1 char:1
+ Create-VM
+ ~~~~~~~~~
    + CategoryInfo          : NotSpecified: (:) [Write-Error], WriteErrorException
    + FullyQualifiedErrorId : Microsoft.PowerShell.Commands.WriteErrorException,Create-VM

The VMnames are : :

PS C:\PowerShell Files> Create-VM -Verbose
VERBOSE: Checking to see if no value was provided
Create-VM : No VM Names were provided
At line:1 char:1
+ Create-VM -Verbose
+ ~~~~~~~~~
    + CategoryInfo          : NotSpecified: (:) [Write-Error], WriteErrorException
    + FullyQualifiedErrorId : Microsoft.PowerShell.Commands.WriteErrorException,Create-VM

VERBOSE: Providing the VM names as output. Typically I would create a VM at this stage
The VMnames are : :
```

Now that we have covered a few of the remaining ways to provide more information for the end users, let's dive into error handling in PowerShell. Actually, PowerShell provides a powerful in-built capability for controlling the behavior of the function/ script if any error is encountered.

$ErrorActionPreference is the variable that controls the behavior of the script when a nonterminating error (an error that does not stop the script) is encountered.

The values that can be provided to this variable are as follows:

- **Stop**: This displays the error and stops the execution of the script.
- **Inquire**: This displays the error message and asks the user whether the execution will continue or not.
- **Continue**: This is the default behavior. With this option, PowerShell displays the error and continues with the execution.
- **Suspend**: With this option, PowerShell automatically suspends a workflow job and allows further investigation. Once the investigation is done, the execution can continue.
- **SilentlyContinue**: With this option, there is no effect of an error on the execution. The error message is not shown and the execution continues.

Providing the $ErrorAction value per command will override the overall $ErrorActionPreference value. Here are some examples:

```
1  $ErrorActionPreference = 'SilentlyContinue'
2
3  Write-Error "This is first error"
4
5  Write-Error "This is Second error"
```

```
PS C:\PowerShell Files> .\ErrorAction.ps1
PS C:\PowerShell Files>
```

Note the difference between SilentlyContinue and Continue. While SilentlyContinue will not show any error, Continue will show the error and continue.

```
1  $ErrorActionPreference = 'Continue'
2
3  Write-Error "This is first error"
4
5  Write-Error "This is Second error"
```

```
PS C:\PowerShell Files> .\ErrorAction.ps1
C:\PowerShell Files\ErrorAction.ps1 : This is first error
At line:1 char:1
+ .\ErrorAction.ps1
+
    + CategoryInfo          : NotSpecified: (:) [Write-Error], WriteErrorException
    + FullyQualifiedErrorId : Microsoft.PowerShell.Commands.WriteErrorException,ErrorAction.ps1

C:\PowerShell Files\ErrorAction.ps1 : This is Second error
At line:1 char:1
+ .\ErrorAction.ps1
+
    + CategoryInfo          : NotSpecified: (:) [Write-Error], WriteErrorException
    + FullyQualifiedErrorId : Microsoft.PowerShell.Commands.WriteErrorException,ErrorAction.ps1

PS C:\PowerShell Files>
```

```
1   $ErrorActionPreference = 'Stop'
2
3   Write-Error "This is first error"
4
5   Write-Error "This is Second error"
```

```
PS C:\PowerShell Files> .\ErrorAction.ps1
C:\PowerShell Files\ErrorAction.ps1 : This is first error
At line:1 char:1
+ .\ErrorAction.ps1
+ ~~~~~~~~~~~~~~~~~
    + CategoryInfo          : NotSpecified: (:) [Write-Error], WriteErrorException
    + FullyQualifiedErrorId : Microsoft.PowerShell.Commands.WriteErrorException,ErrorAction.ps1

PS C:\PowerShell Files>
```

```
1   $ErrorActionPreference = 'Inquire'
2
3   Write-Error "This is first error"
4
5   Write-Error "This is Second error"
```

```
PS C:\PowerShell Files> .\ErrorAction.ps1
```

```
Confirm                                    _  □  ×

This is first error

     Yes        Yes to All     Halt Command     Suspend
```

Next, we can see the $ErrorVariable parameter. With this parameter, we can save the error value in a variable and later use this variable to get the error message:

```
PS C:\PowerShell Files> Write-Error "This is first error" -ErrorVariable MyVar1 -ErrorAction SilentlyContinue
PS C:\PowerShell Files> $MyVar1
Write-Error "This is first error" -ErrorVariable MyVar1 -ErrorAction SilentlyContinue : This is first error
    + CategoryInfo          : NotSpecified: (:) [Write-Error], WriteErrorException
    + FullyQualifiedErrorId : Microsoft.PowerShell.Commands.WriteErrorException

PS C:\PowerShell Files>
```

If you want to debug the script, PowerShell provides an in-built way to do this. Just use the Set-PSDebug cmdlet. This particular cmdlet will allow you to debug the script and set the level at which you want to debug. Setting the trace level to 1 will provide generic information, level 2 will provide more information, and setting it to 0 will bring it back to normal. The following table will show you the values and what each does:

Value	What it does
0	This turns off script tracing.
1	This traces each line of code that is being executed. Non-executed lines are not displayed.
2	This traces each line of code that is being executed. Non-executed lines are not displayed. This displays variable assignments and calls other functions and script blocks.

```
PS C:\PowerShell Files> Set-PSDebug -Trace 1
DEBUG:     1+ >>>> Set-PSDebug -Trace 1

PS C:\PowerShell Files> .\ErrorAction.ps1
DEBUG:     1+ >>>> .\ErrorAction.ps1
DEBUG:     1+ >>>> $ErrorActionPreference = 'Stop'

DEBUG:     3+ >>>> Write-Error "This is first error" -ErrorVariable MyVar1 -ErrorAction SilentlyContinue

DEBUG:     5+ >>>> Write-Error "This is Second error" -ErrorVariable MyVar2 -ErrorAction SilentlyContinue
PS C:\PowerShell Files> Set-PSDebug -Trace 2
DEBUG:     1+ >>>> Set-PSDebug -Trace 2

PS C:\PowerShell Files> .\ErrorAction.ps1
DEBUG:     1+ >>>> .\ErrorAction.ps1
DEBUG:        ! CALL function '<ScriptBlock>'
DEBUG:     1+ >>>> $ErrorActionPreference = 'Stop'

DEBUG:        ! CALL function '<ScriptBlock>'  (defined in file 'C:\PowerShell Files\ErrorAction.ps1')
DEBUG:        ! SET $ErrorActionPreference = 'Stop'.
DEBUG:     3+ >>>> Write-Error "This is first error" -ErrorVariable MyVar1 -ErrorAction SilentlyContinue

DEBUG:     5+ >>>> Write-Error "This is Second error" -ErrorVariable MyVar2 -ErrorAction SilentlyContinue

PS C:\PowerShell Files> Set-PSDebug -Trace 0
DEBUG:     1+ >>>> Set-PSDebug -Trace 0
DEBUG:        ! CALL function '<ScriptBlock>'

PS C:\PowerShell Files>
```

If you want to step through the script, then you can do it using the -Step parameter, as shown in the following example:

```
PS C:\PowerShell Files> Set-PSDebug -Trace 1 -Step

PS C:\PowerShell Files> .\ErrorAction.ps1
DEBUG:     1+ >>>> .\ErrorAction.ps1
DEBUG:     1+ >>>> $ErrorActionPreference = 'Stop'
```

```
Continue with this operation?                        —  ☐  ✕

3+ >>>> Write-Error "This is first error" -ErrorVariable MyVar1 -ErrorAction SilentlyContinue

        Yes   Yes to All   No   No to All   Suspend
```

In this case, in each and every step, you need to provide an input so that debug can step through the entire script.

The next portion talks about two more ways of handling errors in PowerShell scripts: the `Trap` and `try,catch`, and `finally` blocks. Both of them are used to handle terminating errors.

A terminating error in PowerShell is one that stops Shell from continuing further execution. Let's discuss them one by one.

Trap:

The trap keyword will allow us to specify a list of commands to be run if a terminating error occurs. The trap statements handle the errors and allow the execution to continue without stopping.

The syntax for the keyword is as follows:

```
trap [[<error type>]] {<statement list>}
```

Note that, in the place of `<error type>`, we can provide the particular `error type` that we are expecting (if we already know the error type). This is optional and can be omitted. We can also use continue or break in the trap statement list so that it can be decided whether the execution will continue or break once the error occurs. Here are two examples of this:

```
1  Function break_example{
2      trap {"Error trapped"; break;}
3      "This is a test Write"  M:\test.txt
4      Write-Host "completed."
5
6  }
```

```
PS C:\PowerShell Files> break_example
Error trapped
out-file : Cannot find drive. A drive with the name 'M' does not exist.
At line:3 char:6
+     "This is a test Write" > M:\test.txt
+
    + CategoryInfo          : ObjectNotFound: (M:String) [Out-File], DriveNotFoundException
    + FullyQualifiedErrorId : DriveNotFound,Microsoft.PowerShell.Commands.OutFileCommand


PS C:\PowerShell Files>
```

```
1  ⊟ Function continue_example{
2         trap {"Error trapped"; continue;}
3         "This is a test Write"    M:\test.txt
4         Write-Host "completed."
5
6    }
```

```
PS C:\PowerShell Files> continue_example
Error trapped
completed.

PS C:\PowerShell Files> |
```

Try, Catch, and Finally:

We need to use the try block to monitor any error that may occur in PowerShell. If any error occurs in the try block, then first, the error is saved in the $Error automatic variable. PowerShell then searches for the Catch block to handle the error. If there is no matching Catch block for the try block, then PowerShell continues to search for a matching Catch block. Once a Catch block is completed or if a matching Catch block is not found or a trap statement is found, then the Finally block is run. If the error cannot be handled, then it is written to the error stream.

A typical try, catch, finally block syntax is shown here:

```
        try
        {
<Statement Block>
        }
        catch [[<error type>] [',' <error type>]*] {<statement list>}
        }
        catch
        {
<Statement Block>
        }
Finally { <Statement list>}
```

The following is an example of such a function using all the three blocks:

```
1  Function errorcatching{
2      Write-Host "Begin test"
3      try {
4          Write-Host "Attempting to create new file"
5          Get-Content "C:\TestFile.txt" -ErrorAction Stop
6      }
7      Catch {
8          Write-Host "caught an exception"
9          throw "My own Custom message"
10     }
11     Finally {
12         Write-Host "Continued to the end"
13     }
14 }
```

```
PS C:\PowerShell Files> errorcatching
Begin test
Attempting to create new file
caught an exception
Continued to the end
My own Custom message
At line:9 char:9
+           throw "My own Custom message"
+           ~~~~~~~~~~~~~~~~~~~~~~~~~~~~~~~
    + CategoryInfo          : OperationStopped: (My own Custom message:String) [], RuntimeException
    + FullyQualifiedErrorId : My own Custom message

PS C:\PowerShell Files> |
```

For more details on the preceding topics, check out `https://technet.microsoft.com/en-us/library/hh847742.aspx` and `https://technet.microsoft.com/en-us/library/hh847793.aspx`.

Summary

In this chapter, we covered advanced functions, how to write them, and details of different attributes. Next, we learned about help files in PowerShell and how we can write our own help files using comment-based help. At the end, we learned how we can use different methods of error handling in PowerShell or how we can troubleshoot scripts. Although we did not cover all aspects of these topics, we did cover those topics required for advanced script writing.

In the next chapter, we will dive into PowerCLI and cover how to build ESXi images using Image Builder. Next, we will cover how to auto deploy an ESXI host, add a host to a vCenter server, and how to use host profiles in the ESXi environment using PowerCLI.

3
Deploying vSphere Hosts

In the first chapter, we covered the basics of PowerShell and PowerCLI. Next, we covered various advanced topics, such as writing advanced functions in PowerShell and details of parameters and their different attributes. We also covered how to write help files and handle errors in PowerShell. All the previously mentioned topics were introductory topics so that you could use them to build your own advanced scripts. The primary aim of this book is to master PowerCLI, but for obvious reasons we need to master PowerShell to some extent so that we can build upon that. Since we already covered some part of it (the more advance topics of PowerShell will be covered in the upcoming chapters), let's dive into managing VMware environments using PowerCLI. We will start with the installation and configuration of the ESXi server using PowerCLI. Since there are various ways through which you can install the ESXi server, we will limit our discussion to only the portion that requires extensive use of PowerCLI. Keeping this in mind, in this chapter, we will discuss the following topics:

- Image Builder with PowerCLI
- Using host profiles
- Configuring Auto Deploy for ESXi hosts
- Adding hosts to a vCenter server

Note that vSphere Auto Deploy is a process using which you can automatically deploy an ESXi host, but since vSphere Auto Deploy depends heavily on the vSphere Image CLI Builder and host profiles, we will first cover these two topics and then we will cover Auto Deploy. So let's start.

Image Builder with PowerCLI

The vSphere Image Builder CLI is a process or tool used to build custom ESXi images or software bundles, which can later be installed using the update manager. It is actually a collection of PowerCLI cmdlets that gives you the power to do the earlier mentioned tasks. In most cases, VMware partners use it extensively so that they can build their own images. For example, let's assume that particular server hardware requires a few special drivers for the ESXi server to run properly on that platform. So, we have two options: either we need to install these special drivers after the installation of the ESXi server or we can preinclude them in the ESXi image itself so that we don't need to install any drivers later on. In most cases, the second approach is preferred by most hardware vendors, so you will get vanilla ESXi images from the VMware site, but if you download the ESXi image available from a server vendor site, it includes the added drivers required for the proper functioning of the ESXi server.

We can use the same methods to include some other VIBs (vSphere installation bundles) in the ESXi image and create a new ISO; or we can create a software bundle for later use.

We can use Image Builder to manage a software depot, image profile, and VIBs. Note that VIBs are software packages and image profiles are a set of such packages. So, when we apply an image profile, it actually installs a set of VIBs on that server.

The following figure is the architecture of a VMware Image Builder:

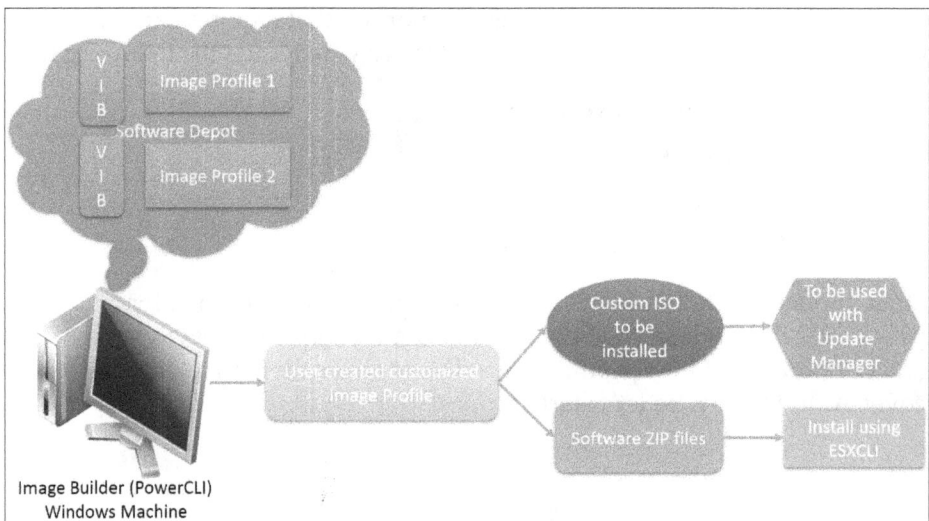

The main use cases and reasons why you need to use Image Builder are as follows:

- We can create image profiles that can be used later by Auto Deploy.
- Add third-party drivers to existing image profiles to make a new custom ISO or software bundle.
- To perform upgrades on the existing environment.
- We can create custom images with a reduced footprint. We can take the default ESXi image and then remove VIBs and create a custom reduced image.

The Image Builder cmdlets take the image profiles and VIBs kept in the software depot as the input and produce either a custom ISO image or offline depot ZIP file. The ZIP file can be used later by the update manager or ESXCLI cmdlets for installation at a later stage.

Before we go ahead and discuss this further, let's take a closer look at few of the common terms that we have used so far:

- VIB: A vSphere installation bundle is an ESXi software package.
- Image profile: An image profile defines an ESXi image and consists of VIBs. They always have a base VIB and can have more VIBs in them.
- Software depot: A software depot is a collection of VIBs and image profiles. It is actually a collection of files and folders. Depending on their nature of availability, they can be an online depot (an HTTP URL access) and offline depot (ZIP file).

Next, let's take a look at the cmdlets that are available in Image Builder. The cmdlets can be grouped into different categories as follows:

- Tasks that can be performed on a software depot:
    - `Add-EsxSoftwareDepot`
    - `Remove-EsxSoftwareDepot`
    - `Get-EsxSoftwareDepot`
- Cmdlets that can manage image profiles:
    - `Get-EsxImageProfile`
    - `New-EsxImageProfile`
    - `Set-EsxImageProfile`
    - `Export-EsxImageProfile`
    - `Compare-EsxImageProfile`
    - `Remove-EsxImageProfile`

- Cmdlets that can work on software packages:
  - ○ Add-EsxSoftwarePackage
  - ○ Remove-EsxSoftwarePackage

To get detailed information on these cmdlets, use their Get-Help cmdlets.

So, let's start with creating a depot. We can add an offline bundle file as a depot and then add it on top of it, or add an online depot. In this example, I have taken an existing online depot provided and maintained by Hewlett Packard (https://vibsdepot.hp.com).

```
PS C:\> Add-EsxSoftwareDepot http://vibsdepot.hp.com

Depot Url
---------
http://vibsdepot.hp.com/index.xml
```

We can download an offline bundle and add it as a software depot as well.

```
PS C:\> Add-EsxSoftwareDepot E:\software-depot\ESXi600-201504001.zip

Depot Url
---------
zip:E:\software-depot\ESXi600-201504001.zip?index.xml
```

So, now you can check that I have two different software depots:

```
PS C:\> Get-EsxSoftwareDepot

Depot Url
---------
http://vibsdepot.hp.com/index.xml
zip:E:\software-depot\ESXi600-201504001.zip?index.xml
```

Since we have added the software depot, let's check the contents. Note that the offline bundle that I downloaded from VMware already has two image profiles: one standard and one without any VMware tools.

```
PS C:\> Get-EsxImageProfile

Name                          Vendor        Last Modified      Acceptance Level
----                          ------        -------------      ----------------
ESXi-6.0.0-20150404001-stan... VMware, Inc.  26-03-2015 0...    PartnerSupported
ESXi-6.0.0-20150404001-no-t... VMware, Inc.  26-03-2015 0...    PartnerSupported
```

We can get a list of available software packages in the depot using the
`Get-EsxSoftwarePackage` cmdlet.

```
PS C:\> Get-EsxSoftwarePackage -SoftwareDepot zip:E:\software-depot\ESXi600-201504001.zip?index.xml

Name                Version                       Vendor    Creation Date
----                -------                       ------    -------------
lsi-msgpt3          06.255.12.00-7vmw.600.0.0.2...  VMware   06-02-2015 02...
ima-qla4xxx         2.02.18-1vmw.600.0.0.2494585  VMware    06-02-2015 02...
sata-ata-piix       2.12-10vmw.600.0.0.2494585    VMware    06-02-2015 02...
sata-sata-sil       2.3-4vmw.600.0.0.2494585      VMware    06-02-2015 02...
lpfc                10.2.309.8-2vmw.600.0.0.249...  VMware   06-02-2015 02...
scsi-ips            7.12.05-4vmw.600.0.0.2494585  VMware    06-02-2015 02...
lsi-mr3             6.605.08.00-6vmw.600.0.0.24...  VMware   06-02-2015 02...
```

Now, let's create a new image profile using the available software packages. In this
example, we will add packages available from the Hewlett Packard site to the existing
VMware profile. As mentioned earlier, since I added the online depot as an existing
depot to my environment, I can get a list of available software packages in the HP site.
From the list of available packages, I will add the `hpbootcfg` package to our existing
image. This is purely an example; I am trying to show you how to add packages to an
existing image. You need to add packages in line with your requirements.

First, I have cloned the existing image profile as `Custom-Profile`; note that I have
mentioned Vendor as `Custom` and AcceptanceLevel as `CommunitySupported`:

**PS C:\> New-EsxImageProfile -CloneProfile ESXi600-201504001-standard
"Custom-Profile" -Vendor Custom -AcceptanceLevel CommunitySupported**

```
PS C:\> New-EsxImageProfile -CloneProfile ESXi-6.0.0-20150404001-standard "Custom-Profile" -vendor Custom -AcceptanceLevel CommunitySupported

Name             Vendor       Last Modified    Acceptance Level
----             ------       -------------    ----------------
Custom-Profile   Custom       26-03-2015 0...  CommunitySupported
```

Now, let's add a software package, `hpbootcfg`, to this new ImageProfile:

**PS C:\> Add-EsxSoftwarePackage -ImageProfile "Custom-Profile" -
SoftwarePackage hpbootcfg**

```
PS C:\> Add-EsxSoftwarePackage -ImageProfile "Custom-Profile" -SoftwarePackage hpbootcfg

Name             Vendor       Last Modified    Acceptance Level
----             ------       -------------    ----------------
Custom-Profile   Custom       03-05-2015 0...  CommunitySupported
```

```
PS C:\> Export-EsxImageProfile -ImageProfile "Custom-Profile" -
ExportToIso C:\Custom-ESXI6.0.iso
```

```
PS C:\> Export-EsxImageProfile -ImageProfile "Custom-Profile" -ExportToIso E:\Custom-ESXI6.0.iso
```

So, we have successfully created a new image profile. Similarly, we can create a new bundle with the `-ExportToBundle` switch. For further details and other supported tasks, you can check individual cmdlets with the `Get-Help` support.

Using host profiles

In the preceding section, we learned how to manipulate and create custom ESXi images using PowerCLI cmdlets. So, now let's take a closer look at how to manipulate host profiles so that we can use both at a later stage in order to automate ESXi deployments. In case of VMware technologies, a host profile is a profile that stores all the configuration information of a host. We can configure an ESXi host as required and mark the host as the golden standard. Next, we create a host profile from the configuration of this host. Once the profile is ready, we can simply apply the profile to other hosts so that they can be automatically configured. This way, we can ensure consistency between host configurations across the entire infrastructure.

For this lab, we will get the following architecture:

We have a **vcenter.lab.com** server as a vCenter server. Under this, we have a datacenter named **Datacenter**. A cluster named **Lab Cluster** is created under **Datacenter**. The cluster has two ESXi hosts: **esxi1.lab.com** and **esxi2.lab.com**. We have chosen **esxi1.lab.com** as the golden host and will apply the host profile to the other host.

First, let's get a list of the commands available to manage a host profile.

```
PS C:\Users\vcadmin> Get-Help "hostprofile"

Name                           Category  Module                        Synopsis
----                           --------  ------                        --------
Get-VMHostProfileRequiredInput Cmdlet    VMware.VimAutomation.Core This cmdlet performs a check whether the available information is sufficient to apply a ...
Invoke-VMHostProfile           Cmdlet    VMware.VimAutomation.Core This cmdlet applies a host profile to the specified host or cluster.
Export-VMHostProfile           Cmdlet    VMware.VimAutomation.Core This cmdlet exports the specified host profile to a file.
Get-VMHostProfile              Cmdlet    VMware.VimAutomation.Core This cmdlet retrieves the available host profiles.
Import-VMHostProfile           Cmdlet    VMware.VimAutomation.Core This cmdlet imports a host profile from a file. The file path must be accessible from th...
New-VMHostProfile              Cmdlet    VMware.VimAutomation.Core This cmdlet creates a new host profile based on a reference host.
Remove-VMHostProfile           Cmdlet    VMware.VimAutomation.Core This cmdlet removes the specified host profiles.
Set-VMHostProfile              Cmdlet    VMware.VimAutomation.Core This cmdlet modifies the specified host profile.
Test-VMHostProfileCompliance   Cmdlet    VMware.VimAutomation.Core This cmdlet tests hosts for profile compliance.
```

So, first create a host profile from the command line using a standard host:

```
PS C:\Users\vcadmin> New-VMHostProfile -Name TestHostProfile -Description
"Test Profile for Auto Deploy" -ReferenceHost esxi1.lab.com
```

```
PS C:\Users\vcadmin> New-VMHostProfile -Name TestHostProfile -Description "Test Profile for Auto Deploy" -ReferenceHost esxi1.lab.com

Name                           Description
----                           -----------
TestHostProfile                Test Profile for Auto Deploy
```

We can check the status of the host profiles with the `Get-VMHostProfile` cmdlet.

Since we have created a host profile, we now need to apply the profile to a host or cluster so that we can run further tasks on the profile.

We can apply a host profile to a host or cluster. In this example, we will apply this on a cluster and keep the level as `-AssociateOnly`. As the name suggests, it will only associate the host profile with the host and will do nothing else.

```
PS C:\Users\vcadmin> $cluster = Get-Cluster -Name "Lab Cluster"
PS C:\Users\vcadmin> Invoke-VMHostProfile -AssociateOnly -Entity $cluster -Profile TestHostProfile -Confirm:$true
```

Now, we can check the compliance of a host in this cluster with the host profile that we attached to it.

```
PS C:\Users\vcadmin> Test-VMHostProfileCompliance -VMHost esxi2.lab.com | Format-List

VMHostId             : HostSystem-host-33
VMHost               : esxi2.lab.com
VMHostUid            : /VIServer=lab\vcadmin@vcenter.lab.com:443/VMHost=HostSystem-host-33/
VMHostProfileId      : HostProfile-hostprofile-1
VMHostProfile        : TestHostProfile
VMHostProfileUid     : /VIServer=lab\vcadmin@vcenter.lab.com:443/VMHostProfile=HostProfile-HostProfile-1/
IncomplianceElementList : {network.vswitch["key-vim-profile-host-VirtualSwitchProfile-vSwitch0"].link-pnicsList:vSwitch vSwitch doesn't have the required NIC
                          devices connected., network.vswitch["key-vim-profile-host-VirtualSwitchProfile-vSwitch0"].networkPolicy-nicOrder:For vSwitch vSwitch0
                          network policy property spec.policy.nicTeaming.nicOrder.activeNic doesn't match,
                          network.hostPortGroup["key-vim-profile-host-HostPortgroupProfile-vMotion"].ipConfig-IpAddress:vmknic not found: vmk1,
                          network.hostPortGroup["key-vim-profile-host-HostPortgroupProfile-vMotion"]-pgExists:Port group vMotion not found...}
Uid                  : /VIServer=lab\vcadmin@vcenter.lab.com:443/VMHost=HostSystem-host-33/VMHostProfileIncompliance=HostProfile-hostprofile-1-5&slash;4&slash
                        ;2015 1:28:38 AM/
ExtensionData        : VMware.Vim.ComplianceResult
Client               : VMware.VimAutomation.ViCore.Impl.V1.VimClient
```

Clearly, the host is not compliant with the profile. So, let's apply the profile now. We can apply the profile with the same `Invoke-VMHostProfile` cmdlet but without the `-AssociateOnly` switch; however, before we go ahead and apply the profile, we need to put the host into maintenance mode. While we apply the policy, we can see that certain values need to be provided first (for example, vMotion IP and so on).

```
PS C:\Users\vcadmin> Invoke-VMHostProfile -Entity esxi2.lab.com -Profile TestHostProfile | Format-List

Name  : network.hostPortGroup["key-vim-profile-host-HostPortgroupProfile-vMotion"].MacAddressPolicy.mac
Value :
Name  : network.hostPortGroup["key-vim-profile-host-HostPortgroupProfile-vMotion"].ipConfig.IpAddressPolicy.address
Value :
Name  : network.hostPortGroup["key-vim-profile-host-HostPortgroupProfile-vMotion"].ipConfig.IpAddressPolicy.subnetmask
Value :
```

We can supply the required values to a variable and then apply the variable to get the end result.

Configuring Auto Deploy for ESXi hosts

Auto Deploy is the VMware feature that can deploy hundreds of ESXi hosts automatically. To understand Auto Deploy, let's take a look at its architecture:

Image source: http://pubs.vmware.com/vsphere-60/index.jsp?topic=%2Fcom.vmware.vsphere.install.
doc%2FGUID-9A827220-177E-40DE-99A0-E1EB62A49408.html

So, we need to work through the installation stages by navigating to **Image Profile** → **Host Profile** → **Auto Deploy**.

The Auto Deploy server stores the following information:

- Image state: This is the required software that needs to be run on an ESXi server. The source of this information is the image profile, created using the Image Builder PowerCLI.

- Configuration state: This is the configuration state of the ESXi server. This information is collected from the host profile UI, which is taken from a golden image/template.

- Dynamic state: This is the runtime state that is generated by running the software. The source of this information is the memory of the host.

- Virtual machine state: This is the status of the virtual machines running on the host. This information is provided by the vCenter server.

- User input: This is the information that cannot be automatically included in the host profile.

When we define Auto Deploy server configurations, we use a certain set of rules. These are rules that are defined using PowerCLI cmdlets.

In case of an ESXi server booting from an Auto Deploy server, the server performs the following steps:

1. The server boots and starts a PXE boot sequence. It contacts a DHCP server and gets an IP address.

2. Next, the server is instructed to contact a TFTP server for the iPXE file and iPXE configuration file.

3. iPXE starts executing and it asks the server to make an HTTP boot request to the Auto Deploy server.

4. The Auto Deploy server in turn queries the rule engine for the information about the host and then streams the required information mentioned in the rule engine to the host.

5. The host boots with the help of the image profile; if a host profile is mentioned, it is then applied to the host.

6. Auto Deploy adds the host to the vCenter server in which the Auto Deploy server is registered.

7. If the host is part of a DRS cluster, then the required tasks related to the DRS server are applied.

For more details on the boot process, check out the VMware online documentation at `http://pubs.vmware.com/vsphere-60/index.jsp#com.vmware.vsphere.` `install.doc/GUID-8C221180-8B56-4E07-88BE-789B25BA372A.html.`

Now, let's start the Auto Deploy server installation process. Since we have already covered the image profile and host profile configuration in the earlier sections, we will focus only on the Auto Deploy configuration here. The steps for the configuration are as follows:

1. First, we need to deploy a TFTP server. For the purpose of my lab, I have used the SolarWinds TFTP server. You can install any TFTP server. In this example, `C:\TFTP-Root` is the default TFTP folder location.

2. Next, we need a DHCP server. For this purpose, I have configured and used a Windows DHCP server that can be configured easily by navigating to **Server Manager Window** and then clicking on the **Add Role** option. You can use your preferred DHCP server. Also, note that building a DHCP server for a network should be carefully planned so that they can provide IPs only to the expected hosts.

3. After configuring the DHCP server, we need to enable and configure Auto Deploy and, using this information, we need to configure the DHCP server for PXE booting. Perform the following steps to configure the Auto Deploy server:

    Log in to a vCenter server Web client with a user ID belonging to a member of the `SystemConfiguration.Administrators` group. You can check and configure this from the Web client by navigating to **Home → Administration → Single Sign On → Users and Groups → Groups.**

4. By default, the Auto Deploy service is disabled in Windows. So, first we need to enable it. To configure Auto Deploy from the Web client, go to **Home → Administrator → Under Deployment → System Configuration → Services → Auto Deploy → Manage**.

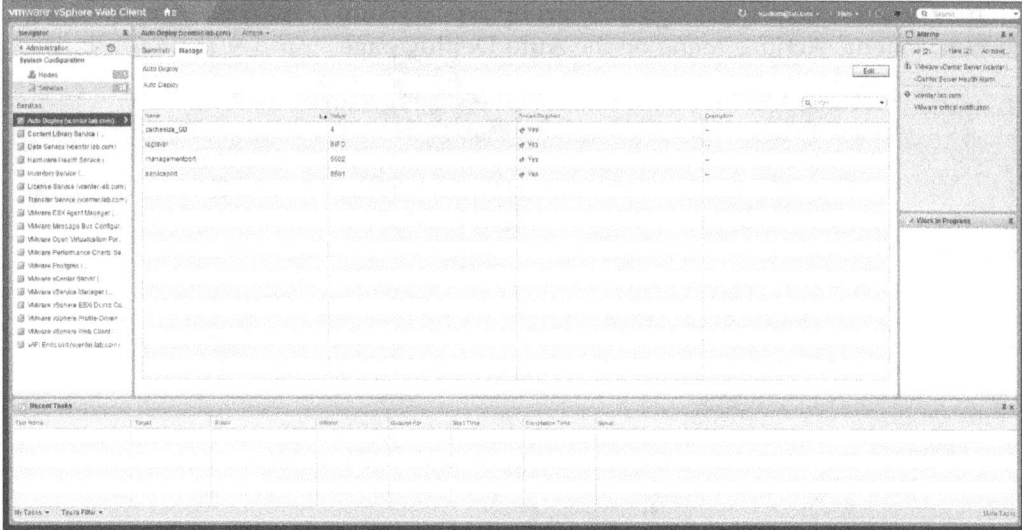

5. Next, click on **Edit** to edit the fields. We can change the following fields:

    o   **cachesize_GB**: This is the Auto Deploy cache size in GB.

    o   **loglevel**: This is the default log level. We can change it to warning errors and fatal errors.

    o   **managementport**: This is the default port for management.

    o   **serviceport**: This is the default service port:

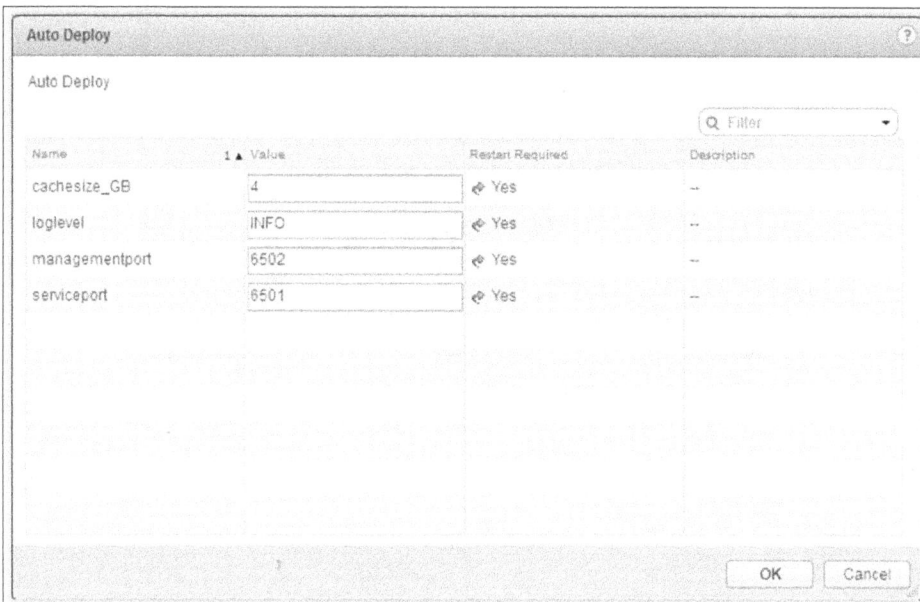

6. Next, we need to change the start up type to **Auto Deploy**. We can do this from the **Actions** menu on the **Auto Deploy** page.

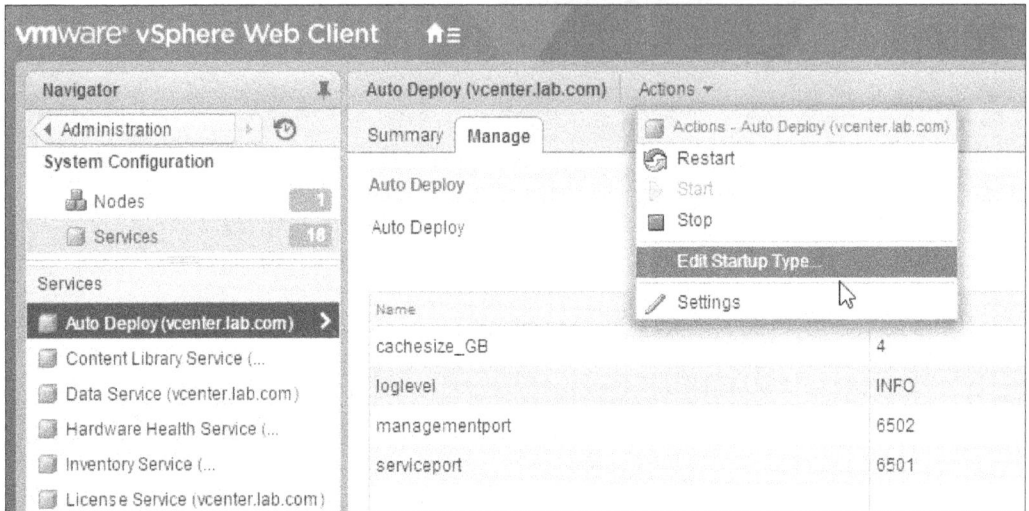

7. The options given are **Automatic**, **Manual**, and **Disabled** (default). For this purpose, we will select **Automatic**.

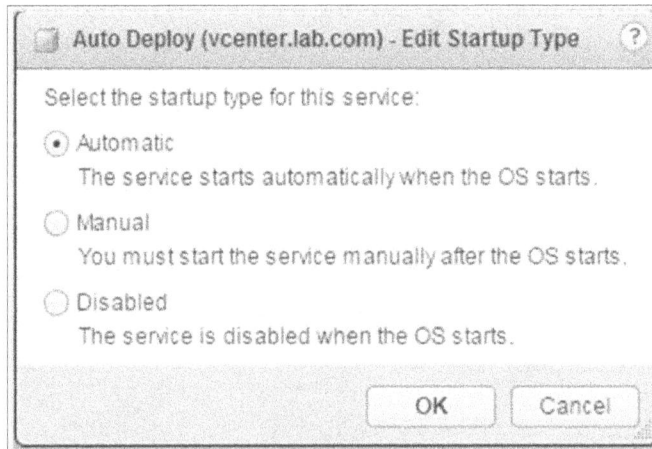

8. Next, we will configure the TFTP server information. To do this, go to
   **Inventory List → vCenter Server System → Manage Tab → Settings →
   Auto Deploy**.

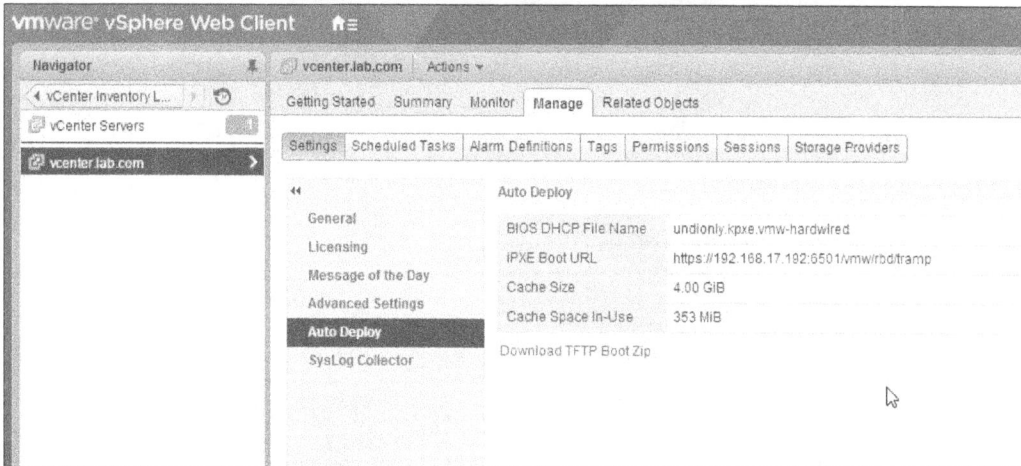

9. Make a note of the BIOS DHCP filename (`undionly.kpxe.vmw-hardwired`).
   On the same page, click on the `Download TFP Boot Zip` option to download
   the TFTP boot files. Download the `deploy-tftp.zip` file to the local directory
   and unzip the contents to the TFTP directory (in my case, it is `C:\TFTP-Root`).

10. Next, we need to further configure the DHCP server to point to this TFTP
    directory. To do this, we need to configure Options 66 and 67 in the DHCP
    server. Note that Options 66 and 67 are mandatory for the basic DHCP
    configuration, but you should really consider the Option Router (003), DNS
    server (006), and DNS domain name (015). You should set these values
    for practical purposes, and I should have kept these in any production
    environment (thanks to Kyle Ruddy for pointing this out).

Option 66 is the boot server hostname. Here, we will provide the TFTP server hostname (in my case, it is the same as the vCenter server).

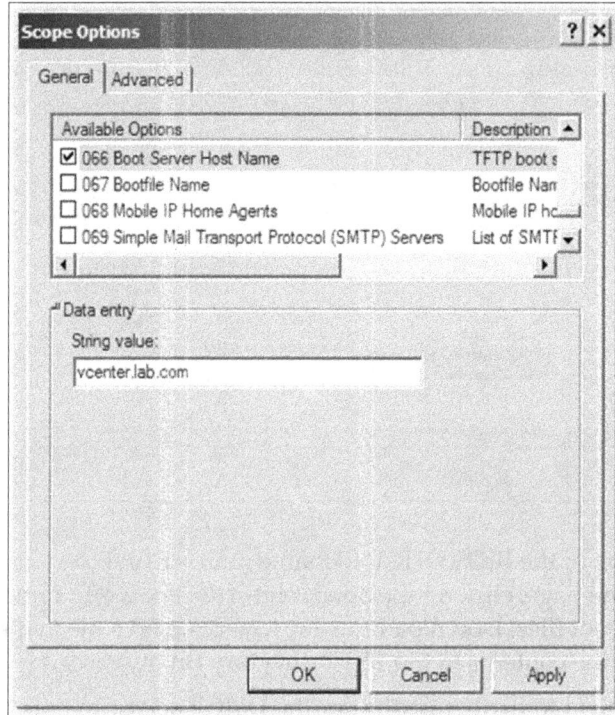

11. The `067` option is the `Bootfile Name` option; here, we will provide the `undionly.kpxe.vmw-hardwired` name.

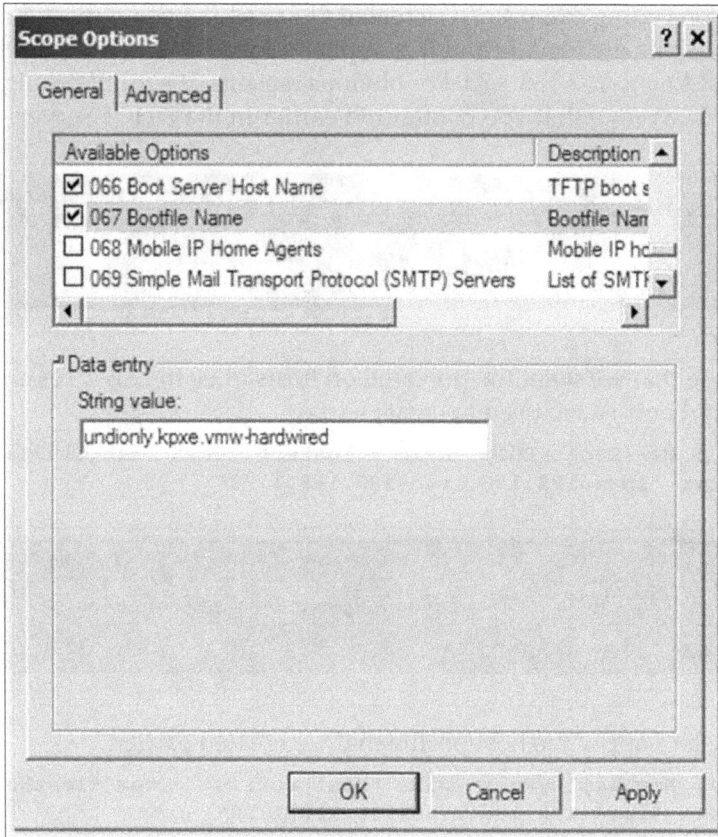

12. Click on **Apply** and then click on **Ok**.

13. Next, we will configure the physical servers to boot using PXE. This will enable the servers to boot using PXE.

14. Next, we need to configure the Auto Deploy rules. We need to start with a software depot and Image profile. In this example, we will use the custom image that we created earlier (check the earlier topic for the details). We will create a new rule using the `New-DeployRule` cmdlet. We used the following cmdlet:

```
PS C:\> New-DeployRule -Name "CustomRule" -Item "Custom-Profile"
-Pattern "ipv4=192.168.1.60-192.168.1.70"
```

15. In the preceding example, we created CustomRule using the "Custom-Profile" image profile, and it is applicable for hosts booting in the IP range 192.168.1.60 to 192.168.1.70. For obvious reasons, it should be aligned with the DHCP range that you configured earlier in the DHCP server.

```
Name        : CustomRule
PatternList : {ipv4=192.168.1.60-192.168.1.70}
ItemList    : {Custom-Profile}


PS C:\Users\vcadmin> New-DeployRule -Name "CustomRule" -Item "Custom-Profile" -Pattern "ipv4=192.168.1.60-192.168.1.70"
```

16. Suppose that we want the powered on hosts to be in Lab Cluster by default. For this, we need to create a rule:

    ```
    PS C:\> New-DeployRule -Name "cluster" -Item "Lab Cluster"
    -Pattern "ipv4=192.168.1.60-192.168.1.70"
    ```

```
PS C:\Users\vcadmin> New-DeployRule -Name "cluster" -Item "Lab Cluster" -Pattern "ipv4=192.168.1.60-192.168.1.70"

Name        : cluster
PatternList : {ipv4=192.168.1.60-192.168.1.70}
ItemList    : {Lab Cluster}
```

17. Lastly, let's apply the host profile that we created earlier:

    ```
    PS C:\> New-DeployRule -Name "hostprofile" -Item "TestHostProfile"
    -Pattern "ipv4=192.168.1.60-192.168.1.70"
    ```

```
PS C:\Users\vcadmin> New-DeployRule -Name "hostprofile" -Item "TestHostProfile" -Pattern "ipv4=192.168.1.60-192.168.1.70"

Name        : hostprofile
PatternList : {ipv4=192.168.1.60-192.168.1.70}
ItemList    : {TestHostProfile}
```

18. So, we have created all three rules; now, let's add them to the active rule set:

    ```
    PS C:\Users\vcadmin> Add-DeployRule CustomRule,Cluster,hostprofile
    ```

    We can check the active rule sets using the following command:

    ```
    Ps C:\> Get-DeployRuleSet
    ```

```
PS C:\Users\vcadmin> Add-DeployRule CustomRule,Cluster,hostprofile


Name        : CustomRule
PatternList : {ipv4=192.168.1.60-192.168.1.70}
ItemList    : {Custom-Profile}

Name        : cluster
PatternList : {ipv4=192.168.1.60-192.168.1.70}
ItemList    : {Lab Cluster}

Name        : hostprofile
PatternList : {ipv4=192.168.1.60-192.168.1.70}
ItemList    : {TestHostProfile}



PS C:\Users\vcadmin> Get-DeployRuleSet


Name        : CustomRule
PatternList : {ipv4=192.168.1.60-192.168.1.70}
ItemList    : {Custom-Profile}

Name        : cluster
PatternList : {ipv4=192.168.1.60-192.168.1.70}
ItemList    : {Lab Cluster}

Name        : hostprofile
PatternList : {ipv4=192.168.1.60-192.168.1.70}
ItemList    : {TestHostProfile}
```

19. Now, it's time to test the setup. I have configured a host to boot using PXE.

```
Copyright (C) 2003-2014  VMware, Inc.
Copyright (C) 1997-2000  Intel Corporation

CLIENT MAC ADDR: 00 0C 29 9E 40 CA  GUID: 564D0BD9-6E0D-0AA0-6C73-5DDD489E40CA
CLIENT IP: 192.168.1.60  MASK: 255.255.255.0  DHCP IP: 192.168.1.39
GATEWAY IP: 192.168.1.1
PXE->EB: !PXE at 9E6E:0070, entry point at 9E6E:0106
         UNDI code segment 9E6E:0BCE, data segment 98F8:5960 (611-638kB)
         UNDI device is PCI 02:01.0, type DIX+802.3
         611kB free base memory after PXE unload
iPXE initialising devices...ok


VMware Build: 2082717 undionly.kpxe.vmw-hardwired
iPXE 1.0.0+ -- Open Source Network Boot Firmware -- http://ipxe.org
Features: HTTP HTTPS iSCSI DNS TFTP AoE bzImage COMBOOT ELF MBOOT PXE PXEXT

net0: 00:0c:29:9e:40:ca on UNDI (open)
  [Link:up, TX:0 TXE:0 RX:0 RXE:0]
DHCP (net0 00:0c:29:9e:40:ca).... ok
net0: 192.168.1.60/255.255.255.0 gw 192.168.1.1
Next server: 192.168.1.40
Filename: tramp
tftp://192.168.1.40/tramp.https://192.168.1.40:6501/vmw/rbd/tramp./vmw/rbd/host-
register?bootmac=00:0c:29:9e:40:ca..._
```

In the following screenshot, we can see that it is booting using the PXE server:

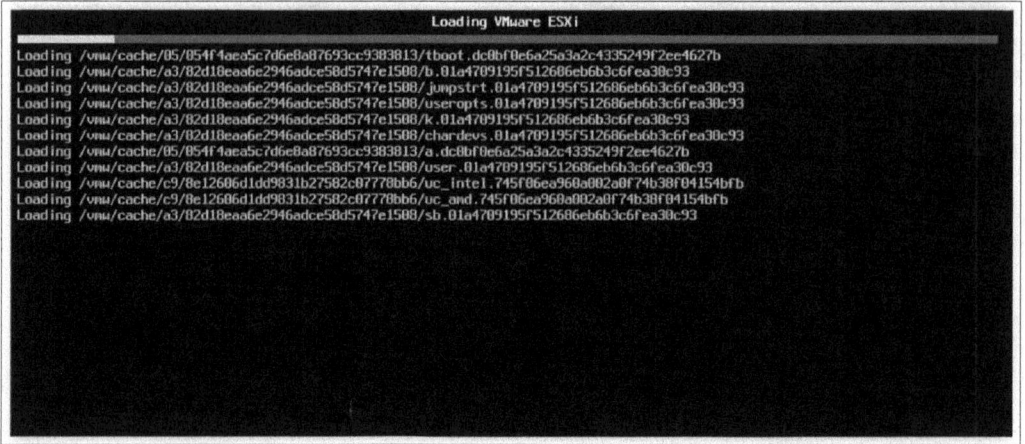

```
                              Loading VMware ESXi

Loading /vmw/cache/05/054f4aea5c7d6e8a87693cc9383813/tboot.dc0bf0e6a25a3a2c4335249f2ee4627b
Loading /vmw/cache/a3/82d18eaa6e2946adce58d5747e1508/b.01a4709195f512686eb6b3c6fea30c93
Loading /vmw/cache/a3/82d18eaa6e2946adce58d5747e1508/jumpstrt.01a4709195f512686eb6b3c6fea30c93
Loading /vmw/cache/a3/82d18eaa6e2946adce58d5747e1508/useropts.01a4709195f512686eb6b3c6fea30c93
Loading /vmw/cache/a3/82d18eaa6e2946adce58d5747e1508/k.01a4709195f512686eb6b3c6fea30c93
Loading /vmw/cache/a3/82d18eaa6e2946adce58d5747e1508/chardevs.01a4709195f512686eb6b3c6fea30c93
Loading /vmw/cache/05/054f4aea5c7d6e8a87693cc9383813/a.dc0bf0e6a25a3a2c4335249f2ee4627b
Loading /vmw/cache/a3/82d18eaa6e2946adce58d5747e1508/user.01a4709195f512686eb6b3c6fea30c93
Loading /vmw/cache/c9/8e12606d1dd9831b27582c07770bb6/uc_intel.745f06ea960a002a0f74b38f04154bfb
Loading /vmw/cache/c9/8e12606d1dd9831b27582c07770bb6/uc_amd.745f06ea960a002a0f74b38f04154bfb
Loading /vmw/cache/a3/82d18eaa6e2946adce58d5747e1508/sb.01a4709195f512686eb6b3c6fea30c93
```

20. Next, we can see that it uses the Auto Deploy server to boot into the ESXi image.

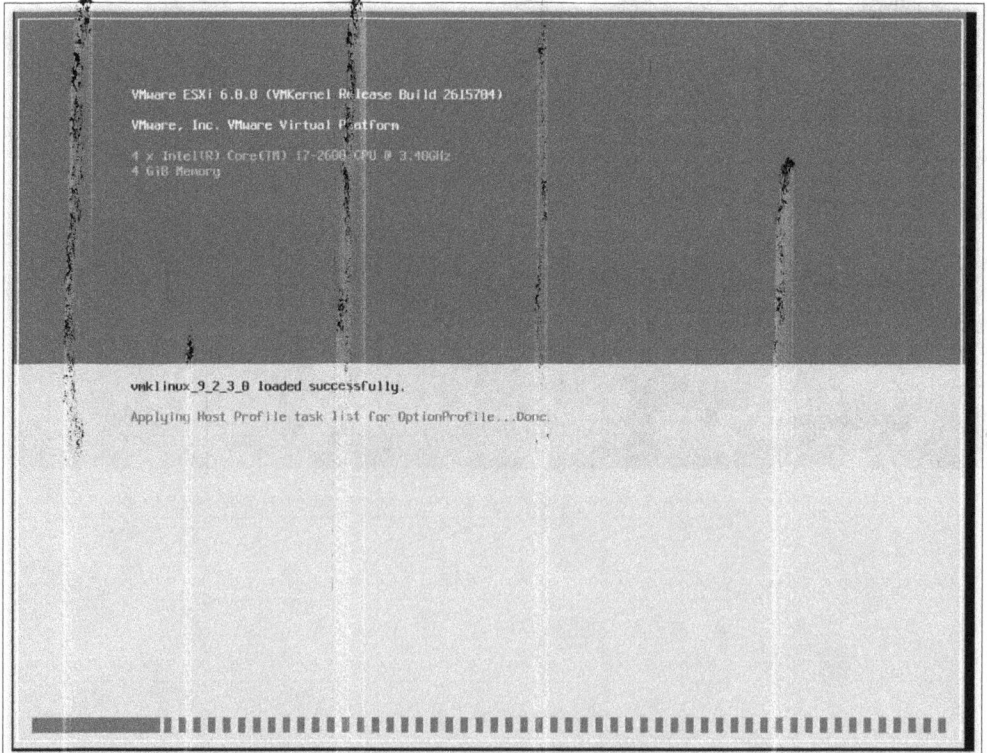

```
VMware ESXi 6.0.0 (VMKernel Release Build 2615704)

VMware, Inc. VMware Virtual Platform

4 x Intel(R) Core(TM) i7-2600 CPU @ 3.40GHz
4 GiB Memory




vmklinux_9_2_3_0 loaded successfully.

Applying Host Profile task list for OptionProfile...Done.
```

21. Also, in the booting process, we can see that it applies the host profile as mentioned earlier. Finally, the server has booted as expected.

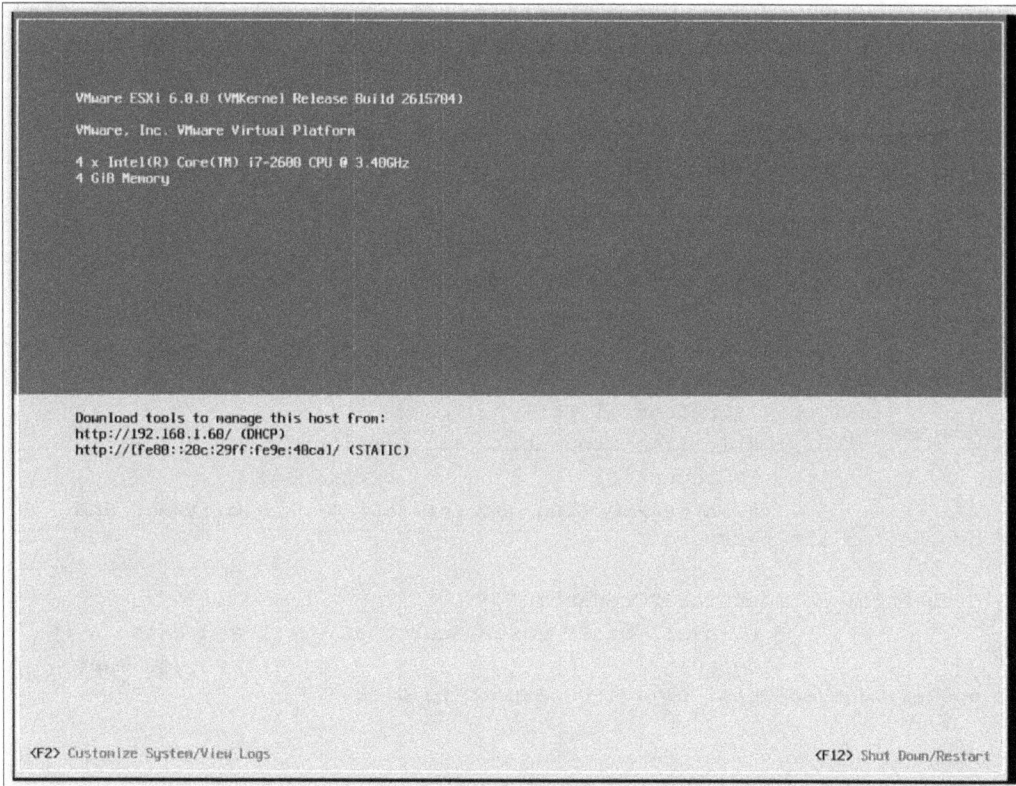

Adding hosts to a vCenter server

To add a host to a vCenter server using the PowerCLI cmdlet, we need to use the Add-VMHost cmdlet. But, for this cmdlet to run successfully, we need to first connect to a vCenter server. We can connect to a vCenter server using the Connect-VIServer cmdlet. So, let's start:

```
PS C:\> Connect-VIServer vcenter.lab.com -User vcadmin@lab.com -
Password Vmware1!
```

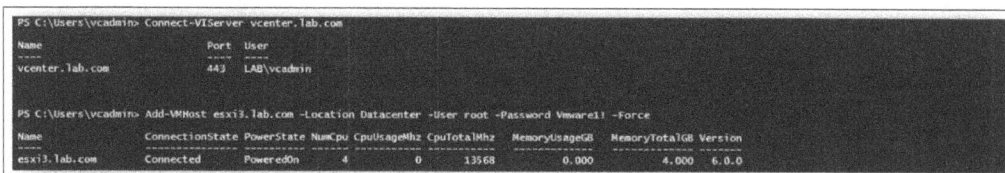

Note that I have provided all the parameter values in the command line itself; if you omit them, then it will display a popup asking for the user ID and password.

There's a better way of providing passwords to a connection: using the `-Credential` option and with `PSCredential`. Hal Rottenberg has written very good functions to incorporate these. The functions are as follows:

The first `Export-PSCredential` function exports the provided credential to a `credentials.enc.xml` file in XML format:

```
function Export-PSCredential {
        param ( $Credential = (Get-Credential), $Path = "credentials.
enc.xml" )

        # Look at the object type of the $Credential parameter to
determine how to handle it
        switch ( $Credential.GetType().Name ) {
                # It is a credential, so continue
                PSCredential            { continue }
                # It is a string, so use that as the username and
prompt for the password
                String                          { $Credential = Get-
Credential -credential $Credential }
                # In all other cases, throw an error and exit
                default                         { Throw "You must
specify a credential object to export to disk." }
        }

        # Create temporary object to be serialized to disk
        $export = New-Object PSObject
        Add-Member -InputObject $export -Name Username -Value
$Credential.Username `
                -MemberType NoteProperty

        # Encrypt SecureString password using Data Protection API
        $EncryptedPassword = $Credential.Password | ConvertFrom-
SecureString
        Add-Member -InputObject $export -Name EncryptedPassword -Value
$EncryptedPassword `
                -MemberType NoteProperty

        # Give object a type name which can be identified later
        $export.PSObject.TypeNames.Insert(0,'ExportedPSCredential')
```

```
        # Export using the Export-Clixml cmdlet
        $export | Export-Clixml $Path
        Write-Host -foregroundcolor Green "Credentials saved to: "
-noNewLine

        # Return FileInfo object referring to saved credentials
        Get-Item $Path
}
```

The other `Import-PSCredential` function imports the credential into a variable from the credential saved in a file:

```
function Import-PSCredential {
        param ( [string]$Path = "credentials-ci.enc.
xml",[string]$cred)

        # Import credential file
        $import = Import-Clixml $Path

        # Test for valid import
        if ( !$import.UserName -or !$import.EncryptedPassword ) {
                Throw "Input is not a valid ExportedPSCredential
object, exiting."
        }
        $Username = $import.Username

        # Decrypt the password and store as a SecureString object for
safekeeping
        $SecurePass = $import.EncryptedPassword | ConvertTo-
SecureString

        # Build the new credential object
        $Credential = New-Object System.Management.Automation.
PSCredential $Username, $SecurePass

        if ($cred) {
                New-Variable -Name $cred -scope Global -value
$Credential
        } else {
                Write-Output $Credential
        }
}
```

For details, check out http://poshcode.org/474.

For my use, I use these functions a lot in all my scripts which I schedule to run at a different time. I use this method for the simple reason that hard coding the credential is never a good idea from security perspective. Also another reason is, if the script waits for user input there may be no one available at that time to provide the input. For example, if I want a script to run at 4 a.m. in the morning it is hard to get someone who will wait in front of the screen to provide the credential.

So, I simply run the Export-PSCredential function to store my credentials in a predefined location and later use this file to get the credential. For example, note the following lines:

```
# Setting the base path
$basePath = "C:\scripts"

# Import the admin credential. Credentialmanagement.ps1 is the
# file which stores the above two functions. I am dot sourcing
# the file so that those two functions will be available in
# current scope
. "$basePath\credentialManagement.ps1"

# Storing the credential in a variable
$credential = Import-PSCredential "$basePath\credentials.enc.xml"

# Connecting to the server using the credential
Connect-VIServer vcenter.lab.com -credential $credential
```

Summary

In this chapter, we discussed how to deploy hosts using image profiles and host profiles using PowerCLI. We also learned how to add a host to a vCenter server using PowerCLI.

In the next chapter, we will learn how to manage standard and advance networking in the vSphere environment in detail using PowerCLI.

4

Managing Networks

In the previous chapter, we saw how to configure a customized image using the image profile, automatically configure hosts using the host profile, and finally, how to automatically deploy ESXi servers using Auto Deploy. Since we deployed the server, we will learn how to configure and manage networking in the vSphere environment using PowerCLI. In this chapter, we will discuss the following topics:

- Managing vSphere standard switches
- Managing host network adapters
- Using port groups
- Managing vSphere distributed switches
- Configuring vSphere network I/O control
- Creating private VLANs
- Configuring Netflow
- Configuring VMware DirectPath IO

We will start with the creation and configuration of standard switches. Next, we will go into the details of distributed switches and then move on to the advanced configurations.

Managing vSphere standard switches

To manage complete vSphere networking, we need two different components. All the cmdlets for standard switches and other one come with the VMware. VimAutomation.Core snap-in/module, and all the cmdlets related to distributed switches are included in the VMware.VimAutomation.Vds module. In this section, we will discuss standard switches; in the next section, we will discuss distributed switches. For all the cmdlets to run successfully, we need to connect to a vCenter server. So, let's connect to a vCenter server and get started.

As you already know, whenever you install an ESXi server, by default a standard vSwitch with the name vSwitch0 is created.

The first thing that we need to do is to get accustomed to the vSwitch in an ESXi host using the PowerCLI cmdlets. For this, we can use the following cmdlets:

- `Get-VirtualSwitch`
- `New-VirtualSwitch`
- `Remove-VirtualSwitch`
- `Set-VirtualSwitch`

First, let's try to get a list of virtual switches available in the entire environment:

```
PS C:\> Get-VirtualSwitch
```

Name	NumPorts	Mtu	Notes
vSwitch0	1536	1500	
vSwitch0	1536	1500	
vSwitch0	1536	1500	

Since I did not mention any specific host, it shows a list of all the standard virtual switches available in the environment. To get a list of vSwitch from a particular host, we need to mention the particular hostname:

```
PS C:\> Get-VirtualSwitch -VMHost Esxi1.lab.com
```

Name	NumPorts	Mtu	Notes
vSwitch0	1536	1500	

Now, let's create a standard virtual switch using a cmdlet. We will create a new standard switch vSwitch1 in the ESXi host Esxi1.lab.com and connect the vmnic1 as an uplink to the newly created switch:

```
PS C:\> New-VirtualSwitch -Name vSwitch1 -VMHost Esxi1.lab.com -Nic
vmnic1
```

Name	NumPorts	Mtu	Notes
vSwitch1	1536	1500	

```
PS C:\> Get-VirtualSwitch -VMHost Esxi1.lab.com
```

Name	NumPorts	Mtu	Notes
vSwitch0	1536	1500	
vSwitch1	1536	1500	

In the preceding examples, we created a new virtual switch named `vSwitch1` in the ESXi host, `Esxi1.lab.com`, which is connected to `vmnic1`.

To configure the different parameters of an existing standard switch, we can use the `Set-VirtualSwitch` cmdlet.

Next, we will check how to add and remove a physical NIC from a virtual switch.

```
PS C:\> Get-VMHostNetworkAdapter -VMHost esxi1.lab.com -VirtualSwitch vSwitch1 -Physical

Name      Mac               DhcpEnabled IP        SubnetMask        DeviceName
----      ---               ----------- --        ----------        ----------
vmnic1    00:0c:29:b8:0b:82 False                                   vmnic1


PS C:\> $nics = Get-VMHostNetworkAdapter -VMHost esxi1.lab.com -Physical
PS C:\> Add-VirtualSwitchPhysicalNetworkAdapter -VirtualSwitch vSwitch1 -VMHostPhysicalNic $nics[3]
PS C:\> Get-VMHostNetworkAdapter -VMHost esxi1.lab.com -VirtualSwitch vSwitch1 -Physical

Name      Mac               DhcpEnabled IP        SubnetMask        DeviceName
----      ---               ----------- --        ----------        ----------
vmnic1    00:0c:29:b8:0b:82 False                                   vmnic1
vmnic3    00:0c:29:b8:0b:96 False                                   vmnic3


PS C:\> Get-VMHost -Name Esxi1.lab.com | Get-VMHostNetworkAdapter -Physical -Name "vmnic3" | Remove-VirtualSwitchPhysicalNetworkAdapter
PS C:\> Get-VMHostNetworkAdapter -VMHost esxi1.lab.com -VirtualSwitch vSwitch1 -Physical

Name      Mac               DhcpEnabled IP        SubnetMask        DeviceName
----      ---               ----------- --        ----------        ----------
vmnic1    00:0c:29:b8:0b:82 False                                   vmnic1
```

In the preceding example, we performed the following steps:

1. First, we checked the available physical network adapters in the `vSwitch1` virtual switch:

    ```
    PowerCLI C:\> Get-VMHostNetworkAdapter -VMHost esxi1.lab.com
    -VirtualSwitch vSwitch1 -Physical
    ```

2. Then, we got a list of physical adapters available in the ESXi server, esxi1.lab. com. With this information, we added the physical NIC vmnic3 card to the virtual switch, vSwitch1:

    ```
    PS :\> $nics = Get-VMHostNetworkAdapter -VMHost esxi1.lab.com -
    Physical
    ```

    ```
    PS :\> Add-VirtualSwitchPhysicalNetworkAdapter -VirtualSwitch
    vSwitch1 -VMHostPhysicalNic $nics[4] -Confirm:$false
    ```

3. Further, we checked the virtual switch to see whether the vmnic3 adapter had been added to vSwitch or not.

4. Lastly, we removed the adapter and again checked the physical adapters attached with the switch. We used the following cmdlets to do this:

```
Add-VirtualSwitchPhysicalNetworkAdapter

Remove-VirtualSwitchPhysicalNetworkAdapter

PS C:\> Get-VMHost -Name esxi1.lab.com | Get-VMHostNetworkAdapter
-Physical -Name 'vmnic4' | Remove-VirtualSwitchPhysicalNetworkAdap
ter
```

Managing networking for ESXi

Cmdlets available for managing ESXi hosts can be categorized in different categories, such as managing the physical NIC and related parameters, managing HBAs, setting the ntp server and snmp, and so on.

The first set of cmdlets is used to check the networking parameters of an ESXi host and the cmdlets are as follows:

- Get-VMHostNetwork
- Set-VMHostNetwork

With the help of the preceding two cmdlets, we can get the details of the configured network setting for an ESXi host, though many of the parameters of these two cmdlets are outdated and will soon be deprecated.

```
PS C:\> Get-VMHostNetwork -VMHost ESXi1.lab.com | Format-list

WARNING: The 'VMKernelGatewayDevice' property of VMHostNetworkInfo type is deprecated and will be removed in a future release.
WARNING: The 'VirtualSwitch' property of VMHostNetworkInfo type is deprecated. Use 'Get-VirtualSwitch' cmdlet instead.
WARNING: The 'PhysicalNic' property of VMHostNetworkInfo type is deprecated. Use 'Get-VMHostNetworkAdapter' cmdlet instead.
WARNING: The 'ConsoleNic' property of VMHostNetworkInfo type is deprecated. Use 'Get-VMHostNetworkAdapter' cmdlet instead.
WARNING: The 'VirtualNic' property of VMHostNetworkInfo type is deprecated. Use 'Get-VMHostNetworkAdapter' cmdlet instead.
WARNING: The value of 'ExtensionData' property of VMHostNetworkInfo type is deprecated and will be changed to the value of 'ExtensionData2'
 property in a future release. Use 'ExtensionData2' property instead.
VMHostId                 : HostSystem-host-29
VMHost                   : esxi1.lab.com
VMKernelGateway          : 192.168.1.1
VMKernelGatewayDevice    :
ConsoleGateway           :
ConsoleGatewayDevice     :
DnsAddress               : {192.168.1.39, 192.168.1.1}
DnsFromDhcp              : False
DnsDhcpDevice            :
DomainName               : lab.com
HostName                 : esxi1
SearchDomain             : {lab.com}
VirtualSwitch            : {vSwitch0, vSwitch1}
PhysicalNic              : {vmnic0, vmnic1, vmnic2, vmnic3}
ConsoleNic               : {}
VirtualNic               : {vmk0, vmk1}
Uid                      : /VIServer=lab\vcadmin@vcenter.lab.com:443/VMHost=HostSystem-host-29/VMHostNetwork=/
IPv6Enabled              : True
ConsoleV6Gateway         :
ConsoleV6GatewayDevice   :
VMKernelV6Gateway        :
VMKernelV6GatewayDevice  :
ExtensionData            : VMware.Vim.HostNetworkInfo
ExtensionData2           : VMware.Vim.HostNetworkSystem
Name                     :
Id                       : HostNetworkSystem-networkSystem-29
Client                   : VMware.VimAutomation.ViCore.Impl.V1.VimClient
```

The `Set-VMHostNetwork` cmdlet is used to update the different parameters of the specified virtual network. For example, the following cmdlets will enable the IPv6 network in the host and then the host must be restarted for any changes to take effect:

```
PS C:\> Get-VMHost -Name ESXi1.lab.com | Get-VMHostNetwork | Set-VMHostNetwork -IPv6Enabled $true
WARNING: Enabling IPv6 will take effect after host reboot.

HostName    DomainName   DnsFro ConsoleGateway  ConsoleGatewayD DnsAddress
                         mDhcp                  evice
--------    ----------   ------ --------------  --------------- ----------
esxi1       lab.com      False                                  {192.168.1.39, 19...


PS C:\> Get-VMHost -Name ESXi1.lab.com | Restart-VMHost -Force -Confirm:$false

Name              ConnectionState PowerState NumCpu CpuUsageMhz CpuTotalMhz  MemoryUsageGB  MemoryTotalGB Version
----              --------------- ---------- ------ ----------- -----------  -------------  ------------- -------
esxi1.lab.com     Connected       PoweredOn    4         80        13568         1.324         4.000      6.0.0
```

We can further control the finer aspects of ESXi host networking with the following set of cmdlets:

- `Get-VMHostNetworkAdapter`
- `New-VMHostNetworkAdapter`
- `Remove-VMHostNetworkAdapter`
- `Set-VMHostNetworkAdapter`

With the help of these cmdlets, we can control the physical network adapters. For example, we can get the details of the physical adapters and the VMkernel adapters by using the following two cmdlets:

```
PS C:\> Get-VMHostNetworkAdapter -VMHost ESXi1.lab.com

Name     Mac                DhcpEnabled IP              SubnetMask        DeviceName
----     ---                ----------- --              ----------        ----------
vmnic0   00:0c:29:b8:0b:78  False                                         vmnic0
vmnic1   00:0c:29:b8:0b:82  False                                         vmnic1
vmnic2   00:0c:29:b8:0b:8c  False                                         vmnic2
vmnic3   00:0c:29:b8:0b:96  False                                         vmnic3
vmk0     00:0c:29:b8:0b:78  False       192.168.1.51    255.255.255.0     vmk0
vmk1     00:50:56:6e:99:05  False       192.168.1.90    255.255.255.0     vmk1


PS C:\> Get-VMHostNetworkAdapter -VMKernel -VMHost ESXi1.lab.com

Name     Mac                DhcpEnabled IP              SubnetMask        DeviceName
----     ---                ----------- --              ----------        ----------
vmk0     00:0c:29:b8:0b:78  False       192.168.1.51    255.255.255.0     vmk0
vmk1     00:50:56:6e:99:05  False       192.168.1.90    255.255.255.0     vmk1
```

We can use the following three cmdlets:

- `New-VMHostNetworkAdapter`
- `Remove-VMHostNetworkAdapter`
- `Set-VMHostNetworkAdapter`

To add a new physical adapter, remove an adapter, and set the parameters for an adapter. You can get details of these cmdlets using the `Get-Help` cmdlets or via online help.

NIC Teaming: One major aspect of networking is to configure NIC Teaming in the vSwitch. Although, we do not change these settings pretty often, but they can come in handy if required. We can check the teaming policy with the `Get-NicTeamingPolicy` cmdlet:

```
PS C:\> Get-VirtualSwitch -VMHost (Get-VMHost esxi1.lab.com) -Name
vSwitch0 | Get-NicTeamingPolicy

VirtualSwitch    ActiveNic        StandbyNic       UnusedNic
FailbackEnabled NotifySwitches

-------------    ---------        ----------       ---------        ---------
------ ---------------

vSwitch0         {vmnic0, vmn...                                    True
True
```

We can set the teaming policy with the `Set-NicTeamingPolicy` cmdlet.

```
PS C:\> $policy = Get-VirtualSwitch -VMHost (Get-VMHost esxi1.lab.com) -Name vSwitch0 | Get-NicTeamingPolicy
PS C:\> $policy

VirtualSwitch    ActiveNic        StandbyNic       UnusedNic        FailbackEnabled NotifySwitches
-------------    ---------        ----------       ---------        --------------- --------------
vSwitch0         {vmnic0, vmn...                                    True            True


PS C:\> $policy | Set-NicTeamingPolicy -FailbackEnabled $false

VirtualSwitch    ActiveNic        StandbyNic       UnusedNic        FailbackEnabled NotifySwitches
-------------    ---------        ----------       ---------        --------------- --------------
vSwitch0         {vmnic0, vmn...                                    False           True
```

Managing vSphere distributed switches

After discussing the different aspects of a standard vSwitch, we will now move on to discus distributed virtual switches. The following is a list of available cmdlets for managing the different aspects of distributed virtual switches:

- `Add-VDSwitchPhysicalNetworkAdapter`
- `Add-VDSwitchVMHost`
- `Export-VDPortGroup`
- `Export-VDSwitch`
- `Get-VDBlockedPolicy`
- `Get-VDPort`
- `Get-VDPortgroup`
- `Get-VDPortgroupOverridePolicy`
- `Get-VDSecurityPolicy`
- `Get-VDSwitch`
- `Get-VDSwitchPrivateVlan`
- `Get-VDTrafficShapingPolicy`
- `Get-VDUplinkLacpPolicy`
- `Get-VDUplinkTeamingPolicy`
- `New-VDPortgroup`
- `New-VDSwitch`
- `New-VDSwitchPrivateVlan`
- `Remove-VDPortGroup`
- `Remove-VDSwitch`
- `Remove-VDSwitchPhysicalNetworkAdapter`
- `Remove-VDSwitchPrivateVlan`
- `Remove-VDSwitchVMHost`
- `Set-VDBlockedPolicy`

- Set-VDPort
- Set-VDPortgroup
- Set-VDPortgroupOverridePolicy
- Set-VDSecurityPolicy
- Set-VDSwitch
- Set-VDTrafficShapingPolicy
- Set-VDUplinkLacpPolicy
- Set-VDUplinkTeamingPolicy
- Set-VDVlanConfiguration

We will start by creating a new dvSwitch using the New-VDSwitch cmdlet.

```
PS C:\> $datacenter = Get-Datacenter -Name "Datacenter"
PS C:\> New-VDSwitch -Name "Test1" -Location $datacenter -Version "6.0.0"

Name                    NumPorts    Mtu      Version    Vendor
----                    --------    ---      -------    ------
Test1                   0           1500     6.0.0      VMware, Inc.


PS C:\> Get-VDSwitch

Name                    NumPorts    Mtu      Version    Vendor
----                    --------    ---      -------    ------
Test1                   0           1500     6.0.0      VMware, Inc.
```

Next, let's add ESXi hosts to the dvSwitch. We will do this using the following cmdlet:

```
PS C:\> Get-VDSwitch -Name "Test1" | Add-VDSwitchVMHost -VMHost "ESXi1.
lab.com", "ESXi2.lab.com"
```

Since we attached the hosts to the dvSwitch, we will now attach physical network adapters to the distributed switch. We will use the Add-VDSwitchPhysicalNetworkAdapter cmdlet:

```
PS C:\> $NetworkAdapter = Get-VMHost -Name "ESXi1.lab.com" | Get-
VMHostNetworkAdapter -Physical -Name vmnic1


PS C:\> Get-VDSwitch "Test1" | Add-VDSwitchPhysicalNetworkAdapter
-VMHostPhysicalNic $NetworkAdapter
```

```
PS C:\> $NetworkAdapter = Get-VMHost -Name "ESXi2.lab.com" | Get-
VMHostNetworkAdapter -Physical -Name vmnic1

PS C:\> Get-VDSwitch "Test1" | Add-VDSwitchPhysicalNetworkAdapter
-VMHostPhysicalNic $NetworkAdapter
```

We can use the other cmdlets to remove a VMHost from a switch or remove a physical adapter from a distributed switch.

Before we move on to other topics, we can take a backup of the distributed switch configuration using the Export-VDSwitch cmdlet.

```
PS C:\> Export-VDSwitch -VDSwitch 'Test1' -Description "VDSwitch Configuration Backup" -Destination "C:\VDSwithConfiguration.zip"

Mode             LastWriteTime         Length Name
----             -------------         ------ ----
-a----      27-05-2015  10:54 PM         4945 VDSwithConfiguration.zip
```

Later, we can use this backup to import the configuration into a newly created distributed switch using the Set-VDSwitch cmdlet along with the BackupPath switch.

Managing port groups

So far, we have created standard and distributed virtual switches as well as checked how to configure the different aspects of networking ESXi hosts. Now, we will take a look at how we can configure port groups in virtual switches. We will start with the different cmdlets that we can use to configure port groups for standard switches, and then we will check the port groups of distributed switches.

The cmdlets related to standard switches are as follows:

* Get-VirtualPortGroup
* New-VirtualPortGroup
* Remove-VirtualPortGroup
* Set-VirtualPortGroup

As the name suggests, we can get details of the `Get-VirtualPortGroup` cmdlet and create a new one with the `New-VirtualPortGroup` cmdlet. We will start with creating a new port group.

```
PS C:\> Get-VirtualPortGroup -VMHost Esxi1.lab.com -Standard

Name                    Key                             VLanId PortBinding NumPorts
----                    ---                             ------ ----------- --------
VM Network              key-vim.host.PortGroup-VM N... 0
vMotion                 key-vim.host.PortGroup-vMotion 0
Management Network      key-vim.host.PortGroup-Mana... 0


PS C:\> Get-VirtualSwitch -VMHost ESXi1.lab.com -Name vSwitch0 | New-VirtualPortGroup -Name "TestPortGroup"

Name                    Key                             VLanId PortBinding NumPorts
----                    ---                             ------ ----------- --------
TestPortGroup           key-vim.host.PortGroup-Test... 0


PS C:\> Get-VirtualPortGroup -VMHost Esxi1.lab.com -Standard

Name                    Key                             VLanId PortBinding NumPorts
----                    ---                             ------ ----------- --------
VM Network              key-vim.host.PortGroup-VM N... 0
vMotion                 key-vim.host.PortGroup-vMotion 0
Management Network      key-vim.host.PortGroup-Mana... 0
TestPortGroup           key-vim.host.PortGroup-Test... 0
```

We can add a VLAN ID to a port group of a virtual switch using the `New-VirtualPortGroup` cmdlet, using the `VLanId` switch.

We can remove a port group using the `Remove-VirtualPortGroup` cmdlet and change the properties of an existing virtual switch using the `Set-VirtualPortGroup` cmdlet.

Next, we will check the different cmdlets related to port group creation for a distributed switch. The following are the cmdlets related to the port group management of a distributed switch:

- `Export-VDPortGroup`
- `Get-VDPortgroup`
- `Get-VDPortgroupOverridePolicy`
- `New-VDPortgroup`
- `Remove-VDPortGroup`
- `Set-VDPortgroup`
- `Set-VDPortgroupOverridePolicy`

Let's first start with a simple dvSwitch port group creation.

```
PS C:\> Get-VDPortgroup

Name                              NumPorts PortBinding
----                              -------- -----------
Test1-DVUplinks-723               8        Static


PS C:\> New-VDPortgroup -VDSwitch "Test1" -Name "TestPortGroup" -VlanTrunkRange "2-7, 20-30"

Name                              NumPorts PortBinding
----                              -------- -----------
TestPortGroup                     128      Static


PS C:\> Get-VDPortgroup

Name                              NumPorts PortBinding
----                              -------- -----------
Test1-DVUplinks-723               8        Static
TestPortGroup                     128      Static
```

As seen in the preceding screenshot, we created a new port group named
TestPortGroup in the distributed switch Test1 with VLAN ranges set to
2-7 and 20-30.

We can check the policy for overriding the port group policy at port
group level using the Get-VDPortgroupOverridePolicy and the
Set-VDPortgroupOverridePolicy cmdlets.

```
PS C:\> Get-VDPortgroupOverridePolicy -VDPortgroup "TestPortGroup"

VDPortgroup         BlockOverride TrafficShapingO SecurityOverride VlanOverride UplinkTeamingOve ResetPortConfig
                    Allowed       verrideAllowed  Allowed          Allowed      rrideAllowed     AtDisconnect
-----------         ------------- --------------- ---------------- ------------ ---------------- ---------------
TestPortGroup       True          False           False            False        False            True
```

As per the distributed switch configuration, we can take a backup of the port group
configuration using the Export-VDPortGroup cmdlet.

```
PS C:\> Export-VDPortGroup -VDPortGroup "TestPortGroup" -Description "Test Port Group Configuration" -Destination "Test.zip"

Mode              LastWriteTime     Length Name
----              -------------     ------ ----
-a----       28-05-2015  12:38 AM     2026 Test.zip
```

We can remove a port group using the Remove-VDPortGroup cmdlet.

Creating private VLANs

In this section, we will discuss how to create a private VLAN in a distributed switch. We will first use the `Get-VDSwitchPrivateVlan` cmdlet to check whether there are any private VLANs configured or not. As can be seen, there is no PVLAN. Next, we created three different types of PVLAN and again checked the status.

```
PS C:\> Get-VDSwitchPrivateVlan -VDSwitch Test1

PS C:\> Get-VDSwitch "Test1" | New-VDSwitchPrivateVlan -PrimaryVlanId 1 -SecondaryVlanId 1 -PrivateVlanType Promiscuous

VDSwitch              PrivateVlanType PrimaryVlanId SecondaryVlanId
--------              --------------- ------------- ---------------
Test1                 Promiscuous     1             1


PS C:\> Get-VDSwitch "Test1" | New-VDSwitchPrivateVlan -PrimaryVlanId 1 -SecondaryVlanId 20 -PrivateVlanType Isolated

VDSwitch              PrivateVlanType PrimaryVlanId SecondaryVlanId
--------              --------------- ------------- ---------------
Test1                 Isolated        1             20


PS C:\> Get-VDSwitch "Test1" | New-VDSwitchPrivateVlan -PrimaryVlanId 1 -SecondaryVlanId 30 -PrivateVlanType Community

VDSwitch              PrivateVlanType PrimaryVlanId SecondaryVlanId
--------              --------------- ------------- ---------------
Test1                 Community       1             30


PS C:\> Get-VDSwitchPrivateVlan -VDSwitch Test1

VDSwitch              PrivateVlanType PrimaryVlanId SecondaryVlanId
--------              --------------- ------------- ---------------
Test1                 Promiscuous     1             1
Test1                 Isolated        1             20
Test1                 Community       1             30
```

We can remove a private VLAN using the `Remove-VDSwitchPrivateVlan` cmdlet.

```
PS C:\> Get-VDSwitchPrivateVlan -VDSwitch Test1

VDSwitch              PrivateVlanType PrimaryVlanId SecondaryVlanId
--------              --------------- ------------- ---------------
Test1                 Promiscuous     1             1
Test1                 Isolated        1             20
Test1                 Community       1             30


PS C:\> $vlan = Get-VDSwitchPrivateVlan -VDSwitch Test1

PS C:\> Remove-VDSwitchPrivateVlan -VDSwitchPrivateVlan $vlan[2]

PS C:\> Get-VDSwitchPrivateVlan -VDSwitch Test1

VDSwitch              PrivateVlanType PrimaryVlanId SecondaryVlanId
--------              --------------- ------------- ---------------
Test1                 Promiscuous     1             1
Test1                 Isolated        1             20
```

Configuring vSphere network I/O control

Configuring network I/O control in the vSphere environment is a great way to control and ensure quality of service for different types of traffic. Though there is no direct cmdlet available to enable and disable network I/O control using PowerCLI, we can do so using the vSphere APIs using PowerCLI. We can get a list of all the methods and properties available in the `VDSwitch` object by inspecting the `ExtensionData` option of the object. In the following screenshot, we can see that there is an `EnableNetworkResourceManagement` method associated with the object that takes a `$true` or `$false` Boolean input, which decides whether `NetworkResourceManagement` will be turned on or off.

```
PS C:\> (Get-VDSwitch -Name Test1).ExtensionData | Get-Member | Where {$_.Name -eq "EnableNetworkResourceManagement"}


   TypeName: VMware.Vim.VmwareDistributedVirtualSwitch

Name                            MemberType Definition
----                            ---------- ----------
EnableNetworkResourceManagement Method     void EnableNetworkResourceManagement(bool enable)
```

> We will see how we can access APIs using PowerCLI in the upcoming chapter in detail. For now, we will just touch upon the subject.

So, we can enable or disable network I/O control by simply using the following method:

```
PS C:\> (Get-VDSwitch -Name Test1).ExtensionData.EnableNetworkResourceManagement($true)
```

```
PS C:\> (Get-VDSwitch -Name Test1).ExtensionData.EnableNetworkResourceManagement($false)
```

To get a list of the available network resource pools, use the following method:

```
PS C:\> (Get-VDSwitch -Name Test1).ExtensionData.NetworkResourcePool | Format-Table

Key            Name                                       Description                                    ConfigVersion AllocationInfo
---            ----                                       -----------                                    ------------- --------------
vsan           Virtual SAN Traffic                        Virtual SAN Traffic Type                       1             VMware.Vim.DVSNetworkRe...
nfs            NFS Traffic                                NFS Traffic Type                               1             VMware.Vim.DVSNetworkRe...
vmotion        vMotion Traffic                            vMotion Traffic Type                           1             VMware.Vim.DVSNetworkRe...
vdp            vSphere Data Protection Backup Traffic     vSphere Data Protection Backup Traffic Type    1             VMware.Vim.DVSNetworkRe...
faultTolerance Fault Tolerance (FT) Traffic               Fault Tolerance (FT) Traffic Type              1             VMware.Vim.DVSNetworkRe...
hbr            vSphere Replication (VR) Traffic           vSphere Replication (VR) Traffic Type          1             VMware.Vim.DVSNetworkRe...
management     Management Traffic                         Management Traffic Type                        1             VMware.Vim.DVSNetworkRe...
iSCSI          iSCSI Traffic                              iSCSI Traffic Type                             1             VMware.Vim.DVSNetworkRe...
virtualMachine Virtual Machine Traffic                    Virtual Machine Traffic Type                   1             VMware.Vim.DVSNetworkRe...
```

Now, we can add a network resource pool using the `AddNetworkResourcePool` method.

```
PS C:\> (Get-VDSwitch -Name Test1).ExtensionData.AddNetworkResourcePool

OverloadDefinitions
-------------------
void AddNetworkResourcePool(VMware.Vim.DVSNetworkResourcePoolConfigSpec[] configSpec)
```

In the preceding screenshot, we can see that this method takes the `VMware.Vim.DVSNetworkResourcePoolConfigSpec[]` type as the input method. So, let's add a new network resource pool to the existing distributed switch. Let's create a new specification for the input. To do this, we will create a `$pSpec` variable that will hold all the required information:

```
$pSpec = New-Object VMware.Vim.DVSNetworkResourcePoolConfigSpec

$pSpec.Name = "TestPool"

$pSpec.Description = "Description"

$pSpec.Key = "Test"

$pSpec.allocationInfo = New-Object        VMware.Vim.
DVSNetworkResourcePoolAllocationInfo

$pSpec.allocationInfo.Limit = -1

$pSpec.allocationInfo.priorityTag = 3

$pSpec.allocationInfo.Shares = New-Object VMware.Vim.SharesInfo

$pSpec.allocationInfo.Shares.Level = "Normal"
```

Now, we will use this variable to create a new resource pool.

> Note that we will cover why we are doing this in this particular way in *Chapter 9, Managing the vSphere API*, where we will cover APIs in detail. For now, please bear with me and follow along.

```
PS C:\> $pSpec = New-Object VMware.Vim.DVSNetworkResourcePoolConfigSpec
$pSpec.Name = "TestPool"
$pSpec.Description = "Description"
$pSpec.Key = "Test"
$pSpec.allocationInfo = New-Object      VMware.Vim.DVSNetworkResourcePoolAllocationInfo
$pSpec.allocationInfo.Limit = -1
$pSpec.allocationInfo.priorityTag = 3
$pSpec.allocationInfo.Shares = New-Object VMware.Vim.SharesInfo
$pSpec.allocationInfo.Shares.Level = "Normal"

PS C:\> (Get-VDSwitch -Name Test1).ExtensionData.AddNetworkResourcePool(@($spec))

PS C:\> (Get-VDSwitch -Name Test1).ExtensionData.NetworkResourcePool | Format-Table

Key                 Name                                        Description                                     ConfigVersion AllocationInfo
---                 ----                                        -----------                                     ------------- --------------
vsan                Virtual SAN Traffic                         Virtual SAN Traffic Type                        1             VMware.Vim.DVSNetwor...
nfs                 NFS Traffic                                 NFS Traffic Type                                1             VMware.Vim.DVSNetwor...
NRP_22680_dvs-723   TestPool                                    Description                                     1             VMware.Vim.DVSNetwor...
vmotion             vMotion Traffic                             vMotion Traffic Type                            1             VMware.Vim.DVSNetwor...
vdp                 vSphere Data Protection Backup Traffic      vSphere Data Protection Backup Traffic Type     1             VMware.Vim.DVSNetwor...
faultTolerance      Fault Tolerance (FT) Traffic                Fault Tolerance (FT) Traffic Type               1             VMware.Vim.DVSNetwor...
hbr                 vSphere Replication (VR) Traffic            vSphere Replication (VR) Traffic Type           1             VMware.Vim.DVSNetwor...
management          Management Traffic                          Management Traffic Type                         1             VMware.Vim.DVSNetwor...
iSCSI               iSCSI Traffic                               iSCSI Traffic Type                              1             VMware.Vim.DVSNetwor...
virtualMachine      Virtual Machine Traffic                     Virtual Machine Traffic Type                    1             VMware.Vim.DVSNetwor...
```

In the following screenshot, a new resource pool **TestPool** has been created:

We can also remove a network resource pool using the RemoveNetworkResourcePool
method.

```
PS C:\> (Get-VDSwitch -Name Test1).ExtensionData | Get-Member | Where {$_.Name -eq "RemoveNetworkResourcePool"}

    TypeName: VMware.Vim.VmwareDistributedVirtualSwitch

Name                      MemberType Definition
----                      ---------- ----------
RemoveNetworkResourcePool Method     void RemoveNetworkResourcePool(string[] key)
```

Note that this method takes a key as the input.

```
PS C:\> (Get-VDSwitch -Name Test1).ExtensionData.RemoveNetworkResourcePool("NRP_22680_dvs-723")

PS C:\> (Get-VDSwitch -Name Test1).ExtensionData.NetworkResourcePool | Format-Table

Key              Name                                    Description                                    ConfigVersion AllocationInfo
---              ----                                    -----------                                    ------------- --------------
vsan             Virtual SAN Traffic                     Virtual SAN Traffic Type                       1             VMware.Vim.DVSNetworkRe...
nfs              NFS Traffic                             NFS Traffic Type                               1             VMware.Vim.DVSNetworkRe...
vmotion          vMotion Traffic                         vMotion Traffic Type                           1             VMware.Vim.DVSNetworkRe...
vdp              vSphere Data Protection Backup Traffic  vSphere Data Protection Backup Traffic Type 1             VMware.Vim.DVSNetworkRe...
faultTolerance   Fault Tolerance (FT) Traffic            Fault Tolerance (FT) Traffic Type              1             VMware.Vim.DVSNetworkRe...
hbr              vSphere Replication (VR) Traffic        vSphere Replication (VR) Traffic Type          1             VMware.Vim.DVSNetworkRe...
management       Management Traffic                      Management Traffic Type                        1             VMware.Vim.DVSNetworkRe...
iSCSI            iSCSI Traffic                           iSCSI Traffic Type                             1             VMware.Vim.DVSNetworkRe...
virtualMachine   Virtual Machine Traffic                 Virtual Machine Traffic Type                   1             VMware.Vim.DVSNetworkRe...
```

Configuring Netflow

To configure Netflow, we need to access APIs. To do this, we will access the `ReconfigureDVPortgroup_Task` method. Alan Renouf has a very good blog and description for this (http://www.virtu-al.net/2013/07/23/disabling-netflow-with-powercli/):

```
PS C:\> (Get-VDPortgroup -Name TestPortGroup).Extensiondata.Config.
defaultPortConfig.ipfixEnabled.Value

False
```

Next, we will change the value. As seen in the following output, it takes a `VMware.Vim.DVPortgroupConfigSpec` type specification:

```
PS C:\> (Get-VDPortgroup -Name "TestPortGroup") Extensiondata.
ReconfigureDVPortgroup_Task


OverloadDefinitions
-------------------

VMware.Vim.ManagedObjectReference ReconfigureDVPortgroup_Task(VMware.Vim.
DVPortgroupConfigSpec spec)
```

To do this, we will first create a specification and then pass the value to the method in order to make the change:

```
$DVPG = Get-VDPortgroup -Name "TestPortGroup"
$pSpec = New-Object VMware.Vim.DVPortgroupConfigSpec
$pSpec.configversion = $DVPG.Extensiondata.Config.ConfigVersion
$pSpec.defaultPortConfig = New-Object VMware.Vim.VMwareDVSPortSetting
$pSpec.defaultPortConfig.ipfixEnabled = New-Object VMware.Vim.BoolPolicy
$pSpec.defaultPortConfig.ipfixEnabled.inherited = $false
$pSpec.defaultPortConfig.ipfixEnabled.value = $true

(Get-VDPortgroup -Name "TestPortGroup" | Get-View).
ReconfigureDVPortgroup_Task($pSpec)
```

> The preceding method is taken from a blog written by Alan Renouf at
> `http://www.virtu-al.net/2013/07/23/disabling-netflow-`
> `with-powercli/`.

The preceding will enable Netflow in the port group. To disable it, change the value accordingly. Note that for this, we need to follow the same process as mentioned earlier but with the exception of one variable value been changed, which is as follows:

`$pSpec.defaultPortConfig.ipfixEnabled.value = $false`

Working with ports

So far, we have worked with host, switch, and port groups; now, let's explore how we can get details of a port and modify it. To manage a port, we will use the following two cmdlets:

* `Get-VDPort`
* `Set-VDPort`

We can get the details of the port using the `Get-VDPort` cmdlet and set details via the `Set-VDPort` cmdlet.

```
PS C:\> Get-VDPort -VDPortgroup "TestPortGroup" -Key 21 | Select Key,Name,Portgroup,Switch,Description | Format-Table

Key Name Portgroup      Switch Description
--- ---- ---------      ------ -----------
21       TestPortGroup Test1


PS C:\> $port = Get-VDPort -VDPortgroup "TestPortGroup" -Key 21

PS C:\> Set-VDPort -VDPort $port -Name "TestPort-1" -Description "Test Port 1"

Key  Name        ConnectedEntity      Portgroup       IsLinkUp  MacAddress     Vlan      Switch
---  ----        ---------------      ---------       --------  ----------     ----      ------
21   TestPort-1                       TestPortGroup                                      Test1


PS C:\> Get-VDPort -VDPortgroup "TestPortGroup" -Key 21 | Select Key,Name,Portgroup,Switch,Description | Format-Table

Key Name       Portgroup      Switch Description
--- ----       ---------      ------ -----------
21  TestPort-1 TestPortGroup Test1  Test Port 1
```

Configuring traffic shaping

We can use PowerCLI to configure traffic shaping in distributed ports, and we can use the following two cmdlets to configure it:

- `Get-VDTrafficShapingPolicy`
- `Set-VDTrafficShapingPolicy`

Obviously, `Get-VDTrafficShapingPolicy` will provide you with the details of the current policy set and `Set-VDTrafficShapingPolicy` will allow us to change the existing settings.

```
PS C:\> $port = Get-VDPort -VDPortgroup "TestPortGroup" -Key 21

PS C:\> Get-VDTrafficShapingPolicy -VDPort $port -Direction In

VDPort                  Direction  Enabled AverageBandwidth  PeakBandwidth  BurstSize
------                  ---------  ------- ----------------  -------------  ---------
21 (TestPort-1)         In         False   100000000         100000000      104857600


PS C:\> Get-VDTrafficShapingPolicy -VDPort $port -Direction Out

VDPort                  Direction  Enabled AverageBandwidth  PeakBandwidth  BurstSize
------                  ---------  ------- ----------------  -------------  ---------
21 (TestPort-1)         Out        False   100000000         100000000      104857600
```

Next, let's set the parameters for traffic shaping.

```
PS C:\> Get-VDTrafficShapingPolicy -VDPortgroup "TestPortGroup" -
Direction In

VDPortgroup                          Direction  Enabled AverageBandwidth
PeakBandwidth  BurstSize
-----------                          ---------  ------- ----------------
--------       ---------
TestPortGroup                        In         False   100000000
100000000      104857600


PS C:\> Get-VDTrafficShapingPolicy -VDPortgroup "TestPortGroup" -
Direction In | Set-VDTrafficShapingPolicy -Enabled $true

VDPortgroup                          Direction  Enabled AverageBandwidth
PeakBandwidth  BurstSize
-----------                          ---------  ------- ----------------
--------       ---------
TestPortGroup                        In         True    100000000
100000000      104857600


PS C:\> Get-VDTrafficShapingPolicy -VDPortgroup "TestPortGroup" -
Direction In | Set-VDTrafficShapingPolicy -Enabled $true -
AverageBandwidth 50000000

VDPortgroup                          Direction  Enabled AverageBandwidth
PeakBandwidth  BurstSize
-----------                          ---------  ------- ----------------
--------       ---------
TestPortGroup                        In         True    50000000
100000000      104857600
```

Configuring port blocking

Next, we will check port blocking options using PowerCLI. The following are the cmdlets available for this purpose:

- Get-VDBlockedPolicy
- Set-VDBlockedPolicy

```
PS C:\> Get-VDPort -VDSwitch "Test1" -ActiveOnly | Get-VDBlockedPolicy

VDPort          Blocked    BlockedInherited
------          -------    ----------------
12 (uplink1)    False      False
16 (uplink1)    False      False


PS C:\> Get-VDPort -VDSwitch "Test1" -ActiveOnly | Get-VDBlockedPolicy | Set-VDBlockedPolicy -Blocked $true

VDPort          Blocked    BlockedInherited
------          -------    ----------------
12 (uplink1)    True       False
16 (uplink1)    True       False


PS C:\> Get-VDPort -VDSwitch "Test1" -ActiveOnly | Get-VDBlockedPolicy

VDPort          Blocked    BlockedInherited
------          -------    ----------------
12 (uplink1)    True       False
16 (uplink1)    True       False
```

Configuring the security policy

To configure the security policy at different levels, we can use the following four cmdlets:

- Get-SecurityPolicy
- Get-VDSecurityPolicy
- Set-SecurityPolicy
- Set-VDSecurityPolicy

The following is an example of how you can make changes to the security policy in a distributed switch using the preceding cmdlets:

```
PS C:\> Get-VDSecurityPolicy -VDPortgroup TestPortGroup

VDPortgroup          AllowPromiscuous MacChanges ForgedTransmits
-----------          ---------------- ---------- ---------------
TestPortGroup        False            False      False


PS C:\> Get-VDSecurityPolicy -VDPortgroup TestPortGroup | Set-VDSecurityPolicy -MacChanges $true

VDPortgroup          AllowPromiscuous MacChanges ForgedTransmits
-----------          ---------------- ---------- ---------------
TestPortGroup        False            True       False
```

Configuring the teaming policy

To configure the uplink teaming policy for distributed ports, we can use the following four cmdlets:

* Get-NicTeamingPolicy
* Get-VDUplinkTeamingPolicy
* Set-NicTeamingPolicy
* Set-VDUplinkTeamingPolicy

The following is an example of setting the teaming policy in a distributed switch:

```
PS C:\> Get-VDUplinkTeamingPolicy -VDPortgroup TestPortGroup

VDPortgroup     LoadBalancingPolicy FailoverDetectionPolicy NotifySwitches EnableFailback ActiveUplinkPort
-----------     ------------------- ----------------------- -------------- -------------- ----------------
TestPortGroup   LoadBalanceSrcId    LinkStatus              True           True           {uplink1, upli...


PS C:\> Get-VDUplinkTeamingPolicy -VDPortgroup TestPortGroup | Set-VDUplinkTeamingPolicy -NotifySwitches $false

VDPortgroup     LoadBalancingPolicy FailoverDetectionPolicy NotifySwitches EnableFailback ActiveUplinkPort
-----------     ------------------- ----------------------- -------------- -------------- ----------------
TestPortGroup   LoadBalanceSrcId    LinkStatus              False          True           {uplink1, upli...
```

Summary

In this chapter, we covered the different aspects of networking in the vSphere environment, starting with how to manage standard switches using PowerCLI. Next, we covered how to manage ESXi hosts and distributed switches. After this, we covered the different parameters and aspects of distributed switches that we can configure using PowerCLI.

In the next chapter, we will cover how to configure the different aspects of storage in the vSphere environment. For example, how we can add different types of storage in an ESXi host, create a new data store, and so on, and how we can create and configure VSAN using PowerCLI.

5
Managing Storage

To build a virtual environment using VMware solutions, we start with the installation and then we configure the network in the setup. What follows next is the configuration of storage. In the previous chapters, we talked about installing ESXi hosts and then managing networking through PowerCLI. Logically, next we should configure storage in the environment. In this chapter, we are going to talk about managing different aspects of storage in the vSphere environment using PowerCLI. Before we start discussing types of storage and how we can manage them through PowerCLI, there are three basic tasks that we should be able to perform from the command line:

- Refreshing the storage
- Rescanning all HBA
- Rescanning all datastores

The first one will refresh the existing storage in the environment. As the name suggests, the second will rescan all the HBAs; this particular option is very helpful if you are going to work with SAN storage. The third one will rescan all the available datastores. We can do all this using a single cmdlet which is the Get-VMHostStorage cmdlet.

To refresh all storage, we can use the cmdlet:

```
PS C:\> Get-VMHostStorage -VMHost ESXi1.lab.com -Refresh
```

To rescan all HBA, we can use the same cmdlet:

```
PS C:\> Get-VMHostStorage -VMHost ESXi1.lab.com -RescanAllHba
```

To rescan all Vmfs, we use this cmdlet:

```
PS C:\> Get-VMHostStorage -VMHost ESXi1.lab.com -RescanVmfs
```

Managing datastores

Before we go ahead and start a discussion on how we can add different types of storage to an ESXi host, we will discuss a few basic tasks, such as copy and move operations on datastores. In the following example, we have the cmdlets that we can use to generally achieve the tasks:

- `Copy-DatastoreItem`
- `Get-Datastore`
- `Move-Datastore`
- `New-Datastore`
- `Remove-Datastore`
- `Set-Datastore`

The first cmdlet `Copy-DatastoreItem` lets you copy data from a local machine disk to a remote datastore:

```
PS C:\> Copy-DatastoreItem vmstore:\Datacenter\vsanDatastore\Test-VM\*
C:\VMFolder\Test-VM\ -Force
```

This will copy the files related to `Test-VM` to a local folder in the local system.

As the name suggests, the `Get-Datastore` cmdlet provides a list of datastores in the systems:

```
PS C:\> Get-Datastore
```

Name	FreeSpaceGB	CapacityGB
datastore1	11.628	12.500
datastore1 (3)	11.628	12.500
iSCSI-1	48.798	49.750
iSCSI-2	48.798	49.750
iSCSI-3	48.798	49.750
datastore1 (1)	11.628	12.500
iSCSI-4	48.798	49.750
iSCSI-5	48.798	49.750
NFS_SHARE	17.595	17.595
vsanDatastore	585.258	593.977

The `Move-Datastore` cmdlet moves a datastore from one location to another, be it under one folder, another cluster, or even a datacenter. For example, I am moving the `NFS_SHARE` datastore to a new location `NFS`, which can be a folder, a cluster, or a datacenter:

```
PS C:\> Move-Datastore "NFS_SHARE" -Destination "NFS"
```

In the next sections, we will take a closer look at how we can add different types of storage in an ESXi host. First, we will start with how we can add fibre channel storage to an ESXi host.

Before we start our discussion about managing fibre channel storage, let's have a look at the device naming format and the `CanonicalName` of the devices. We will discuss about device naming convention for ESXi 5.x/6.0 only. There are five different ways a storage device can be named or represented:

- `naa.<NAA>:<Partition>` or `eui.<EUI>:<Partition>`: **NAA** stands for **Network Addressing Authority** identifier. **EUI** stands for **Extended Unique Identifier**. This is the preferred way of representing a device, as the number is guaranteed to be unique for that device. This number is generated by the storage device and so remains unique. It is presented in the same way to all the ESXi hosts.

- `mpx.vmhba<Adapter>:C<Channel>:T<Target>:L<LUN>` or `mpx.vmhba<Adapter>:C<Channel>:T<Target>:L<LUN>:<Partition>`:

  Some devices do not provide the NAA number as mentioned in the preceding point. In such cases, an MPX identifier is generated by ESXi to represent the LUN or disk.

- `vml.<VML>` or `vml.<VML>:<Partition>`: The VML Identifier can be used interchangeably with the NAA identifier and the MPX identifier. Appending `:<Partition>` works in the same way as described previously. This identifier is generally used for operations with utilities such as `vmkfstools`.

  To find out the VML ID, run the following command:

  vmkfstools -q <vm-disk>.vmdk

- `vmhba<Adapter>:C<Channel>:T<Target>:L<LUN>`: This identifier is used exclusively to identify a path to LUN. This identifier is not used as frequently as the preceding ones, as this is a runtime naming convention and may be different from hosts to hosts.

- `<UUID>`: `<UUID>` is a unique number assigned to a VMFS volume upon the creation of the volume. It may be included in syntax, where you need to specify the full path of specific files on a datastore.

The preceding portion was taken from VMware KB Article 1014953. For further reference, it is strongly recommended to visit the website at `http://kb.vmware.com/selfservice/microsites/search.do?language=en_US&cmd=displayKC&externalId=1014953` or search by the KB Article number.

For more explanation, please visit the documentation from VMware at `https://pubs.vmware.com/vsphere-60/index.jsp#com.vmware.vsphere.storage.doc/GUID-A36810F4-00EC-4EA8-A242-2A0DBBF56731.html`.

Configuring Fibre Channel storage

To add **Fibre Channel (FC)** storage, we first get a list of LUNs added to the host. To get a list, we can use the `Get-ScsiLun` cmdlet. The format is as follows:

```
PS C:\> Get-ScsiLun -VmHost Esxi1.lab.com | Select CanonicalName
CanonicalName
-------------
naa.60060e801660c500000160c500000107
naa.60060e801660c500000160c500000108
naa.60060e801660c500000160c500000109
```

Once we get a list of the attached LUNs and identify the particular LUN that we want to add to the host, we create a new datastore using the `New-Datastore` cmdlet:

```
PS C:\> New-Datastore -Name SAN-1 -VMHost Esxi1.lab.com -Path naa.60060e8
01660c500000160c500000109 -Vmfs
```

This will create a new VMFS datastore with the name `SAN-1`. If we rescan all the HBAs, then it will be visible to other hosts as well.

Configuring iSCSI storage

In this section, we will configure iSCSI storage for the ESXi server. There can be primarily two types of iSCSI adapters:

- **Software iSCSI adapter**: A software iSCSI adapter is a VMware code built into the VMkernel. It allows the host to connect to the iSCSI storage device through standard network adapters. The software iSCSI adapter handles iSCSI processing while communicating with the network adapter. With the software iSCSI adapter, we don't need any specialized hardware adapter.

- **Hardware iSCSI adapter**: A hardware iSCSI adapter is a third-party adapter that offloads iSCSI and network processing from the host. Hardware iSCSI adapters are divided into different categories:

  - **Dependent hardware iSCSI adapter**: This type of adapter can be a card that presents a standard network adapter and iSCSI offload functionality for the same port. The iSCSI offload functionality depends on the host's network configuration to obtain the IP, MAC, and other parameters used for iSCSI sessions.

  - **Independent hardware iSCSI adapter**: This is a card that either presents only iSCSI offload functionality, or iSCSI offload functionality and standard NIC functionality. The iSCSI offload functionality has independent configuration management that assigns the IP, MAC, and other parameters used for the iSCSI sessions.

For this example, we will discuss configuring software iSCSI adapters. Configuring software iSCSI adapters and dependent hardware iSCSI adapter are quite similar; the only difference is that for the software iSCSI adapter we need to install the adapter in the first place. Let's first check whether a software iSCSI adapter is installed in the ESXi server or not. To find out whether a software iSCSI adapter is already installed or not, we can use the Get-VMHostStorage cmdlet:

```
Get-VMHostStorage -VMHost <Hostname>
```

The result of the preceding command is shown in the following screenshot:

```
PS C:\> Get-VMHostStorage -VMHost ESXi1.lab.com

SoftwareIScsiEnabled
--------------------
False
```

As you can see from the preceding example, a software iSCSI is not enabled in the server. Let's enable the software iSCSI in the server. To enable the software iSCSI adapter, we will take help of the Set-VMHostStorage cmdlet:

```
Set-VMHostStorage -SoftwareIScsiEnabled $True
```

The result of the preceding command is shown in the following screenshot:

```
PS C:\> Get-VMHostStorage -VMHost ESXi1.lab.com | Set-VMHostStorage -SoftwareIScsiEnabled $True

SoftwareIScsiEnabled
--------------------
True
```

Now, the software iSCSI adapter is enabled in the server. We can get the details of the adapter by using the `Get-VMHostHba` cmdlet in conjunction with the `-Type` parameter:

```
PS C:\> Get-VMHostHba -VMHost ESXi1.lab.com -Type IScsi
```

The result of the preceding command is shown in the following screenshot:

```
PS C:\> Get-VMHostHba -VMHost ESXi1.lab.com -Type IScsi

Device     Type      Model                    Status
------     ----      -----                    ------
vmhba33    IScsi     iSCSI Software Adapter    online
```

Next, let's check whether any iSCSI target is already configured in the server. As you can see in the following screenshot, no iSCSI target is configured in the server:

```
PS C:\> Get-IScsiHbaTarget -IScsiHba vmhba33 -Type Send

PS C:\>
```

Now, we will add a target in the server by using the `New-IScsiHbaTarget` cmdlet:

```
PS C:\> New-IScsiHbaTarget -IScsiHba vmhba33 -Address freenas.lab.com
WARNING: Parameter 'IScsiHba' is obsolete. This parameter no longer accepts multiple values.
WARNING: Parameter 'Address' is obsolete. This parameter no longer accepts multiple values.

Address             Port  Type
-------             ----  ----
freenas.lab.com     3260  Send
freenas.lab.com     3260  Send
freenas.lab.com     3260  Send
```

Note the warning in the preceding output. It is a warning saying that the parameters `IScsiHba` and `Address` are obsolete and these parameters no longer accept multiple values. These warnings are very helpful to remind us that we should avoid using these parameters. If you want to suppress them, you can do that using the following cmdlet:

```
PS C:\> Set-PowerCLIConfiguration -DisplayDeprecationWarnings $false -
Scope User
```

We again checked to see whether the target was properly added or not:

```
PS C:\> Get-IScsiHbaTarget -IScsiHba vmhba33 -Type Send

Address          Port  Type
-------          ----  ----
freenas.lab.com  3260  Send
freenas.lab.com  3260  Send
freenas.lab.com  3260  Send
```

Next, let's rescan all HBA adapters so that the changes will take effect. We will rescan using the `RescanAllHba` parameter along with the `Get-VMHostStorage` cmdlet:

```
PS C:\> Get-VMHost | Get-VMHostStorage -RescanAllHba

SoftwareIScsiEnabled
--------------------
True
True
True
```

Now all the paths and devices will be visible. So let's go ahead and add the datastores. Before we do that, let's check the available devices so that we can add that device as a datastore. To get a list of available devices, we will use the `Get-ScsiLun` cmdlet:

```
PS C:\> Get-ScsiLun -VmHost ESXi1.lab.com | Select CanonicalName

CanonicalName
-------------
mpx.vmhba1:C0:T2:L0
t10.FreeBSD_iSCSI_Disk_____000c2905f550000_____
mpx.vmhba1:C0:T1:L0
t10.FreeBSD_iSCSI_Disk_____000c2905f550001_____
mpx.vmhba1:C0:T0:L0
mpx.vmhba32:C0:T0:L0
t10.FreeBSD_iSCSI_Disk_____000c2905f550002_____
t10.FreeBSD_iSCSI_Disk_____000c2905f550003_____
t10.FreeBSD_iSCSI_Disk_____000c2905f550004_____
t10.FreeBSD_iSCSI_Disk_____000c2905f550005_____
```

As you can see from the preceding example, there are six iSCSI devices available in the system. We will add the first device as a datastore. Before we do that, let's check the currently available datastores in the host:

```
PS C:\> Get-VMHost -Name ESXi1.lab.com | Get-Datastore

Name                                    FreeSpaceGB        CapacityGB
----                                    -----------        ----------
datastore1                                   11.628            12.500
NFS-Datastore1                               17.595            17.595
```

Now, let's add the datastore using the New-Datastore cmdlet. Though an example is provided here, I strongly recommend that you visit the documentation reference of this cmdlet. This is a pretty important cmdlet and you should be familiar with its parameters. You can check the details from https://www.vmware.com/support/developer/PowerCLI/PowerCLI60R1/html/New-Datastore.html.

We will first select the path using the following cmdlet:

```
PS C:\> $path = Get-ScsiLun -VmHost ESXi1.lab.com | Select `
CanonicalName | Where { $_.CanonicalName.Contains('FreeBSD')}
```

The output of the variable $path is as follows:

```
PS C:\> $path

CanonicalName
-------------
t10.FreeBSD_iSCSI_Disk_____000c2905f550000_____
t10.FreeBSD_iSCSI_Disk_____000c2905f550001_____
t10.FreeBSD_iSCSI_Disk_____000c2905f550002_____
t10.FreeBSD_iSCSI_Disk_____000c2905f550003_____
t10.FreeBSD_iSCSI_Disk_____000c2905f550004_____
t10.FreeBSD_iSCSI_Disk_____000c2905f550005_____
```

Next we will create the datastore using the New-Datastore cmdlet:

```
PS C:\> New-Datastore -VMHost ESXi1.lab.com -Name iSCSI-1 -Path `
$path[0].CanonicalName -Vmfs
```

The result of the preceding command is shown in the following screenshot:

```
PS C:\> New-Datastore -VMHost ESXi1.lab.com -Name iSCSI-1 -Path $path[0].CanonicalName -Vmfs
WARNING: Parameter 'VMHost' is obsolete. This parameter no longer accepts multiple values.

Name                            FreeSpaceGB      CapacityGB
----                            -----------      ----------
iSCSI-1                              48.801          49.750
```

Since the datastore is added now, let's check the available datastores in the host:

```
PS C:\> Get-VMHost -Name ESXi1.lab.com | Get-Datastore

Name                            FreeSpaceGB      CapacityGB
----                            -----------      ----------
datastore1                           11.628          12.500
iSCSI-1                              48.799          49.750
NFS-Datastore1                       17.595          17.595
```

From the preceding example, we can see that the datastore has been added. In the following screenshot from the Web client, we can see that the datastore has been added:

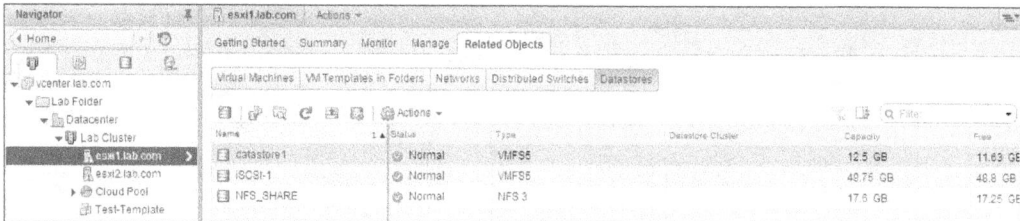

For further configurations, we can use other commands related to the preceding commands. For example, to remove a datastore, use the `Remove-Datastore` cmdlet.

Configuring NFS storage

We can add NFS storage by again using the `New-Datastore` cmdlet. Now, we will use the parameter `-Nfs`:

```
PS C:\> Get-VMHost | New-Datastore -Nfs -Name NFS_SHARE -Path /mnt/NFS_SHARE -NfsHost freenas.lab.com
WARNING: Parameter 'VMHost' is obsolete. This parameter no longer accepts multiple values.

Name                            FreeSpaceGB      CapacityGB
----                            -----------      ----------
NFS_SHARE                            17.595          17.595
```

We can see that the NFS share has been added successfully to all the ESXi hosts. To check this, we can see the listing of the available datastores in the following screenshot:

```
PS C:\> Get-VMHost | Get-Datastore

Name                          FreeSpaceGB        CapacityGB
----                          -----------        ----------
datastore1                         11.628            12.500
iSCSI-1                            48.798            49.750
NFS_SHARE                         17.595            17.595
datastore1 (3)                    11.628            12.500
datastore1 (2)                    11.628            12.500
```

Configuring virtual SAN

In order to configure virtual SAN, certain prerequisites need to be met. For example, we need a SSD in the server and a VMkernel portgroup needs to be configured, which will require a VSAN network. Let's first check the portgroups available in the server:

```
PS C:\> Get-VirtualPortGroup -VMHost ESXi1.lab.com -VirtualSwitch vSwitch0 -Standard

Name                   Key                             VLanId PortBinding NumPorts
----                   ---                             ------ ----------- --------
TestPortGroup          key-vim.host.PortGroup-Test... 0
VM Network             key-vim.host.PortGroup-VM N... 0
vMotion                key-vim.host.PortGroup-vMotion 0
Management Network     key-vim.host.PortGroup-Mana... 0
```

Then, check whether VSAN traffic is enabled in any of the portgroups. We will do this using the Get-VMHostNetworkAdapter cmdlet. Note the Where {...} check; here, I am checking each object for the existence of VsanTraffic:

```
PS C:\> Get-VMHostNetworkAdapter -VMHost ESXi1.lab.com -VMKernel | Where
{$_.VsanTrafficEnabled -eq $true}
```

The result of the preceding command is shown in the following screenshot:

```
PS C:\> Get-VMHostNetworkAdapter -VMHost ESXi1.lab.com -VMKernel | Where { $_.VsanTrafficEnabled -eq $true }
PS C:\>
```

As you can see from the preceding example, VSAN traffic is not enabled in any of the existing portgroups. So, we will first create a portgroup VSAN in the distributed switch. Remember you need to import the VMware.VimAutomation.Vds module first, as we are going to work with a distributed switch:

```
PS C:\> New-VDPortgroup -VDSwitch 'Cloud dvSwitch' -Name VSAN


Name                           NumPorts PortBinding

----                           -------- -----------

VSAN                           128      Static
```

Next, we will add the VMkernel adapters from the host and enable VSAN traffic in it. To do so, we will run the following command:

```
PS C:\>New-VMHostNetworkAdapter -VMHost ESXi1.lab.com –PortGroup ` VSAN
-VirtualSwitch 'Cloud dvSwitch' -IP 192.168.1.100 `
 –SubnetMask 255.255.255.0 -VsanTrafficEnabled $true
```

The result of the preceding command is shown in the following screenshot:

```
PS C:\> New-VMHostNetworkAdapter  VMHost esxi1.lab.com  PortGroup VSAN  VirtualSwitch vSwitch0  IP 192.168.168.100  SubnetMask 255.255.255.0  VsanTrafficEnabled $true

Name      Mac                 DhcpEnabled IP            SubnetMask     DeviceName
----      ---                 ----------- --            ----------     ----------
vmk2      00:50:56:64:20:39 False         192.168.168.100 255.255.255.0      vmk2


PS C:\> New-VMHostNetworkAdapter  VMHost esxi2.lab.com  PortGroup VSAN  VirtualSwitch vSwitch0  IP 192.168.168.101  SubnetMask 255.255.255.0  VsanTrafficEnabled $true

Name      Mac                 DhcpEnabled IP            SubnetMask     DeviceName
----      ---                 ----------- --            ----------     ----------
vmk2      00:50:56:69:d2:33 False         192.168.168.101 255.255.255.0      vmk2


PS C:\> New-VMHostNetworkAdapter –VMHost esxi3.lab.com  PortGroup VSAN  VirtualSwitch vSwitch0  IP 192.168.168.102  SubnetMask 255.255.255.0  VsanTrafficEnabled $true

Name      Mac                 DhcpEnabled IP            SubnetMask     DeviceName
----      ---                 ----------- --            ----------     ----------
vmk2      00:50:56:6b:13:f7 False         192.168.168.102 255.255.255.0      vmk2
```

Now let's check the VSAN traffic status again:

```
PS C:\> Get-VMHostNetworkAdapter –VMHost ESXi1.lab.com –VMKernel | Where { $_.VsanTrafficEnabled -eq $true }

Name      Mac                 DhcpEnabled IP            SubnetMask     DeviceName
----      ---                 ----------- --            ----------     ----------
vmk2      00:50:56:6d:0f:8c False         192.168.168.100 255.255.255.0      vmk2
```

As you can see from the preceding example, a vmkernel portgroup named VSAN has been created with VSAN traffic enabled in it. Next, we will go ahead and enable the VSAN cluster. First, let's check the available clusters in the environment:

```
PS C:\> Get-Cluster

Name            HAEnabled HAFailover DrsEnabled DrsAutomationLevel
                          Level
----            --------- ---------- ---------- ------------------
Lab Cluster     False     1          False      FullyAutomated
```

As you can see from the preceding example, there is only one cluster named `Lab Cluster` available in the environment. So, let's check whether the VSAN cluster is enabled in it or not. We can do so by using the `VsanEnabled` property in the `Get-Cluster` cmdlet:

```
PS C:\> (Get-Cluster -Name "Lab Cluster").VsanEnabled
False
```

As you can see from the preceding example, VSAN is not enabled in the cluster. Next, we enable VSAN in the cluster along with other options and again check the status:

```
PS C:\> Get-Cluster -Name "Lab Cluster" | Set-Cluster -VsanEnabled:$true -VsanDiskClaimMode Automatic -Confirm:$false

Name                HAEnabled  HAFailover  DrsEnabled  DrsAutomationLevel
                               Level
----                ---------  ----------  ----------  ------------------
Lab Cluster         False      1           False       FullyAutomated


PS C:\> (Get-Cluster -Name "Lab Cluster").VsanEnabled
True
```

Since VSAN is enabled on the cluster, we can check the diskgroups or disks that are part of VSAN. We can use the following cmdlets to monitor those parameters:

- `Get-VsanDisk`
- `Get-VsanDiskGroup`
- `New-VsanDisk`
- `New-VsanDiskGroup`
- `Remove-VsanDisk`
- `Remove-VsanDiskGroup`

In the following screenshot, we can see the different aspects:

```
PS C:\> Get-VsanDisk | Sort IsSsd

CanonicalName          DevicePath                                  IsSsd
-------------          ----------                                  -----
mpx.vmhba1:C0:T2:L0    /vmfs/devices/disks/mpx.vmhba1:C0:T2:L0     False
mpx.vmhba1:C0:T2:L0    /vmfs/devices/disks/mpx.vmhba1:C0:T2:L0     False
mpx.vmhba1:C0:T2:L0    /vmfs/devices/disks/mpx.vmhba1:C0:T2:L0     False
mpx.vmhba1:C0:T1:L0    /vmfs/devices/disks/mpx.vmhba1:C0:T1:L0     True
mpx.vmhba1:C0:T1:L0    /vmfs/devices/disks/mpx.vmhba1:C0:T1:L0     True
mpx.vmhba1:C0:T1:L0    /vmfs/devices/disks/mpx.vmhba1:C0:T1:L0     True


PS C:\> Get-VsanDiskGroup

Name                                             VMHost
----                                             ------
Disk group (0000000000766d686261313a313a30)      esxi1.lab.com
Disk group (0000000000766d686261313a313a30)      esxi2.lab.com
Disk group (0000000000766d686261313a313a30)      esxi3.lab.com
```

Using datastore clusters

Since we have configured the different types of datastores, let's configure the datastore cluster. We can use following cmdlets to manage different aspects of a datastore cluster:

- `Get-DatastoreCluster`
- `New-DatastoreCluster`
- `Remove-DatastoreCluster`
- `Set-DatastoreCluster`

Let's start by checking whether we already have a datastore cluster configured or not:

```
PS C:\> Get-DatastoreCluster
PS C:\>
```

We can see that there is no `DatastoreCluster` configured in the environment. So let's first create `DatastoreCluster`. As you can see in the following screenshot, we have created a datastore cluster named `iSCSI-Cluster` in `Datacenter`:

```
PS C:\> New-DatastoreCluster -Name 'iSCSI-Cluster' -Location 'Datacenter'

Name            CapacityGB      FreeSpaceGB     SdrsAutomationLevel
----            ----------      -----------     -------------------
iSCSI-Cluster   0.000           0.000           Disabled
```

We can again check whether a datastore is present in the environment or not. As you can see in the following screenshot, a `DatastoreCluster` has been created:

```
PS C:\> Get-DatastoreCluster

Name              CapacityGB       FreeSpaceGB      SdrsAutomationLevel
----              ----------       -----------      -------------------
iSCSI-Cluster     0.000            0.000            Disabled
```

But as you can see from the preceding example, no datastore has been added to the cluster and the storage DRS automation level has not been set. So let's check how we can set those parameters. First, let's add datastores in the existing cluster:

```
PS C:\> Get-Datastore "iSCSI-1", "iSCSI-2", "iSCSI-3" | Move-Datastore -Destination "iSCSI-Cluster"

Name            FreeSpaceGB     CapacityGB
----            -----------     ----------
iSCSI-1             48.798          49.750
iSCSI-2             48.798          49.750
iSCSI-3             48.798          49.750
```

Since we added datastores, let's check them:

```
PS C:\> Get-DatastoreCluster -Name "iSCSI-Cluster"

Name                    CapacityGB      FreeSpaceGB     SdrsAutomationLevel
----                    ----------      -----------     -------------------
iSCSI-Cluster           149.250         146.394         Disabled
```

As you can see from the preceding screenshot, datastores have been added but the SDRS automation level is still not set. To set the automation level, we can take help of the `Set-DatastoreCluster` cmdlet:

```
PS C:\> Set-DatastoreCluster -DatastoreCluster "iSCSi-Cluster" -SdrsAutomationLevel FullyAutomated

Name                    CapacityGB      FreeSpaceGB     SdrsAutomationLevel
----                    ----------      -----------     -------------------
iSCSI-Cluster           149.250         146.394         FullyAutomated
```

It can be seen from the preceding example that `SdrsAutomationLevel` has been set to `FullyAutomated`. Next, we will further check three different parameters that we can set for a datastore cluster: `IOLoadBalanceEnabled`, `IOLatencyThresholdMillisecond`, and `SpaceUtilizationThresholdPercent`. The tasks of these parameters are explained in the following list:

- `IOLoadBalanceEnabled`: By setting this parameter, we can define whether IO will be load-balanced between datastores or not

- `IOLatencyThresholdMillisecond`: This parameter will define what the triggering latency in IO is in milliseconds

- `SpaceUtilizationThresholdPercent`: This parameter defines the triggering percent for datastore space utilization

```
PS C:\> Get-DatastoreCluster -Name iSCSI-Cluster | Select-Object * | Format-List

Name                             : iSCSI-Cluster
SpaceUtilizationThresholdPercent : 80
IOLatencyThresholdMillisecond    : 15
IOLoadBalanceEnabled             : True
SdrsAutomationLevel              : Manual
ExtensionData                    : VMware.Vim.StoragePod
CapacityGB                       : 149.25
FreeSpaceGB                      : 146.3935546875
Id                               : StoragePod-group-p952
Uid                              : /VIServer=lab\vcadmin@vcenter.lab.com:443/DatastoreCluster=StoragePod-group-p952/
Client                           : VMware.VimAutomation.ViCore.Impl.V1.VimClient
```

First, we need to set these parameters. We will use the `Set-DatastoreCluster` cmdlet to set these parameters:

```
PS C:\> Set-DatastoreCluster -DatastoreCluster "iSCSI-Cluster" -IOLoadBalanceEnabled $True

Name                  CapacityGB        FreeSpaceGB       SdrsAutomationLevel
----                  ----------        -----------       -------------------
iSCSI-Cluster         149.250           146.394           FullyAutomated


PS C:\> Set-DatastoreCluster -DatastoreCluster "iSCSI-Cluster" -IOLatencyThresholdMillisecond 10

Name                  CapacityGB        FreeSpaceGB       SdrsAutomationLevel
----                  ----------        -----------       -------------------
iSCSI-Cluster         149.250           146.394           FullyAutomated


PS C:\> Set-DatastoreCluster -DatastoreCluster "iSCSI-Cluster" -SpaceUtilizationThresholdPercent 70

Name                  CapacityGB        FreeSpaceGB       SdrsAutomationLevel
----                  ----------        -----------       -------------------
iSCSI-Cluster         149.250           146.394           FullyAutomated
```

Now, let's check whether those parameters have really been changed or not. Here, we are checking individual parameters one at a time:

```
PS C:\> (Get-DatastoreCluster -Name "iSCSI-Cluster").IOLoadBalanceEnabled
True
PS C:\> (Get-DatastoreCluster -Name "iSCSI-Cluster").IOLatencyThresholdMillisecond
10
PS C:\> (Get-DatastoreCluster -Name "iSCSI-Cluster").SpaceUtilizationThresholdPercent
70
```

As you can see from the preceding screenshot, those parameters have been set according to the values set by us.

Using Raw Device Mapping

Though **Raw Device Mapping** (**RDM**) disks are added to a VM, we will cover this topic here as we are discussing storage-related topics here. A RDM is a pointer mapping file, which is kept in a VMFS datastore that acts as a proxy for a raw physical storage device. By using RDM, a virtual machine can directly access the raw physical device. Typically, we use RDM disks when we need to access raw disks—for example, configuring an OS cluster inside a guest OS, configuring database clusters, and so on. To add a device as a RDM disk to a VM, let's first get a list of devices available to a host. We do this using a list of SCSI devices available per host using the `Get-SCSILun` cmdlet:

```
PS C:\> Get-ScsiLun -VmHost ESXi1.lab.com | Select ConsoleDeviceName |
Sort ConsoleDeviceName
```

The result of the preceding command is shown in the following screenshot:

```
PS C:\> Get-ScsiLun –VMHost ESXi1.lab.com | Select ConsoleDeviceName | Sort ConsoleDeviceName

ConsoleDeviceName
-----------------
/vmfs/devices/cdrom/mpx.vmhba32:C0:T0:L0
/vmfs/devices/disks/mpx.vmhba1:C0:T0:L0
/vmfs/devices/disks/mpx.vmhba1:C0:T1:L0
/vmfs/devices/disks/mpx.vmhba1:C0:T2:L0
/vmfs/devices/disks/t10.FreeBSD_iSCSI_Disk_____000c2905f550000
/vmfs/devices/disks/t10.FreeBSD_iSCSI_Disk_____000c2905f550001
/vmfs/devices/disks/t10.FreeBSD_iSCSI_Disk_____000c2905f550002
/vmfs/devices/disks/t10.FreeBSD_iSCSI_Disk_____000c2905f550003
/vmfs/devices/disks/t10.FreeBSD_iSCSI_Disk_____000c2905f550004
/vmfs/devices/disks/t10.FreeBSD_iSCSI_Disk_____000c2905f550005
```

From the device list shown in the preceding screenshot, we will take /vmfs/devices/disks/t10.FreeBSD_iSCSI_Disk_____000c290 5f550005_____ as a RDM device. Next let's check the available VMs. We will do that using the Get-VM cmdlet:

```
PS C:\> Get-VM


Name                PowerState Num CPUs MemoryGB
----                ---------- -------- --------
Test-VM2            PoweredOff 1        1.000
Test-VM1            PoweredOff 1        1.000
```

We want to add the disk as a RDM disk to Test-VM1. For this, we will use the New-HardDisk cmdlet. Before we do that, let's check whether there are any existing RDM's in the environment:

```
PS C:\> Get-VM | Get-HardDisk –DiskType 'RawPhysical' | Select Parent,Nam
e,DiskType,ScsiCanonicalName,DeviceName,CapacityGB| Format-List
```

The result of the preceding command is shown in the following screenshot:

```
PS C:\> Get-VM | Get-HardDisk –DiskType "RawPhysical" | Select Parent,Name,DiskType,ScsiCanonicalName,DeviceName,CapacityGB | fl
PS C:\>
```

As you can see from the preceding example, there is no RDM device in the environment. So, we added the device as a RDM disk to VM Test-VM1:

```
PS C:\> Get-VM Test-VM1 | New-HardDisk -DiskType RawPhysical `
 -DeviceName /vmfs/devices/disks/t10.FreeBSD_iSCSI_Disk_____000c290
5f550005_____
```

The result of the preceding command is shown in the following screenshot:

```
PS C:\> Get-VM Test-VM1 | New-HardDisk -DiskType RawPhysical -DeviceName `
 /vmfs/devices/disks/t10.FreeBSD_iSCSI_Disk_____000c2905f550005
WARNING: Parameter 'VM' is obsolete. Passing multiple values to this parameter is obsolete.

CapacityGB      Persistence                                            Filename
----------      -----------                                            --------
50.000          IndependentPersis...                    [iSCSI-1] Test-VM1/Test-VM1_1.vmdk
```

We used the `New-HardDisk` cmdlet with the following options:

```
New-HardDisk -VM "Test-VM1" -DiskType RawPhysical -DeviceName <Device
Name> -Datastore "datastore1"
```

The option `DiskType` lets you choose whether you want the format to be `RawPhysical` or `RawVirtual`. With the option datastore, we can mention which datastore we want to use to store the pointer file. If we do not mention any datastore, then the file is stored with the virtual machine (as I have done in the example).

- In physical mode RDM, minimal SCSI virtualization of the mapped device is done. In this mode, VMKernel passes all SCSI commands except the REPORT LUN command. So this provides better performance but lesser flexibility.

- In Virtual Mode RDM, full virtualization of the mapped device is done. Only the READ and WRITE commands are sent to the mapped device. So, you get more flexibility as it supports more vmfs functions, but it provides less performance.

The differences between these two modes are detailed in the VMware KB Article 2009226. I strongly suggest you to visit the following website and check it:

```
http://kb.vmware.com/selfservice/microsites/search.do?language=en_US&
cmd=displayKC&externalId=2009226
```

If we check the RDM status, we will see the details of the RDM LUN:

```
PS C:\> Get-VM | Get-HardDisk -DiskType "RawPhysical" | Select Parent,Name,DiskType,ScsiCanonicalName,DeviceName,CapacityGB

Parent            : Test-VM1
Name              : Hard disk 2
DiskType          : RawPhysical
ScsiCanonicalName : t10.FreeBSD_iSCSI_Disk_____000c2905f550005
DeviceName        : vml.02000500003000000124e6369695343534920
CapacityGB        : 49.9999990463256835937
```

As you can see from the preceding screenshot, a new RDM LUN has been added to the VM Test-VM1.

Managing storage using storage policy-based management

Storage policy-based management is the foundation for new software-defined storage. In VSAN environment, control is not at the storage end; it is at the VM end. All the policies are applied on a per VM basis and decide different aspects of the storage for the VM.

The cmdlets available under this category can be subdivided into different categories, as discussed in the following sections.

Cmdlets related to policy rules

The cmdlets related to policy rules are used to set the `Rule` or `Ruleset`:

- `New-SpbmRule`
- `New-SpbmRuleSet`

Cmdlets related to storage policy

The cmdlets related to storage policy are used to define different aspects of storage policy:

- `New-SpbmStoragePolicy`
- `Remove-SpbmStoragePolicy`
- `Set-SpbmStoragePolicy`
- `Get-SpbmStoragePolicy`

Cmdlets related to Spbm capabilities and compatible storage

The cmdlets related to `Spbm` capabilities and compatible storage are used to gather information about `Spbm` capabilities and the capabilities of the storage:

- `Get-SpbmCapability`
- `Get-SpbmCompatibleStorage`

Cmdlets related to policy application

Using the cmdlets related to policy application, we can get the information or set the spbm policies to an endpoint:

* `Get-SpbmEntityConfiguration`
* `Set-SpbmEntityConfiguration`

Cmdlets related to policy backup and migration

Using the cmdlets related to policy backup, we can get the information or set the spbm policies to an endpoint:

* `Export-SpbmStoragePolicy`
* `Import-SpbmStoragePolicy`

Storage policies are mainly composed of three main components:

* Storage capabilities provided by storage provider
* Rules [Key Value Pair: Storage Capability + (Value for Quantity or Quality)]
* Rule sets

Here is a screenshot from the Web client:

Let's take a closer look at these three components. First, let's discuss the storage capabilities. While defining storage policies for a VM, there are two types of storage capabilities:

- User-defined metadata tags
- Vendor-specific storage capabilities

Here is a list of capabilities that are available from the VSAN storage provider that can be consumed at the time of policy definition:

Storage capability (key)	Quantity or quality (value)
Number of failures to tolerate	Default value is 1 and maximum value is 3
Number of disk stripes per object	Default value is 1 and maximum value is 12
Object space reservation	Default value is 0 percent and maximum value is 100 percent
Flash read cache reservation	Default value is 0 percent and maximum value is 100 percent
Force provisioning	Default value is No and optional value is Yes

A rule is a combination of storage capability and quantity, which when presented together, forms a rule and is a condition that must be met for compliance.

As the name suggests, a rule set is a *collection of rules* or *set of rules*. The point to remember here is the rules must be from a single storage provider.

Let's test the cmdlets now; we will first check out the storage capabilities that are available:

```
PS C:\> Get-SpbmCapability | Select Name,ValueType,Description | Format-List

Name        : VSAN.cacheReservation
ValueType   : System.Int32
Description : Flash capacity reserved as read cache for the storage object. Specified as a percentage of the logical size of the object.
              To be used only for addressing read performance issues. Reserved flash capacity cannot be used by other objects. Unreserved
              flash is shared fairly among all objects. Default value: 0%, Maximum value: 100%.

Name        : VSAN.forceProvisioning
ValueType   : System.Boolean
Description : If this option is enabled, the object will be provisioned even if the policy specified in the storage policy is not
              satisfiable with the resources currently available in the cluster. Virtual SAN will try to bring the object into compliance
              if and when resources become available. Default Value: Disabled.

Name        : VSAN.hostFailuresToTolerate
ValueType   : System.Int32
Description : Defines the number of host, disk or network failures a storage object can tolerate. For n failures tolerated, "n+1" copies
              of the object are created and "2n+1" hosts contributing storage are required. If fault domains are configured, "2n+1" fault
              domains with hosts contributing storage are required. Note: A host which is not part of a fault domain is counted as its own
              single-host fault domain. Default value: 1, Maximum value: 3.

Name        : VSAN.proportionalCapacity
ValueType   : System.Int32
Description : Percentage of the logical size of the storage object that will be reserved (thick provisioned) upon VM provisioning. The
              rest of the storage object is thin provisioned. Default value: 0%, Maximum value: 100%.

Name        : VSAN.stripeWidth
ValueType   : System.Int32
Description : The number of HDDs across which each replica of a storage object is striped. A value higher than 1 may result in better
              performance (for e.g. when flash read cache misses need to get serviced from HDD), but also results in higher use of system
              resources. Default value: 1, Maximum value: 12.
```

Next, we will create a rule. We can create a rule with the `New-SpbmRule` cmdlet. With the rule, we need to mention the `capability` for that rule. Let's create a rule that will set the *number of host failures to tolerate* to 2. First, we have created a rule named `FirstRule` and then created `RuleSet` named `Set_Of_Rules`. At the end, we created a new `SpbmStoragePolicy` named `TestPolicy` using these values.

```
PS C:\> $Storage_Policy = "TestPolicy"
PS C:\> $Rule_Set = "TestRuleSet"
PS C:\> $FirstRule = New-SpbmRule -Capability VSAN.hostFailuresToTolerate 2
PS C:\> $Set_Of_Rules = New-SpbmRuleSet -Name $RuleSet -AllOfRules @(($FirstRule))
PS C:\> New-SpbmStoragePolicy -Name $Storage_Policy -RuleSet $Set_Of_Rules

Name            Description            Rule Set                      CommonRule
----            -----------            --------                      ----------
TestPolicy                             {(VSAN.hostFailuresToTolera... {}
```

As you can see from the preceding screenshot, we have created a new policy. Let's check the new policy:

```
PS C:\> Get-SpbmStoragePolicy -Name "TestPolicy"

Name            Description            Rule Set                      CommonRule
----            -----------            --------                      ----------
TestPolicy                             {(VSAN.hostFailuresToTolera... {}
```

We can make changes to the preceding policy using the `Set-SpbmStoragePolicy` cmdlet. In the preceding example, we did not set any description. So we will set the description using this cmdlet:

```
PS C:\> Set-SpbmStoragePolicy -StoragePolicy "TestPolicy" -Description "This is a Test Rule"

Name            Description            Rule Set                      CommonRule
----            -----------            --------                      ----------
TestPolicy      This is a Test Rule    {(VSAN.hostFailuresToTolera... {}


PS C:\> Get-SpbmStoragePolicy -Name "TestPolicy"

Name            Description            Rule Set                      CommonRule
----            -----------            --------                      ----------
TestPolicy      This is a Test Rule    {(VSAN.hostFailuresToTolera... {}
```

Since the policy is set, now we can assign the policy to a VM. For this, we will first create a VM:

```
PS C:\> New-VM -Name Test-VM -Datastore "vsanDatastore" -VMHost esxi2.
lab.com
```

Name	PowerState Num CPUs MemoryGB
----	---------- -------- --------
Test-VM	PoweredOff 1 0.250

Now, let's apply the new policy to the VM that we created:

```
PS C:\> Get-VM -Name Test-VM | Set-SpbmEntityConfiguration -StoragePolicy TestPolicy

Entity                     Storage Policy              Status          Time Of Check
------                     --------------              ------          -------------
Test-VM                    TestPolicy                  compliant       23-05-2015 18:05:36
```

We can always check for compliant storage for a particular storage policy using the `Get-SpbmCompatibleStorage` cmdlet:

```
PS C:\> Get-SpbmCompatibleStorage -StoragePolicy TestPolicy

Name                            FreeSpaceGB            CapacityGB
----                            -----------            ----------
vsanDatastore                       585.258               593.977
```

We can also check configuration data related to `spbm` for a VM, hard disk, or cluster. We can get this information using the `Get-SpbmEntityConfiguration` cmdlet:

```
PS C:\> $VM = Get-VM -Name Test-VM

PS C:\> Get-SpbmEntityConfiguration -VM $VM -CheckComplianceNow

Entity                     Storage Policy              Status          Time Of Check
------                     --------------              ------          -------------
Test-VM                    TestPolicy                  notApplicable   15-06-2015 22:23:03
```

We can remove a storage policy using the `Remove-SpbmStoragePolicy` cmdlet.

Finally, let's check the export and import options for the Spbm storage policy. We can export the configuration of an existing storage policy using Export-SpbmStoragePolicy cmdlet:

```
PS C:\> Export-SpbmStoragePolicy -StoragePolicy TestPolicy -FilePath C:\Users\chandragupta\Desktop\

Mode                LastWriteTime        Length Name
----                -------------        ------ ----
-a----      15-06-2015   11:12 PM          1399 TestPolicy.xml
```

We can import an existing configuration using the Import-SpbmStoragePolicy cmdlet. An example is provided in the following screenshot:

```
PS C:\> Import-SpbmStoragePolicy -FilePath C:\Users\chandragupta\Desktop\TestPolicy.xml -Name Test2

Name                Description                      Rule Set                        CommonRule
----                -----------                      --------                        ----------
Test2                                                {(VSAN.hostFailuresToTolera...  {}
```

Applying VMFS resignaturing

Since we are talking about managing storage in vSphere environments in this chapter, I felt we should cover one extra topic here. One of the common tasks in vSphere is VMFS resignature. First, let's try to find out what a VMFS resignaturing task is.

By default, ESXi mounts all the datastores that are visible to the host. Each datastore has a unique UUID that is stored in the datastore superblock. Also, the unique LUN ID is store in the VMFS metadata. When a LUN is replicated, all the information is copied block by block and we get an identical LUN. If the original datastore had an UUID as X, the copied LUN also has an UUID as X.

Consider the case when you want to mount the replicated LUN; ESXi will see a duplicate LUN and will not mount the LUN automatically.

To mount the replicated LUN, we can either force-mount the copy in case we are sure the original is not in use, or we can resignature the copy so that it will have another UUID.

Though there are other ways of resignaturing a snapshot LUN, we will cover a more direct and easy way here. We will cover the advanced way of doing it in a later chapter, where we will discuss how we can use vSphere APIs to get the same result. Here, we will use Esxcli commands through PowerCLI and do it in a more direct way.

To use the Esxcli commands in PowerCLI, we will use the `Get-EsxCli` cmdlet. First, we will establish a connection to an Esxi host:

```
PS C:\> $esxcli = Get-EsxCli -VMHost esxi1.lab.com
```

Now, the variable `$esxcli` has the required information and we can simply use it as the Esxcli command. For example, if you want to see the available options, we can simply type `$esxcli` and get the output:

```
PS C:\> $esxcli = Get-EsxCli -VMHost esxi1.lab.com

PS C:\> $esxcli

===================
EsxCli: esxi1.lab.com

    Elements:
    ---------
    device
    elxnet
    esxcli
    fcoe
    graphics
    hardware
    iscsi
    network
    rdma
    sched
    software
    storage
    system
    vm
    vsan
```

We want to see a list of filesystems available in the ESXi host, but we want to do that using the Esxcli commands. We can do so by running the following command:

```
PS C:\> $esxcli.storage.filesystem.list() | Format-Table
```

The result of the preceding cmdlet is shown in the following screenshot:

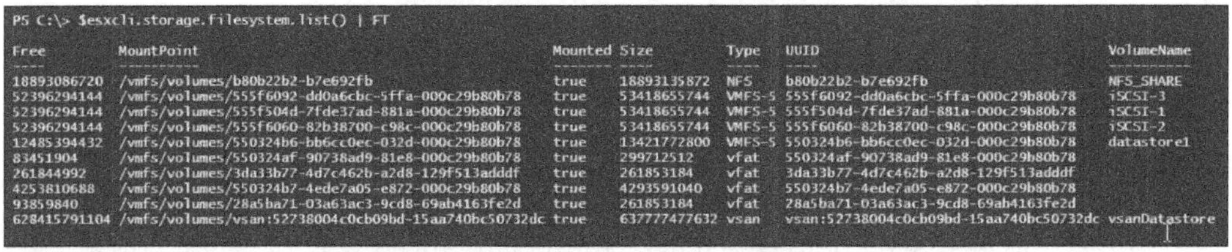

```
PS C:\> $esxcli.storage.filesystem.list() | FT

Free          MountPoint                                             Mounted Size          Type   UUID                                       VolumeName
----          ----------                                             ------- ----          ----   ----                                       ----------
18893086720   /vmfs/volumes/b80b22b2-b7e692fb                        true    18893135872   NFS    b80b22b2-b7e692fb                          NFS_SHARE
52396294144   /vmfs/volumes/555f6092-dd0a6cbc-5ffa-000c29b80b78      true    53418655744   VMFS-5 555f6092-dd0a6cbc-5ffa-000c29b80b78        iSCSI-3
52396294144   /vmfs/volumes/555f504d-7fde37ad-881a-000c29b80b78      true    53418655744   VMFS-5 555f504d-7fde37ad-881a-000c29b80b78        iSCSI-1
52396294144   /vmfs/volumes/555f6060-82b38700-c98c-000c29b80b78      true    53418655744   VMFS-5 555f6060-82b38700-c98c-000c29b80b78        iSCSI-2
12485394432   /vmfs/volumes/550324b6-bb6cc0ec-032d-000c29b80b78      true    134217772800  VMFS-5 550324b6-bb6cc0ec-032d-000c29b80b78        datastore1
83451904      /vmfs/volumes/550324af-90738ad9-81e8-000c29b80b78      true    299712512     vfat   550324af-90738ad9-81e8-000c29b80b78
261844992     /vmfs/volumes/3da13b77-4d7c462b-a2d8-129f513adddf      true    261853184     vfat   3da13b77-4d7c462b-a2d8-129f513adddf
4253810688    /vmfs/volumes/550324b7-4ede7a05-e872-000c29b80b78      true    4293591040    vfat   550324b7-4ede7a05-e872-000c29b80b78
93859840      /vmfs/volumes/28a5ba71-03a63ac3-9cd8-69ab4163fe2d      true    261853184     vfat   28a5ba71-03a63ac3-9cd8-69ab4163fe2d
628415791104  /vmfs/volumes/vsan:52738004c0cb09bd-15aa740bc50732dc   true    637777477632  vsan   vsan:52738004c0cb09bd-15aa740bc50732dc     vsanDatastore
```

Now, we can fully utilize all the options available with the Esxcli commands. To get a list of snapshot LUNs, we can use the following command:

```
PS C:\> $esxcli.storage.vmfs.snapshot.list()
```

Once we get a list of snapshot LUNs, we can apply resignaturing on them using the following command:

```
PS C:\> $esxcli.storage.vmfs.snapshot.resignature(<volume label>|<volume uuid>)
```

The preceding command will resignature the LUN and then you should be able to mount it accordingly.

Configuring vFLASH using PowerCLI Extensions

PowerCLI Extensions is a VMware fling that provides extra cmdlets to manage the Virtual Flash in an ESXi host. To get the fling and install it, follow the procedure mentioned in this link: `https://labs.vmware.com/flings/powercli-extensions`. The cmdlets provided in this module are as follows:

We can configure virtual flash in an ESXi hosts using the following cmdlets:

- `Get-VMHostVFlashConfiguration`
- `Set-VMHostVFlashConfiguration`

The following cmdlets can be used to configure vFlash Cache for a particular hard disk:

- `Get-HardDiskVFlashConfiguration`
- `Set-HardDiskVFlashConfiguration`

The last three cmdlets are the ones related to instant cloning of the VMs:

- `Enable-InstantCloneVM`
- `Get-InstantCloneVM`
- `New-InstantCloneVM`

A very detailed and interesting blog regarding instant cloning was written by Brian Graf, and you can find it at `https://blogs.vmware.com/PowerCLI/2015/08/using-vmware-instant-clone-via-powercli-extensions-fling.html`.

As mentioned previously, to check the vFlash Configuration for a host, we can use the Get-VMHostVFlashConfiguration cmdlet. As you can see from the following screenshot, vFlash is already configured for ESXi hosts esxi1 and esxi2, but not for esxi3:

```
PS C:\> Get-VMHostVFlashConfiguration

Name                    CapacityGB SwapCacheReservationGB Extents
----                    ---------- ---------------------- -------
esxi2.lab.com           19.75      0                      {mpx.vmhba1:C0:T3:L0:P1}
esxi3.lab.com           0          0                      {}
esxi1.lab.com           19.75      0                      {mpx.vmhba1:C0:T3:L0:P1}
```

To configure vFlash for esxi3, we need to use the Set-VMHostVFlashConfiguration cmdlet. To use it, we will gather information in two variables and use it later:

PS C:\> $vFlashConfig = Get-VMHostVFlashConfiguration -VMHost ` esxi3. lab.com

The result of the preceding cmdlet is shown in the following screenshot:

```
PS C:\> $vFlashConfig = Get-VMHostVFlashConfiguration -VMHost esxi3.lab.com

PS C:\> $vFlashConfig

Name                    CapacityGB SwapCacheReservationGB Extents
----                    ---------- ---------------------- -------
esxi3.lab.com           0          0                      {}
```

The other variable is the disk which we will use:

PS C:\> $vFlashDisk = Get-VMHostDisk -VMHost esxi3.lab.com | `

Where { $_.DeviceName.Contains('mpx') }

Note the Where{} clause. I know in my environment that the SSD disks are marked with the mpx naming convention, so I listed only those disks:

```
PS C:\> $vFlashDisk = Get-VMHostDisk -VMHost esxi3.lab.com | where { $_.DeviceName.Contains('mpx')}

PS C:\> $vFlashDisk

DeviceName                                        TotalSectors
----------                                        ------------
/vmfs/devices/disks/mpx.vmhba1:C0:T2:L0           419430400
/vmfs/devices/disks/mpx.vmhba1:C0:T1:L0           41943040
/vmfs/devices/disks/mpx.vmhba1:C0:T0:L0           41943040
/vmfs/devices/disks/mpx.vmhba1:C0:T3:L0           41943040
```

In my environment, I know `mpx.vmhba1:C0:T3:L0` is the disk that I want to use. We will access that value with `$vFlashDisk[3].DeviceName`. Now, we are ready to add the device:

```
PS C:\> Set-VMHostVFlashConfiguration -VFlashConfiguration `
$vFlashConfig -AddDevice $vFlashDisk

Name          CapacityGB SwapCacheReservationGB Extents

----          ---------- ---------------------- -------

esxi3.lab.com 19.75         0     {mpx.vmhba1:C0:T3:L0:P1}
```

As you can see from the following screenshot, vFlash is enabled. We can further configure the SWAP space using the same cmdlet. I am leaving it to you to further explore the cmdlet.

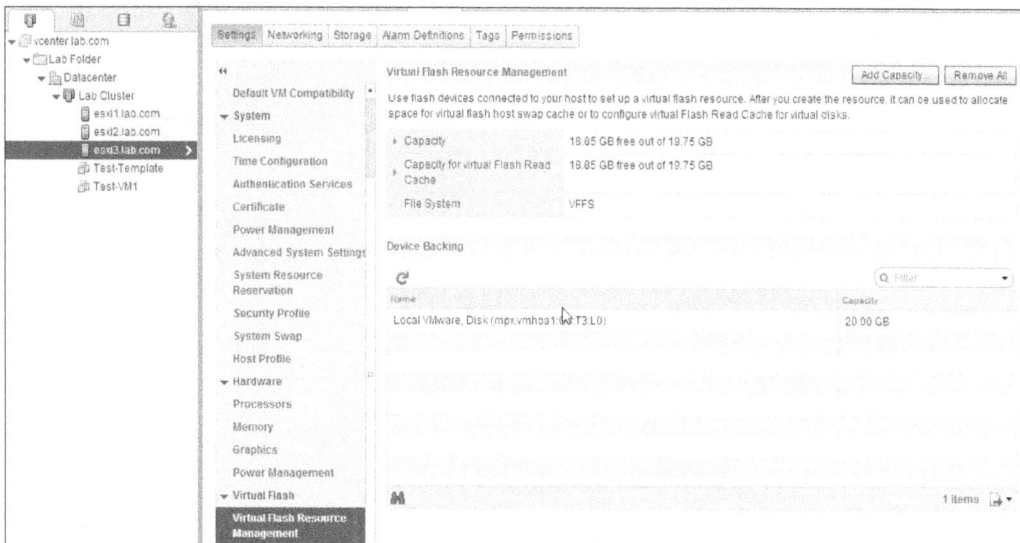

Similarly, the other set of cmdlets can be used to enable vFlash in a hard disk. It is pretty similar to the examples shown in this chapter, so I am not covering it here and leave it to you to explore it further.

Summary

In this chapter, we talked about configuring and managing storage in a vSphere environment. So far, we have covered the configuration of the physical aspects of an ESXi host. If you have followed till this point, then you have a physical host with ESXi installed in it. Also, networking and storage in the host are configured.

In the next chapter, we are going to talk about the last aspect of building a vSphere environment, that is, the logical constructs of the vSphere setup. In the next chapter, we will talk about configuring the datacenter, cluster, HA, DRS, and so on.

6
Managing Clusters and Other Constructs

In the last few chapters, we discussed the configuration of the physical aspects of a vSphere environment. For example, how to automate the installation of ESXi servers and configure networking and storage aspects of an ESXi host. In this chapter, we are going to talk about the logic aspects of a vSphere environment. In particular, we will discuss the following topics:

- Configuring vCenter logical constructs
- Configuring the **Enhanced vMotion Compatibility (EVC)** mode
- Configuring **High Availability (HA)**
- Using **Dynamic Resource Scheduling (DRS)**
- Using the DRS affinity and anti-affinity rules
- Managing resource pools
- Managing alarms

To discuss and showcase these topics, we will take a freshly installed environment with just the ESXi hosts and vCenter installed. We will then build the constructs such as a datacenter, cluster, resource pool, and so on. Using PowerCLI, we will then check the other things that we can do related to this topic. So, let's first start by building a vCenter environment as this is the first step toward building a vSphere virtual environment. For all the following topics, we will assume that we are already connected to a vCenter server. For our lab purpose, we will take it as `vcenter.lab.com`. We will take three ESXi hosts: `ESXi1.lab.com`, `ESXi2.lab.com`, and `ESXi3.lab.com`. Also, to showcase other configurations, we will create the two `Test1` and `Test2` VMs.

Configuring vCenter logical constructs

In this section, we will discuss the different components, which are as follows:

- A folder
- A datacenter
- A cluster

Folder

We are connected to a vCenter server with nothing configured in it. We will start with creating a **folder**. A folder is the most basic component of the logical constructs in a vCenter environment. We create folders to organize different constructs. We can use the following cmdlets to manage folders in an environment:

- `Get-Folder`
- `Move-Folder`
- `New-Folder`
- `Remove-Folder`
- `Set-Folder`

First, we will create a folder under the root folder. To get the root folder, we can use the following cmdlet:

```
PS C:\> Get-Folder -NoRecursion

Name                         Type
----                         ----
Datacenters                  Datacenter
```

> Notice the –NoRecursion switch, by default the Get-Folder cmdlet is recursive in nature, it starts with the root folder, and shows the rest. Here, we want to see only the root folder, so I disabled the recursive nature with this switch, resulting in the root folder.

Next, we will create a new folder under the root folder:

```
PS C:\> Get-Folder -NoRecursion | New-Folder -Name "Lab Folder"

Name                         Type
----                         ----
Lab Folder                   Datacenter
```

We can check the folder that we just created using the following cmdlet:

```
PS C:\> Get-Folder -Name "Lab Folder"

Name                          Type
----                          ----

Lab Folder                    Datacenter
```

> Here, the folder type is mentioned as Datacenter. Since it is a
> root folder, it is of the Datacenter type. The other types are VM,
> HostAndCluster, Datastore, and Network. Depending on
> where they are created or what data they store, the type changes.

Next, we will create another folder named Test under the root folder using the same cmdlet, as shown in the following screenshot:

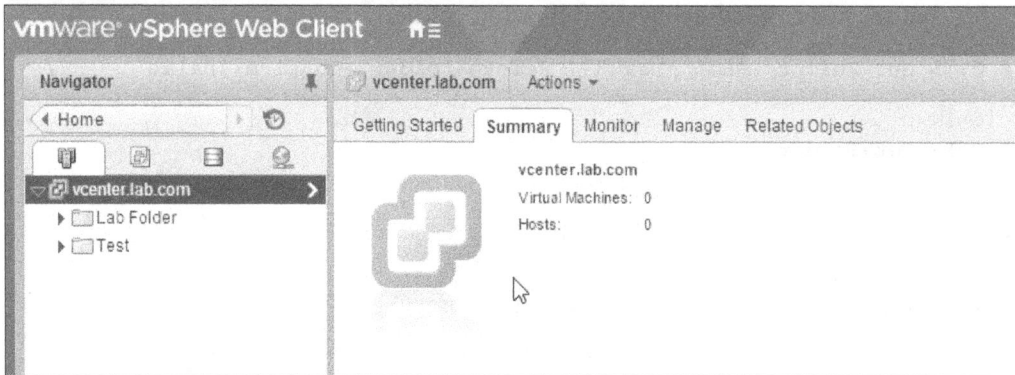

We will check the Move-Folder cmdlet that helps you move a folder to another location. We will use this cmdlet to move the Test folder into the Lab Folder:

```
PS C:\> Get-Folder -Name "Test" | Move-Folder -Destination "Lab Folder"

Name                          Type
----                          ----

Test                          Datacenter
```

As shown in the following screenshot, the folder has now been moved to a new destination:

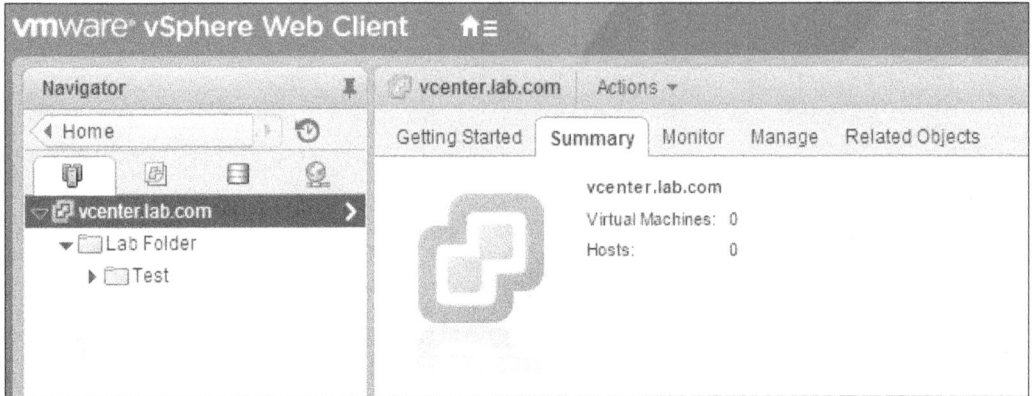

We can remove a folder using the `Remove-Folder` cmdlet. Let's remove the `Test` folder that we just created using the following cmdlet:

```
PS C:\> Get-Folder -Name "Test" | Remove-Folder -Confirm:$false


PS C:\> Get-Folder


Name                     Type
----                     ----

Datacenters              Datacenter
Lab Folder               Datacenter
```

Just for your reference, you can see in the following screenshot that when we try to create a folder under `Datacenter`, it asks for the different types of folders (a folder to hold a type of entity). This will make it easy to understand the different types of folders:

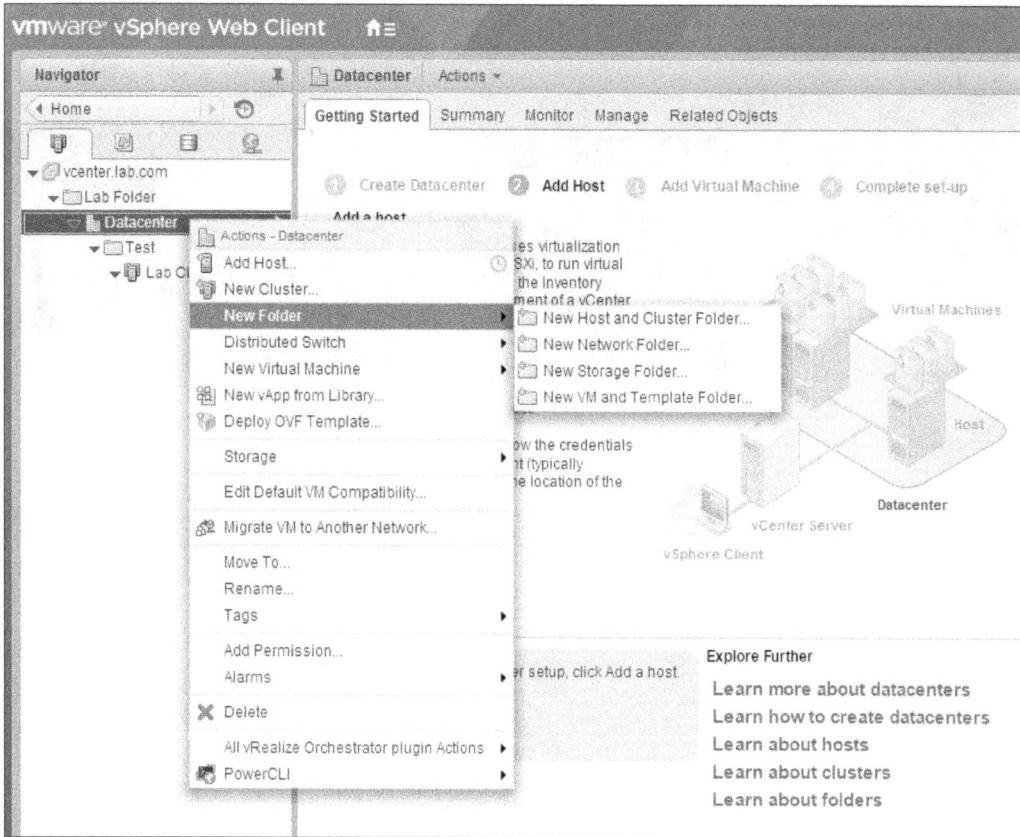

Datacenter

We discussed how to create and manage a folder in a vCenter environment. Our next task is to create a **datacenter**. To manage a datacenter in a vCenter server, we can utilize the following cmdlets:

- `Get-Datacenter`
- `Move-Datacenter`
- `New-Datacenter`
- `Remove-Datacenter`
- `Set-Datacenter`

Since this is a new environment, we will start by creating a new datacenter, and as the name suggests, New-Datacenter will help us create that. Here, we will create a new datacenter named Lab Datacenter under the Lab Folder:

```
PS C:\> New-Datacenter -Location "Lab Folder" -Name "Lab Datacenter" | Format-List

WARNING: PowerCLI scripts should not use the 'Client' property. The property will be removed in a future release.
ParentFolderId    : Folder-group-d781
ParentFolder      : Lab Folder
Name              : Lab Datacenter
CustomFields      : {}
ExtensionData     : VMware.Vim.Datacenter
Id                : Datacenter-datacenter-783
Uid               : /VIServer=lab\vcadmin@vcenter.lab.com:443/Datacenter=Datacenter-datacenter-783/
Client            : VMware.VimAutomation.ViCore.Impl.V1.VimClient
DatastoreFolderId : Folder-group-s786
```

As shown in the following screenshot, a datacenter has been created:

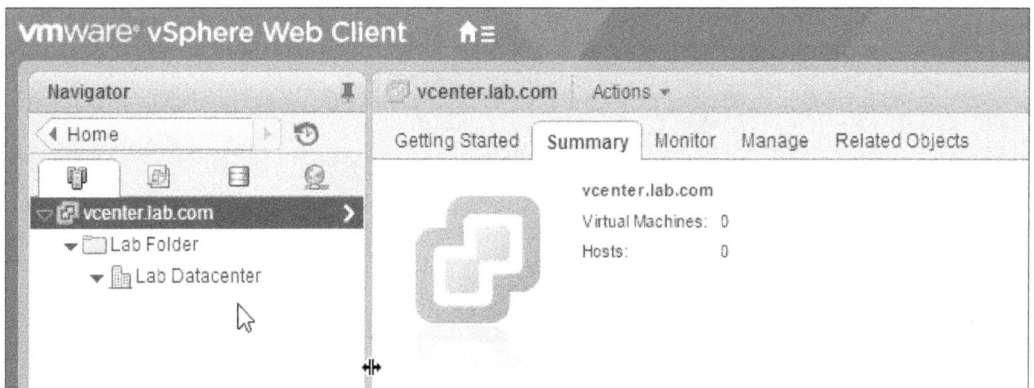

We can check the status of the new datacenter with the Get-Datacenter cmdlet:

PS C:\> Get-Datacenter

Name

Lab Datacenter

We can use Set-Datacenter to change the name of a datacenter:

PS C:\> Set-Datacenter -Datacenter "Lab Datacenter" -Name "Datacenter"

Name

Datacenter

We can use the `Move-Datacenter` cmdlet to move a datacenter to another folder:

```
PS C:\> Move-Datacenter Datacenter -Destination Test


Name

----

Datacenter
```

In the following screenshot, the datacenter name has been changed and moved to another folder named `Test`:

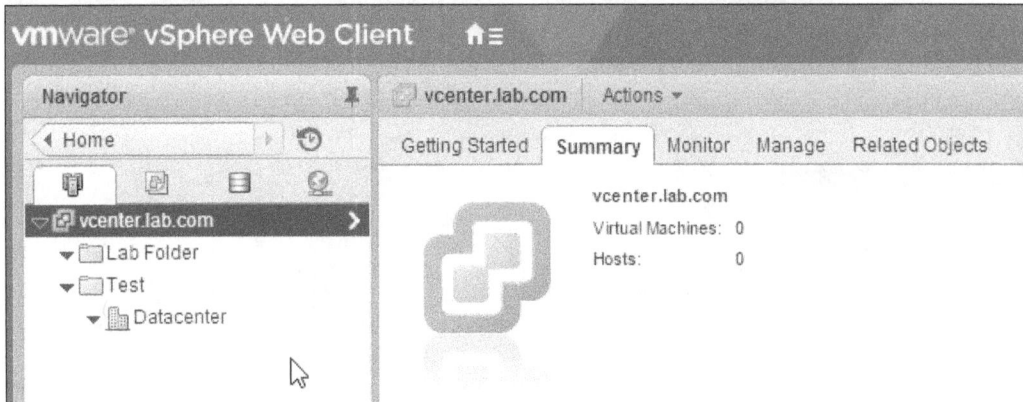

We can use the `Remove-Datacenter` cmdlet to delete a `Datacenter`. For example, when we run the following command, it will delete the `Datacenter`:

```
PS C:\> Remove-Datacenter Datacenter -Confirm:$false
```

Cluster

Since we created a datacenter, the next thing that we need to create is a **cluster**. To manage a cluster, we can utilize the following cmdlets:

* `Get-Cluster`
* `Move-Cluster`
* `New-Cluster`
* `Remove-Cluster`
* `Set-Cluster`

Let's first create a cluster with the `New-Cluster` cmdlet:

```
PS C:\> New-Cluster -Name "Lab Cluster" -Location "Datacenter"

Name              HAEnabled  HAFailover  DrsEnabled  DrsAutomationLevel
                             Level
----              ---------  ----------  ----------  ------------------
Lab Cluster       False      1           False       FullyAutomated
```

In the following screenshot, a new cluster has been created in the environment:

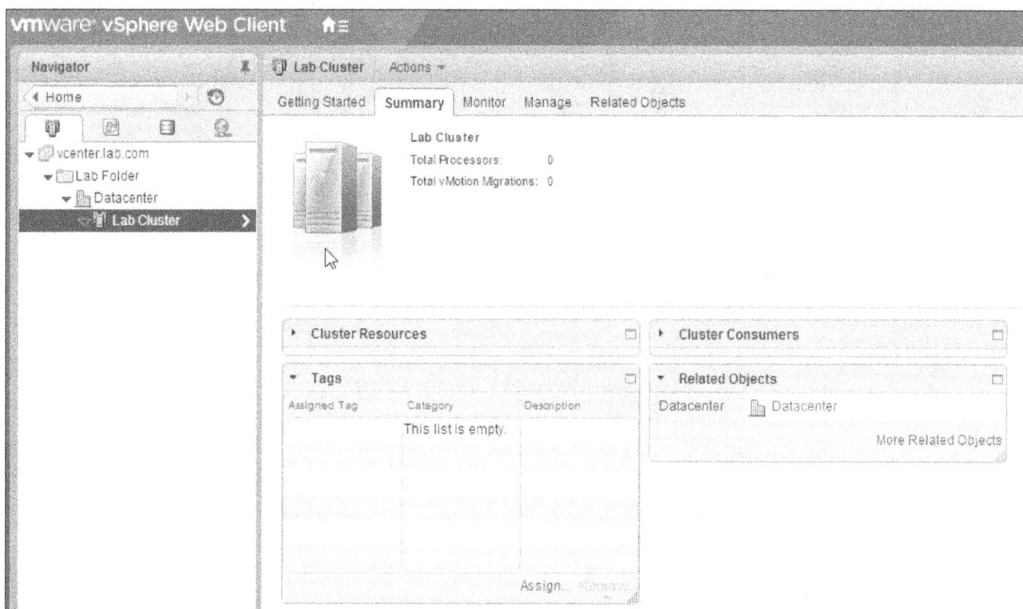

We can use the `Move-Cluster` cmdlet to move a cluster to another folder, as shown in the following screenshot:

```
PS C:\> Move-Cluster "Lab Cluster" -Destination Test

Name              HAEnabled  HAFailover  DrsEnabled  DrsAutomationLevel
                             Level
----              ---------  ----------  ----------  ------------------
Lab Cluster       False      1           False       FullyAutomated
```

In the following screenshot, the cluster has been moved to the `Test` folder:

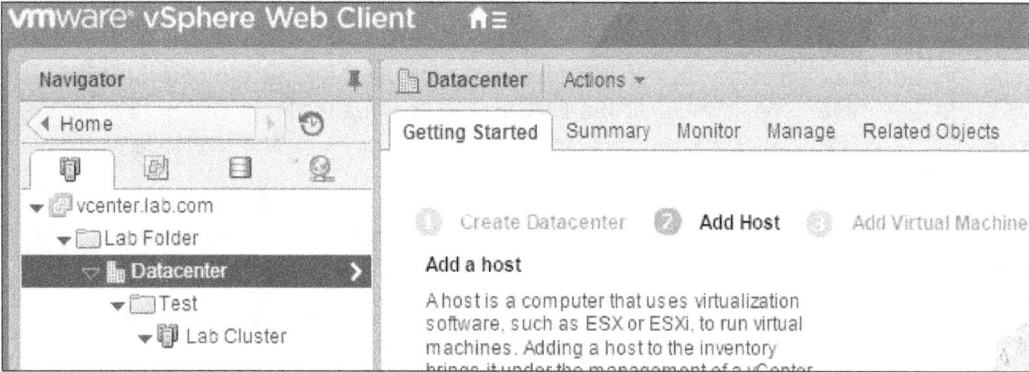

We can use `Set-Cluster` to change the different aspects of a cluster. We will use this cmdlet later in detail while configuring other aspects of a cluster. We can use the `Remove-Cluster` cmdlet to delete a cluster.

In the next section, we will remove the `Test` folder, add the three hosts to the cluster, and then configure the next part. To move an ESXi host to the cluster, we will use the `Move-VMHost` cmdlet:

```
PS C:\> Get-VMHost | Move-VMHost -Destination 'Lab Cluster'
```

In the following screenshot, the hosts have been added under the `Lab Cluster`:

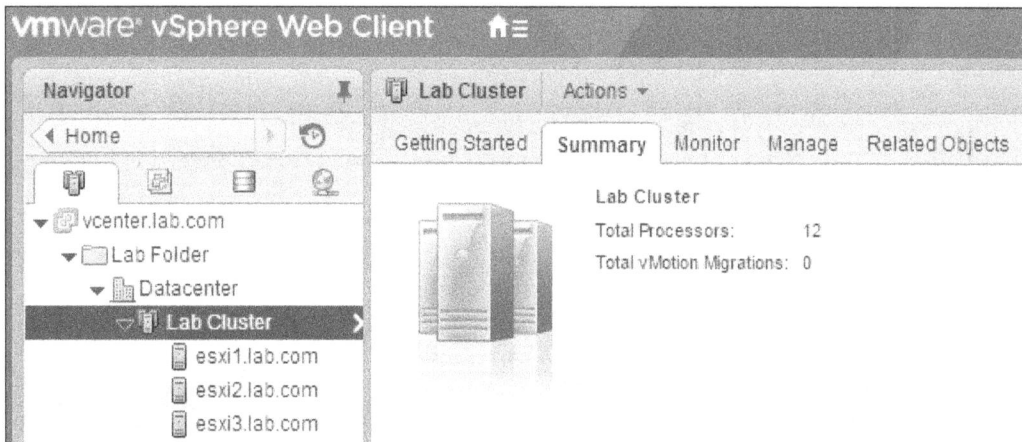

Configuring the Enhanced vMotion Compatibility mode

The EVC mode is a feature that enables us to maximize the vMotion compatibility of hosts in a cluster. We can check the EVC mode at a cluster level and on a per-host basis. We can check the EVC mode on a cluster using the EVCMode property of a cluster.

For example, we can check the EVC mode for the cluster that we just created, using the following cmdlet:

```
PS C:\> Get-Cluster -Name "Lab Cluster" | Select -Property Name,EVCMode


Name          EVCMode

----          -------

Lab Cluster
```

As seen in the preceding example, no EVC mode has been set on this cluster.

Next, let's check the maximum supported EVC mode on the ESXi hosts. To do this, we can check the MaxEVCMode property of the host:

```
PS C:\> Get-VMHost -Name Esxi1.lab.com | Select Name, MaxEVCMode


Name          MaxEVCMode

----          ----------

esxi1.lab.com intel-sandybridge
```

In the preceding example, the host supports the intel-sandybridge mode. We will set this EVC mode to the cluster and then add ESXi hosts to this cluster.

To set the EVC mode to a cluster, we will use the Set-Cluster cmdlet:

```
PS C:\> Set-Cluster 'Lab Cluster' -EVCMode 'intel-sandybridge'
```

The result of the preceding command is shown in the following screenshot:

```
PS C:\> Set-Cluster -Cluster "Lab Cluster" -EVCMode 'intel-sandybridge'

Name                 HAEnabled   HAFailover   DrsEnabled   DrsAutomationLevel
                                 Level

----                 ---------   ----------   ----------   ------------------
Lab Cluster          False       1            False        FullyAutomated
```

Now, let's check the status of the EVCMode parameter in the cluster:

```
PS C:\> Get-Cluster "Lab Cluster" | Select -Property Name, EVCMode


Name          EVCMode

----          -------

Lab Cluster intel-sandybridge
```

We can disable the EVC mode on a cluster by passing a $null value to the EVCMode parameter. The following screenshot shows you an example of how to disable the EVC mode:

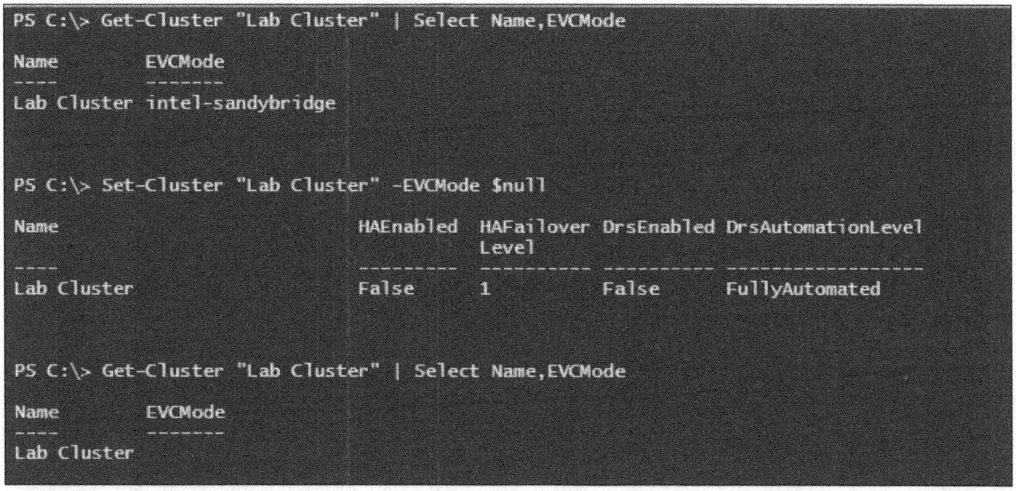

```
PS C:\> Get-Cluster "Lab Cluster" | Select Name,EVCMode

Name          EVCMode
----          -------
Lab Cluster intel-sandybridge


PS C:\> Set-Cluster "Lab Cluster" -EVCMode $null

Name                          HAEnabled  HAFailover DrsEnabled DrsAutomationLevel
                                         Level
----                          ---------  ---------- ---------- ------------------
Lab Cluster                   False      1          False      FullyAutomated


PS C:\> Get-Cluster "Lab Cluster" | Select Name,EVCMode

Name          EVCMode
----          -------
Lab Cluster
```

For details on the EVC mode and different available EVC modes, refer to the VMware KB Article 1005764 at http://kb.vmware.com/selfservice/microsites/search.do?language=en_US&cmd=displayKC&externalId=1005764.

Configuring High Availability

In this section, we will discuss how to configure HA in a cluster and the other advanced parameters related to HA.

As shown in the preceding examples, HA is not enabled for this cluster. To enable the cluster, we will again make use of the Set-Cluster cmdlet. In the following example, HA in the cluster has been enabled:

```
PS C:\> Set-Cluster -Cluster "Lab Cluster" -HAEnabled:$true

Name                      HAEnabled  HAFailover DrsEnabled DrsAutomationLevel
                                     Level

----                      ---------  ---------- ---------- ------------------
Lab Cluster               True       1          False      FullyAutomated
```

Next, we will enable the HAAdmissionControl property. Let's first check whether HAAdmissionControl is enabled or not:

```
PS C:\> Get-Cluster "Lab Cluster" | Select -Property HAEnabled,HAAdmissio
nControlEnabled


HAEnabled HAAdmissionControlEnabled

--------- -------------------------

    True                      False
```

To enable this property, we will use the Set-Cluster cmdlet. The process of enabling this parameter is shown in the following example:

```
PS C:\> Set-Cluster "Lab Cluster" -HAAdmissionControlEnabled:$true

Name                      HAEnabled  HAFailover DrsEnabled DrsAutomationLevel
                                     Level

----                      ---------  ---------- ---------- ------------------
Lab Cluster               True       1          False      FullyAutomated


PS C:\> Get-Cluster "Lab Cluster" | Select -Property HAEnabled,HAAdmissionControlEnabled

HAEnabled HAAdmissionControlEnabled
--------- -------------------------
    True                      True
```

Next, we will set `HAFailoverLevel`. To do this, we will set the `HAFailoverLevel` property of the cluster. In the following example, we have changed the failover level to 2 (the default value is 1):

```
PS C:\> Get-Cluster "Lab Cluster" | Select -Property HAEnabled, HAFailoverLevel

HAEnabled HAFailoverLevel
--------- ---------------
     True               1


PS C:\> Set-Cluster "Lab Cluster" -HAFailoverLevel 2

Name                        HAEnabled  HAFailover DrsEnabled DrsAutomationLevel
                                       Level
----                        ---------  ---------- ---------- ------------------
Lab Cluster                 True       2          False      FullyAutomated
```

In the next step, we need to configure the `HAIsolationResponse` property. This value determines whether the virtual machines running on top of an isolated host should be powered off or not. The valid values for this property are as follows:

* `PowerOff`
* `DoNothing`
* `ShutDown`

In the following example, we have changed the default value of `DoNothing` to `PowerOff`:

```
PS C:\> Get-Cluster "Lab Cluster" | Select -Property HAEnabled, HAIsolationResponse

HAEnabled HAIsolationResponse
--------- -------------------
     True          DoNothing


PS C:\> Set-Cluster "Lab Cluster" -HAIsolationResponse PowerOff

Name                        HAEnabled  HAFailover DrsEnabled DrsAutomationLevel
                                       Level
----                        ---------  ---------- ---------- ------------------
Lab Cluster                 True       1          False      FullyAutomated


PS C:\> Get-Cluster "Lab Cluster" | Select -Property HAEnabled, HAIsolationResponse

HAEnabled HAIsolationResponse
--------- -------------------
     True           PowerOff
```

The last property that we need to set is `HARestartPriority`. The valid values for this parameter are as follows:

- `Disabled`
- `High`
- `Low`
- `Medium`

The default value is `Medium`. In the following example, we will change the default value to `High`:

```
PS C:\> Get-Cluster "Lab Cluster" | Select -Property HAEnabled, HARestartPriority

HAEnabled HARestartPriority
--------- -----------------
     True            Medium


PS C:\> Set-Cluster "Lab Cluster" -HARestartPriority High

Name                              HAEnabled  HAFailover DrsEnabled DrsAutomationLevel
                                             Level
----                              ---------  ---------- ---------- ------------------
Lab Cluster                       True       1          False      FullyAutomated


PS C:\> Get-Cluster "Lab Cluster" | Select -Property HAEnabled, HARestartPriority

HAEnabled HARestartPriority
--------- -----------------
     True              High
```

Using Dynamic Resource Scheduling

In the preceding examples, for `Lab Cluster`, DRS is not enabled. So, first we will enable DRS for this cluster. In the following example, we have enabled DRS and the default automation level is `FullyAutomated`:

```
PS C:\> Set-Cluster "Lab Cluster" -DrsEnabled:$true

Name                              HAEnabled  HAFailover DrsEnabled DrsAutomationLevel
                                             Level
----                              ---------  ---------- ---------- ------------------
Lab Cluster                       True       1          True       FullyAutomated
```

Next, we will change the automation level using the `DrsAutomationLevel` property. The valid values that we can use are as follows:

- `FullyAutomated`
- `Manual`
- `PartiallyAutomated`

In this example, we will change the value to `PartiallyAutomated`:

```
PS C:\> Set-Cluster "Lab Cluster" -DrsAutomationLevel PartiallyAutomated

Name                 HAEnabled   HAFailover  DrsEnabled  DrsAutomationLevel
                                 Level
----                 ---------   ----------  ----------  ------------------
Lab Cluster          True        1           True        PartiallyAutomated
```

We can use the `Get-DrsRecommendation` cmdlet to get the DRS recommendations for a cluster. For example, to get the DRS recommendation, we can run the following command:

```
PS C:\> Get-DrsRecommendation -Cluster 'Lab Cluster' -Refresh
```

This will refresh the cluster and show the recommendations, as shown in the following example:

```
PS C:\> Get-DrsRecommendation -Cluster 'Lab Cluster' -Refresh

Priority Recommendation                                                      Reason
-------- --------------                                                      ------
2        Migrate VM 'Test1' from host 'esxi1.lab.com' to host 'esxi2.lab.com'.   Balance average memory loads
2        Migrate VM 'Test2' from host 'esxi1.lab.com' to host 'esxi3.lab.com'.   Balance average memory loads
```

Next, we will discuss the advanced settings of a DRS cluster.

Using the DRS affinity and anti-affinity rules

In this section, we will discuss the advanced settings of a cluster. We can use the following cmdlets for this section:

- `Get-DrsRule`
- `New-DrsRule`
- `Remove-DrsRule`
- `Set-DrsRule`

First, we will create a new anti-affinity rule with the two `Test1` and `Test2` VMs that we created for this purpose. We want to always keep them separate in such a way that they will not run on a single host at any point of time. For this, we will use the `New-DrsRule` cmdlet to create a rule. We will use the following command for this:

```
PS C:\> New-DrsRule –Cluster 'Lab Cluster' –Name `  antiAffinityTest1
-KeepTogether $false –VM Test1, Test2
```

The result of the preceding command is shown in the following screenshot:

```
PS C:\> New-DrsRule –Cluster "Lab Cluster" –Name antiAffinityTest1 –KeepTogether $false –VM Test1, Test2
WARNING: Parameter 'Cluster' is obsolete. This parameter no longer accepts multiple values.

Name                          Enabled Type            VMIDs
----                          ------- ----            -----
antiAffinityTest1             True    VMAntiAffinity  {VirtualMachine-vm-821, VirtualMachine-vm-822}

PS C:\> Get-DrsRule –Cluster "Lab Cluster" –Name antiAffinityTest1

Name                          Enabled Type            VMIDs
----                          ------- ----            -----
antiAffinityTest1             True    VMAntiAffinity  {VirtualMachine-vm-821, VirtualMachine-vm-822}
```

Note the warning about the `Cluster` parameter. This warning is displayed to show you that this parameter is obsolete and should be avoided. We can check the details of the rule using the `Get-DrsRule` cmdlet.

We can change a rule using the `Set-DrsRule` cmdlet. In the following example, we have changed the association of the VMs with the rule. Instead of the `Test1` and `Test2` VMs, now the `Test3` and `Test4` VMs are associated with the rule:

```
PS C:\> Get-DrsRule –Name antiAffinityTest1 –Cluster "Lab Cluster" | Set-DrsRule –VM Test3, Test4 –Enabled $true
Name                          Enabled Type            VMIDs
----                          ------- ----            -----
antiAffinityTest1             True    VMAntiAffinity  {VirtualMachine-vm-823, VirtualMachine-vm-824}
```

We can remove a rule using the `Remove-DrsRule` cmdlet. In the following example, we removed the `antiAffinityTest1` rule:

```
PS C:\> Get-DrsRule -Name antiAffinityTest1 -Cluster "Lab Cluster" |
Remove-DrsRule


PS C:\> Get-DrsRule -Cluster "Lab Cluster"
```

Managing resource pools

Here, we will discuss how to create and manage resource pools in a vCenter environment. We can use the following cmdlets to manage resource pools:

- Get-ResourcePool

- Move-ResourcePool

- New-ResourcePool

- Remove-ResourcePool

- Set-ResourcePool

As the name suggests, Get-ResourcePool provides you the details of the existing resource pools. Since we have enabled DRS in Lab Cluster, a default resource pool is already created (a root resource pool). The following are the details of this pool with default values:

```
PS C:\> Get-ResourcePool

Name            CpuSharesL CpuReserva CpuLimitMH MemSharesL MemReservationG MemLimitGB
                evel       tionMHz    z          evel       B
----            ---------- ---------- ---------- ---------- --------------- ----------
Resources       Normal     32256      32256      Normal     3.088           3.088
```

Next, we will create a new resource pool named Mgmt with the following characteristics:

- It will be created under the default Resources resource pool

- The CpuExpandableReservation parameter is set to True

- The CpuReservationMhz parameter is set to 500

- The CpuSharesLevel parameter is set to High

- The MemExpandableReservation parameter is set to True

- The MemReservationGB parameter is set to 1

- The MemSharesLevel parameter is set to High

In the following example, we have run the same parameters with the New-ResourcePool cmdlet to create the resource pool. The following commands are run:

```
PS C:\> $rpool1 = Get-ResourcePool -Location 'Lab Cluster' -Name
Resources

PS C:\> $rpool1
```

The following is an example of the preceding command:

```
PS C:\> $rpool1 = Get-ResourcePool -Location 'Lab Cluster' -Name Resources
PS C:\> $rpool1

Name              CpuSharesL CpuReserva CpuLimitMH MemSharesL MemReservationG MemLimitGB
                  evel       tionMHz    z          evel       B
----              ---------- ---------- ---------- ---------- --------------- ----------
Resources         Normal     32256      32256      Normal     3.191           3.191
```

Next, we will create the Mgmt resource pool:

```
PS C:\> New-ResourcePool -Location $rpool1 -Name Mgmt `
-CpuExpandableReservation $true -CpuReservationMhz 500 `
-CpuSharesLevel High -MemExpandableReservation $true `
 -MemReservationGB 1 -MemSharesLevel High
```

The following is an example of the preceding command:

```
PS C:\> New-ResourcePool -Location $rpool1 -Name Mgmt -CpuExpandableReservation $true `
 -CpuReservationMhz 500 -CpuSharesLevel High -MemExpandableReservation $true `
 -MemReservationGB 1 -MemSharesLevel High

Name              CpuSharesL CpuReserva CpuLimitMH MemSharesL MemReservationG MemLimitGB
                  evel       tionMHz    z          evel       B
----              ---------- ---------- ---------- ---------- --------------- ----------
Mgmt              High       500        -1         High       1.000           -1.000
```

We can get the details of the newly created resource pool with the Get-ResourcePool cmdlet:

```
PS C:\> Get-ResourcePool -Name Mgmt

Name              CpuSharesL CpuReserva CpuLimitMH MemSharesL MemReservationG MemLimitGB
                  evel       tionMHz    z          evel       B
----              ---------- ---------- ---------- ---------- --------------- ----------
Mgmt              High       500        -1         High       1.000           -1.000
```

We can use the Move-ResourcePool cmdlet to move a resource pool to another location. The format of the cmdlet is as follows:

```
PS C:\>Move-ResourcePool -ResourcePool ResourcePool -Destination Host
```

If a host or a cluster is specified for the -Destination parameter, the resource pool is moved to a resource pool named Resources. The Resources resource pool is a system resource pool and is guaranteed to exist.

We can move a VM to a resource pool using the Move-VM cmdlet:

```
PS C:\> Move-VM Test1, Test2 -Destination Mgmt
```

Name	PowerState	Num CPUs	MemoryGB
Test1	PoweredOff	1	0.016
Test2	PoweredOff	1	0.016

```
PS C:\> Move-VM Test3, Test4 -Destination Prod
```

Name	PowerState	Num CPUs	MemoryGB
Test3	PoweredOff	1	0.016
Test4	PoweredOff	1	0.016

We can use the Set-ResourcePool cmdlet to change the different aspects of an existing resource pool. To remove a Resource pool, we can use the Remove-ResourcePool cmdlet:

```
PS C:\> Remove-ResourcePool Prod
```

The preceding command will remove the Prod resource pool.

Managing alarms

To manage the different aspects of an alarm, we can use the following cmdlets:

- Get-AlarmAction
- New-AlarmAction
- Remove-AlarmAction
- Get-AlarmDefinition
- Set-AlarmDefinition
- Get-AlarmActionTrigger
- New-AlarmActionTrigger
- Remove-AlarmActionTrigger

There is no direct cmdlet available to create an alarm. We can create an alarm using the vSphere APIs, which we will cover in a later chapter. So, in this section, we will cover how to define and manage the different aspects of an existing alarm.

An alarm has main three parts: an alarm definition, alarm action, and alarm action trigger.

In the following screenshot, the definition is where you will define the name, description, type, and whether it is enabled or not:

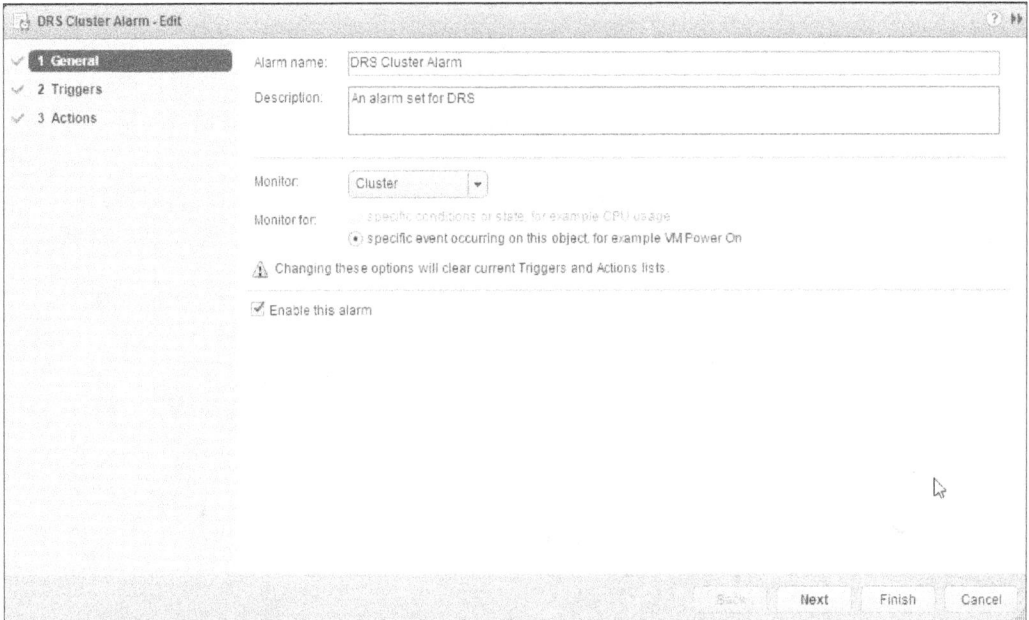

We can use the `Get-AlarmDefinition` cmdlet to get the details regarding the definition of an existing alarm:

```
PS C:\> Get-AlarmDefinition "DRS Cluster Alarm"

Name                    Description                    Enabled
----                    -----------                    -------
DRS Cluster Alarm       An alarm set for DRS           True
```

Next, we will make changes to the different points. We will use the Set-AlarmDefinition cmdlet for this. In the following example, we changed the name of an existing alarm DRS Cluster Alarm to DRS Alarm, the Description to Changed the Name of the Alarm, and changed the Enabled status. The following is the cmdlet:

```
PS C:\> Get-AlarmDefinition -Name 'DRS Cluster Alarm' `
| Set-AlarmDefinition -Name 'DRS Alarm' -Description `
'Changed the Name of the Alarm' -Enabled:$false
```

The following is an example of the preceding command:

```
PS C:\> Get-AlarmDefinition -Name 'DRS Cluster Alarm' | Set-AlarmDefinition `
-Name 'DRS Alarm' -Description 'Changed the Name of the Alarm'`
 -Enabled:$false

Name                    Description                                      Enabled
----                    -----------                                      -------
DRS Alarm               Changed the Name of the Alarm                    False
```

As shown in the following screenshot, these changes have been made:

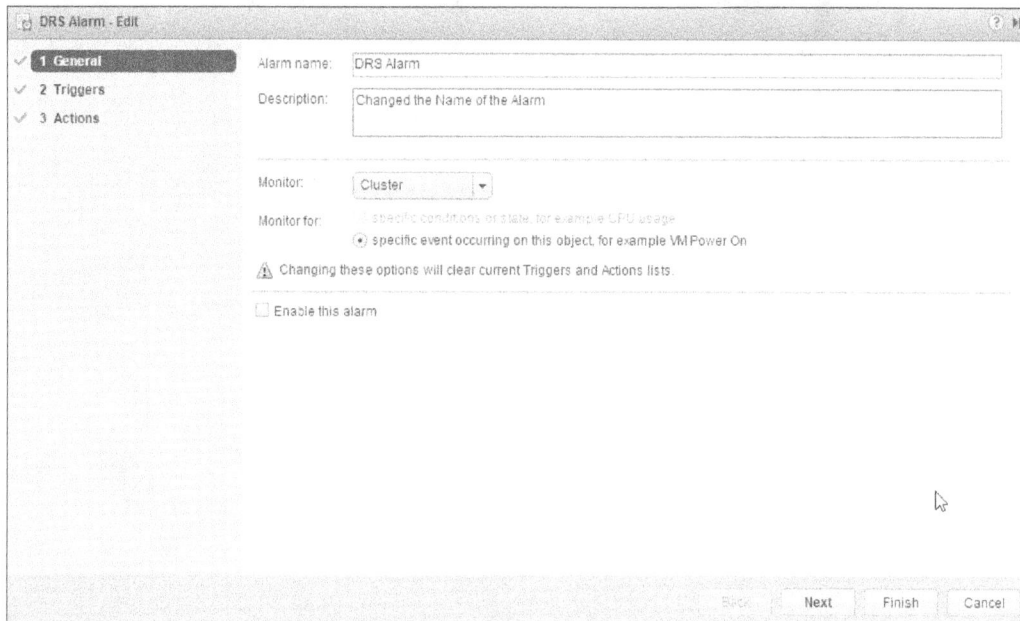

Next, we will manage alarm triggers. We can use the following cmdlets to manage the alarm action triggers:

- `Get-AlarmActionTrigger`
- `New-AlarmActionTrigger`
- `Remove-AlarmActionTrigger`

Let's first start with checking the current `AlarmActionTrigger` for `DRS Alarm`:

```
PS C:\> Get-AlarmAction -AlarmDefinition (Get-AlarmDefinition -Name "DRS Alarm") | Get-AlarmActionTrigger

StartStatus      EndStatus      Repeat
-----------      ---------      ------
Yellow           Red            False
```

In the preceding screenshot, we can see that the `DRS Alarm` will be triggered when the status changes from `Yellow` to `Red` and there would be no `Repeat` of the alarm.

Next, we will create a new alarm action trigger using the `New-AlarmActionTrigger` cmdlet:

```
PS C:\> Get-AlarmDefinition -Name "DRS Alarm" | Get-AlarmAction | New-AlarmActionTrigger -StartStatus 'Red' -EndStatus 'Yellow' -Repeat

StartStatus      EndStatus      Repeat
-----------      ---------      ------
Red              Yellow         True
```

In the following screenshot, we can see that the new changes have been made:

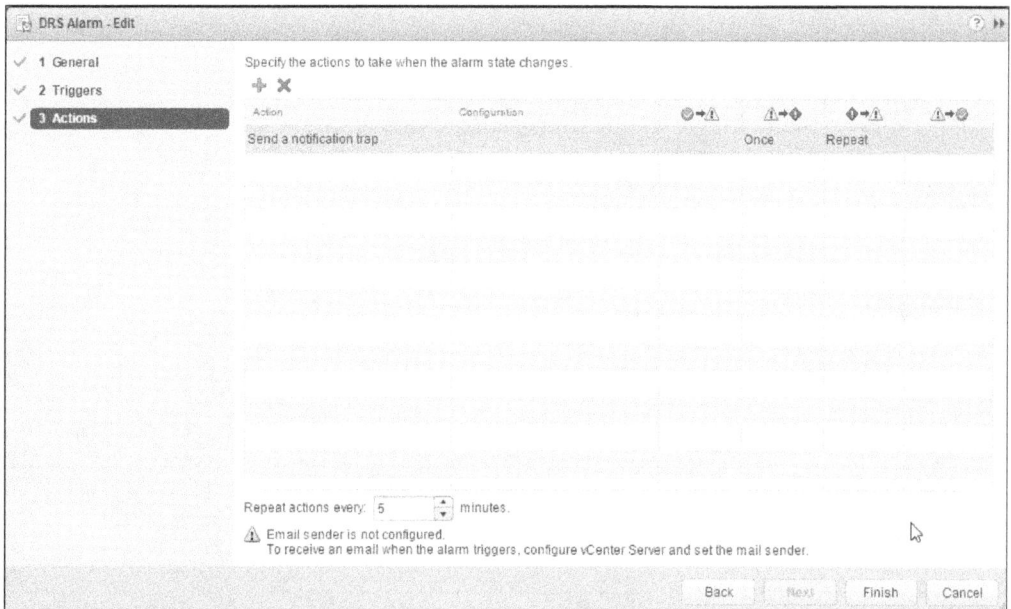

To remove a trigger, we can use the `Remove-AlarmActionTrigger` cmdlet. In the following example, we have used this cmdlet to remove a set trigger:

```
PS C:\> Get-AlarmDefinition -Name "DRS Alarm" | Get-AlarmAction | Get-AlarmActionTrigger

StartStatus      EndStatus      Repeat
-----------      ---------      ------
Yellow           Red           False
Red              Yellow        True


PS C:\> Get-AlarmDefinition -Name "DRS Alarm" | Get-AlarmAction | Get-AlarmActionTrigger | Select -First 1 | Remove-AlarmActionTrigger -Confirm:$false
PS C:\> Get-AlarmDefinition -Name "DRS Alarm" | Get-AlarmAction | Get-AlarmActionTrigger

StartStatus      EndStatus      Repeat
-----------      ---------      ------
Red              Yellow        True
```

Lastly, we will check the alarm actions. To manage the alarm actions, we can use the following cmdlets:

- `Get-AlarmAction`
- `New-AlarmAction`
- `Remove-AlarmAction`

We can use the `Get-AlarmAction` cmdlet to get the details of `ActionType`, `Trigger`, and other details of `AlarmDefinition`:

```
PS C:\> Get-AlarmAction -AlarmDefinition "DRS Alarm" | Format-List

ActionType       : SendSNMP
AlarmDefinition  : DRS Alarm
Trigger          : {Red -> Yellow (Repeat)}
Uid              : /VIServer=lab\vcadmin@vcenter.lab.com:443/Alarm=Alarm-alarm-201/SendSNMPAction=-1381748622/
AlarmVersion     : 105
Client           :
```

Next, we will use the `New-AlarmAction` cmdlet to define a new action for the alarm `DRS Alarm`:

```
PS C:\> Get-AlarmDefinition -Name "DRS Alarm" | New-AlarmAction -Script -ScriptPath 'C:\test.ps1' | Format-List

ScriptFilePath   : C:\test.ps1
ActionType       : ExecuteScript
AlarmDefinition  : DRS Alarm
Trigger          : {Yellow -> Red (Once)}
Uid              : /VIServer=lab\vcadmin@vcenter.lab.com:443/Alarm=Alarm-alarm-201/RunScriptAction=-921260669/
AlarmVersion     : 105
Client           :
```

As shown in the following screenshot, this change has taken place:

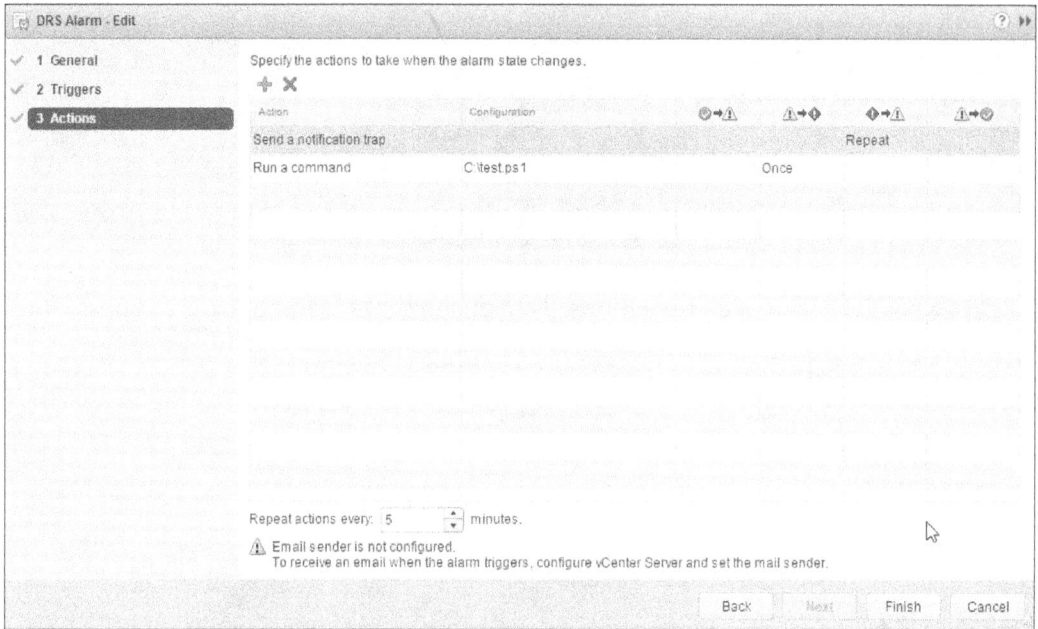

We can use `Remove-AlarmAction` to remove a defined action from an alarm. For example, note the following cmdlet:

```
PS C:\> Get-AlarmDefinition -Name 'DRS Alarm' | `
Get-AlarmAction | Select -First 1 | Remove-AlarmAction `
-Confirm:$false
```

In the following example, the first defined alarm action has been removed:

Summary

In this chapter, we covered how to configure and manage different logical aspects of a vCenter environment. We started by configuring constructs such as a datacenter, cluster, and so on. Next, we discussed how to manage EVC modes, HA, and DRS followed by a discussion on resource pools. At the end of the chapter, we discussed how to manage alarms.

In the next chapter, we will discuss how to create and manage virtual machines in a vSphere environment. We will cover how to modify settings in a virtual machine, run commands in a guest OS, configure fault tolerance, and so on.

7
Managing Virtual Machines

In the previous chapters, we discussed the different aspects of building and automating a vSphere environment using PowerCLI. In this chapter, we will discuss how to manage virtual machines. In general, we will discuss the following topics:

- Creating and managing virtual machines
- Modifying virtual machines
- Managing templates
- Managing OS customization specifications
- Managing the guest OS
- Managing vApps

We will start our discussion with the creation of VMs and other hardware-related aspects of a VM.

Creating virtual machines

We will use the following cmdlets to manage the different aspects of managing a virtual machine in a vSphere environment using PowerCLI cmdlets:

- `Get-VM`
- `Move-VM`
- `New-VM`
- `Remove-VM`
- `Set-VM`

We will start by creating a simple virtual machine. To do this, we will use the New-VM cmdlet:

```
PS C:\> New-VM -Name Test3 -ResourcePool Mgmt -Datastore iSCSI-4 `
-NumCPU 1 -MemoryGB 1 -DiskGB 10 -NetworkName "VM Network" `
-Floppy -CD -DiskStorageFormat Thin -GuestID winNetDatacenterGuest


Name                    PowerState Num CPUs MemoryGB

----                    ---------- -------- --------

Test3                   PoweredOff 1        1.000
```

The output will be as follows:

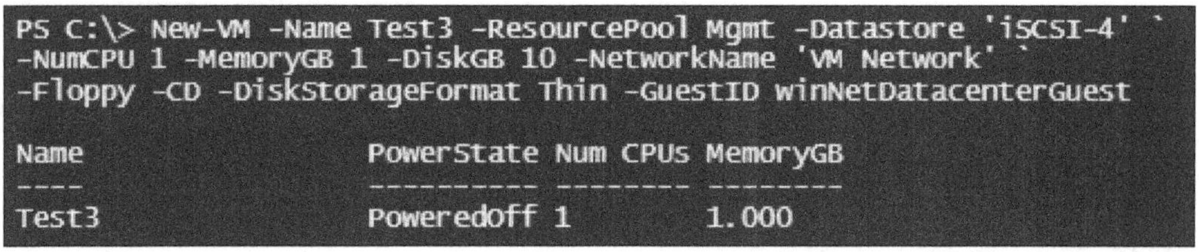

```
PS C:\> New-VM -Name Test3 -ResourcePool Mgmt -Datastore 'iSCSI-4' `
-NumCPU 1 -MemoryGB 1 -DiskGB 10 -NetworkName 'VM Network' `
-Floppy -CD -DiskStorageFormat Thin -GuestID winNetDatacenterGuest

Name                    PowerState Num CPUs MemoryGB
----                    ---------- -------- --------
Test3                   PoweredOff 1        1.000
```

Note that the ResourcePool parameter accepts ResourcePool, Cluster, VApp, and standalone VMHost as input options. For example, in the following screenshot, I am creating a VM directly under the cluster, Lab Cluster:

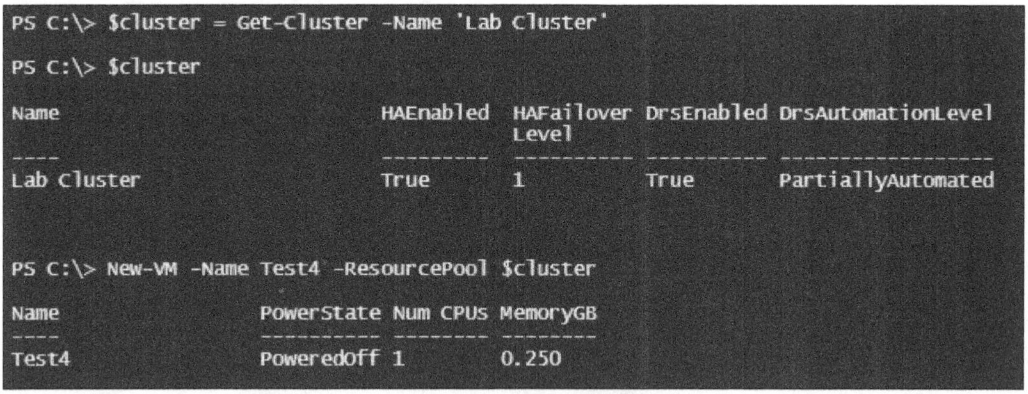

```
PS C:\> $cluster = Get-Cluster -Name 'Lab Cluster'
PS C:\> $cluster

Name                  HAEnabled HAFailover DrsEnabled DrsAutomationLevel
                                Level
----                  --------- ---------- ---------- ------------------
Lab Cluster           True      1          True       PartiallyAutomated


PS C:\> New-VM -Name Test4 -ResourcePool $cluster
Name                  PowerState Num CPUs MemoryGB
----                  ---------- -------- --------
Test4                 PoweredOff 1        0.250
```

We can use the Get-VM cmdlet to check the list of available VMs or a particular VM:

```
PS C:\> Get-VM

Name                    PowerState Num CPUs MemoryGB
----                    ---------- -------- --------
Test3                   PoweredOff 1          1.000
Test2                   PoweredOff 1          0.016
Test1                   PoweredOff 1          0.016


PS C:\> Get-VM -Name Test3

Name                    PowerState Num CPUs MemoryGB
----                    ---------- -------- --------
Test3                   PoweredOff 1          1.000
```

To create a VM by cloning an existing VM, we can again use the New-VM cmdlet. In the following example, we created a new VM Test3Cloned by cloning an existing VM Test3:

```
PS C:\> New-VM -Name Test3Cloned -VM Test3 -Datastore iSCSI-5 `
-VMHost Esxi2.lab.com

Name                    PowerState Num CPUs MemoryGB
----                    ---------- -------- --------
Test3Cloned             PoweredOff 1          1.000
```

To create a new VM using a template, we can specify the Template parameter:

```
PS C:\> New-VM -Name Test-1 -Template Test1 -ResourcePool 'Lab Cluster'

Name                    PowerState Num CPUs MemoryGB
----                    ---------- -------- --------
Test-1                  PoweredOff 1          0.016
```

We can use many other advanced options with the New-VM cmdlet. For example, we can create a VM with a specific guest OS customization or we can put the VM in a cluster or storage cluster with affinity rules set for it.

Since we are talking about cloning a VM, we will next cover creating a linked clone of a VM. But before we go ahead and create a linked clone of a VM, we need to take a snapshot of the original VM. We will discuss how to create a snapshot using PowerCLI shortly but, for the time being, we will create a snapshot named `LinkedClone` of the `Test1` VM using GUI. Next we will create a linked clone VM using this snapshot. The commands are as follows:

First, we collected information of the source VM:

```
PS C:\> $sourceVM = Get-VM -Name Test1
```

Next we collected the information about the snapshot:

```
PS C:\> $snapshot = Get-Snapshot -VM $sourceVM -Name 'LinkedClone'
```

Finally, we created the linked clone VM:

```
PS C:\> New-VM -LinkedClone -Name TestLinkedClone -VM $sourceVM `
-ReferenceSnapshot $snapshot -ResourcePool Mgmt `
-Datastore 'iSCSI-Cluster'
```

The output will be as follows:

```
PS C:\> $sourceVM = Get-VM -Name Test1
PS C:\> $sourceVM

Name                      PowerState Num CPUs MemoryGB
----                      ---------- -------- --------
Test1                     PoweredOff 1            0.125


PS C:\> $snapshot = Get-Snapshot -VM $sourceVM -Name "LinkedClone"
PS C:\> $snapshot

Name                      Description                    PowerState
----                      -----------                    ----------
LinkedClone               Snapshot for LinkedClone       PoweredOff


PS C:\> New-VM -LinkedClone -Name TestLinkedClone -VM $sourceVM `
-ReferenceSnapshot $snapshot -ResourcePool Mgmt `
-Datastore 'iSCSI-Cluster'

Name                      PowerState Num CPUs MemoryGB
----                      ---------- -------- --------
TestLinkedClone           PoweredOff 1            0.125
```

For all the detailed options, check the online documentation for the `New-VM` cmdlet at `https://www.vmware.com/support/developer/PowerCLI/PowerCLI60R1/html/New-VM.html`.

We can use the `Move-VM` cmdlet to move a VM from one location to another. For example, if we want to move the VM from one folder to another folder, we can use the following cmdlet:

First, we will move a VM to another folder:

```
PS C:\> Move-VM -VM Test-1 -Destination "TestFolder"


Name                    PowerState Num CPUs MemoryGB
----                    ---------- -------- --------
Test-1                  PoweredOff 1        0.016
```

Next we will move a VM to another host, another datastore, and change the disk format. We will do this again using the `Move-VM` cmdlet:

```
PS C:\> Get-VM -Name Test-1 | Move-VM -Destination Esxi2.lab.com
-Datastore iSCSI-2 -DiskStorageFormat Thin


Name                    PowerState Num CPUs MemoryGB
----                    ---------- -------- --------
Test-1                  PoweredOff 1        0.016
```

There are other parameters that we can use to move a VM to a datastore cluster and set affinity rules for the disks.

We can use the `Remove-VM` cmdlet to remove a VM from the inventory; this will not delete it from the disk. We can use the `-DeletePermanently` parameter to delete a VM permanently from the environment and disk.

In the next section, we will check how we can manage the power state of a VM. We can use the following cmdlets to start, stop, restart, or suspend a VM:

- `Restart-VM`
- `Start-VM`
- `Stop-VM`
- `Suspend-VM`

Before we go ahead and start the VMs, let's check the current status. In the following example, there are two VMs: `Test-1` and `Test-2` and both are in the powered-off state:

```
PS C:\> Get-VM


Name               PowerState Num CPUs MemoryGB
----               ---------- -------- --------
Test-2             PoweredOff 0           0.000
Test-1             PoweredOff 1           0.016
```

We can use the following command to power on all the powered-off VMs in the environment. You can modify the command to customize it to your requirements:

```
PS C:\> Get-VM | Where {$_.PowerState -eq "PoweredOff"} | Start-VM
-Confirm:$false


Name               PowerState Num CPUs MemoryGB
----               ---------- -------- --------
Test-2             PoweredOn  1           0.016
Test-1             PoweredOn  1           0.016
```

Note that, in the preceding example, we are getting a list of all the VMs using the `Get-VM` cmdlet. Next we are filtering the output and selecting only those VMs that are in the `PoweredOff` state. Finally, we are simply starting those VMs using the `Start-VM` cmdlet.

Similarly, we can use the `Stop-VM` cmdlet to power off the required VMs. Again, we will use a slightly changed version of the preceding command to power off all the powered-on VMs in the environment:

```
PS C:\> Get-VM | Where {$_.PowerState -eq "PoweredOn"} | Stop-VM
-Confirm:$false


Name               PowerState Num CPUs MemoryGB
----               ---------- -------- --------
Test-2             PoweredOff 1           0.016
Test-1             PoweredOff 1           0.016
```

Note that the `Stop-VM` cmdlet does a hard power-off of the VM. It is equivalent to the `Power Off` option of the GUI; it is not a `Shutdown Guest` equivalent.

To restart the VM or to suspend the VM, we can use the `Restart-VM` and `Suspend-VM` cmdlets respectively.

In the next section, we will cover how to modify different aspects of a virtual machine.

Modifying virtual machines

Modifying a virtual machine can be divided into many categories. We have divided it as follows:

- CD drives and floppy drives
- Hard disks
- Network adapters and USB devices
- Passthrough devices
- Snapshots
- Resource configuration and policies
- Managing VMware tools

As given in the preceding list, we will start with managing CD drives and floppy drives:

We will use the following cmdlets to manage the CD drives and floppy drives in a VM:

- `Get-CDDrive` / `Get-FloppyDrive`
- `New-CDDrive` / `New-FloppyDrive`
- `Remove-CDDrive` / `Remove-FloppyDrive`
- `Set-CDDrive` / `Set-FloppyDrive`

To get a list of connected CD or floppy drives, we can use the `Get-CDDrive` or `Get-FloppyDrive` cmdlet. For example, by running this cmdlet, we can find out that the `Test-1` VM is currently not connected to any CD drive:

```
PS C:\> Get-CDDrive -VM Test-1


PS C:\>
```

So, let's first add a CD drive to the VM using the `New-CDDRive` cmdlet:

```
PS C:\> New-CDDrive -VM Test-1

WARNING: Parameter 'VM' is obsolete. Passing multiple values to this
parameter is obsolete.


IsoPath                 HostDevice                 RemoteDevice
-------                 ----------                 ------------
```

So, let's connect an ISO image to the VM using the `Set-CDDrive` cmdlet. The following cmdlets are used to do this:

```
PS C:\> $cd = Get-CDDrive -VM Test-1

PS C:\> Set-CDDrive -CD $cd -IsoPath '[NFS_SHARE] VMware-VMVisor-
Installer-6.0.0-2494585.x86_64.iso' -Confirm:$false
```

The output will be as follows:

```
PS C:\> $cd = Get-CDDrive -VM Test-1

PS C:\> Set-CDDrive -CD $cd -IsoPath "[NFS_SHARE] VMware-VMVisor-Installer-6.0.0-2494585.x86_64.iso" -Confirm:$false

IsoPath                 HostDevice                 RemoteDevice
-------                 ----------                 ------------
[NFS_SHARE] VMwar...


PS C:\> Get-CDDrive -VM Test-1

IsoPath                 HostDevice                 RemoteDevice
-------                 ----------                 ------------
[NFS_SHARE] VMwar...
```

> Note that the ISO path requires the following specific format:
>
> `[<Datastore Name>]`**`<A single space>`**`<Folder>/<ISO File Name>`
>
> Also, note that we need to use a forward slash; there is no back slash. The ISO path given as an example in the `Set-CDDrive` cmdlet is not correct. For example, in the preceding example, the datastore name is `NFS_SHARE` and the ISO name is `VMware-VMVisor-Installer-6.0.0-2494585.x86_64.iso`. So, the used path was `[NFS_SHARE] <space> VMware-VMVisor-Installer-6.0.0-2494585.x86_64.iso`. In my case, the file was kept in the root folder. If it was kept in any folder, then the format of the path would be as given earlier. You need to be aware of the space and the forward slash.

We can use the `-Connected` parameter to disconnect a CD drive, and use the `-NoMedia` parameter to remove a connected ISO.

To remove a CD drive, we can use the `Remove-CDDrive` cmdlet:

`PS C:\> Get-CDDrive -VM Test-1 | Remove-CDDrive -Confirm:$false`

Similar cmdlets can be used to manage a floppy drive as well.

Hard disks

Next we will check the cmdlets used to manage the different aspects of hard disks in a VM. We can use the following cmdlets to manage hard disks:

- `Copy-HardDisk`
- `Move-HardDisk`
- `Get-HardDisk`
- `New-HardDisk`
- `Remove-HardDisk`
- `Set-HardDisk`

We can use the `Get-HardDisk` cmdlet to get a list of hard disks available in a VM:

`PS C:\> Get-HardDisk -VM Test-1`

CapacityGB	Persistence	Filename
2.000	Persistent	[iSCSI-2] Test-1/Test-1.vmdk

We can add a new hard disk to an existing VM using the `New-HardDisk` cmdlet:

```
PS C:\> Get-VM -Name Test-1 | New-HardDisk -CapacityGB 2 -Persistence Persistent -StorageFormat Thin -Confirm:$false
WARNING: Parameter 'VM' is obsolete. Passing multiple values to this parameter is obsolete.

CapacityGB   Persistence              Filename
----------   -----------              --------
2.000        Persistent               [iSCSI-2] Test-1/Test-1_2.vmdk

PS C:\> Get-HardDisk -VM Test-1

CapacityGB   Persistence              Filename
----------   -----------              --------
2.000        Persistent               [iSCSI-2] Test-1/Test-1.vmdk
2.000        Persistent               [iSCSI-2] Test-1/Test-1_2.vmdk
```

We can use other options with the `New-HardDisk` cmdlet to attach an existing disk to a VM or set affinity rules for the disks. In *Chapter 5, Managing Storage*, we discussed how to set raw disks (RDM disks) to a VM using the `New-HardDisk` cmdlet.

We can use the `Copy-HardDisk` and `Move-HardDisk` cmdlets to copy a hard disk to another location and move a hard disk to another location.

To change an existing hard disk, we can use the `Set-HardDisk` cmdlet, respectively:

```
PS C:\> $harddisk = Get-HardDisk -VM Test-1
PS C:\> Set-HardDisk -HardDisk $harddisk -CapacityGB 4 -Confirm:$false

CapacityGB      Persistence                                       Filename
----------      -----------                                       --------
4.000           Persistent                        [iSCSI-2] Test-1/Test-1.vmdk
```

We can use the same cmdlet to change the guest partition using the `-ResizeGuestPartition` parameter. So, we can use this parameter along with the `-CapacityGB` parameter to increase the disk size and, at the same time, increase the size from within the guest OS as well. For more options on how to manage disk size, check the documentation of this cmdlet at https://www.vmware.com/support/developer/PowerCLI/PowerCLI60R1/html/Set-HardDisk.html. To remove a hard disk, we can use the `Remove-HardDisk` cmdlet.

Next, we are going to talk about how to manage network adapters.

Network adapters and USB devices

To manage network adapters, we can use the following cmdlets:

- `Get-NetworkAdapter`
- `New-NetworkAdapter`
- `Remove-NetworkAdapter`
- `Set-NetworkAdapter`

To get a list of network adapters in a VM, we can utilize the `Get-NetworkAdapter` cmdlet:

```
PS C:\> Get-NetworkAdapter -VM Test-1

Name                Type        NetworkName   MacAddress        WakeOnLan
                                                                Enabled
----                ----        -----------   ----------        ---------
Network adapter 1   Flexible    TestPortG...  00:50:56:9a:1f:19      True
```

We can add a new network adapter to a VM using the `New-NetworkAdapter` cmdlet:

```
PS C:\> Get-VM -Name Test-1 | New-NetworkAdapter -NetworkName "VM Network" -Type Flexible
WARNING: Parameter 'VM' is obsolete. Passing multiple values to this parameter is obsolete.

Name                    Type        NetworkName    MacAddress          WakeOnLan
                                                                       Enabled
----                    ----        -----------    ----------          ---------
Network adapter 2       Flexible    VM Network     00:50:56:9a:1a:33      False


PS C:\> Get-NetworkAdapter -VM Test-1

Name                    Type        NetworkName    MacAddress          WakeOnLan
                                                                       Enabled
----                    ----        -----------    ----------          ---------
Network adapter 1       Flexible    TestPortG...   00:50:56:9a:1f:19       True
Network adapter 2       Flexible    VM Network     00:50:56:9a:1a:33      False
```

To make any changes to an existing network adapter, we can use the `Set-NetworkAdapter` cmdlet:

```
PS C:\> Get-VM Test-1 | Get-NetworkAdapter | Where { $_.NetworkName -eq "VM Network"} | Set-NetworkAdapter -Type e1000 -Confirm:$false
Name               Type      NetworkName    MacAddress         WakeOnLan
                                                               Enabled
----               ----      -----------    ----------         ---------
Network adapter 2  e1000     VM Network     00:50:56:9a:1a:33    False
```

In the preceding example, we used the `Set-NetworkAdapter` cmdlet to change the type of an existing adapter to `e1000`.

In a similar way, we can use the following two cmdlets to manage USB devices attached to a VM:

- `Get-UsbDevice`
- `Remove-UsbDevice`

Passthrough devices

To manage the passthrough devices in a VM, we can use the following cmdlets:

- `Add-PassthroughDevice`
- `Get-PassthroughDevice`
- `Remove-PassthroughDevice`

Let's take a look at the following example:

```
PS C:\> Get-PassthroughDevice -VM Test-1

PS C:\> $scsidev =  Get-PassthroughDevice -VMHost esxi1.lab.com -Type Scsi

PS C:\> Add-PassthroughDevice -VM (Get-VM Test-1) -PassthroughDevice $scsidev

Key         Name                                  VendorName              Type
---         ----                                  ----------              ----
2000        /vmfs/devices/cdrom/mpx.vmh...        NECVMWar                Scsi


PS C:\> Get-PassthroughDevice -VM Test-1

Key         Name                                  VendorName              Type
---         ----                                  ----------              ----
2000        /vmfs/devices/cdrom/mpx.vmh...        NECVMWar                Scsi
```

In the preceding example, we can see that, to get a list of passthrough devices attached to a VM, we can use the Get-PassthroughDevice cmdlet; to add a device, we can use the Add-PassthroughDevice cmdlet.

Snapshots

One of the most important and utilized features of a VM is the snapshot functionality. To manage a snapshot for a VM, we can use the following cmdlets:

- Get-Snapshot

- New-Snapshot

- Remove-Snapshot

- Set-Snapshot

To get a list of snapshots for a VM, we will use the Get-Snapshot cmdlet. To add a new snapshot, we will use the New-Snapshot cmdlet:

```
PS C:\> Get-VM Test-1 | New-Snapshot -Name Snapshot1 -Description "First Snapshot"
WARNING: Parameter 'VM' is obsolete. This parameter no longer accepts multiple values.

Name              Description                   PowerState
----              -----------                   ----------
Snapshot1         First Snapshot                PoweredOff


PS C:\> Get-Snapshot -VM Test-1

Name              Description                   PowerState
----              -----------                   ----------
Snapshot1         First Snapshot                PoweredOff
```

We can use the `Set-Snapshot` cmdlet to change an existing snapshot, and use the `Remove-Snapshot` cmdlet to remove a snapshot.

Resource configuration and policies

Before we discuss how to manage the resources of a VM, we will provide some information on how to open a console of a VM using PowerCLI and manage questions for a VM.

We can use the `Open-VMConsoleWindow` cmdlet to open a console of a powered-on virtual machine:

```
PS C:\> Open-VMConsoleWindow -VM Test-1 -FullScreen
```

We can use the `Get-VMQuestion` and `Set-VMQuestion` cmdlets to get a question from a virtual machine and then set the answer to that question.

With regard to managing resources on a VM, we can use the following cmdlets:

- `Get-VMResourceConfiguration`
- `Set-VMResourceConfiguration`

Using `Get-VMResourceConfiguration`, we can get the details of the resource configuration of a VM:

```
PS C:\> Get-VMResourceConfiguration -VM Test-1
```

VM	NumCpuShares	CpuSharesLevel	NumMemShares	MemSharesLevel
Test-1	1000	Normal	160	Normal

We can use the `Set-VMResourceConfiguration` cmdlet to make changes to the existing resource configuration of a VM:

```
PS C:\> Get-VM Test-1 | Get-VMResourceConfiguration | Set-VMResourceConfiguration -NumCpuShares 1500 -CpuSharesLevel Custom -MemSharesLevel High
VM             NumCpuShares   CpuSharesLevel   NumMemShares   MemSharesLevel
Test-1         1500           Custom           320            High
```

We can get the start policy of a VM and set the value for it using the following cmdlets:

- `Get-VMStartPolicy`
- `Set-VMStartPolicy`

As shown in the following example, we have changed the start delay for the `Test-1` VM from `120` to `60`:

```
PS C:\> Get-VMStartPolicy -VM Test-1

VM                         StartAction  StartDelay    StartOrder
--                         -----------  ----------    ----------
Test-1                     None         120           1


PS C:\> Get-VMStartPolicy -VM Test-1 | Set-VMStartPolicy -StartDelay 60

VM                         StartAction  StartDelay    StartOrder
--                         -----------  ----------    ----------
Test-1                     None         60            1
```

Managing VMware tools in a VM

This is the last subtopic in this topic. We can use the `Mount-Tools` cmdlet to mount the VMware tool's ISO image to a VM, whereas `Dismount-Tools` dismounts the image.

We can use `Update-Tools` to update the tools in a VM, and the `Wait-Tools` cmdlet is used to wait for the VMware tools on a VM to load.

Managing templates

One of the major aspects of managing a vSphere environment is managing templates. In any virtualized data center, invariably, there will be many templates that are maintained in it. In this section, we will check the PowerCLI cmdlets related to template management. Here is a list of the available cmdlets used for managing templates:

- `Get-Template`
- `Move-Template`
- `New-Template`
- `Remove-Template`
- `Set-Template`

Like all the other topics, in this topic too, we will start with getting a list of the available templates. We can do this using the Get-Template cmdlet:

```
PS C:\> Get-Template


Name

----

Template1


PS C:\> Get-Template -Location 'Lab Folder'


Name

----

Template1


PS C:\> Get-Template -Datastore NFS_SHARE


Name

----

Template1
```

In the preceding set of examples, we can use the Get-Template cmdlet to get a list of all the templates available in the environment, in a particular location or data center. We can also use this to get the details of a particular template as well.

Next let's create a new template from an existing virtual machine. We will use the New-Template cmdlet for this purpose:

```
PS C:\> $vm = Get-VM -Name Test-1


PS C:\> New-Template -VM $vm -Name Template2 -Datastore iSCSI-3 -Location
TestFolder


Name

----

Template2
```

In the preceding example, we created a new template with the name `Template2` from an existing `Test-1` VM and kept the template in the `iSCSI-3` datastore. We can use the same cmdlet to register an already existing template to a vCenter server.

We can use the `Move-Template` cmdlet to move a template from one location to another.

To convert an existing VM, we can use the `Set-VM` cmdlet:

```
PS C:\> Set-VM -VM Test-1 -ToTemplate -Confirm:$false


Name
----
Test-1
```

In the preceding example, we converted the `Test-1` VM into a template.

To rename an existing template, we can use the `Set-Template` cmdlet. We can use the same template to convert an existing template into a VM:

```
PS C:\> Set-Template -Template Test-1 -ToVM


Name                  PowerState Num CPUs MemoryGB
----                  ---------- -------- --------
Test-1                PoweredOff 1        0.250
```

In the preceding example, the `Test-1` template that we created in the earlier example has been converted back into a VM.

Managing OS customization specifications

In this topic, we will discuss how to manage OS customization specifications in a vSphere environment. We can use the following cmdlets to manage customization specifications:

- `Get-OSCustomizationSpec`
- `New-OSCustomizationSpec`
- `Remove-OSCustomizationSpec`
- `Set-OSCustomizationSpec`

To create a new guest OS customization specification, we can use the New-OSCustomizationSpec cmdlet. Using this cmdlet, we can specify the specification for both Windows and Linux VMs. To use it with Windows, there are certain mandatory parameters, which we need to specify. These are as follows:

- A name
- A domain or workgroup
- A FullName and OrgName

In the case of a Linux VM, only a name and domain name need to be specified.

We can use the -OSType parameter to mention whether the VM is a Windows or Linux type. This parameter accepts only Windows and Linux as valid values. The cmdlet and the output is shown in the following example:

```
PS C:\> New-OSCustomizationSpec -Name 'TestSpec1' -FullName `
'administrator' -OrgName 'lab' -Domain 'lab.com' -DomainUsername` 'user1'
-DomainPassword 'Passw0rd' -OSType Windows


Name    Description Type       OSType   LastUpdate            Server

----    ----------- ----       ------   ----------            ------

TestSpec1           Persistent Windows 7/6/2015 10:47:05 PM vcenter.lab.com
```

```
PS C:\> New-OSCustomizationSpec -Name 'TestSpec1' -FullName 'administrator' `
-OrgName 'lab' -Domain 'lab.com' -DomainUsername 'user1' -DomainPassword 'Passw0rd' -OSType Windows

Name                            Description Type        OSType  LastUpdate            Server
----                            ----------- ----        ------  ----------            ------
TestSpec1                                   Persistent  Windows 9/22/2015 11:42:1... vcenter.lab.com
```

Let's create another specification but this time for the Linux environment. The cmdlet for this is as follows:

```
PS C:\> New-OSCustomizationSpec -Name 'TestSpec2' -Domain ` 'lab.com' -
OSType Linux -DnsServer '192.168.1.39'
```

```
PS C:\> New-OSCustomizationSpec -Name 'TestSpec2' -Domain 'lab.com' -OSType Linux -DnsServer '192.168.1.39'
Name                            Description Type        OSType  LastUpdate            Server
----                            ----------- ----        ------  ----------            ------
TestSpec2                                   Persistent  Linux   9/22/2015 11:47:0... vcenter.lab.com
```

Note that we used the -DnsServer parameter to mention the DNS server details.

We can also use the -Type parameter to mention whether the specification is Persistent or NonPersistent.

Next let's apply this policy to a VM. To do this, we will use the `Set-VM` cmdlet:

```
PS C:\> Set-VM -VM Test-1 -OSCustomizationSpec TestSpec1 -Confirm:$false
Name                PowerState Num CPUs MemoryGB
----                ---------- -------- --------
Test-1              PoweredOff 1        0.250
```

We can use `Remove-OSCustomizationSpec` to remove an existing customization specification. To make changes to an existing specification, we can use the `Set-OSCustomizationSpec` cmdlet.

We can use the following cmdlets to add a network customization specification to a specified OS customization specification, and manage it:

- `Get-OSCustomizationNicMapping`
- `New-OSCustomizationNicMapping`
- `Remove-OSCustomizationNicMapping`
- `Set-OSCustomizationNicMapping`

For example, we can get the `Get-OSCustomizationNicMapping` cmdlet to get the details of an existing NIC customization:

```
PS C:\> Get-OSCustomizationNicMapping -OSCustomizationSpec TestSpec1


Position IPMode      IPAddress       DefaultGateway
-------- ------      ---------       --------------
       1 UseDhcp
```

We can use the `New-OSCustomizationNicMapping` cmdlet to make a custom specification for NIC. In the following example, we created a custom specification with a static IP, subnet mask, and default gateway set:

```
PS C:\> New-OSCustomizationNicMapping –OSCustomizationSpec "TestSpec1" –
IpMode UseStaticIP -IpAddress "192.168.1.100" –SubnetMask "255.255.255.0"
-DefaultGateway "192.168.1.1" –Dns "192.168.1.39"
WARNING: Parameter 'OSCustomizationSpec' is obsolete. This parameter no
longer accepts multiple values.


Position IPMode      IPAddress       DefaultGateway
-------- ------      ---------       --------------
       2 UseStaticIP 192.168.1.100   192.168.1.1
```

Managing the guest OS

In this category, we will discuss how to manage the guest OS of a VM using PowerCLI. To manage the different aspects of the guest OS, we can use the following cmdlets:

- Get-VMGuest
- Restart-VMGuest
- Stop-VMGuest
- Suspend-VMGuest
- Copy-VMGuestFile
- Get-VMGuestNetworkInterface
- Set-VMGuestNetworkInterface
- Get-VMGuestRoute
- New-VMGuestRoute
- Remove-VMGuestRoute
- Invoke-VMScript

We can use the Get-VMGuest cmdlet to get the guest operating system of the VM. Using the next three cmdlets, that is, Restart-VMGuest, Stop-VMGuest, and Suspend-VMGuest, we can control the power state of a VM guest operating system. The Get-VMGuest cmdlet gives the current status of a VM guest. Similarly, we can use the restart, stop, and suspend cmdlets to restart, stop, and suspend the state of a virtual machine:

```
PS C:\> Get-VMGuest "LAB AD"


State          IPAddress          OSFullName
-----          ---------          ----------
Running        {fe80::acd6:aa2f:... Microsoft Windows Server 2008 R2 (64-
bit)
```

Next we can use the Copy-VMGuestFile cmdlet to copy files to and from the guest OS of the specified virtual machine using VMware tools:

```
PS C:\> Copy-VMGuestFile -Source C:\test.txt -Destination C:\temp\ -VM
"LAB AD" -GuestToLocal -GuestUser Administrator -GuestPassword Vmware1!
```

Next the two `Get-VMGuestNetworkInterface` and `Set-VMGuestNetworkInterface`
cmdlets allow us to manage and configure the network configuration of the guest
OS of a VM. In the following example, the current network policy for the LAB AD
VM is set to use a static IP and the IP set is `192.168.1.150` with a subnet mask of
`255.255.255.0`. Note the following example:

```
PS C:\> Get-VMGuestNetworkInterface -VM 'Lab AD' -GuestUser `
Administrator -GuestPassword VMware1!
```

The output is as follows:

```
PS C:\> Get-VMGuestNetworkInterface -VM "Lab AD" -GuestUser Administrator -GuestPassword Vmware1!

VM            Name                       IP              IPPolicy   SubnetMask
--            ----                       --              --------   ----------
LAB AD        Local Area Connection      192.168.1.150   Static     255.255.255.0
LAB AD        isatap.{17DDE053-67F6-...                  Static
LAB AD        Local Area Connection* 11                  Static
```

We can use the `Set-VMGuestNetworkInterface` cmdlet to set the network of a VM
using VMware tools.

The `Get-VMGuestRoute`, `New-VMGuestRoute`, and `Remove-VMGuestRoute` cmdlets
allow us to manage the route for the network interface of a guest operating system
of a VM. In the following example, we can see the default gateway set for the
LAB AD VM:

```
PS C:\> Get-VMGuestRoute -VM "Lab AD" -GuestUser Administrator -GuestPassword Vmware1!

Interface        Destination       Netmask          Gateway
---------        -----------       -------          -------
192.168.1.150    0.0.0.0           0.0.0.0          192.168.1.1
127.0.0.1        127.0.0.0         255.0.0.0        On-link
127.0.0.1        127.0.0.1         255.255.255.255  On-link
127.0.0.1        127.255.255.255   255.255.255.255  On-link
192.168.1.150    192.168.0.0       255.255.252.0    On-link
192.168.1.150    192.168.1.150     255.255.255.255  On-link
192.168.1.150    192.168.3.255     255.255.255.255  On-link
127.0.0.1        224.0.0.0         240.0.0.0        On-link
192.168.1.150    224.0.0.0         240.0.0.0        On-link
127.0.0.1        255.255.255.255   255.255.255.255  On-link
192.168.1.150    255.255.255.255   255.255.255.255  On-link
```

With the help of the last `Invoke-VMScript` cmdlet, we can remotely run a script
in the operating system, in the virtual machine. In the following example, we
are remotely executing the `Dir C:\` command in the LAB AD VM to get a list of
directories and files in the C drive:

```
PS C:\> Invoke-VMScript -VM 'Lab AD' -ScriptText 'Dir C:\' `
-GuestUser Administrator -GuestPassword Vmware1!
```

The output is as follows:

```
PS C:\> Invoke-VMScript -VM "LAB AD" -ScriptText "Dir C:\" -GuestUser Administrator -GuestPassword Vmware1!

ScriptOutput
---------------------------------------------------------------------------------------|

    Directory: C:\


  Mode                LastWriteTime     Length Name
  ----                -------------      ------ ----
  d----      7/14/2009    8:50 AM              PerfLogs
  d-r--      5/27/2015    5:58 AM              Program Files
  d-r--      3/13/2015    9:58 PM              Program Files (x86)
  d----      5/27/2015    5:55 AM              temp
  d-r--      3/14/2015    9:53 AM              Users
  d----      5/27/2015    6:10 AM              Windows
  -a---      5/27/2015    6:07 AM         1024 .rnd
  -a---      5/27/2015    5:55 AM            0 test.txt


---------------------------------------------------------------------------------------
```

We can use the same cmdlet to remotely execute any PowerShell script or BAT script in the guest VM. For more details, check out the help for this cmdlet.

Managing vApps

So far, we have worked with creating and managing the different aspects of a virtual machine. In this section, I am going to discuss how to manage vApps in a vSphere environment and also import or export OVF or OVA VMs.

We can use the Get-OvfConfiguration cmdlet to get and control the required parameters of an OVF or OVA template.

First, let's check the Get-OvfConfiguration cmdlet to get the configuration of an OVF template:

```
PS C:\> $ovfPath = "E:\Virtual Machine\VMware-Identity-Appliance-2.0.0.0-1445146_OVF10.ova"

PS C:\> $ovfConfig = Get-OvfConfiguration -Ovf $ovfPath

PS C:\> $ovfConfig.ToHashTable() | FT -AutoSize

Name                                          Value
----                                          -----
vami.gateway.VMware_Identity_Appliance
varoot-password
vami.netmask0.VMware_Identity_Appliance
vami.hostname
vami.ip0.VMware_Identity_Appliance
vami.DNS.VMware_Identity_Appliance
NetworkMapping.Network 1
IpAssignment.IpProtocol
```

In *Chapter 9*, *Managing the vSphere API*, we will discuss how to modify these parameters in order to supply the values from the command line.

We can use the `Import-VApp` cmdlet to import an existing vApp:

```
PS C:\> $vmHost = Get-VMHost -Name ESXi1.lab.com
PS C:\> Import-VApp -Source "E:\Virtual Machine\Identity-Appliance-2-OVF.ova" -VMHost $vmHost

Name                    PowerState Num CPUs MemoryGB
----                    ---------- -------- --------
VMware_Identity_A...    PoweredOff 1        2.000
```

In the preceding example, we imported the existing OVA template into an ESXi host, `ESXi1.lab.com`.

Next, we will discuss how to manage vApps in a vSphere environment. We can use the following cmdlets to manage vApps:

* `Export-VApp`
* `Get-VApp`
* `Import-VApp`
* `Move-VApp`
* `New-VApp`
* `Remove-VApp`
* `Set-VApp`
* `Start-VApp`
* `Stop-VApp`

First, let's get a list of all the existing vApps:

```
PS C:\> Get-VApp

Name       Status   CpuSharesL CpuReserva CpuLimitMh MemSharesL MemReservationG    MemLimitGB
                    evel       tionMhz    z          evel       B
----       ------   ---------- ---------- ---------- ---------- ---------------    ----------
Test-vAPP  Stopped  Normal     0          -1         Normal     0.000              -1.000
```

We can see that there is already an existing vApp called `Test-vAPP`. Let's create a new one with the `New-VApp` cmdlet. The cmdlet is as follows:

```
PS C:\> New-VApp -Name Test-VApp2 -CpuLimitMhz 200 ` -CpuReservationMhz
100 -Location ESXi2.lab.com
```

The output is as follows:

```
PS C:\> New-VApp -Name Test-VApp-2 -CpuLimitMhz 200 -CpuReservationMhz 100 -Location ESXi2.lab.com

Name              Status     CpuSharesL CpuReserva CpuLimitMh MemSharesL MemReservationG      MemLimitGB
                             evel       tionMhz    z          evel       B
----              ------     ---------- ---------- ---------- ---------- ---------------      ----------
Test-VApp-2       Stopped    Normal     100        200        Normal     0.000                -1.000


PS C:\> Get-VApp

Name              Status     CpuSharesL CpuReserva CpuLimitMh MemSharesL MemReservationG      MemLimitGB
                             evel       tionMhz    z          evel       B
----              ------     ---------- ---------- ---------- ---------- ---------------      ----------
Test-VApp-2       Stopped    Normal     100        200        Normal     0.000                -1.000
Test-vAPP         Stopped    Normal     0          -1         Normal     0.000                -1.000
```

In the preceding example, we successfully created a vApp named `Test-VApp-2`.

We can make changes to an existing vApp using the `Set-VApp` cmdlet or move a vApp to another location using the `Move-VApp` cmdlet. To remove a vApp, we can use the `Remove-VApp` cmdlet. To power on a vApp, we can use the `Start-VApp` cmdlet; to power off a vApp, we can use the `Stop-VApp` cmdlet.

Lastly, to import a vApp, we can use the `Import-VApp` cmdlet; to export a vApp, we can use the `Export-VApp` cmdlet:

```
PS C:\> Export-VApp -VApp Test-VApp-2 -Destination "E:\"

Mode                LastWriteTime         Length Name
----                -------------         ------ ----
-a----          7/8/2015   1:09 AM          1340 Test-VApp-2.ovf
-a----          7/8/2015   1:09 AM            64 Test-VApp-2.mf
```

As shown earlier, we can simply use the `Import-VApp` cmdlet to import an OVF or OVA template:

```
PS C:\> Import-VApp -Source "E:\Test-VApp-2\Test-VApp-2.ovf" -VMHost ESXi2.lab.com

Name              Status     CpuSharesL CpuReserva CpuLimitMh MemSharesL MemReservationG      MemLimitGB
                             evel       tionMhz    z          evel       B
----              ------     ---------- ---------- ---------- ---------- ---------------      ----------
Test-VApp-2       Stopped    Normal     100        200        Normal     0.000                -1.000
```

In the preceding example, we successfully imported the previously exported template.

Summary

In this chapter, we discussed how to manage the different aspects of a virtual machine in a vSphere environment using PowerCLI. We started this chapter with a discussion on how to create and manage virtual machines. We then discussed how to modify a virtual machine using PowerCLI followed by a discussion on how to manage templates in a vSphere environment. Next we covered how to manage OS customization specifications and guest OS management using PowerCLI. Finally, we covered how to manage vApps in a vSphere environment.

In the next chapter, we will discuss how to implement security best practices using PowerCLI and Update Manager. Then, we will cover how to automate DR using PowerCLI and SRM. Finally, we will discuss how to manage vCloud Air workloads followed by a discussion on managing vRealize Operations Manager using PowerCLI.

Managing vSphere Security, SRM, vCloud Air, and vROps

So far, we have discussed how to install and configure ESXi servers and how to configure and manage networks and storage in a vSphere environment. Then we discussed logical constructs in a vCenter environment. In the previous chapter, we covered how to manage the different aspects of a virtual machine, thus making life easier for the virtual administrator. In this chapter, we will discuss the additional aspects of a vCenter environment, which are as follows:

- The vSphere Security Hardening Guide
- Managing vSphere Update Manager
- Configuring firewall and services in an ESXi host
- Managing host profiles
- Managing vCenter Site Recovery Manager
- Managing vCloud Air
- Managing vRealize Operations Manager

We will start this chapter with a discussion on the Security Hardening Guide in a vSphere environment.

The vSphere Security Hardening Guide

The Security Hardening Guides provided by VMware gives a prescriptive guidance for end users on how to securely deploy and operate VMware products. Typically, vSphere guides are provided in a spreadsheet format. The document also includes script examples in various formats used for automating the security implementation. To get the latest version of the document, visit the website and download the version applicable to you from:

`https://www.vmware.com/security/hardening-guides.`

In this book, we will cover and discuss the vSphere 6.0 Hardening Guide. There is a total of 75 points regarding security best practices that should be checked and implemented. In *Chapter 12, Best Practices and Sample Scripts* we will provide you with a script that will cover all these points, and automate the environment to check for the points; if they are not set, the script will set them for you.

Note that many of the points can be set and checked using Update Manager and host profiles. So, here, we will cover Update Manager and revisit host profiles so that we can utilize these features.

Managing vSphere Update Manager

VMware vSphere Update Manager is a tool used to automate patch management and remove manual tracking and patching for ESXi hosts and virtual machines. We can use the following cmdlets to manage Update Manager in a vSphere environment using PowerCLI:

- `Attach-Baseline`
- `Detach-Baseline`
- `Get-Baseline`
- `Remove-Baseline`
- `Get-Compliance`
- `Download-Patch`
- `Get-Patch`
- `Stage-Patch`
- `Get-PatchBaseline`
- `New-PatchBaseline`
- `Set-PatchBaseline`
- `Remediate-Inventory`
- `Scan-Inventory`

If you take a look at the cmdlets, you will notice that there are few categories in which we can place the cmdlets. The first of these groups is the one that manages `Patch`. The following are the three cmdlets for this group:

- `Download-Patch`
- `Get-Patch`
- `Stage-Patch`

Using the first `Download-Patch` cmdlet, we can download the patches. This cmdlet initiates the download of new patches and returns a task object. To get the status of the task, we can use the `Get-Task` cmdlet:

```
PS C:\> $task = Download-Patch -RunAsync

PS C:\> Get-Task

Name                         State     % Complete Start Time  Finish Time
----                         -----     ---------- ----------  -----------
Download patch definitions   Success          100 11:39:19 PM 11:39:24 PM
```

As you can see in the preceding example, we downloaded the latest defined patches.

> We ran the patch download task asynchronously, so the console will not wait for the completion of the task; it will simply come back to the user prompt. The original task will continue in the background, while you can run other commands. So, I saved the task in a `$task` variable that will enable me to monitor the task for completion or kill the task if necessary. This is a handy way of doing and managing some background jobs.

Next let's check all the downloaded patches that are already available. We will use the `Get-Patch` cmdlet for this:

```
PS C:\> Get-Patch -Severity Critical -After "1/1/2015"

Name             Product         Release Date    Severity   Vendor Id
----             -------         ------------    --------   ---------
Updates esx-base {embeddedEsx... 2/26/2015 1:... Critical   ESXi500-201502401-BG
Updates esx-base {embeddedEsx... 1/22/2015 1:... Critical   ESXi550-201501401-BG
Updates esx-base {embeddedEsx... 4/7/2015 1:3... Critical   ESXi550-201504201-BG
Updates esx-base {embeddedEsx... 5/8/2015 1:3... Critical   ESXi550-201505401-BG
Updates tools-light {embeddedEsx... 5/8/2015 1:3... Critical   ESXi550-201505402-BG
Updates net-ixgbe {embeddedEsx... 5/8/2015 1:3... Critical   ESXi550-201505403-BG
Updates esx-base {embeddedEsx... 4/9/2015 1:3... Critical   ESXi600-201504401-BG
Updates esx-base {embeddedEsx... 7/7/2015 1:3... Critical   ESXi600-201507101-SG
Updates esx-base {embeddedEsx... 7/7/2015 1:3... Critical   ESXi600-201507401-BG
Updates tools-light {embeddedEsx... 7/7/2015 1:3... Critical   ESXi600-201507403-BG
Updates lsu-lsi-l... {embeddedEsx... 7/7/2015 1:3... Critical   ESXi600-201507406-BG
Updates lsu-lsi-m... {embeddedEsx... 7/7/2015 1:3... Critical   ESXi600-201507407-BG
```

In the preceding example, we checked the list for only those patches for which `Severity` is marked as `Critical` and that were available after January 01, 2015. You can use other available parameters to get a list restricted to the required patches.

The third cmdlet `Stage-Patch` will stage all the patches included in a baseline against a vmhost entity.

The next set of cmdlets will manage the patch baselines because we need to first create a patch baseline and then apply this patch base line as a baseline:

- `Get-PatchBaseline`
- `New-PatchBaseline`
- `Set-PatchBaseline`

We will create a new patch baseline using the patch list that we created earlier. The used cmdlets are follows:

```
PS C:\> $latest_patches = Get-Patch -Severity Critical `
-After '1/1/2015'


PS C:\> New-PatchBaseline -Dynamic -Name 'Latest Baseline' `
-IncludePatch $latest_patches -Description `
'Baseline including latest critical Patches'
```

The output will be as follows:

```
PS C:\> $latest_patches = Get-Patch -Severity Critical -After "1/1/2015"

PS C:\> New-PatchBaseline -Dynamic -Name "Latest Baseline" -IncludePatch $latest_patches -Description "Baseline including latest critical patches"

Name                Description          Id    Type   Targe LastUpdateTime        Numbe
                                                      tType                       rOfPa
                                                                                  tches
----                -----------          --    ----   ----- --------------        -----
Latest Baseline     Baseline includin... 10    Patch  Host  7/13/2015 12:08:2...  231
```

To get a list of the existing patch baseline, we can use the `Get-PatchBaseline` cmdlet:

```
PS C:\> Get-PatchBaseline

Name                Description          Id    Type   Targe LastUpdateTime        Numbe
                                                      tType                       rOfPa
                                                                                  tches
----                -----------          --    ----   ----- --------------        -----
Critical Host Pat... A predefined base... 1     Patch  Host  7/12/2015 9:41:32 PM  50
Non-Critical Host... A predefined base... 2     Patch  Host  7/12/2015 9:41:32 PM  181
New Custom Baseline                       7     Patch  Host  7/12/2015 10:12:0...  2
Latest Baseline     Baseline includin... 10    Patch  Host  7/13/2015 12:08:2...  231
```

We can use the `Set-PatchBaseline` cmdlet to make changes to an existing patch baseline. For details of this cmdlet, check out the help that is available.

Next we will attach these baselines to hosts. We will use the following set of cmdlets to manage the baselines:

- `Attach-Baseline`
- `Detach-Baseline`
- `Get-Baseline`
- `Remove-Baseline`

We will use the `Attach-Baseline` cmdlet to attach a previously created cmdlet to multiple hosts:

```
PS C:\> $latest_baseline = New-PatchBaseline -Dynamic -Name "Latest
Baseline" -IncludePatch $latest_patches -Description "Baseline including
latest critical patches"


PS C:\> Attach-Baseline -Baseline $latest_baseline -Entity esxi1.lab.com,
esxi2.lab.com
```

We can use the `Get-Baseline` cmdlet to get a list of the current available baselines:

```
PS C:\> Get-Baseline -Name "Latest Baseline"

Name              Description       Id    Type  Targe LastUpdateTime      Numbe
                                                tType                     rOfPa
                                                                          tches

----              -----------       --    ----  ----- --------------      -----
Latest Baseline   Baseline includin... 11  Patch Host  7/13/2015 12:24:4... 231
```

We can get a list of the attached baseline to a host using the same `Get-Baseline` cmdlet:

```
PS C:\> Get-VMHost -Name ESXi1.lab.com | Get-Baseline

Name              Description       Id    Type  Targe LastUpdateTime      Numbe
                                                tType                     rOfPa
                                                                          tches

----              -----------       --    ----  ----- --------------      -----
New Custom Baseline                 7     Patch Host  7/12/2015 10:12:0... 2
Latest Baseline   Baseline includin... 11  Patch Host  7/13/2015 12:24:4... 231
```

We can use the `Detach-Baseline` cmdlet to detach a baseline from an entity. In the following example, we have detached `"New Custom Baseline"` from the hosts:

```
PS C:\> $baseline = Get-Baseline -Name "New Custom Baseline"
PS C:\> Detach-Baseline -Entity Esxi1.lab.com, Esxi2.lab.com -Baseline $baseline -Confirm:$false
PS C:\> Get-VMHost -Name ESXi1.lab.com | Get-Baseline

Name                Description        Id    Type   Targe LastUpdateTime      Numbe
                                                    tType                     rOfPa
                                                                              tches
----                -----------        --    ----   ----- --------------      -----
Latest Baseline     Baseline includin... 11  Patch  Host  7/13/2015 12:24:4... 231
```

We can use the `Remove-Baseline` cmdlet to remove a baseline:

```
PS C:\> Remove-Baseline -Baseline $baseline -Confirm:$false
```

Next we will check the set of cmdlets and remediate an ESXi host against a baseline:

- `Get-Compliance`
- `Remediate-Inventory`
- `Scan-Inventory`

We can use the `Scan-Inventory` cmdlet to scan an entity against the baseline set against it:

```
PS C:\> Scan-Inventory -Entity ESXi1.lab.com
```

To get the compliance of an entity against the baseline set against it, we can use the `Get-Compliance` cmdlet:

```
PS C:\> Get-VMHost -Name ESXi1.lab.com | Get-Compliance

Entity                        Baseline                Status
------                        --------                ------
esxi1.lab.com                 Custom  Baseline        Incompatible
esxi1.lab.com                 Latest Baseline         NotCompliant
```

We can use the `Remediate-Inventory` cmdlet to remediate the entities in order to make them compliant.

We can use the `Stage-Patch` cmdlet to stage patches on the entities without actually applying them.

Configuring a firewall and services in an ESXi host

Configuring a firewall in any environment is one of the main security configurations that anyone does. To configure a firewall in a vSphere environment, we can use the following cmdlets:

- `Get-VMHostFirewallDefaultPolicy`
- `Set-VMHostFirewallDefaultPolicy`
- `Get-VMHostFirewallException`
- `Set-VMHostFirewallException`

Also, we can use the following cmdlets to manage the services in an ESXi host:

- `Get-VMHostService`
- `Restart-VMHostService`
- `Set-VMHostService`
- `Start-VMHostService`
- `Stop-VMHostService`

We will start with the firewall cmdlets, and then we will take a look at the services that control the cmdlets.

We can get a list and status of the services in an ESXi server using the
`Get-VMHostFirewallException` cmdlet:

```
PS C:\> Get-VMHostFirewallException -VMHost ESXi1.lab.com

Name                 Enabled IncomingPorts    OutgoingPorts     Protocols  ServiceRunning
----                 ------- -------------    -------------     ---------  --------------
CIM Server           True    5988                               TCP        True
CIM Secure Server    True    5989                               TCP        True
CIM SLP              True    427              427               UDP, TCP
DHCPv6               True    546              547               TCP, UDP
DVFilter             False   2222                               TCP
DVSSync              True    8301, 8302       8302, 8301        UDP
HBR                  True                     31031, 44046      TCP
IKED                 False   500              500               UDP
NFC                  True    902              902               TCP
WOL                  True                     9                 UDP
Active Directory All False                    88, 123, 13...    UDP, TCP
Virtual SAN Clust... False   12345, 23451     12345, 23451      UDP
DHCP Client          True    68               68                UDP
DNS Client           True    53               53                UDP, TCP
esxupdate            False                    443               TCP
Fault Tolerance      True    8100, 8200,...   80, 8100, 8...    TCP, UDP
vSphere High Avai... True    8182             8182              TCP, UDP   True
FTP Client           False   20               21                TCP
gdbserver            False   1000-9999, ...                     TCP
httpClient           False                    80, 443           TCP
Software iSCSI Cl... True                     3260              TCP
iofiltervp           False   9080                               TCP
NSX Distributed L... False   6999             6999              UDP
nfs41Client          False                    2049              TCP
NFS Client           True                     0-65535           TCP
NTP Client           False                    123               UDP        False
rabbitmqproxy        True                     5671              TCP
Virtual SAN Trans... False   2233             2233              TCP
VM serial port co... False   23, 1024-65535   0-65535           TCP
SNMP Server          True    161                                UDP        False
SSH Client           False                    22                TCP
SSH Server           True    22                                 TCP
syslog               False                    514, 1514         UDP, TCP
vCenter Update Ma... True                     80, 9000-9100     TCP
vMotion              True    8000             8000              TCP
VM serial port co... False                    0-65535           TCP
vSphere Web Client   True    902, 443                           TCP
vprobeServer         False   57007                              TCP        False
VMware vCenter Agent True                     902               UDP        True
vsanvp               True    8080             8080              TCP
vvold                False                    0-65535           TCP
vSphere Web Access   True    80                                 TCP
```

We can get a selective list as well; for example, to get a list of enabled services,
we can use the same cmdlet with the `-Enabled` parameter:

PS C:\> Get-VMHostFirewallException -VMHost ESXi1.lab.com -Enabled:$true

We can use the `Set-VMHostFirewallException` cmdlet to set the exception.

In the following example, we used this cmdlet to enable an exception for SSH:

```
PS C:\> Get-VMHostFirewallException -VMHost ESXi1.lab.com | Where { $_.Name.StartsWith("SSH")}

Name              Enabled IncomingPorts OutgoingPorts Protocols ServiceRunning
----              ------- ------------- ------------- --------- --------------
SSH Client        False                 22            TCP
SSH Server        True    22                          TCP


PS C:\> $SSHException = Get-VMHostFirewallException -VMHost ESXi1.lab.com | Where { $_.Name.StartsWith('SSH')}

PS C:\> $SSHException | Set-VMHostFirewallException -Enabled $true

Name              Enabled IncomingPorts OutgoingPorts Protocols ServiceRunning
----              ------- ------------- ------------- --------- --------------
SSH Client        True                  22            TCP
SSH Server        True    22                          TCP
```

To get the default firewall policy for a host, we can use the
Get-VMHostFirewallDefaultPolicy cmdlet:

```
PS C:\> Get-VMHostFirewallDefaultPolicy -VMHost ESXi1.lab.com


IncomingEnabled OutgoingEnabled

--------------- ---------------

False           False
```

To change the default firewall policy, we can use the
Set-VMHostFirewallDefaultPolicy cmdlet.

Next we will check the cmdlets that we can use to manage the services in an
ESXi host. We can use the Get-VMHostService cmdlet to get a list of the available
services in the host:

```
PS C:\> Get-VMHostService -VMHost ESXi1.lab.com

Key              Label                         Policy   Running   Required
---              -----                         ------   -------   --------
DCUI             Direct Console UI             on       True      False
TSM              ESXi Shell                    off      False     False
TSM-SSH          SSH                           on       False     False
lbtd             Load-Based Teaming Daemon     on       True      False
lwsmd            Active Directory Service      off      False     False
ntpd             NTP Daemon                    off      False     False
pcscd            PC/SC Smart Card Daemon       off      False     False
sfcbd-watchdog   CIM Server                    on       True      False
snmpd            SNMP Server                   on       False     False
vmsyslogd        Syslog Server                 on       True      True
vmware-fdm       vSphere High Availability A...on       True      False
vprobed          VProbe Daemon                 off      False     False
vpxa             VMware vCenter Agent          on       True      False
xorg             X.Org Server                  on       False     False
```

To get a selective list of services, we can use further queries. For example, to get a list of all the running services, we can use the following cmdlet:

```
PS C:\> Get-VMHostService -VMHost ESXi1.lab.com | Where {$_.Running -eq "True"}

Key                    Label                            Policy    Running  Required
---                    -----                            ------    -------  --------
DCUI                   Direct Console UI                on        True     False
lbtd                   Load-Based Teaming Daemon        on        True     False
sfcbd-watchdog         CIM Server                       on        True     False
vmsyslogd              Syslog Server                    on        True     True
vmware-fdm             vSphere High Availability A...   on        True     False
vpxa                   VMware vCenter Agent             on        True     False
```

We can change the status of a service using the `Set-VMHostService` cmdlet:

```
PS C:\> Get-VMHostService -VMHost ESXi1.lab.com | Where {$_.Key -eq "ntpd"} | Set-VMHostService -Policy "Automatic"

Key           Label                    Policy       Running   Required
---           -----                    ------       -------   --------
ntpd          NTP Daemon               automatic    False     False
```

We can use the `Start-VMHostService` and `Stop-VMHostService` cmdlets to start or stop a service:

```
PS C:\> $vmHostService = Get-VMHostService -VMHost ESXi1.lab.com | Where { $_.Key -eq "ntpd"}

PS C:\> Stop-VMHostService -HostService $vmHostService -Confirm:$false

Key           Label                    Policy       Running   Required
---           -----                    ------       -------   --------
ntpd          NTP Daemon               on           False     False


PS C:\> Start-VMHostService -HostService $vmHostService -Confirm:$false

Key           Label                    Policy       Running   Required
---           -----                    ------       -------   --------
ntpd          NTP Daemon               on           True      False
```

Also, we can use the `Restart-VMHostService` cmdlet to restart a service.

Managing host profiles

In *Chapter 3*, *Deploying vSphere Hosts* we touched upon host profile concepts. In this section, we will go more in-depth on the topic. To manage host profiles, we can use the following cmdlets:

- `Export-VMHostProfile`
- `Get-VMHostProfile`

- Get-VMHostProfileRequiredInput

- Import-VMHostProfile

- Invoke-VMHostProfile

- New-VMHostProfile

- Remove-VMHostProfile

- Set-VMHostProfile

- Test-VMHostProfileCompliance

We have already checked how we can utilize the New-VMHostProfile, Get-VMHostProfile, and Invoke-VMHostProfile cmdlets.

Here is a set of examples to show you the preceding cmdlets:

```
PS C:\> Export-VMHostProfile -Profile "Configuration-Profile" -FilePath C:\

Mode                LastWriteTime         Length Name
----                -------------         ------ ----
-a----       7/23/2015   10:44 PM        1174979 Configuration-Profile.vpf


PS C:\> Remove-VMHostProfile -Profile "Configuration-Profile" -Confirm:$false

PS C:\> Get-VMHostProfile

PS C:\> Import-VMHostProfile -FilePath C:\Configuration-Profile.vpf -Name "Host-Profile"

Name                            Description
----                            -----------
Host-Profile


PS C:\> Get-VMHostProfile

Name                            Description
----                            -----------
Host-Profile


PS C:\> Set-VMHostProfile -Profile "Host-Profile" -Description "Custom Host Profile"

Name                            Description
----                            -----------
Host-Profile                    Custom Host Profile


PS C:\> Get-VMHostProfile

Name                            Description
----                            -----------
Host-Profile                    Custom Host Profile
```

Here are the explanations of the preceding cmdlets.

In the first `Export-VMHostProfile` cmdlet, we are taking a backup of the profile `Configuration-Profile` in the C drive. Note the extension of the profile; it is saved as a `.vpf` file.

In the second cmdlet, we are removing an existing profile `Configuration-Profile` using the `Remove-VMHostProfile` cmdlet. Next we run the `Get-VMHostProfile` cmdlet to check whether the profile was actually deleted or not.

In the next cmdlet, we are importing an existing profile from a file stored earlier in the local directory. But this time, we are importing it by another name, **Host-Profile**. We are using the `Import-VMHostProfile` cmdlet for this purpose.

Next we are again checking the available profiles using the `Get-VMHostProfile` cmdlet.

Finally, we are using the `Set-VMHostProfile` cmdlet to make changes to the existing cmdlet.

Next, we will utilize `Test-VMHostProfileCompliance` to test the compliance against an entity:

```
PS C:\> Test-VMHostProfileCompliance -Profile 'Host-Profile'
PS C:\> Test-VMHostProfileCompliance -VMHost ESXi1.lab.com
```

The output is as follows:

```
PS C:\> Test-VMHostProfileCompliance -Profile "Host-Profile"

IncomplianceElementList
-----------------------
{option["key-vim-profile-host-OptionProfile-Misc_HeartbeatPanicTimeout"]-optionFixed:Option Misc.HeartbeatPanicTimeou...
{option["key-vim-profile-host-OptionProfile-Misc_HeartbeatPanicTimeout"]-optionFixed:Option Misc.HeartbeatPanicTimeou...


PS C:\> Test-VMHostProfileCompliance -VMHost ESXi1.lab.com

IncomplianceElementList
-----------------------
{option["key-vim-profile-host-OptionProfile-Misc_HeartbeatPanicTimeout"]-optionFixed:Option Misc.HeartbeatPanicTimeou...
```

We are checking the compliance of an entity using this cmdlet. Note that I am saying an "entity" here, as I can check the compliance of the profile (we did this earlier). It will show you the compliance status of all the hosts attached to the profile. Or we can check the compliance directly for an ESXi host, as we did in the second command. We can apply the profile where it is not compliant to the `Invoke-VMHostProfile` cmdlet. You can refer to *Chapter 3, Deploying vSphere Hosts*, for more details.

Managing vCenter Site Recovery Manager

Here, we will discuss how we can use PowerCLI cmdlets to manage Site Recovery Manager. To manage SRM, we can use two cmdlets: `Connect-SrmServer` and `Disconnect-SrmServer`.

To connect to an SRM server, we first need to connect to a vCenter server where SRM is already configured and attached to the vCenter server. Once we connect to the vCenter server using the `Connect-VIServer` cmdlet, we can connect to the SRM server using the `Connect-SrmServer` cmdlet:

```
PS C:\> $srmServer = Connect-SrmServer
PS C:\> $srmServer
```

```
Name                     Port  User
----                     ----  ----
192.168.12.20            9007  lab.com\Administrator
```

To disconnect from an SRM server, we can use the `Disconnect-SrmServer` cmdlet. To get more information from the SRM server and to manage further aspects, we need to access the extension data information. We will go into details of how we can access this information. Here, we will just cover how we can get the information; details of the explanation will be provided in the next chapter.

To get the details of a paired site, we can use the following cmdlet:

```
PS C:\> $srmServer.ExtensionData.GetPairedSite() | FL
```

```
Name   : TEST-DR
Uuid   : 494351b7-9789-4a97-aaf2-720889cf2122
VcHost : 192.168.19.11
VcPort : 80
```

To get the site name, we can use the following option:

```
PS C:\> $srmServer.ExtensionData.GetSiteName()
TEST-DC
```

To get a list of the protection groups, we can utilize the following option:

```
$srmApi=$srmServer.ExtensionData
$protectionGroups=$srmApi.Protection.ListProtectionGroups()
PS C:\> $protectionGroups | Foreach{ $_.GetInfo() } | FL
```

```
Name        : PG-DATABASE
Description : Database Cluster
Type        : san


Name        : PG-TEST
Description :
Type        : san


Name        : PG-WEB
Description : WEB CLUSTER
Type        : san
```

We can use similar options to get a list of protected VMs, recovery groups, and other information. We will discuss these topics in detail in the next chapter.

Managing vCloud Air

In this section, we will discuss how to manage vCloud Air using PowerCLI cmdlets. Earlier, we had vCloud director available as a cloud solution, and we could use vSphere PowerCLI for tenants to manage the in-house vCloud director environments. With the availability of the vCloud Air and vCloud Air network environments and discontinuity of a standalone vCloud director environment, we now have updated PowerCLI cmdlets with which we can directly manage the workload hosted in the vCloud Air environment. To manage the vCloud Air environment, at the time of the PowerCLI installation, we need to install the `vCloud Air/vCD PowerCLI` module as well. It is not installed by default:

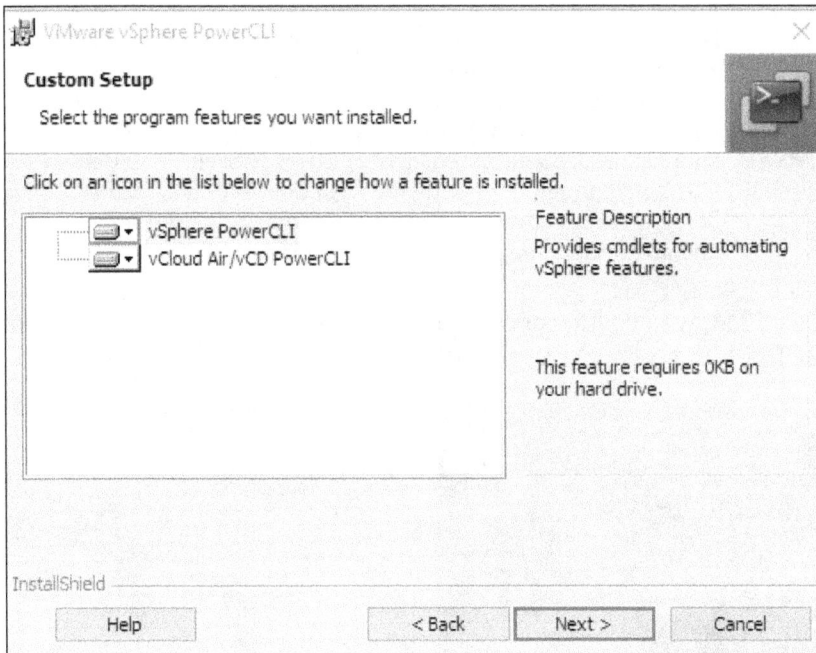

The vCloud Air/vCD PowerCLI module has two different modules: VMware.VimAutomation.Cloud and VMware.VimAutomation.PCloud. To get a list of the available cmdlets in these two modules, we can use the Get-Command cmdlet:

```
PowerCLI C:\> Get-Command -Module Vmware.VimAutomation.PCloud | Select
Name

Name
----
Connect-PIServer
Disconnect-PIServer
Get-PIComputeInstance
Get-PIDatacenter
```

Coming back to these modules, the VMware.VimAutomation.PCloud module is a new module that enables us to connect to a vCloud Air environment and locate the resources hosted in vCloud Air. The cloud module is the refined version of vSphere PowerCLI for tenants and helps us manage the resources in the vCloud director environment. It also supports all vCloud Air networks. So, in order to manage vCloud Air resources, we need to first connect to a vCloud Air environment using the PCloud module and then use the Cloud module cmdlets to manage the resources.

> Note that, as of PowerCLI 6.0 R1, we do not have a cmdlet available to manage an on-demand-based environment in vCloud Air. The cmdlets support only a subscription-based environment. Currently, work is going on cmdlets that will support on-demand-based environments as well. Alan Renouf was kind enough to provide me with the cmdlets currently being worked on; these support an on-demand environment, and are going to be part of a future release.

So, let's start. First, we need to connect to the vCloud Air environment. For this, we will use the `Connect-PIServer` cmdlet:

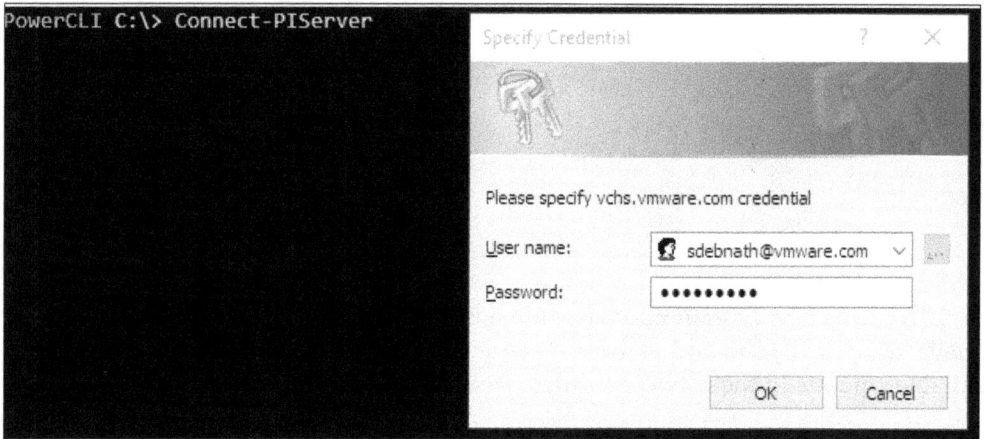

```
PowerCLI C:\> Connect-PIServer
```

Note that I did not have to provide details of the server because it already knows that it needs to connect to `vchs.vmware.com`. Also, since I did not provide any user ID and password, it prompted me for the ID and password. Otherwise, we can pass the ID and password from the command line as well. Also, we can use the `New-VICredentialStoreItem` cmdlet to store the credentials in a file. Next time, when we try to connect to the server and do not provide a credential, it searches in the file; once a match is found, it uses that password to connect to the server:

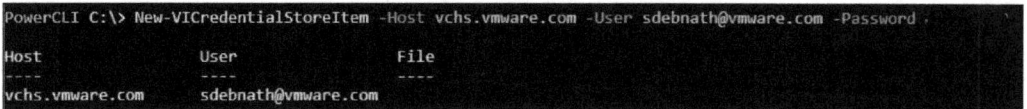

```
PowerCLI C:\> New-VICredentialStoreItem -Host vchs.vmware.com -User sdebnath@vmware.com -Password ·

Host                 User                    File
----                 ----                    ----
vchs.vmware.com      sdebnath@vmware.com
```

The next time I tried to connect, it simply got connected and returned the details:

```
PowerCLI C:\> Connect-PIServer
```

```
Name                           User
----                           ----
vchs.vmware.com                sdebnath@vmware.com
```

So, now we are connected to the server. Next, we need to get a list of the available datacenters using the `Get-PIDatacenter` cmdlet. Note that `Get-PIDatacenter` works only with a subscription-based environment and will not work in an on-demand environment.

Since I have an on-demand account and I am using the updated module, I need to connect to the on-demand account using the `-vCA` parameter:

```
PowerCLI C:\> Connect-PIServer -vCA
```

```
Name                           User
----                           ----
vca.vmware.com                 sdebnath@vmware.com
```

Note that the server also changes; now it is vca.vmware.com instead of the default vchs.vmware.com.

Since I am connected to the on-demand environment, I need to get a list of the compute environments available for me. Note that earlier I provided you with a list of available cmdlets with the `PCloud` module. Since this is an updated module that I am using, this module provides a new `Get-PIComputeInstance` cmdlet, which works with on-demand accounts and returns a list of the available computer resources. For our purpose, I will use this cmdlet:

```
PowerCLI C:\> Get-PIComputeInstance

Region                         ServiceGroup              Name
------                         ------------              ----
jp-japanwest-1-10.vchs.vmware.com   M879839286           Virtual Private Cloud OnDemand
```

In the list, I can see that I have resources from Japan datacenter. Next we need to connect to this server. We will use the `Connect-CIServer` cmdlet:

```
PowerCLI C:\> $CI | Connect-CIServer

Name                      User                   Org
----                      ----                   ---
https://jp-japanwest-1-10.v...  sdebnath@vmware.com    5e6cbe38-2e04-4607-a2b9-2dd...
```

Since we are connected to the vCD server, we can use all the cmdlets available in the cloud module to manage the environment. Remember that, since we are connected as a tenant, we cannot use the cmdlets for system admin.

Another point to note is that all the cmdlets have an equivalent alias to manage the vCD environment. For example, Get-CIVM has an alias of Get-PIVM:

```
PowerCLI C:\> Get-Alias -Definition Get-CIVM


CommandType     Name            Version     Source
-----------     ----            -------     ------

Alias           Get-PIVM        6.0.0.0     VMware.VimAutomation.Cloud
```

This is because all the old vCD cmdlets are still available, so you can utilize your existing PowerShell scripts. If you are writing a new script, you can use the PI version instead of CI so that it would be evident that you are working with vCloud Air.

Now, let's take a look at the available vApps and their respective VMs in the vCD server:

```
PowerCLI C:\> Get-CIVApp

Name                    Enabled InMaintenanceMode   Owner
----                    ------- -----------------   -----
Test1-VApp              True    False               sdebnath@vmware.com


PowerCLI C:\> Get-CIVM

Name            Status              GuestOSFullName             CpuCount MemoryGB
----            ------              ---------------             -------- --------
Test1           PoweredOff          CentOS 4/5/6 (32-bit)       1        2.000
```

First, let's take a look at the templates available for me in this environment:

```
PowerCLI C:\> Get-CIVAppTemplate

Name                       Status      Owner           StorageUsedGB
----                       ------      -----           -------------
CentOS63-32bit             Resolved    catalog_admin   20.000
CentOS63-32bit-JP          Resolved    catalog_admin   20.000
CentOS63-64bit             Resolved    catalog_admin   20.000
CentOS63-64bit-JP          Resolved    catalog_admin   20.000
CentOS64-32bit             Resolved    catalog_admin   20.000
CentOS64-32bit-JP          Resolved    catalog_admin   20.000
CentOS64-64bit             Resolved    catalog_admin   20.000
CentOS64-64bit-JP          Resolved    catalog_admin   20.000
UbuntuServer12.04LTS(amd642...  Resolved   catalog_admin   10.000
UbuntuServer12.04LTS(i38620...  Resolved   catalog_admin   10.000
W2K12-STD-64BIT            Resolved    catalog_admin   40.000
W2K12-STD-64BIT-JP         Resolved    catalog_admin   40.000
W2K12-STD-R2-64BIT         Resolved    catalog_admin   40.000
W2K12-STD-R2-64BIT-JP      Resolved    catalog_admin   40.000
W2K8-STD-R2-64BIT          Resolved    catalog_admin   40.000
W2K8-STD-R2-64BIT-JP       Resolved    catalog_admin   40.000
```

Before we create anything else, let's first take a look at the organization's available VDCs in the environment that I created:

```
PowerCLI C:\> Get-OrgVdc

Name    Enabled CpuUsedGHz      MemoryUsedGB    StorageUsedGB    AllocationModel
----    ------- ----------      ------------    -------------    ---------------
VDC1    True    0.00 (0.0%)     0.000 (0.0%)    22.000 (0.5%)    PayAsYouGo
VDC2    True    0.00 (0.0%)     0.000 (0.0%)    0.000 (0.0%)     PayAsYouGo
```

Since we got two organization VDCs, we can create new vApps or VMs in these VDCs. We will use the `New-PIVApp` cmdlet for this:

```
PowerCLI C:\> $Template = Get-PIVAppTemplate -Name 'CentOS63-32bit-JP'
PowerCLI C:\> $OrgVdc = Get-OrgVdc -Name 'VDC2'
PowerCLI C:\> New-PIVApp -Name 'Test-vApp' -Description "This vApp is created from PowerCLI" -OrgVdc $OrgVdc -VAppTemplate $Template

Name        Enabled InMaintenanceMode   Owner
----        ------- -----------------   -----
Test-vApp   True    False               sdebnath@vmware.com
```

Since we have created the vApp, now let's check the cmdlets available to manage a VM. Here is a list of cmdlets that are used to manage a VM or VM guest:

- `Get-PIVM`
- `New-PIVM`
- `Restart-PIVM`
- `Restart-PIVMGuest`
- `Start-PIVM`
- `Stop-PIVM`
- `Stop-PIVMGuest`
- `Suspend-PIVM`

Before we create a new VM, let's check the available VM templates in the environment:

```
PowerCLI C:\> Get-PIVMTemplate

Name                              Status       GuestOSFullName                          CpuCount MemoryGB
----                              ------       ---------------                          -------- --------
CentOS63-32bit                    PoweredOff   CentOS 4/5/6 (32-bit)                    1        1
CentOS63-32bit-JP                 PoweredOff   CentOS 4/5/6 (32-bit)                    1        1
CentOS63-64bit                    PoweredOff   CentOS 4/5/6/7 (64-bit)                  1        1
CentOS63-64bit-JP                 PoweredOff   CentOS 4/5/6/7 (64-bit)                  1        1
CentOS64-32bit                    PoweredOff   CentOS 4/5/6 (32-bit)                    1        1
CentOS64-32bit-JP                 PoweredOff   CentOS 4/5/6 (32-bit)                    1        1
CentOS64-64bit                    PoweredOff   CentOS 4/5/6/7 (64-bit)                  1        1
CentOS64-64bit-JP                 PoweredOff   CentOS 4/5/6/7 (64-bit)                  1        1
Ubuntu Server 12.04 LTS (am...    PoweredOff   Ubuntu Linux (64-bit)                    1        1
Ubuntu Server 12.04 LTS (i3...    PoweredOff   Ubuntu Linux (32-bit)                    1        1
W2K12-STD-64BIT                   PoweredOff   Microsoft Windows Server 2012 (64-bit)   1        4
W2K12-STD-64BIT-JP                PoweredOff   Microsoft Windows Server 2012 (64-bit)   1        4
W2K12-STD-R2-64BIT                PoweredOff   Microsoft Windows Server 2012 (64-bit)   1        4
W2K12-STD-R2-64BIT-JP             PoweredOff   Microsoft Windows Server 2012 (64-bit)   1        4
W2K8-STD-R2-64BIT                 PoweredOff   Microsoft Windows Server 2008 R2 (64-... 1        2
W2K8-STD-R2-64BIT-JP              PoweredOff   Microsoft Windows Server 2008 R2 (64-... 1        4
```

Let's create a new VM using one of these templates:

```
PowerCLI C:\> $VmTemplate = Get-PIVMTemplate -Name 'CentOS63-32bit-JP'
PowerCLI C:\> Get-PIVApp "Test-vApp" | New-PIVM -Name "Test-VM1" -VMTemplate $VmTemplate

Name        Status       GuestOSFullName          CpuCount MemoryGB
----        ------       ---------------          -------- --------
Test-VM1    PoweredOff   CentOS 4/5/6 (32-bit)    1        1.000
```

Since we created the new VM, let's power on the vApp. We will do this using the `Start-PIVApp` cmdlet:

```
PowerCLI C:\> Start-PIVApp Test-vApp

Name                    Enabled  InMaintenanceMode  Owner
----                    -------  -----------------  -----
Test-vApp               True     False              sdebnath@vmware.com


PowerCLI C:\> Get-PIVM Test-VM1

Name         Status      GuestOSFullName          CpuCount  MemoryGB
----         ------      ---------------          --------  --------
Test-VM1     PoweredOn   CentOS 4/5/6 (32-bit)    1         1.000
```

To manage the network in the environment, we can use the following cmdlets:

```
PowerCLI C:\> Get-Command -Module Vmware.VimAutomation.Cloud | Where {$_.
Name.Contains("Network")} | Select Name


Name
----

Get-PINetworkAdapter

Get-PIVAppNetwork

New-PIVAppNetwork

Remove-PIVAppNetwork

Set-PINetworkAdapter

Set-PIVAppNetwork

Get-CINetworkAdapter

Get-OrgVdcNetwork

Set-OrgNetwork
```

In the preceding list, I have removed the original CI cmdlets and kept only PI cmdlets. We can utilize these cmdlets to manage the different aspects of networking in the environment. For example, to get a list of the available networks in an Org VDC, we can utilize the `Get-OrgVdcNetwork` cmdlet:

```
PowerCLI C:\> Get-OrgVdcNetwork

Name                      OrgVdc                       DefaultGateway  NetworkType
----                      ------                       --------------  -----------
default-routed-network    VDC2                         192.168.109.1   Routed
default-routed-network    VDC1                         192.168.109.1   Routed
```

In the preceding example, we can see that we have two default routed networks in the two Org VDCs.

You can utilize the rest of the cmdlets as per your requirement or use your old scripts without modifying them.

Finally, to disconnect from VDC, we will use `Disconnect-CIServer`, `Disconnect-PIComputeInstance`, and `Disconnect-PIServer`, in that order:

```
PowerCLI C:\> Disconnect-CIServer

Confirm
Are you sure you want to perform this action?
Performing the operation "Disconnect CIServer" on target "User: sdebnath@vmware.com, Server: https://jp-japanwest-1-10.vchs.vmware.com/api/compute, Port:
443".
[Y] Yes  [A] Yes to All  [N] No  [L] No to All  [S] Suspend  [?] Help (default is "Y"): y
PowerCLI C:\> Disconnect-PIComputeInstance

Confirm
Are you sure you want to perform this action?
Performing the operation "Disconnect CIServer" on target "User: sdebnath@vmware.com, Server: https://jp-japanwest-1-10.vchs.vmware.com/api/compute, Port:
443".
[Y] Yes  [A] Yes to All  [N] No  [L] No to All  [S] Suspend  [?] Help (default is "Y"): y
PowerCLI C:\> Disconnect-PIServer

Confirm
Are you sure you want to perform this action?
Performing the operation "Disconnect vCloud Air server" on target ""User: sdebnath@vmware.com, Server: https://vca.vmware.com/"".
[Y] Yes  [A] Yes to All  [N] No  [L] No to All  [S] Suspend  [?] Help (default is "Y"): y
```

Managing vRealize Operations Manager

By the time I finished writing the first draft of this book, PowerCLI Version 6.0 Release 2 came out. The major changes are listed here:

- The license snap-in has been converted into a module.

- vSphere Update Manager (VUM): This is used as a separate installable snap-in. This has been converted into a `VMware.VumAutomation` module and is included in the main installable.

- vRealize Operations Support. With this release, support for vRealize Operations is included.

- vCloud Air support for an on-demand environment is included in this release with the addition of a new cmdlet.

- Cmdlets are added to get more host hardware information.

- New cmdlets have been added to VASA, NFS 4.1, and VAIO filters.

There are other pretty interesting enhancements too. For a detailed coverage, visit the VMware official blog at `https://blogs.vmware.com/PowerCLI/2015/09/powercli-6-0-release-2-is-now-generally-available.html`.

In this topic, I plan to cover the vRealize Operations support in detail. As mentioned earlier, with this release there is support for vRealize Operations; currently, the support is only for vRealize Operations 6.0.3 and later.

To get the new release, you can download it from `https://my.vmware.com/group/vmware/details?downloadGroup=PCLI600R2&productId=491` and install it.

Once the installation is complete, import the module with the `Import-Module` cmdlet:

```
PS C:\> Import-Module VMware.VimAutomation.VROps
```

There are a total of 12 cmdlets that have been included in this release. We will cover the cmdlets one by one:

- `Connect-OMServer`
- `Disconnect-OMServer`
- `Set-OMAlert`
- `Get-OMAlert`
- `Get-OMAlertDefinition`
- `Get-OMAlertSubType`
- `Get-OMAlertType`
- `Get-OMRecommendation`
- `Get-OMResource`
- `Get-OMStat`
- `Get-OMStatKey`
- `Get-OMUser`

The first two cmdlets are related to connecting and disconnecting to an Operations Manager instance. To connect, we will use the `Connect-OMServer` cmdlet. As the name suggests, this cmdlet will connect us to an instance of the vRealize Operations Manager server:

```
PS C:\> Connect-OMServer 10.25.10.10 -user admin -Password Vmware1!
```

The output is as follows:

Note that I have covered the most basic authentication method. There are other ways to authenticate. For example, you can connect using the vCenter server authentication source, using the -AuthSource parameter:

```
PS C:\> Connect-OMServer -Server 'server_name' –AuthSource
'vCenterServer_name_in_vROps' -User 'vCenterServer_admin -Password 'user_
password'
```

The preceding cmdlet will allow you to use the vCenter server that the user imported from the connected vCenter server. There is an option to connect using an existing session or credential store. You can check the documentation for examples using the following command:

```
PS C:\> Get-Help Connect-OMServer –Examples
```

To disconnect from the active session, we can simply use the Disconnect-OMServer cmdlet. For example, in the following command, we can disconnect from the active connection, and I am disconnecting without any confirmation. For multiple connections, you can select the connection to disconnect using the hostname:

```
PS C:\> Disconnect-OMServer -Confirm:$false
```

The following set of cmdlets is related to alerts in the vROps environment. The cmdlets are as follows:

- Set-OMAlert
- Get-OMAlert
- Get-OMAlertDefinition
- Get-OMAlertSubType
- Get-OMAlertType

The first cmdlet that we will try from this set is Get-OMAlertType. This cmdlet will return a set of defined alert types in the vRealize Operations Manager server. For example, run the following command:

```
PS C:\> Get-OMAlertType
PS C:\> Get-OMAlertType -Name 'Network Alerts'
```

The output is as follows:

```
PS C:\> Get-OMAlertType

Name                                    Description
----                                    -----------
Application Alerts                      Application Alerts description
Virtualization/Hypervisor Alerts       Virtualization/Hypervisor Alerts description
Hardware (OSI) Alerts                   Hardware (OSI) Alerts description
Storage Alerts                         Storage Alerts description
Network Alerts                         Network Alerts description


PS C:\> Get-OMAlertType -Name 'Network Alerts'

Name                                    Description
----                                    -----------
Network Alerts                         Network Alerts description
```

The first example returned a list of all the alert types, whereas in the second example we used a specific query for only 'Network Alerts'.

The next cmdlet that we will check is Get-OMAlertSubType. As the name suggests, this cmdlet will get a list of alert subtypes from the specified server. If we run only the cmdlet, then we will get a list of all the subtypes in the environment. We can be specific by mentioning either the Name of a subtype or the AlertType parameter:

```
PS C:\> Get-OMAlertSubType -AlertType 'Application Alerts'
PS C:\> Get-OMAlertSubType -Name Performance
```

The output is as follows:

```
PS C:\> Get-OMAlertSubType -AlertType 'Application Alerts'

Name              Description                AlertType
----              -----------                ---------
Availability      Availability description   Application Alerts
Performance       Performance description    Application Alerts
Capacity          Capacity description       Application Alerts
Compliance        Compliance description     Application Alerts
Configuration     Configuration description  Application Alerts


PS C:\> Get-OMAlertSubType -Name Performance

Name              Description                AlertType
----              -----------                ---------
Performance       Performance description    Application Alerts
Performance       Performance description    Virtualization/Hypervisor Alerts
Performance       Performance description    Hardware (OSI) Alerts
Performance       Performance description    Storage Alerts
Performance       Performance description    Network Alerts
```

The next cmdlet is the `Get-OMAleterDefinition` cmdlet. Again, as the name suggests, this cmdlet will get the alerts defined in the environment. We can further drill-down the query using multiple parameters. Here are a few such examples that are pretty self-explanatory:

```
PS C:\> Get-OMAlertDefinition -Criticality Critical

PS C:\> Get-OMAlertDefinition –AdapterKind VMWARE –ResourceKind
VirtualMachine

PS C:\> Get-OMAlertDefinition -Name *storage*
```

The output is as follows:

```
PS C:\> Get-OMAlertDefinition -Name *storage*

Name                         Type                SubType         Criticality   Impact    WaitCycle CancelCycle
----                         ----                -------         -----------   ------    --------- -----------
vCenter storage data collec... Virtualization/Hy... Availability   SymptomBased  Health    1         1
Database storage capacity i... Application Alerts  Performance     SymptomBased  Health    1         1
Storage Lun Thin Provisione... Hardware (OSI) Al... Availability   Critical      Health    1         1
Storage Lun Thin Provisione... Hardware (OSI) Al... Availability   Warning       Health    1         1
Permanent Device Loss on a ... Hardware (OSI) Al... Availability   Critical      Health    1         1
Storage sensors are reporti... Hardware (OSI) Al... Availability   SymptomBased  Health    1         1
Datastore has lost connecti... Storage Alerts     Availability    Critical      Health    1         1
Datastore has one or more h... Storage Alerts     Availability    Immediate     Health    1         1
A storage device for a data... Storage Alerts     Availability    Critical      Health    1         1
```

Now it is time to have some real fun. We can get a list of all the alerts with the `Get-OMAlert` cmdlet. If the cmdlet is used as it is, then it will return all the alerts in the environment. For a big environment, this may be a big list. So, we can further drill-down our query to be more specific. For example, we can query for a particular resource with the following query:

```
PS C:\> Get-OMAlert -Resource Test-VM
```

The output is as follows:

```
PS C:\> Get-OMAlert -Resource

Name                             Type                Subtype       Impact  Criticality  Resource
----                             ----                -------       ------  -----------  --------
Virtual machine has unexpected... Virtualization/Hy... Performance   Health  Critical
Virtual machine has unexpected... Virtualization/Hy... Performance   Health  Critical
```

Here is an example of a set of such queries:

```
PS C:\> $resource = Get-OMResource -Name

PS C:\> $resource

Name                         Health  ResourceKind    Description
----                         ------  ------------    -----------
                             Green   HostSystem


PS C:\> Get-OMAlert -Resource $resource -Status Active

PS C:\> Get-OMAlert -Criticality Critical -Status Active

Name                    Type             Subtype      Impact  Criticality  Resource
----                    ----             -------      ------  -----------  --------
Datastore is projected to run ... Storage Alerts  Capacity     Risk    Critical
Datastore is projected to run ... Storage Alerts  Capacity     Risk    Critical
Virtual machine has chronic hi... Virtualization/Hy.. Performance  Risk    Critical
```

Again, to get details, take help of the Get-Help cmdlet.

The last one in this category is the Set-OMAlert cmdlet. As the name suggests, this cmdlet is used to configure and manage vRealize Operations Manager alerts.

If you check the cmdlet using Get-Help, you can see that the first example is as follows:

```
PS C:\>$alert = Get-OMAlert -Id 'ID'
PS C:\> Set-OMAlert -Alert $alert -Cancel
```

The question is: How do you get the ID? As mentioned in the preceding example, by default the ID of an alert is not shown. So, let's find out how we can get the ID of an alert. If we get the members of the object returned by the Get-OMAlert cmdlet, we can see that they have a property ID. We can also see from the following screenshot that the returned object is of the type VMware.VimAutomation.vROps.Impl. V1.OMAlertImpl. This will be helpful for you if you want to play with the APIs:

```
PS C:\> Get-OMAlert -Resource 10.25.114.242 | GM


    TypeName: VMware.VimAutomation.vROps.Impl.V1.OMAlertImpl

Name             MemberType  Definition
----             ----------  ----------
ConvertToVersion Method      T ConvertToVersion[T](), T VersionedObjectInterop.ConvertToVersion[T]()
Equals           Method      bool Equals(System.Object obj)
GetHashCode      Method      int GetHashCode()
GetType          Method      type GetType()
IsConvertableTo  Method      bool IsConvertableTo(type toType), bool VersionedObjectInterop.IsConvertableTo(type type)
ToString         Method      string ToString()
AlertDefinition  Property    VMware.VimAutomation.vROps.Types.V1.OMAlertDefinition AlertDefinition {get;}
AssignedUser     Property    VMware.VimAutomation.vROps.Types.V1.OMUser AssignedUser {get;}
CancelTime       Property    System.Nullable[datetime] CancelTime {get;}
Client           Property    VMware.VimAutomation.vROps.Interop.V1.OMClient Client {get;}
ControlState     Property    System.Nullable[VMware.VimAutomation.vROps.Types.V1.OMAlertControlState] ControlState {get;}
Criticality      Property    System.Nullable[VMware.VimAutomation.vROps.Types.V1.OMCriticality] Criticality {get;}
ExtensionData    Property    System.Object ExtensionData {get;}
Id               Property    string Id {get;}
Impact           Property    System.Nullable[VMware.VimAutomation.vROps.Types.V1.OMImpact] Impact {get;}
Name             Property    string Name {get;}
Resource         Property    VMware.VimAutomation.vROps.Types.V1.OMResource Resource {get;}
StartTime        Property    System.Nullable[datetime] StartTime {get;}
Status           Property    System.Nullable[VMware.VimAutomation.vROps.Types.V1.OMAlertStatus] Status {get;}
Subtype          Property    VMware.VimAutomation.vROps.Types.V1.OMAlertSubtype Subtype {get;}
SuspendedUntil   Property    System.Nullable[datetime] SuspendedUntil {get;}
Type             Property    VMware.VimAutomation.vROps.Types.V1.OMAlertType Type {get;}
Uid              Property    string Uid {get;}
UpdateTime       Property    System.Nullable[datetime] UpdateTime {get;}
```

So, let's assume that we want to cancel a critical alert that is related to a particular entity. So, let's first get all the critical alerts related to the entity:

```
PS C:\> $info = Get-OMAlert -Resource 192.168.1.20 -Criticality `
Critical
```

> Note that earlier we got a list of all the alerts related to a particular resource. Here, we are further narrowing down the list with the criticality parameter. This is will return only critical alerts. I would strongly recommend that you make a note of all the parameters. We can use them to further narrow down our search. For example, let's take a look at the following command:
>
> ```
> PS C:\> Get-OMAlert -Resource 192.168.1.20 -Criticality
> Critical` -Status Active -Impact Health
> ```
>
> Here, I am trying to find out all the alerts of the resource 192.168.1.20, which are critical, active, and impact health.
>
> This is pretty impressive! This is what you can do with all these parameters.

The $info cmdlet will give the following output:

```
PS C:\> $info

Name                              Type               Subtype       Impact  Criticality  Resource
----                              ----               -------       ------  -----------  --------
Host in a non-DRS cluster has ... Virtualization/Hy... Performance   Health  Critical     10.
Host in a non-DRS cluster has ... Virtualization/Hy... Performance   Health  Critical     10.
Host in a non-DRS cluster has ... Virtualization/Hy... Performance   Health  Critical     10.
Host in a non-DRS cluster has ... Virtualization/Hy... Performance   Health  Critical     10.
Host in a non-DRS cluster has ... Virtualization/Hy... Performance   Health  Critical     10.
Host in a non-DRS cluster has ... Virtualization/Hy... Performance   Health  Critical     10.
Host in a non-DRS cluster has ... Virtualization/Hy... Performance   Health  Critical     10.
Host in a non-DRS cluster has ... Virtualization/Hy... Performance   Health  Critical     10.
Host in a non-DRS cluster has ... Virtualization/Hy... Performance   Health  Critical     10.
Host in a non-DRS cluster has ... Virtualization/Hy... Performance   Health  Critical     10.
Host in a non-DRS cluster has ... Virtualization/Hy... Performance   Health  Critical     10.
Host in a non-DRS cluster has ... Virtualization/Hy... Performance   Health  Critical     10.
Host in a non-DRS cluster has ... Virtualization/Hy... Performance   Health  Critical     10.
```

Now, we can get the ID of the first alert by accessing the ID parameter:

```
PS C:\> $info[0].id
47c53bcb-2591-40e8-a748-c8b60e9ba9e8
```

We can now use this ID to get information about this particular alert only:

```
PS C:\> $alert = Get-OMAlert -Id '47c53bcb-2591-40e8-a748-c8b60e9ba9e8'
PS C:\> $alert
```

The output is as follows:

```
PS C:\> $alert = Get-OMAlert -Id '47c53bcb-2591-40e8-a748-c8b60e9ba9e8'
PS C:\> $alert

Name                              Type                Subtype        Impact  Criticality   Resource
----                              ----                -------        ------  -----------   --------
Host in a non-DRS cluster has ... Virtualization/Hy... Performance    Health  Critical
```

Next we will use the `Set-OMAlert` cmdlet to cancel this alert:

PS C:\> Set-OMAlert -Alert $alert -Cancel

The output is as follows:

```
PS C:\> Set-OMAlert -Alert $alert -Cancel

Name                              Type                Subtype        Impact  Criticality   Resource
----                              ----                -------        ------  -----------   --------
Host in a non-DRS cluster has ... Virtualization/Hy... Performance    Health  Critical
```

In the following example, we will take ownership of all the alerts by a particular name in a server:

PS C:\> Get-OMAlert -Id '47c53bcb-2591-40e8-a748-c8b60e9ba9e8'| Select Name

PS C:\> $alertname = 'Host in a non-DRS cluster has CPU contention caused by less than half of the virtual machines'

PS C:\> Set-OMAlert -Alert $alertname -Server 10.25.114.188 `
-TakeOwnership

The output is as follows:

```
PS C:\> Get-OMAlert -Id '47c53bcb-2591-40e8-a748-c8b60e9ba9e8'| Select Name

Name
----
Host in a non-DRS cluster has CPU contention caused by less than half of the virtual machines


PS C:\> $alertname = 'Host in a non-DRS cluster has CPU contention caused by less than half of the virtual machines'

PS C:\> Set-OMAlert -Alert $alertname -Server             -TakeOwnership

Name                              Type                Subtype        Impact  Criticality   Resource
----                              ----                -------        ------  -----------   --------
Host in a non-DRS cluster has ... Virtualization/Hy... Performance    Health  Critical
Host in a non-DRS cluster has ... Virtualization/Hy... Performance    Health  Immediate
Host in a non-DRS cluster has ... Virtualization/Hy... Performance    Health  Critical
Host in a non-DRS cluster has ... Virtualization/Hy... Performance    Health  Immediate
Host in a non-DRS cluster has ... Virtualization/Hy... Performance    Health  Critical
```

Again, I would suggest that you check the online documentation for more references at:

```
https://www.vmware.com/support/developer/PowerCLI/PowerCLI60R2/html/
Set-OMAlert.html
```

The next cmdlet that we will check is the `Get-OMRecommendation` cmdlet. By default, this cmdlet will show you a list of recommendations for the entire server. We can further drill-down using different parameters. For example, run the following command:

```
PS C:\> $alert = Get-OMAlert -Id '47c53bcb-2591-40e8-a748-c8b60e9ba9e8'
PS C:\> Get-OMRecommendation -Alert $alert | Format-List
```

The output is as follows:

```
PS C:\> $alert = Get-OMAlert -Id '47c53bcb-2591-40e8-c8b60e9ba9e8'

PS C:\> Get-OMRecommendation -Alert $alert | Format-List

AlertDefinition : Host in a non-DRS cluster has CPU contention caused by less than half of the virtual machines
ExtensionData   : VMware.VimAutomation.VROps.Views.Recommendation
Id              : Recommendation-df-VMWARE-MoveSomeVMsToOtherHostForCPU
Description     : Use vMotion to migrate some virtual machines with high CPU workload to other hosts that have available CPU capacity
Alert           : Host in a non-DRS cluster has CPU contention caused by less than half of the virtual machines
Client          : VMware.VimAutomation.vROps.Impl.V1.OMClientImpl
Uid             : /OMServer=admin@          :443/OMAlertRecommendation=Recommendation-df-VMWARE-MoveSomeVMsToOtherHostForCPU/
```

The `Get-OMResource` cmdlet returns vRealize Operations Manager resource objects. As returned by the Get-Help cmdlet, for this cmdlet, we can query the Operations Manager for a particular resource using the information from the vCenter server. Remember that, in the following example, we need to connect to a vCenter server. Obviously, the entity that we are querying for must be added to the vRealize Operations Manager server:

```
PS C:\> $vCenterCluster = Get-Cluster "MyCluster"
PS C:\> $clusterResource = Get-OMResource -Entity $vCenterCluster
```

Also, we can query the server directly using an entity or resource name:

```
PS C:\> Get-OMResource -Name esxi1.lab.com
```

The output is as follows:

```
PS C:\> Get-OMResource -Name

Name                          Health   ResourceKind     Description
----                          ------   ------------     -----------
                        ...   Green    HostSystem
```

For example, we want to get a list of the resources of `AdapterKind VMWARE` and `ResourceKind HostSystem`:

```
PS C:\> Get-OMResource –AdapterKind VMWARE –ResourceKind ` HostSystem
```

So far, we have discussed alerts, resources, and so on, but what is the point of vRealize Operations Manager cmdlets if we do not talk about statistics. The most interesting part of these cmdlets is to be able to get statistics directly from the command line. So, let's get our hands dirty with this. The following are the two cmdlets that we will use to get this information:

- `Get-OMStatKey`
- `Get-OMStat`

To get any information, we first need to know what to look for. To be able to get statistical information, we first need to work with the statistics keys. Once we are familiar with the keys, we will use these to get the respective information. `Get-OMStatKey` is the cmdlet that is used to get statistics keys.

The first example shows you a list of statistic keys available for a `HostSystem` resource. It is a pretty long list with a total of 2224 keys. Here is an example:

```
PS C:\> (Get-OMStatKey -ResourceKind HostSystem).Count
2224
PS C:\> Get-OMStatKey -ResourceKind HostSystem
```

The output is as follows:

```
PS C:\> (Get-OMStatKey -ResourceKind HostSystem).Count
2224
PS C:\> Get-OMStatKey -ResourceKind HostSystem

Name                                    Unit     ResourceKind     Description
----                                    ----     ------------     -----------
diskspace-waste|activeNotShared|ac...   gb       HostSystem       Current Size
diskspace|alloc|consumer.demand_av...   gb       HostSystem       Average Consumer Demand with committed projects...
cpu|alloc|capacityRemaining_whatif      percent  HostSystem       Capacity Remaining with committed projects
net|usage|stress_whatif                 percent  HostSystem       Stress with committed projects
mem|alloc|capacityRemainingUsingCo...            HostSystem       Capacity Remaining (Small consumer profile)
```

We can get the statistics keys related to a particular entity by directly querying that resource. In the following example, we will get a list of all the statistics keys related to a particular host:

```
PS C:\> Get-OMResource 'esxi1.lab.com' | Get-OMStatKey
```

There are other parameters that we can use with this cmdlet. For a detailed list and other options, I suggest that you check the online documentation at `https://www.vmware.com/support/developer/PowerCLI/PowerCLI60R2/html/Get-OMStatKey.html`.

Great! We got a list of all the available statistics keys that we can use. The problem is that it is a huge list and how do you search for what you're looking for? The answer is very simple; just check; metric definitions in the vRealize Operations Manager documentation set. You can check the definitions at `http://pubs.vmware.com/vrealizeoperationsmanager-61/index.jsp#com.vmware.vcom.core.doc/GUID-ACF48F67-B877-45DB-910C-4BFADC86F794.html`.

The output of the preceding URL is as follows:

CPU Usage Metrics		
Metric Key	Metric Name	Description
cpu|capacity_usagepct_average	Capacity Usage	Percent capacity used.
cpu|capacity_contentionPct	CPU Contention	Percent CPU contention.
cpu|demandPct	Demand (%)	CPU demand percentage.
cpu|demandmhz	Demand (MHz)	Demand in megahertz.
cpu|demand_average	Demand	CPU demand in megahertz.

(Left panel: Metric Definitions in vRealize Operations Manager → Metrics for vCenter Server Components → vSphere Metrics, vCenter Server Metrics, Virtual Machine Metrics, Host System Metrics, Cluster Compute Resource Metrics, Resource Pool Metrics, Datacenter Metrics, Custom Datacenter Metrics, Storage Pod Metrics, VMware Distributed Virtual Switch Metrics, Distributed Virtual Port Group Metrics, Datastore Metrics)

On the left-hand side, you will find a list of the entities against which you can get a list of the available statistics. For example, under the metric definition of vRealize Operations Manager, there are metrics for vCenter Server components; under this, we can get a list of all the metrics for vSphere. Also, on the details page, the metrics are categorized under multiple categories, such as **CPU Usage Metrics**, **Memory Metrics**, and so on.

Metric Definitions in vRealize Operations Manager | Metric for vCenter Server Components | vSphere Metrics.

For example, the first CPU usage metric for the vSphere host is `cpu|capacity_usagepct_average`.

Now, if we try to get details of the key, we find that this key returns the Capacity Usage percentage, and if available for `ClusterComputeResource`, `Datacenter`, `HostSystem`, `VMwareAdapter Instance`, and `vSphere World`:

```
PS C:\> Get-OMStatKey -Name 'cpu|capacity_usagepct_average'

Name                             Unit     ResourceKind             Description
----                             ----     ------------             -----------
cpu|capacity_usagepct_average    percent  ClusterComputeResource   Capacity Usage (%)
cpu|capacity_usagepct_average    percent  Datacenter               Capacity Usage (%)
cpu|capacity_usagepct_average    percent  HostSystem               Capacity Usage (%)
cpu|capacity_usagepct_average    percent  VMwareAdapter Instance   Capacity Usage (%)
cpu|capacity_usagepct_average    percent  vSphere World            Capacity Usage (%)
```

So, we got to know which information to look for. Now, let's find the information. For example, for a particular host system, I want to know what was the CPU capacity usage percentage is. We will use the `Get-OMStat` cmdlet for this:

```
PS C:\>Get-OMStat -Resource 'esxi1.lab.com' -Key ` 'cpu|capacity_
usagepct_average'
```

The output is as follows:

```
PS C:\> Get-OMStat -Resource '                              ' -Key 'cpu|capacity_usagepct_average'

Resource                              Key                              Value              Time
--------                              ---                              -----              ----
                        ... cpu|capacity_usagepct_average    10.9584655761719   11-12-2014 00:29:59
                        ... cpu|capacity_usagepct_average    15.7571992874146   11-12-2014 01:29:59
                        ... cpu|capacity_usagepct_average    15.7810173034668   11-12-2014 02:29:59
                        ... cpu|capacity_usagepct_average    10.0802364349365   11-12-2014 03:29:59
                        ... cpu|capacity_usagepct_average    12.2236251831055   11-12-2014 04:29:59
```

Note that it returns a list of all the values for this host from the time it was added to the vRealize Operations Manager server. Again, this list is huge depending on the date on which it was configured. We can further narrow down the list using the `-From` parameter:

```
PS C:\> Get-OMStat -Resource 'esxi1.lab.com' `

-Key 'cpu|capacity_usagepct_average' -From `

([DateTime]::Now).AddDays(-7)
```

The preceding command will return the value for the last seven days.

The following example will return the Health of the esxi1.lab.com host between 06/24/2015 and 09/25/2015 with an `IntervalType` as `Months` and `IntervalCount` 2. The `RollupType` is `Avg`:

```
PS C:\> $startdate = Get-Date -Year 2015 -Month 06 -Day 24


PS C:\> $enddate = Get-Date -Year 2015 -Month 09 -Day 25
PS C:\> Get-OMStat -Resource 'esxi1.lab.com' -Key 'badge|health' `

  -IntervalType 'Months'  -IntervalCount '2' -RollupType 'Avg' `

-From $startDate -To $endDate
```

The output is as follows:

```
PS C:\> Get-OMStat -Resource '                         ' -Key 'badge|health' `
  -IntervalType 'Months'  -IntervalCount '2' -RollupType 'Avg' -From $startDate -To $endDate

Resource                    Key              Value         Time
--------                    ---              -----         ----
                   ... badge|health          100           31-07-2015 23:59:59
                   ... badge|health          100           30-09-2015 23:59:59
```

Note the `IntervalType` and `IntervalCount` should fit the chosen time.

As always, doing is learning. So, I strongly suggest that you dive into these and start getting your hands dirty.

The last cmdlet is `Get-OMUser`. By default, this cmdlet will return a list of all the defined users in the server if not used with any parameters. But this will not return the details of the admin user. To query for a particular user, we can use the `Name` parameter:

```
PS C:\> Get-OMUser -Name bas4
```

The output is as follows:

```
PS C:\> Get-OMUser -Name bas4

Name                              FirstName           LastName            Enabled
----                              ---------           --------            -------
bas4                              BAS4                BAS4                False
```

This concludes the section on managing vRealize Operations Manager. This is an interesting addition to the weaponry. I am pretty eager to see how this turns out and all the scripts that appear in the community.

Summary

In this chapter, we discussed how to manage security and other aspects of a vSphere environment, starting with host profile and moving on to Update Manager and firewall services. Then we touched upon managing SRM servers and the vCloud Air environment. At the end of the chapter, we discussed the latest release of PowerCLI: Version 6.0 Release2. We also discussed cmdlets for managing the vRealize Operations Manager environment.

In the next chapter, we will move on to more interesting and fun topics involved in managing the APIs in a vSphere environment using PowerCLI.

Managing the vSphere API

So far, we have discussed how to configure and manage different aspects of ESXi and vCenter Server and its peripheral services. We used the cmdlets available in PowerCLI, but the real fun begins now. In this chapter, we will dive into the deep end of the pool and work directly with .NET objects and the vSphere API. It is an amazing way to manage the vSphere world. As we move into the chapter, we will discuss the following topics:

- Using the `Get-View` cmdlet to return .NET View objects
- Using the `ExtensionData` property to return .NET View objects
- Using the vSphere API
- Creating a vSphere scheduled task
- Configuring Distributed Power Management
- Configuring Fault Tolerance
- Managing Content Libraries
- Managing SRM advanced configurations
- Generating PowerCLI code using Onyx
- PowerActions for the vSphere Web client

So, let's start the discussion on how we can use the `Get-View` cmdlet to get .NET View objects.

Using the Get-View cmdlet to return .NET View objects

When we use any cmdlet, it does a lot of background work and provides us nice, formatted output. This has the positive effect of making our life easier and we can be blissfully ignorant of the underlying complexities. But, due to the same reason, it also runs a bit slower and hides a lot of information. If we want to get more information about objects, then we need to use the `Get-View` cmdlet. For example, let's look at the output of the following two cmdlets:

```
PS C:\> Get-VMHost -Name ESXi1.lab.com

PS C:\> Get-VMHost -Name ESXi1.lab.com | Get-View
```

The results of the preceding commands are shown in the following screenshot:

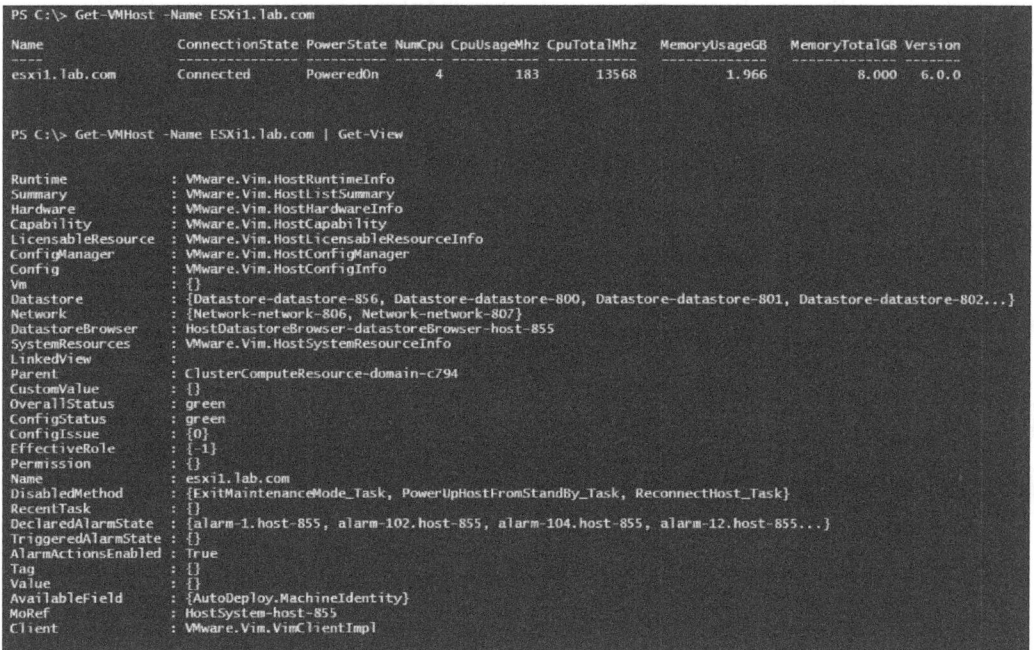

```
PS C:\> Get-VMHost -Name ESXi1.lab.com

Name              ConnectionState PowerState NumCpu CpuUsageMhz CpuTotalMhz  MemoryUsageGB  MemoryTotalGB Version
----              --------------- ---------- ------ ----------- -----------  -------------  ------------- -------
esxi1.lab.com     Connected       PoweredOn       4         183       13568          1.966          8.000 6.0.0


PS C:\> Get-VMHost -Name ESXi1.lab.com | Get-View

Runtime             : VMware.Vim.HostRuntimeInfo
Summary             : VMware.Vim.HostListSummary
Hardware            : VMware.Vim.HostHardwareInfo
Capability          : VMware.Vim.HostCapability
LicensableResource  : VMware.Vim.HostLicensableResourceInfo
ConfigManager       : VMware.Vim.HostConfigManager
Config              : VMware.Vim.HostConfigInfo
Vm                  : {}
Datastore           : {Datastore-datastore-856, Datastore-datastore-800, Datastore-datastore-801, Datastore-datastore-802...}
Network             : {Network-network-806, Network-network-807}
DatastoreBrowser    : HostDatastoreBrowser-datastoreBrowser-host-855
SystemResources     : VMware.Vim.HostSystemResourceInfo
LinkedView          :
Parent              : ClusterComputeResource-domain-c794
CustomValue         : {}
OverallStatus       : green
ConfigStatus        : green
ConfigIssue         : {0}
EffectiveRole       : {-1}
Permission          : {}
Name                : esxi1.lab.com
DisabledMethod      : {ExitMaintenanceMode_Task, PowerUpHostFromStandBy_Task, ReconnectHost_Task}
RecentTask          : {}
DeclaredAlarmState  : {alarm-1.host-855, alarm-102.host-855, alarm-104.host-855, alarm-12.host-855...}
TriggeredAlarmState : {}
AlarmActionsEnabled : True
Tag                 : {}
Value               : {}
AvailableField      : {AutoDeploy.MachineIdentity}
MoRef               : HostSystem-host-855
Client              : VMware.Vim.VimClientImpl
```

As you can see from the preceding screenshot, `Get-View` provides much more detailed information than the simple `Get-VMHost` cmdlet. We can further pinpoint the data that we are looking for by using the `-ViewType` and `-Filter` parameters. The `ViewType` parameter lets us select the data for a particular type of object data. Here is a list of the permissible types:

- **ComputeResource**: This provides details of Cluster type objects
- **Datacenter**: This provides details of Datacenter type objects
- **Datastore**: This provides details of Datastore type objects
- **DistributedVirtualSwitch**: This provides details of vDS type objects
- **Folder**: This provides details of Folder type objects
- **HostSystem**: This provides details of ESX Host type objects
- **Network**: This provides details of Virtual network type objects
- **ResourcePool**: This provides details of Resource Pool type objects
- **VirtualMachine**: This provides details of Virtual Machine type objects

For example, if we want to see the details of the ESXi hosts, we can use the following command:

```
PS C:\> Get-View -ViewType HostSystem
```

But this will return the details of all the hosts available in the system, which we do not want. To solve this problem, we can further pinpoint and get the information by filtering the output. To filter the output, we need to provide the parameter in a Hash Table format. For example, if we want to get information about the ESXi host `ESXi1.lab.com` only, then we can use the command as shown in the following screenshot:

```
PS C:\> Get-View -ViewType HostSystem -Filter @{"NAME"="ESXi1.lab.com"}

Runtime               : VMware.Vim.HostRuntimeInfo
Summary               : VMware.Vim.HostListSummary
Hardware              : VMware.Vim.HostHardwareInfo
Capability            : VMware.Vim.HostCapability
LicensableResource    : VMware.Vim.HostLicensableResourceInfo
ConfigManager         : VMware.Vim.HostConfigManager
Config                : VMware.Vim.HostConfigInfo
Vm                    : {}
Datastore             : {Datastore-datastore-856, Datastore-datastore-800, Datastore-datastore-801, Datastore-datastore-802...}
Network               : {Network-network-806, Network-network-807}
DatastoreBrowser      : HostDatastoreBrowser-datastoreBrowser-host-855
SystemResources       : VMware.Vim.HostSystemResourceInfo
LinkedView            :
Parent                : ClusterComputeResource-domain-c794
CustomValue           : {}
OverallStatus         : green
ConfigStatus          : green
ConfigIssue           : {0}
EffectiveRole         : {-1}
Permission            : {}
Name                  : esxi1.lab.com
DisabledMethod        : {ExitMaintenanceMode_Task, PowerUpHostFromStandBy_Task, ReconnectHost_Task}
RecentTask            : {}
DeclaredAlarmState    : {alarm-1.host-855, alarm-102.host-855, alarm-104.host-855, alarm-12.host-855...}
TriggeredAlarmState   : {}
AlarmActionsEnabled   : True
Tag                   : {}
Value                 : {}
AvailableField        : {AutoDeploy.MachineIdentity}
MoRef                 : HostSystem-host-855
Client                : VMware.Vim.VimClientImpl
```

We can get the same information by passing the -VIObject parameter:

```
PS C:\> Get-View -VIObject ESXi1.lab.com

Runtime             : VMware.Vim.HostRuntimeInfo
Summary             : VMware.Vim.HostListSummary
Hardware            : VMware.Vim.HostHardwareInfo
Capability          : VMware.Vim.HostCapability
LicensableResource  : VMware.Vim.HostLicensableResourceInfo
ConfigManager       : VMware.Vim.HostConfigManager
Config              : VMware.Vim.HostConfigInfo
Vm                  : {}
Datastore           : {Datastore-datastore-856, Datastore-datastore-800, Datastore-datastore-801, Datastore-datastore-802...}
Network             : {Network-network-806, Network-network-807}
DatastoreBrowser    : HostDatastoreBrowser-datastoreBrowser-host-855
SystemResources     : VMware.Vim.HostSystemResourceInfo
LinkedView          :
Parent              : ClusterComputeResource-domain-c794
CustomValue         : {}
OverallStatus       : green
ConfigStatus        : green
ConfigIssue         : {0}
EffectiveRole       : {-1}
Permission          : {}
Name                : esxi1.lab.com
DisabledMethod      : {ExitMaintenanceMode_Task, PowerUpHostFromStandBy_Task, ReconnectHost_Task}
RecentTask          : {}
DeclaredAlarmState  : {alarm-1.host-855, alarm-102.host-855, alarm-104.host-855, alarm-12.host-855...}
TriggeredAlarmState : {}
AlarmActionsEnabled : True
Tag                 : {}
Value               : {}
AvailableField      : {AutoDeploy.MachineIdentity}
MoRef               : HostSystem-host-855
Client              : VMware.Vim.VimClientImpl
```

The Get-View cmdlet, along with the -ViewType parameter, returns the details of a View Object. However, VIObject is different. It is a vSphere Inventory Object that is returned by the PowerCLI cmdlet. The object returned by Get-View is a vSphere .NET View Object that is the client copy of a managed object. Therefore, while providing the -VIObject parameter, we could use the direct hostname ESXi1.lab. com as it is a recognizable vSphere Inventory object. While using the -ViewType parameter, we are querying all the objects that are of the type HostSystem.

From that perspective, -ViewType is more basic and granular. We will discuss the practical implications of these two in more detail in further sections.

Now that we know how to access the detailed object information, what do we do with it? Let's explore the fields one by one. For this, we will assume we do not have any idea about where we would get the required information. For example, we want to get the information about the CPU of the host. So let's start with the details of the object. We will store the information in a variable so that we can work with it later. The command is as follows:

```
PS C:\> $hostView = Get-View -ViewType HostSystem -Filter @
{"NAME"="ESXi1.lab.com"}
```

Now, the $hostView parameter has the details of the object. As we saw in the earlier examples, the HostSystem object returns information about Runtime, Summary, Hardware, Vm, Datastore, Name, and so on.

For our current purpose, Hardware seems to be a promising one. Let's explore that field. We can get the details by simply using the list of the fields in the format $hostView.Hardware:

```
PS C:\> $hostView.Hardware

SystemInfo             : VMware.Vim.HostSystemInfo
CpuPowerManagementInfo : VMware.Vim.HostCpuPowerManagementInfo
CpuInfo                : VMware.Vim.HostCpuInfo
CpuPkg                 : {0, 1, 2, 3}
MemorySize             : 8589398016
NumaInfo               : VMware.Vim.HostNumaInfo
SmcPresent             : False
PciDevice              : {0000:00:00.0, 0000:00:01.0, 0000:00:07.0, 0000:00:07.1...}
CpuFeature             : {VMware.Vim.HostCpuIdInfo, VMware.Vim.HostCpuIdInfo, VMware.Vim.HostCpuIdInfo, VMware.Vim.HostCpuIdInfo...}
BiosInfo               : VMware.Vim.HostBIOSInfo
ReliableMemoryInfo     : VMware.Vim.HostReliableMemoryInfo
```

This provides us with further information on what information we can get about CPU, Memory, BIOS, and so on. We can get further information about CPU using the CpuInfo field, as shown here:

```
PS C:\> $hostView.Hardware.CpuInfo


NumCpuPackages NumCpuCores NumCpuThreads          Hz
-------------- ----------- -------------          --
             4           4             4 3392311000
```

Likewise, we can use other fields to get information about other hardware-related information. For example, using the BiosInfo field, we can get the information about the BIOS:

```
PS C:\> $hostView.Hardware.BiosInfo


BiosVersion ReleaseDate
----------- -----------
6.00        5/20/2014 12:00:00 AM
```

Using Get-View, we can find detailed information about an entity and use it. Now the question is how we can use this information. We can use this information for reporting purpose or do something on it; reporting is easy because we can directly use the values.

We can take two different approaches to do something on these entities. The first approach is to use the PowerCLI cmdlets and achieve something. For example, if we want to shut down the ESXi host, we will have to do it in the following way.

Since it is native .NET view object format, we cannot directly use the PowerCLI cmdlet on it. If we want to power off the host using the Stop-VMHost cmdlet, we get an error message as follows:

```
PS C:\> $hostView | Stop-VMHost

Stop-VMHost : The input object cannot be bound to any parameters for the
command either because the command does not take pipeline input or the
input and its properties do not match any of the parameters that take
pipeline input.

At line:1 char:13

+ $hostView | Stop-VMHost

+               ~~~~~~~~~~~~

    + CategoryInfo          : InvalidArgument: (VMware.Vim.
HostSystem:PSObject) [Stop-VMHost], ParameterBindingException

    + FullyQualifiedErrorId : InputObjectNotBound,VMware.VimAutomation.
ViCore.Cmdlets.Commands.StopVMHost
```

The result of the preceding commands is as shown in the following screenshot:

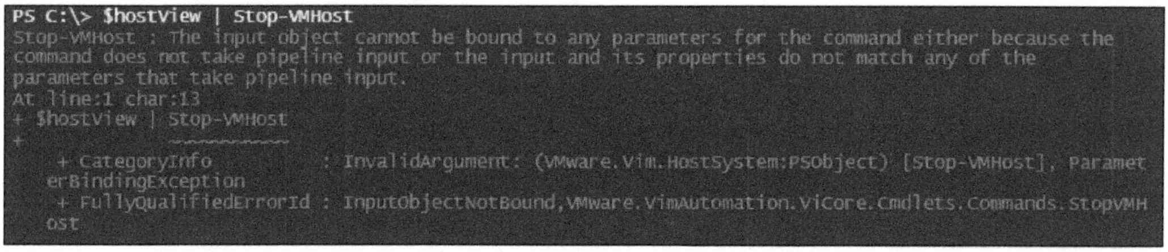

This is because PowerCLI cmdlets work on VIObject but the information that we get from Get-View cmdlet is not formatted in VIObject format. So, we need to convert the .NET view object type to the VIObject type first and then we can use PowerCLI cmdlets on them to perform actions. This is shown in the following screenshot:

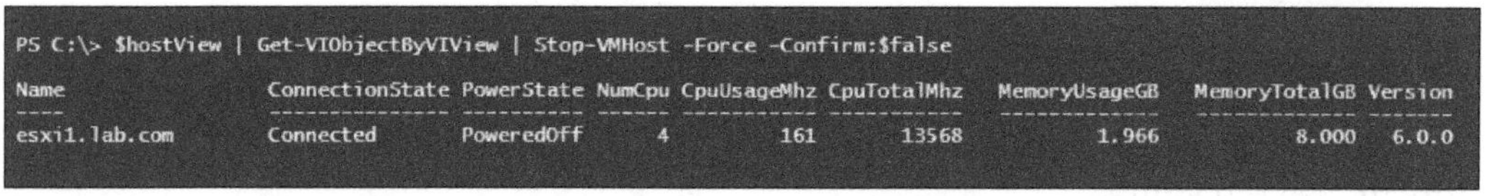

The second approach is more direct and works faster than the first method, but it requires more digging and knowledge. We will directly use the methods available to this object. For this, we will use the Get-Member cmdlet to explore the available methods and properties of the returned object. For example, when we use the Get-Member cmdlet on the $hostView variable holding the HostSystem object, we see that a long list of methods and properties are associated with the object. Also, details of each method are provided (Name, MemberType, and Definition). A small list of methods and properties can be seen in the following screenshot:

```
PS C:\> $hostView | Get-Member


   TypeName: VMware.Vim.HostSystem

Name                      MemberType Definition
----                      ---------- ----------
AcquireCimServicesTicket  Method     VMware.Vim.HostServiceTicket AcquireCimServicesTicket()
Destroy                   Method     void Destroy()
Destroy_Task              Method     VMware.Vim.ManagedObjectReference Destroy_Task()
DisconnectHost            Method     void DisconnectHost()
DisconnectHost_Task       Method     VMware.Vim.ManagedObjectReference DisconnectHost_Task()
EnterLockdownMode         Method     void EnterLockdownMode()
```

A truncated list of properties is provided here:

```
AlarmActionsEnabled   Property   bool AlarmActionsEnabled {get;}
AvailableField        Property   VMware.Vim.CustomFieldDef[] AvailableField {get;}
Capability            Property   VMware.Vim.HostCapability Capability {get;}
Client                Property   VMware.Vim.VimClient Client {get;}
Config                Property   VMware.Vim.HostConfigInfo Config {get;}
ConfigIssue           Property   VMware.Vim.Event[] ConfigIssue {get;}
ConfigManager         Property   VMware.Vim.HostConfigManager ConfigManager {get;}
ConfigStatus          Property   VMware.Vim.ManagedEntityStatus ConfigStatus {get;}
CustomValue           Property   VMware.Vim.CustomFieldValue[] CustomValue {get;}
Datastore             Property   VMware.Vim.ManagedObjectReference[] Datastore {get;}
DatastoreBrowser      Property   VMware.Vim.ManagedObjectReference DatastoreBrowser {get;
DeclaredAlarmState    Property   VMware.Vim.AlarmState[] DeclaredAlarmState {get;}
DisabledMethod        Property   string[] DisabledMethod {get;}
```

This is a very interesting list. Notice the ShutdownHost method:

```
ShutdownHost          Method     void ShutdownHost(bool force)
```

It returns nothing and takes a Boolean value for forcing the action. So the value can be either $true or $false. Now, let's use this method to shut down the host instead of using the Stop-VMHost cmdlet:

```
PS C:\> $hostView.Shutdownhost($true)


PS C:\>
```

It simply takes the input and does the job without much fuss.

So why use the `Get-View` cmdlet? We use it because it is much faster than the other cmdlets. Taking the same examples, if we try to measure the time taken by both the approaches, we will get the following results:

```
PS C:\> Measure-Command { $hostView | Get-VIObjectByVIView | Stop-VMHost -Force -Confirm:$false }


Days              : 0
Hours             : 0
Minutes           : 0
Seconds           : 2
Milliseconds      : 212
Ticks             : 22125461
TotalDays         : 2.56081724537037E-05
TotalHours        : 0.000614596138888889
TotalMinutes      : 0.0368757683333333
TotalSeconds      : 2.2125461
TotalMilliseconds : 2212.5461




PS C:\> Measure-Command { $hostView.Shutdownhost($true) }


Days              : 0
Hours             : 0
Minutes           : 0
Seconds           : 0
Milliseconds      : 418
Ticks             : 4186959
TotalDays         : 4.84601736111111E-06
TotalHours        : 0.000116304416666667
TotalMinutes      : 0.006978265
TotalSeconds      : 0.4186959
TotalMilliseconds : 418.6959
```

While the use of the `Stop-VMHost` cmdlt approach took 2 seconds and 212 milliseconds, the direct object methods took only 418 milliseconds. So, using native methods and properties are typically faster than the other methods.

> There's an excellent blog series by Brian Graf about `Get-View` and the last one in the series, `Get-View Part 3: Peformance Impact - Is it really THAT much different?` details the performance impact of using `Get-View` in comparison to normal cmdlets (`http://blogs.vmware.com/PowerCLI/2015/06/get-view-part-3-peformance-really-much-different.html`).

The `Get-View` cmdlet provides the server-side information at the time of query. When we store it in a variable and use it later, the values remain same but in the meantime the server-side data can change. So, to update the information, we can use the `UpdateViewData()` method to update the data. Here is an example.

We can check from the following example that the server ESXi1.lab.com is in the maintenance mode:

```
PS C:\> $hostView = Get-View -ViewType HostSystem -Filter @
{"NAME"="ESXi1.lab.com"}


PS C:\> $hostView.Runtime.InMaintenanceMode
True
```

Next, we will bring the host out of maintenance mode:

```
PS C:\> $hostView.ExitMaintenanceMode(1)


PS C:\> $hostView.Runtime.InMaintenanceMode
True
```

As you can see from the preceding example, the host is not in maintenance mode but the InMaintenanceMode parameter still holds the old value. Now, let's try to update the values:

```
PS C:\> $hostView.Runtime.InMaintenanceMode
True


PS C:\> $hostView.UpdateViewData()


PS C:\> $hostView.Runtime.InMaintenanceMode
False
```

With the help of the UpdateViewData() method, we have updated the value of the Object. Remember that we have updated the values of the entire Object. We can update selective parameters as well.

So keep this in mind and be careful while using the Get-View cmdlet and the information related to it. If you are using a value that is updated frequently, then use the UpdateViewData() method before using the values.

Using the ExtensionData property to return .NET View objects

In the previous section, we saw how to access minute details of the objects using the Get-View cmdlet. We can do the same without using the Get-View cmdlet as well. The magic property is ExtensionData. By using this property, we can access the details of an object. Let's examine this in more detail. First, we will get the information of a host and store it in a variable:

```
PS C:\> $hostInfo = Get-VMHost -Name ESXi1.lab.com
```

The result of the preceding command is shown in the following screenshot:

```
PS C:\> $hostInfo

Name          ConnectionState PowerState NumCpu CpuUsageMhz CpuTotalMhz MemoryUsageGB MemoryTotalGB Version
----          --------------- ---------- ------ ----------- ----------- ------------- ------------- -------
esxi1.lab.com Connected       PoweredOn       4         141       13568         1.940         8.000 6.0.0
```

Now, let's add the ExtensionData parameter to the variable $hostInfo:

```
PS C:\> $hostInfo.ExtensionData

Runtime             : VMware.Vim.HostRuntimeInfo
Summary             : VMware.Vim.HostListSummary
Hardware            : VMware.Vim.HostHardwareInfo
Capability          : VMware.Vim.HostCapability
LicensableResource  : VMware.Vim.HostLicensableResourceInfo
ConfigManager       : VMware.Vim.HostConfigManager
Config              : VMware.Vim.HostConfigInfo
Vm                  : {}
Datastore           : {Datastore-datastore-856, Datastore-datastore-800, Datastore-datastore-801, Datastore-datastore-802...}
Network             : {Network-network-806, Network-network-807}
DatastoreBrowser    : HostDatastoreBrowser-datastoreBrowser-host-855
SystemResources     : VMware.Vim.HostSystemResourceInfo
LinkedView          :
Parent              : ClusterComputeResource-domain-c794
CustomValue         : {}
OverallStatus       : green
ConfigStatus        : gray
ConfigIssue         : {0}
EffectiveRole       : {-1}
Permission          : {}
Name                : esxi1.lab.com
DisabledMethod      : {ExitMaintenanceMode_Task, PowerUpHostFromStandBy_Task, ReconnectHost_Task}
RecentTask          : {}
DeclaredAlarmState  : {alarm-1.host-855, alarm-102.host-855, alarm-104.host-855, alarm-12.host-855...}
TriggeredAlarmState : {}
AlarmActionsEnabled : True
Tag                 : {}
Value               : {}
AvailableField      : {AutoDeploy.MachineIdentity}
MoRef               : HostSystem-host-855
Client              : VMware.Vim.VimClientImpl
```

As we can see, it provides the exact same information that we got earlier by using the Get-View cmdlet.

```
PS C:\> $hostInfo.ExtensionData.Hardware.CpuInfo


NumCpuPackages NumCpuCores NumCpuThreads          Hz
-------------- ----------- -------------          --
             4           4             4 3392312000
```

For rest of the operations, we can do what we did earlier with Get-View. For example, if we want to put the host in maintenance mode, then we can check the parameter as follows:

```
PS C:\> $hostInfo.ExtensionData.EnterMaintenanceMode
OverloadDefinitions
-------------------
void EnterMaintenanceMode(int timeout, System.Nullable[bool] evacuatePoweredOffVms)
void EnterMaintenanceMode(int timeout, System.Nullable[bool] evacuatePoweredOffVms, VMware.Vim.HostMaintenanceSpec maintenanceSpec)
```

As you can see from the preceding screenshot, the method takes two values, one is the timeout value and another is a Boolean value to decide if the powered off VMs will be evacuated or not:

```
PS C:\> $hostInfo.ExtensionData.EnterMaintenanceMode(1, $false)
```

So, we can put the host into maintenance mode by using this method and providing the respective values. Thus, we can utilize the Get-View cmdlet or the ExtensionData property to access the .NET objects and work with them.

For the next parts of the chapter, we will utilize these processes to get results that we cannot obtain in the normal way, because direct cmdlets are unavailable to perform those tasks. Note that each object has a field **MoRef** (**Managed Object Reference**), which typically refers to the host itself or to another managed object.

Using the vSphere API

Before we move ahead and talk about performing various tasks using vSphere APIs, let's first see how we can utilize them to our advantage. The vSphere API reference is available at vSphere 6.0 Documentation Center (`http://pubs.vmware.com/vsphere-60/index.jsp`). On the documentation page, you need to go to **vSphere API/SDK Documentation | vSphere Management SDK | vSphere Web Services SDK Documentation | VMware vSphere API Reference**:

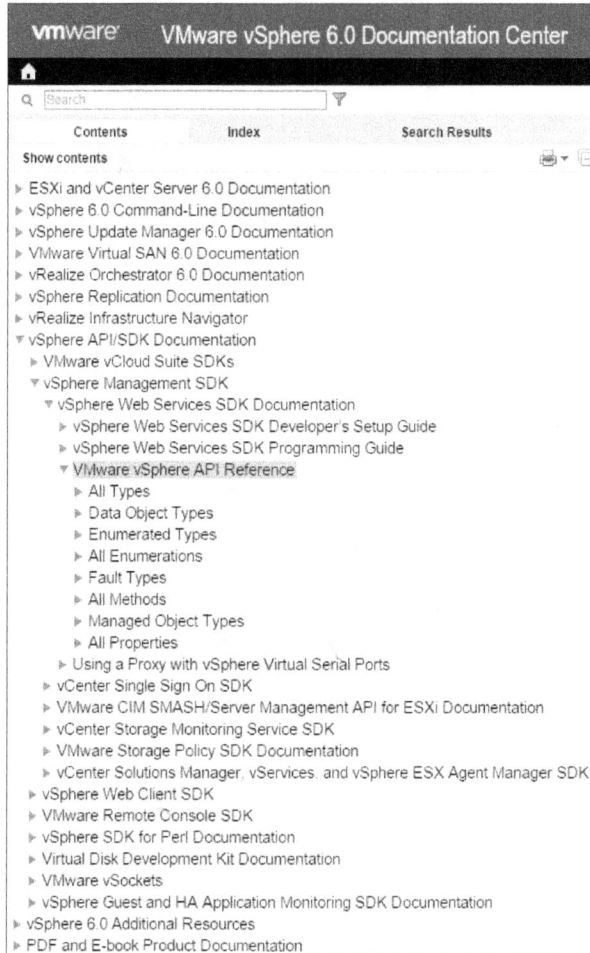

If you look closely, you will see that there are different types of Object categories available:

- **Managed Object types**: This is a core data structure of the server-side object model. Instances of various managed object types are referred to generically as *managed objects*.

- **Data Object types**: This is a core data structure of the server-side object model. Data objects are similar to abstract data types (in Java) and the `struct` data type (in C++). The VMware vSphere management object model uses basic object-oriented features, such as composition and inheritance. For example, managed object types are composed of data object types and primitive data types. Some managed object types extend other managed object types, and some data object types extend other data object types.

- **Enumerated types**: An enumerated data type (or, simply, an **enumeration**) is a data object that stores a specific set of predefined values or objects. Enumerated data types serve the same purpose as constants. For example, a `VirtualMachinePowerState` enumerated type comprises a set of three predefined string values that can be used to convey the runtime state of a virtual machine:

    ○ `poweredOff`

    ○ `poweredOn`

    ○ `suspended`

- **Fault types**: A fault type is a data structure that conveys information about errors, such as processing errors, raised by the server. Information can include the nature of the problem, such as `Not Supported` or `NoPermission`.

> The preceding definition and information was taken from the vSphere API reference documentation. For more details, please check the documentation.

Once we understand the different object types in the vSphere environment, we can check how to achieve a task. To achieve a task, you can either check the details of a .NET View Object or access the details of `VIObject` through the `ExtentensionData` property and check the methods available to the object. Also, we can search in the API reference document for the task that we want to do and find a suitable method. For example, to create a Cluster, we can search for `Create` and get the information that two methods `CreateCluster` and `CreateClusterEx` are available for this task. On closer inspection, we can see that the `CreateCluster` method is deprecated. So we would use the `CreateClusterEx` method. On checking this method, we can see that it takes two inputs, a name (a simple string) and a data object spec (detailed specification).

To invoke the method, we will have to create a data object. Creating the object is pretty simple; just create a new object using the `New-Object` cmdlet:

```
New-Object VMware.Vim.ClusterConfigSpecEx
```

The interesting point to note here is the Object type. Remember to decide which type of object to create, and just add the data object type name to the end of `VMware.Vim`. Since we have a new object of the type `ClusterConfigSpecEx` now, we need to supply the different values it requires. On checking the API documentation we can see that this Object Type has few Properties which we need to set. Check the following screen shot for details:

Properties		
NAME	**TYPE**	**DESCRIPTION**
dasConfig	ClusterDasConfigInfo	HA configuration; includes default settings for virtual machines.
dasVmConfigSpec	ClusterDasVmConfigSpec[]	HA configuration for individual virtual machines. The entries in this array override the cluster default settings (ClusterDasConfigInfo.defaultVmSettings). You cannot specify an HA override for a secondary FT virtual machine. The secondary virtual machine will inherit whatever settings apply to its primary virtual machine. If you include an entry for a secondary, the reconfigure method will throw the fault CannotChangeHaSettingsForFtSecondary.
dpmConfig	ClusterDpmConfigInfo	DPM configuration; includes default settings for hosts.
dpmHostConfigSpec	ClusterDpmHostConfigSpec[]	DPM configuration for individual hosts. The entries in this array override the cluster default settings (ClusterDpmConfigInfo.defaultDpmBehavior).

Note that the properties marked with a red asterisk need not be set. You can safely omit them. But if you want to set a particular value, then go deep into that and set a value. If that property is a simple value, then simply setting it is ok. If the property points to another linked object then again we need to create an object of that type and set the values for it. We need to reiterate this process until we set the values for all the properties. For example, if we need to set HA properties at this stage, then we need to set the values for `dasConfig`. On checking again, we see that we need to create another object `VMware.Vim.ClusterDasConfigInfo` and set the values for it. To set the values, we again go through the same process of checking, creating, and setting values.

At the end, while tying everything together we need to set the values of the properties first and call the method at the end. In a way, the task can be compared to traversing an inverted tree. We work on all the branches first and at the end come to the trunk.

Hopefully, this sheds some light on the whole concept. There is nothing better than examples. So let's start with the examples.

Creating a vSphere scheduled task

In this section, we will discuss ways in which we can create a vSphere scheduled task using the vSphere API through PowerCLI. For this, we will use the `ServiceInstance` managed object. This is the singleton root object in the inventory.

> For more details, please check the vSphere API documentation at **Managed Object Types | ServiceInstance** (http://pubs. vmware.com/vsphere-60/index.jsp#com.vmware. wssdk.apiref.doc/vim.ServiceInstance.html).

To create a scheduled task, we will use the CreateScheduledTask method. If we examine the method, we can see that this method takes two inputs: an entity (MoRef) and a specification (ScheduledTaskSpec).

To create a task, we need to create a scheduled task specification. This in turn takes six different inputs:

NAME	TYPE	DESCRIPTION
action	Action	The action of the scheduled task, to be done when the scheduled task runs.
description	xsd:string	Description of the scheduled task.
enabled	xsd:boolean	Flag to indicate whether the scheduled task is enabled or disabled.
name	xsd:string	Name of the scheduled task.
notification	xsd:string	The email notification. If not set, this property is set to empty string, indicating no notification.
scheduler	TaskScheduler	The time scheduler that determines when the scheduled task runs.

The rest of the values are static but notice action and scheduler. These need to be defined as objects. Note that we defined an Action, which in turn calls the CreateSnapshot_Task method to create the snapshot. As the action argument, we provided the necessary arguments to the CreateSnapshot_Task method (for details, check the vSphere API documentation for the CreateSnapshot_Task method).

Here's the script that will create a scheduled snapshot:

```
# Get the details of the VM for which snapshot needs to be created

$VM = Get-View -ViewType VirtualMachine -Filter @{"Name" = "Test-1"}

# Create the Action Object with the CreateSnapshot_Task

$ma = New-Object VMware.Vim.MethodAction
$ma.Name = "CreateSnapshot_Task"
$ma.Argument = New-Object VMware.Vim.MethodActionArgument[] (4)

($ma.argument[0] = New-Object VMware.Vim.MethodActionArgument).Value = "$vm.Name scheduled snapshot"
($ma.argument[1] = New-Object VMware.Vim.MethodActionArgument).Value = "Snapshot created"
```

```
($ma.argument[2] = New-Object VMware.Vim.MethodActionArgument).Value =
$false # Snapshot memory

($ma.argument[3] = New-Object VMware.Vim.MethodActionArgument).Value =
$false # quiesce guest file system (requires VMware Tools)


# Setting the values for schedule time


$dts = New-Object VMware.Vim.DailyTaskScheduler

$dts.Hour = 20

$dts.Minute = 0

$dts.Interval = 7


# Creating object for ScheduledTask specification and setting
# values


$spec = New-Object VMware.Vim.ScheduledTaskSpec

$spec.Name = "Snapshot" + $VM.Name

$spec.Description = "Snapshot" + $VM.Name

$spec.Enabled = $true

$spec.Notification = "sdebnath@vmware.com"

$spec.Action = $ma

$spec.Scheduler = $dts


# Finally creating the task


$si = Get-View ServiceInstance

$stm = Get-View $si.Content.ScheduledTaskManager

$stm.CreateScheduledTask($vm.MoRef,$Spec)
```

When we run the preceding commands, it will create a new scheduled task. This is
shown in the following screenshot:

```
PS C:\> # Get the details of the VM for which snapshot needs to be created

$VM = Get-View -ViewType VirtualMachine -Filter @{"Name" = "Test-1"}

# Create the Action Object with the CreateSnapshot_Task

$ma = New-Object VMware.Vim.MethodAction
$ma.Name = "CreateSnapshot_Task"
$ma.Argument = New-Object VMware.Vim.MethodActionArgument[] (4)

($ma.argument[0] = New-Object VMware.Vim.MethodActionArgument).Value = "$vm.Name scheduled snapshot"
($ma.argument[1] = New-Object VMware.Vim.MethodActionArgument).Value = "Snapshot created"
($ma.argument[2] = New-Object VMware.Vim.MethodActionArgument).Value = $false # Snapshot memory
($ma.argument[3] = New-Object VMware.Vim.MethodActionArgument).Value = $false # quiesce guest file system (requires VMware Tools)

# Setting the values for schedule time

$dts = New-Object VMware.Vim.DailyTaskScheduler
$dts.Hour = 20
$dts.Minute = 0
$dts.Interval = 7

# Creating object for ScheduledTask specification and setting
# values

$spec = New-Object VMware.Vim.ScheduledTaskSpec
$spec.Name = "Snapshot" + $VM.Name
$spec.Description = "Snapshot" + $VM.Name
$spec.Enabled = $true
$spec.Notification = "sdebnath@vmware.com"
$spec.Action = $ma
$spec.Scheduler = $dts

# Finally creating the task

$si = Get-View ServiceInstance
$stm = Get-View $si.Content.ScheduledTaskManager
$stm.CreateScheduledTask($vm.MoRef,$Spec)


Type          Value
----          -----
ScheduledTask schedule-104
```

We can also check the details of the created task by using the following methods:

```
PS C:\> $si = Get-View ServiceInstance

PS C:\> $stm =  Get-View $si.Content.ScheduledTaskManager

PS C:\> $info =  Get-View $stm.ScheduledTask

PS C:\> $info.Info
```

The output is as follows:

```
ScheduledTask    : ScheduledTask-schedule-104

Entity           : VirtualMachine-vm-850

LastModifiedTime : 7/27/2015 6:36:27 PM

LastModifiedUser : LAB\vcadmin

NextRunTime      : 7/27/2015 8:00:00 PM

PrevRunTime      :

State            : success
```

```
Error             :
Result            :
Progress          :
ActiveTask        :
TaskObject        : VirtualMachine-vm-850
LinkedView        :
Name              : SnapshotTest-1
Description       : SnapshotTest-1
Enabled           : True
Scheduler         : VMware.Vim.DailyTaskScheduler
Action            : VMware.Vim.MethodAction
Notification      : sdebnath@vmware.com
```

Configuring Distributed Power Management

Next, we will configure Distributed Power Management using the vSphere API and PowerCLI. To achieve this, we will use the `ReconfigureComputeResource_Task` method, which is defined under the *All Methods* section in VMware vSphere API documentation.

On further inspection, we can see that this method takes two inputs. First, a set of configuration changes to apply to the compute resource in the form of `ComputeResourceConfigSpec` specification. If we check `ComputeResourceConfigSpec`, further we can see that we can extend its use to the `ClusterConfigSpecEx` data object that has the properties that can configure the services listed here:

- **High Availability (HA)**
- **Distributed Resource Scheduling (DRS)**
- **Distributed Power Management (DPM)**
- VSAN

We can see that we can use the following properties:

- `dasConfig`
- `dasVmConfigSpec`
- `dpmConfig`

- dpmHostConfigSpec
- drsConfig
- drsVmConfigSpec
- groupSpec
- rulesSpec
- vsanConfig
- vsanHostConfigSpec

The property that we need to use and set is dpmConfig. So let's examine it further. We can see that we can further set the following properties:

- defaultDpmBehavior
- enabled
- hostPowerActionRate
- option

To sum it all, we need to first define the ClusterConfigSpecEx object, set the DpmConfig parameter, define a ClusterDpmConfigInfo object, and then set the parameters.

Here's the code sample that will set the DPM configuration:

```
# Set parameters

$Cluster = "Lab Cluster"
$Type = "automated"
$Enabled = $true


$Cluster = Get-Cluster $Cluster | Get-View


# Create the specification object

$specs = New-Object vmware.Vim.ClusterConfigSpecEx


# Define the values for the object
$specs.dpmConfig = New-Object VMware.Vim.ClusterDpmConfigInfo
$specs.DpmConfig.DefaultDpmBehavior = $Type
```

```
$specs.DpmConfig.Enabled = $Enabled

# Reconfigure the Cluster to set the DPM
$Cluster.ReconfigureComputeResource_Task($specs, $true)
```

Here's the code snippet in console:

```
PS C:\> $Cluster = "Lab Cluster"
$Type = "automated"
$Enabled = $true

$Cluster = Get-Cluster $Cluster | Get-View
$specs = New-Object vmware.Vim.ClusterConfigSpecEx
$specs.dpmConfig = New-Object VMware.Vim.ClusterDpmConfigInfo
$specs.DpmConfig.DefaultDpmBehavior = $Type
$specs.DpmConfig.Enabled = $Enabled
$Cluster.ReconfigureComputeResource_Task($specs, $true)

Type Value
---- -----
Task task-2966
```

We can see that a task has been created to set the DPM configuration, and it can be seen in the following screenshot that the configuration has been set:

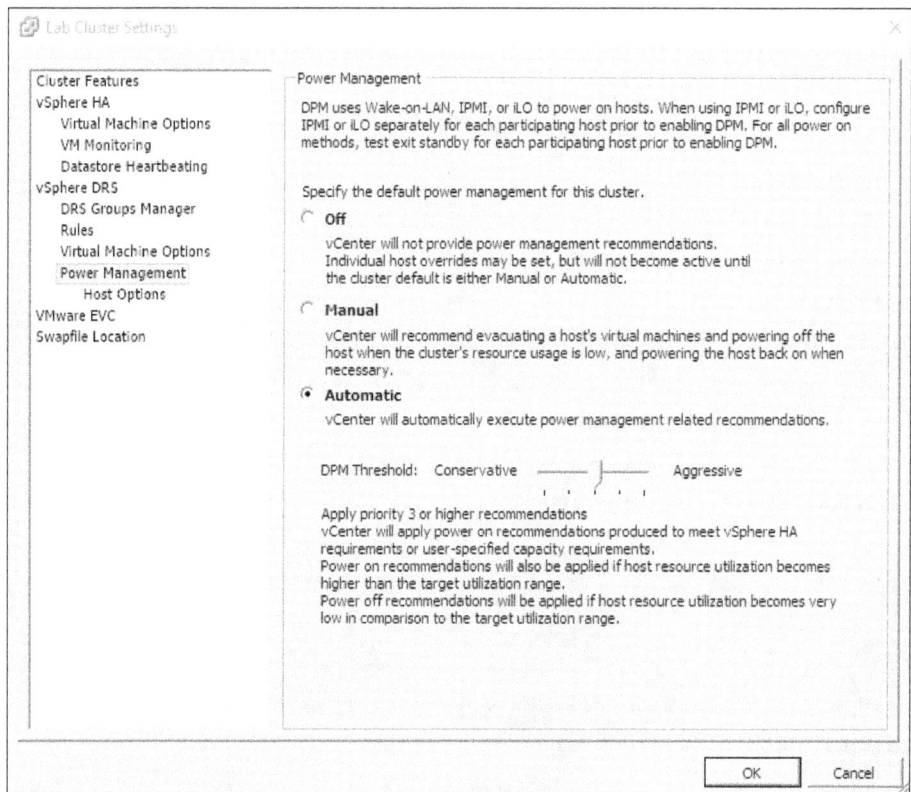

Configuring Fault Tolerance

In this section, we will discuss how we can use vSphere API's to configure FT through PowerCLI. For this, let's explore the methods and properties that we need to access.

If we access the APIs, we can see that there are two methods, `CreateSecondaryVMEx_Task` and `CreateSecondaryVM_Task`, which we can use to configure **Fault Tolerance (FT)**. If we check, we can see that `CreateSecondaryVM_Task` is the deprecated method. So for this example, we will use the `CreateSecondaryVMEx_Task` method.

If we check the `CreateSecondaryVMEX_Task` method, we can see that it takes two different parameters, `host` and `spec`. The `host` parameter is for specifying a host system where the secondary VM should be placed, and `spec` is a Data Object of type `FaultToleranceVMConfigSpec` and is used for specifying the values for fault tolerance VM configuration. If we check, we can see that it takes two parameters: `disks` of type `FaultToleranceDiskSpec` and `vmConfig` of type `ManagedObjectReference` to a datastore.

The idea of building a solution is to go from bottom up. We need to first define the minor parameters first and then build the final piece. So let's build the code:

```
# First we will define the FaultToleranceMetaSpec

$meta = New-Object VMware.Vim.FaultToleranceMetaSpec

$meta.metaDataDatastore = (Get-Datastore NFS_SHARE).Extensiondata.MoRef


# We will next create VM Config specification
$vmc = New-Object VMware.Vim.FaultToleranceVMConfigSpec

$vmc.vmConfig = (Get-Datastore iSCSI-1).Extensiondata.MoRef

$vmc.disks = $null


# Last we will create and configure Fault Tolerance Config Spec
$Config = New-Object VMware.Vim.FaultToleranceConfigSpec

$Config.MetadataPath = $meta
```

```
$Config.secondaryVmSpec = $vmc


# Finally pass the parameters to the method to configure FT
$VM.ExtensionData.CreateSecondaryVMEX_Task($null, $Config)
```

Now let's run the code and see the result.

```
PS C:\> $VM = Get-VM Test-1
```

I am using the value of variable $VM in the following example to make changes in the VM Test-1:

```
PS C:\> # First we will define the FaultToleranceMetaSpec

$meta = New-Object VMware.Vim.FaultToleranceMetaSpec

$meta.metaDataDatastore = (Get-Datastore NFS_SHARE).Extensiondata.MoRef

# We will next create VM Config specification
$vmc = New-Object VMware.Vim.FaultToleranceVMConfigSpec

$vmc.vmConfig = (Get-Datastore iSCSI-1).Extensiondata.MoRef

$vmc.disks = $null

# Last we will create and configure Fault Tolerance Config Spec
$Config = New-Object VMware.Vim.FaultToleranceConfigSpec

$Config.MetadataPath = $meta

$Config.secondaryVmSpec = $vmc

# Finally pass the parameters to the method to configure FT
$VM.ExtensionData.CreateSecondaryVMEX_Task($null, $Config)

Type Value
---- -----
Task task-2991
```

To disable FT, we can use the TurnOffFaultToleranceForVM_Task() method.

```
PS C:\> $VM.ExtensionData.TurnOffFaultToleranceForVM_Task()


Type Value
---- -----
Task task-2992
```

Managing Content Libraries

In this section, we will discuss how we can utilize the vCloud Suite SDK and combine it with the vCenter Server APIs to manage a content library in vCenter Server. To do this, first we need to import the module `VMware.VimAutomation.Cis.Core`. We can check the cmdlets available with this module by running the following command:

```
PS C:\> Get-Command -Module VMware.VimAutomation.Cis.Core | Select Name


Name
----
Connect-CisServer
Disconnect-CisServer
Get-CisService
```

So let's first connect to the vCloud Suite SDK server:

```
PS C:\> Connect-CisServer vcenter.lab.com -User vcadmin@lab.com -Password Vmware1!

Name                          User                          Port
----                          ----                          ----
vcenter.lab.com               vcadmin@lab.com               443
```

To get a list of all the services available and their description, run the cmdlet `Get-CisService`:

```
$Library = Get-CisService com.vmware.content.local_library
```

The result of the preceding command is shown in the following screenshot:

```
PS C:\> $Library = Get-CisService com.vmware.content.local_library
PS C:\> $Library

                    Name Documentation
                    ---- -------------
com.vmware.content.local_library   The {@name LocalLibrary} {@term service} manages local libraries. <p> The {@name LocalLibrary} {@term service} provides support for
                                   creating and maintaining local library instances. A local library may also use the {@link Library} {@term service} to manage general
                                   library functionality.
```

As you can see from the description in the screenshot, this service manages the local libraries. So, we will use this service to manage the content library.

To get a list of available libraries, we can use the `list()` method of the service:

```
PS C:\> $Library.list()
```

```
Value
-----
8a33ede4-122c-4d66-9666-87a93e70c7f6
```

So, we can see that there is a single library. To get the details of this library, we can use the `get()` method as shown:

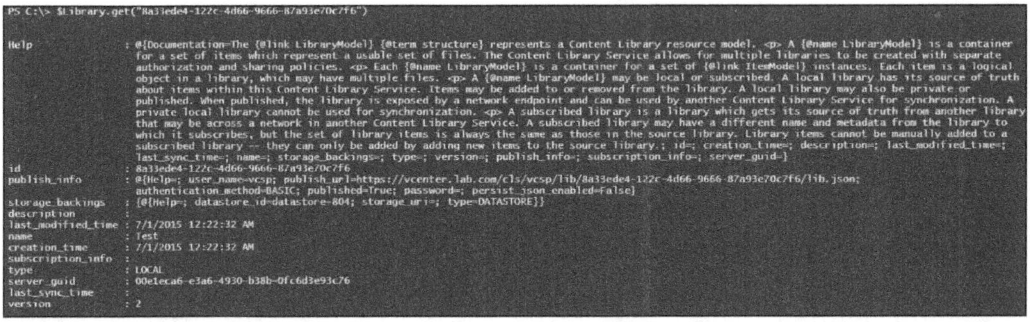

On inspecting the object, we can see that currently it supports the following methods:

- `Create`
- `Delete`
- `Get`
- `List`
- `Update`

We can use the `Create` method to create a content library. Details of this can be found on vSphere PowerCLI 6.0 documentation (`http://pubs.vmware.com/vsphere-60/topic/com.vmware.ICbase/PDF/vsp_powercli_60_usg.pdf`).

Managing SRM advanced configurations

In this section, we will discuss how to manage SRM through APIs. To manage a SRM server, we first need to connect to vCenter Server. Once we are connected to vCenter Server, we can connect to the SRM server using the following cmdlet:

```
PS C:\ $SrmServer = Connect-SrmServer
```

To access the SRM APIs, we can use the following command:

```
PS C:\ $SrmApi = $SrmServer.ExtensionData
PS C:\ > $SrmApi |FL


Content     : VMware.VimAutomation.Srm.Views.SrmServiceInstanceContent
Recovery    : VMware.VimAutomation.Srm.Views.SrmRecovery
Protection  : VMware.VimAutomation.Srm.Views.SrmProtection
MoRef       : SrmServiceInstance-SrmServiceInstance
```

As you can see from the preceding example, the SRM APIs are divided into three groups: `Content`, `Recovery`, and `Protection`.

To check what is available under Protection, we can use the following command:

```
PS C:\Users\administrator.SPWSVCD1> $SrmApi.Protection | Get-Member | Select Name


Name
----
CreateAbrProtectionGroup
CreateHbrProtectionGroup
Equals
GetHashCode
GetProtectionGroupRootFolder
GetType
ListInventoryMappings
ListProtectedDatastores
ListProtectedVms
ListProtectionGroups
ListReplicatedDatastores
ListUnassignedReplicatedDatastores
ListUnassignedReplicatedVms
ToString
```

To get a list of all the Protection groups, we can use the following command:

```
PS C:\ > $SrmApi.Protection.ListProtectionGroups()
```

```
MoRef
-----
SrmProtectionGroup-srm-protection-group-530337
SrmProtectionGroup-srm-protection-group-502249
SrmProtectionGroup-srm-protection-group-566515
SrmProtectionGroup-srm-protection-group-3953105
SrmProtectionGroup-srm-protection-group-556040
```

To get a list of protected datastores, we can use the following command:

```
PS C:\ > $SrmApi.Protection.ListProtectedDatastores()
```

Running the following command will provide us a list of available methods for recovery plans:

```
PS C:\ > $SrmApi.Recovery | GM | Select Name
```

```
Name
----
Equals
GetHashCode
GetHistory
GetRecoveryPlanRootFolder
GetType
ListPlans
ToString
```

To get a list of recovery plans, we can use the ListPlans method:

```
PS C:\ > $SrmApi.Recovery.ListPlans()
```

```
MoRef
-----
SrmRecoveryPlan-srm-recovery-plan-539251
```

```
SrmRecoveryPlan-srm-recovery-plan-539204

SrmRecoveryPlan-srm-recovery-plan-3991693

SrmRecoveryPlan-srm-recovery-plan-562193

SrmRecoveryPlan-srm-recovery-plan-581991
```

To get the history for a particular plan, we can use the following command:

```
PS C:\ > $SrmApi.Recovery.GetHistory("SrmRecoveryPlan-srm-recovery-
plan-539251")


MoRef

-----

SrmRecoveryHistory-srm-recovery-history--539250
```

Using the processes mentioned in the preceding examples, we can manage SRM environment.

Generating PowerCLI code using Onyx

Onyx is a very useful fling that we could use with the C# client to record the actions taken in the client and generate equivalent PowerCLI .NET code. It is a script recorder that sits between vSphere Client and vCenter Server, and it records what scripts were called whenever you do something within the C# Client. It can output the scripts as raw SOAP messages, C#, and vCO (or vRO) JavaScript code.

vSphere 5.5 Web Client has become the main focus for managing vSphere environment and supports many features that are not available in C# client. Now, we have an updated fling, Onyx for the Web Client, that supports Web Client operations. This version translates actions taken in the vSphere Web Client to PowerCLI .NET code. The resulting code can then be used to understand how VMware performs an action in the API and also better define functions. You can download the fling from https://labs.vmware.com/flings/onyx-for-the-web-client.

There's an excellent blog written by Brian Graf (https://labs.vmware.com/flings/onyx-for-the-web-client), which details how to install the fling in the VCSA environment. I will cover the Windows vCenter Installation here.

Remember that Onyx for Web Client requires vSphere Web Client Version 6.0.0 Build 2559277 to work properly. To install it in vCenter, we need to start PowerShell as an administrator. Assuming that the proper `ExecutionPolicy` is set, we can go to the folder where the Onyx files are unzipped and install the fling by simply executing the `install.ps1` file. Before starting the installation, stop the `VMware vSphere Web Client service`. The installation will automatically start the service once it is complete. While executing, it provides a warning. Accept the warning and the installation will start:

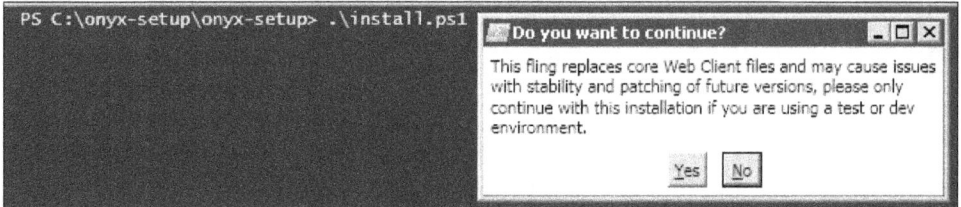

Once the installation is complete, it will show you the following information:

Once the fling is installed, if you open the web client, there will be three different areas where new icons will be available related to Onyx. As you can see in the following screenshot, the parts that are highlighted by the red boxes are added in the Web Client:

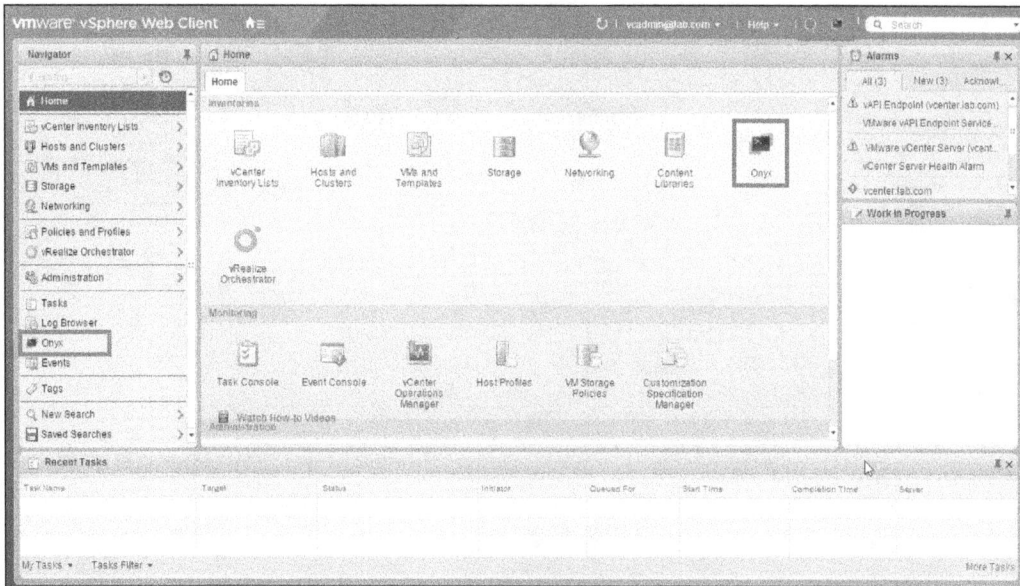

The Onyx buttons will take you to the Onyx console, where you can start the recording by clicking on the red dot positioned in the upper right corner of the **Web Client** (just beside the **Help** option). Once the recording starts, the red button becomes the **Stop** button. Once the task is complete, click on the **Stop** button and the code can be reviewed from the Onyx console.

For example, I recorded the HA and DRS enabling actions. I started the recording and, once the task was done, I clicked on the **Stop** button. Next, I opened the Onyx console to review the code.

Once we review the code, we can save the code by clicking on the **Save** button:

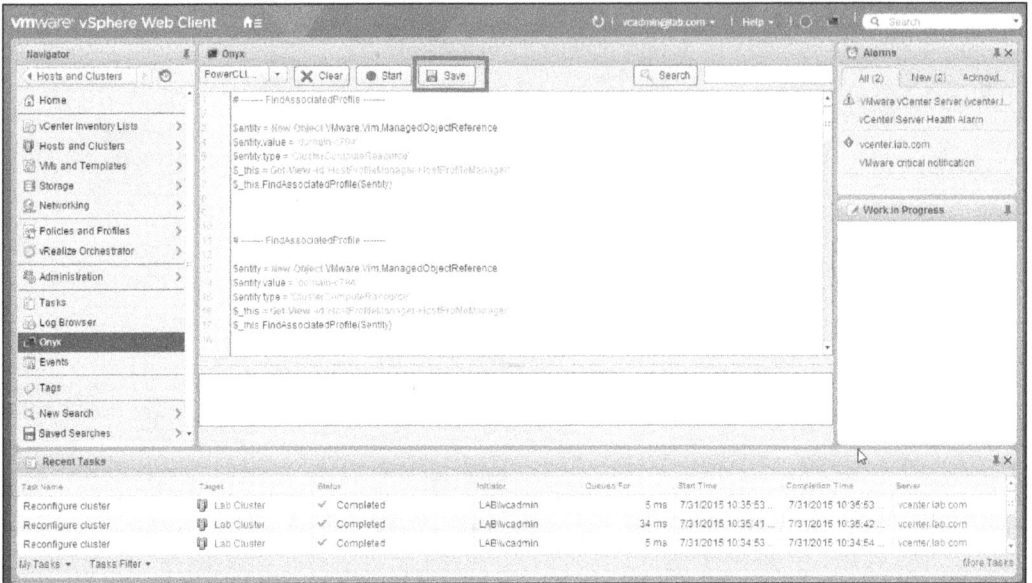

After following the preceding steps, we got the following code:

```
# ------- FindAssociatedProfile -------


$entity = New-Object VMware.Vim.ManagedObjectReference
$entity.value = 'domain-c794'
$entity.type = 'ClusterComputeResource'
$_this = Get-View -Id 'HostProfileManager-HostProfileManager'
$_this.FindAssociatedProfile($entity)


# ------- FindAssociatedProfile -------


$entity = New-Object VMware.Vim.ManagedObjectReference
$entity.value = 'domain-c794'
$entity.type = 'ClusterComputeResource'
$_this = Get-View -Id 'HostProfileManager-HostProfileManager'
$_this.FindAssociatedProfile($entity)
```

```
# ------- RetrieveDasAdvancedRuntimeInfo -------


$_this = Get-View -Id 'ClusterComputeResource-domain-c794'
$_this.RetrieveDasAdvancedRuntimeInfo()


# ------- RetrieveDasAdvancedRuntimeInfo -------


$_this = Get-View -Id 'ClusterComputeResource-domain-c794'
$_this.RetrieveDasAdvancedRuntimeInfo()


# ------- QueryLastEvent -------


# Method QueryLastEvent is not available in the public API.


# ------- QueryLastEvent -------


# Method QueryLastEvent is not available in the public API.


# ------- ReconfigureComputeResource_Task -------


$spec = New-Object VMware.Vim.ClusterConfigSpecEx
$spec.dpmConfig = New-Object VMware.Vim.ClusterDpmConfigInfo
$spec.dpmConfig.enabled = $true
$spec.dpmConfig.hostPowerActionRate = 3
$spec.dpmConfig.defaultDpmBehavior = 'automated'
$spec.drsConfig = New-Object VMware.Vim.ClusterDrsConfigInfo
$spec.drsConfig.enabled = $true
$spec.drsConfig.vmotionRate = 3
$spec.drsConfig.defaultVmBehavior = 'fullyAutomated'
$spec.drsConfig.option = New-Object VMware.Vim.OptionValue[] (0)
$spec.drsConfig.enableVmBehaviorOverrides = $true
$modify = $true
$_this = Get-View -Id 'ClusterComputeResource-domain-c794'
$_this.ReconfigureComputeResource_Task($spec, $modify)
```

```
# ------- RetrieveDasAdvancedRuntimeInfo -------


$_this = Get-View -Id 'ClusterComputeResource-domain-c794'
$_this.RetrieveDasAdvancedRuntimeInfo()


# ------- QueryEventsById -------


# Method QueryEventsById is not available in the public API.


# ------- QueryEventsById -------


# Method QueryEventsById is not available in the public API.


# ------- ReconfigureComputeResource_Task -------


$spec = New-Object VMware.Vim.ClusterConfigSpecEx
$spec.dasConfig = New-Object VMware.Vim.ClusterDasConfigInfo
$spec.dasConfig.vmComponentProtecting = 'disabled'
$spec.dasConfig.enabled = $true
$spec.dasConfig.admissionControlEnabled = $false
$spec.dasConfig.vmMonitoring = 'vmMonitoringDisabled'
$spec.dasConfig.hostMonitoring = 'enabled'
$spec.dasConfig.HBDatastoreCandidatePolicy =
'allFeasibleDsWithUserPreference'
$spec.dasConfig.defaultVmSettings = New-Object VMware.Vim.
ClusterDasVmSettings
$spec.dasConfig.defaultVmSettings.vmComponentProtectionSettings = New-
Object VMware.Vim.ClusterVmComponentProtectionSettings
$spec.dasConfig.defaultVmSettings.vmComponentProtectionSettings.
vmReactionOnAPDCleared = 'none'
$spec.dasConfig.defaultVmSettings.vmComponentProtectionSettings.
enableAPDTimeoutForHosts = $true
$spec.dasConfig.defaultVmSettings.vmComponentProtectionSettings.
vmStorageProtectionForAPD = 'disabled'
$spec.dasConfig.defaultVmSettings.vmComponentProtectionSettings.
vmTerminateDelayForAPDSec = 180
```

```
$spec.dasConfig.defaultVmSettings.vmComponentProtectionSettings.
vmStorageProtectionForPDL = 'disabled'
```

```
$spec.dasConfig.defaultVmSettings.vmToolsMonitoringSettings = New-Object
VMware.Vim.ClusterVmToolsMonitoringSettings
```

```
$spec.dasConfig.defaultVmSettings.vmToolsMonitoringSettings.
failureInterval = 30
```

```
$spec.dasConfig.defaultVmSettings.vmToolsMonitoringSettings.maxFailures =
3
```

```
$spec.dasConfig.defaultVmSettings.vmToolsMonitoringSettings.
maxFailureWindow = -1
```

```
$spec.dasConfig.defaultVmSettings.vmToolsMonitoringSettings.minUpTime =
120
```

```
$spec.dasConfig.defaultVmSettings.restartPriority = 'high'
```

```
$spec.dasConfig.defaultVmSettings.isolationResponse = 'powerOff'
```

```
$spec.dasConfig.option = New-Object VMware.Vim.OptionValue[] (0)
```

```
$spec.dasConfig.heartbeatDatastore = New-Object VMware.Vim.
ManagedObjectReference[] (0)
```

```
$spec.dasConfig.hBDatastoreCandidatePolicy =
'allFeasibleDsWithUserPreference'
```

```
$modify = $true
```

```
$_this = Get-View -Id 'ClusterComputeResource-domain-c794'
```

```
$_this.ReconfigureComputeResource_Task($spec, $modify)
```

```
# ------- RetrieveDasAdvancedRuntimeInfo -------
```

```
$_this = Get-View -Id 'ClusterComputeResource-domain-c794'
```

```
$_this.RetrieveDasAdvancedRuntimeInfo()
```

We can further use this code to modify it according to our requirement or further use it.

Before we move onto next set of actions, we can click on the **Clear** button and Onyx will be clear and ready for next action.

PowerActions for vSphere Web Client

The last topic of this chapter is PowerActions for vSphere Web Client. This is an amazing fling that integrates the vSphere Web Client and PowerCLI to provide complex automation solutions from within the standard vSphere Web Client.

This is actually deployed as a plugin for the vSphere Web Client and allows the end users access to PowerCLI commands and scripts in the vSphere Web Client integrated PowerShell Console. In addition to that, this enables the users to right-click on entity in Web Client and run a script against that entity. Sounds amazing, right? Also, Mac and Linux users get the PowerShell console from their environment directly.

The fling can be installed from `https://labs.vmware.com/flings/poweractions-for-vsphere-web-client`. The prerequisites for this fling installation are as follows:

- VMware vSphere 5.1 to 6.0 (earlier than 5.1 has not been tested)
- PowerShell host machine
- Windows 2003 Server or newer
- .NET 4.0 or 4.5
- PowerShell v1, v2, v3, or v4
- PowerCLI version supporting your current VMware vSphere version
- Administrative privileges for installation

When an action is run, the commands are sent to a machine running the PowerCLI and PowerActions software. Now, let's start the installation. Remember, the machine where we want to install the PowerActions software needs to have PowerShell and PowerCLI installed.

To start the installation, just double-click on the downloaded installation file.

Next, accept the license agreement:

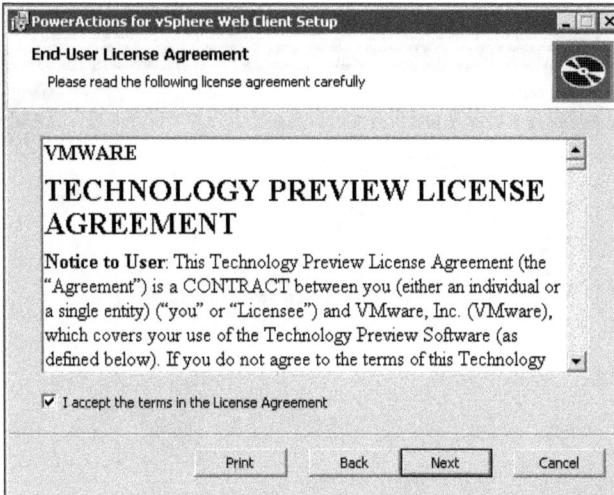

In the next screen, you can select different locations and click on **Next**:

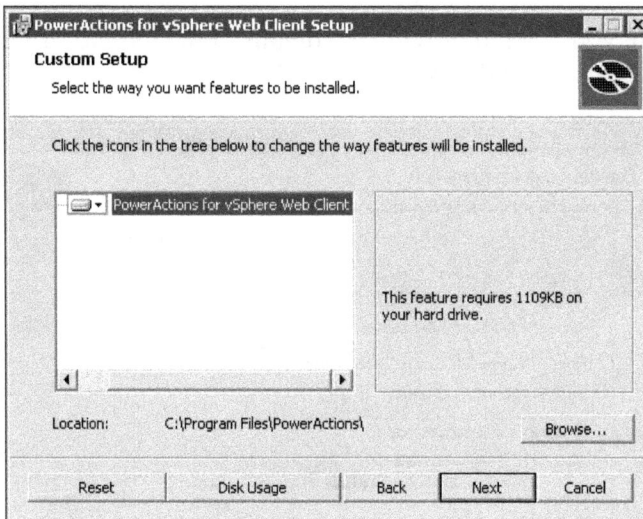

Then, you need to provide the required port and the hostname with which it will be registered with the lookup service:

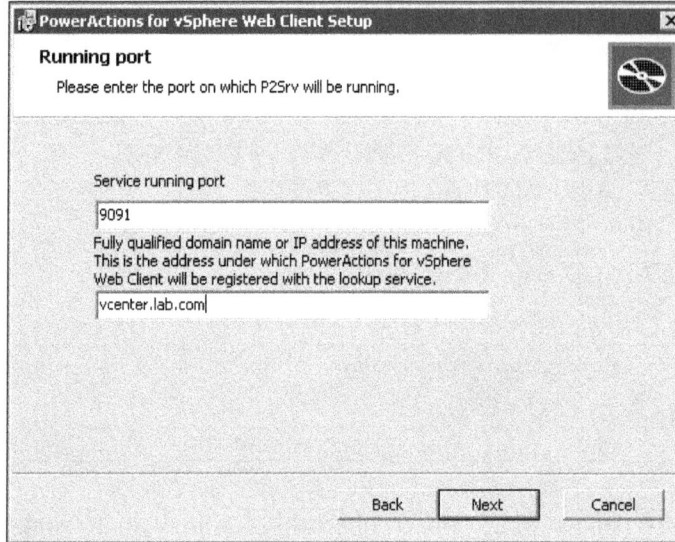

In the next screen, you need to provide the details of the lookup service server and the SSO Administrator ID and password:

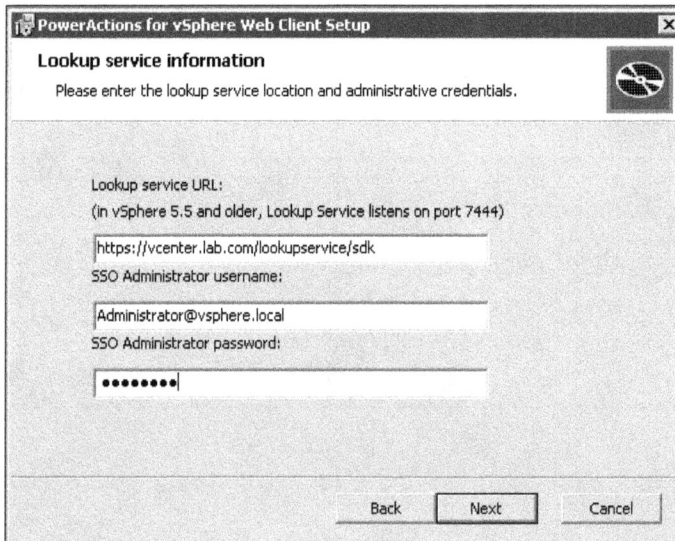

In the next screen, you can start the installation by clicking on **Install**:

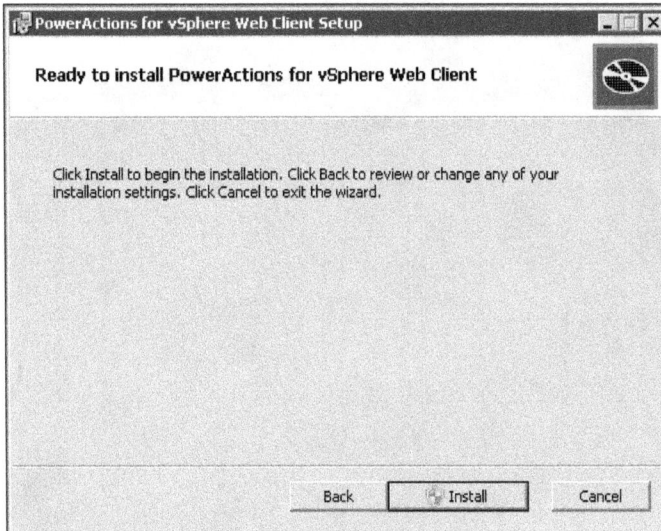

In the next screen, you can start the installation by clicking on **Install**:

You will be prompted for administrative permission:

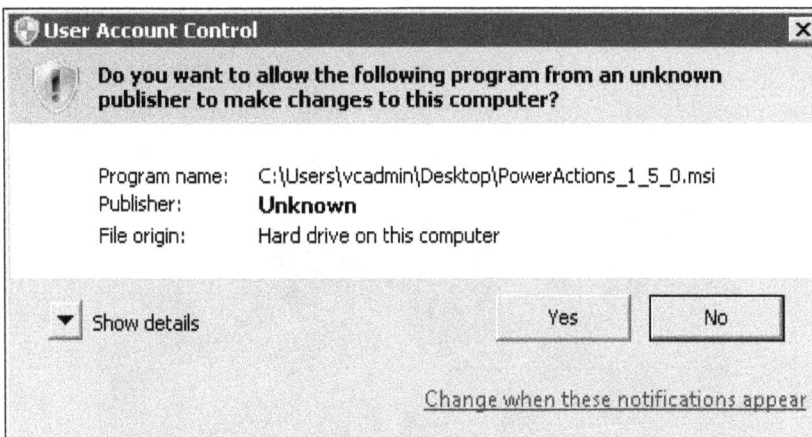

Once you click on **Yes**, the installation will start. Afterwards, click on the **Finish** button to finish the task.

If we open the Web Client after the installation, we can see that two extra buttons have been added: **PowerCLI Console** and **PowerCLI Scripts**. These are highlighted in the following screenshot:

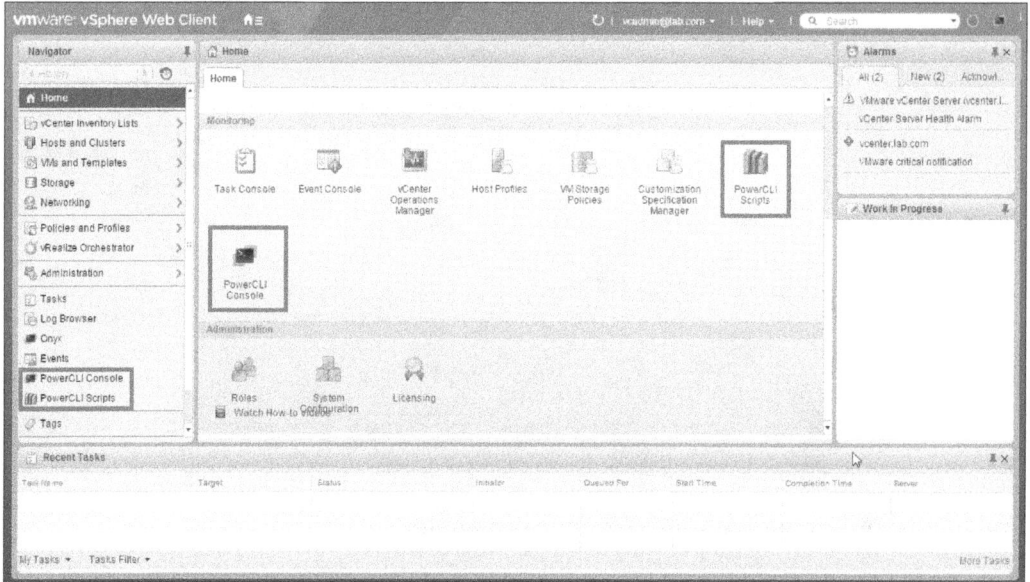

The PowerCLI console provides a PowerCLI console in the Web Client itself (yes, I know it sounds amazing), as you can see in the following screenshot:

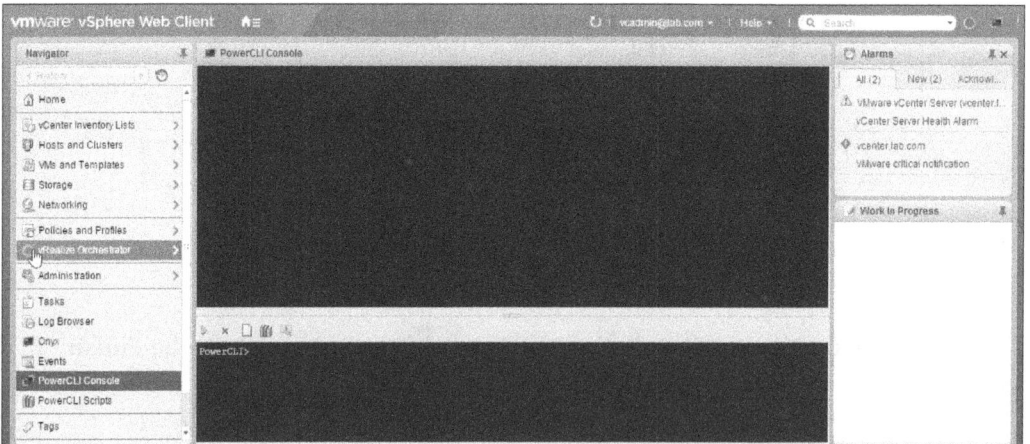

PowerCLI Scripts is a repository for PowerCLI scripts. It allows you to store your scripts or share the script with other admins as well.

In the PowerCLI Scripts window, we can add a new script by clicking on the new script button. Then, we need to provide `Target Type`, which is the object against which we need to run the script:

In the next screen, we need to provide a name and description for the script. Also, we need to mention **Output format** — that is, whether the script will do an action (**Action**) or report something (**Report**):

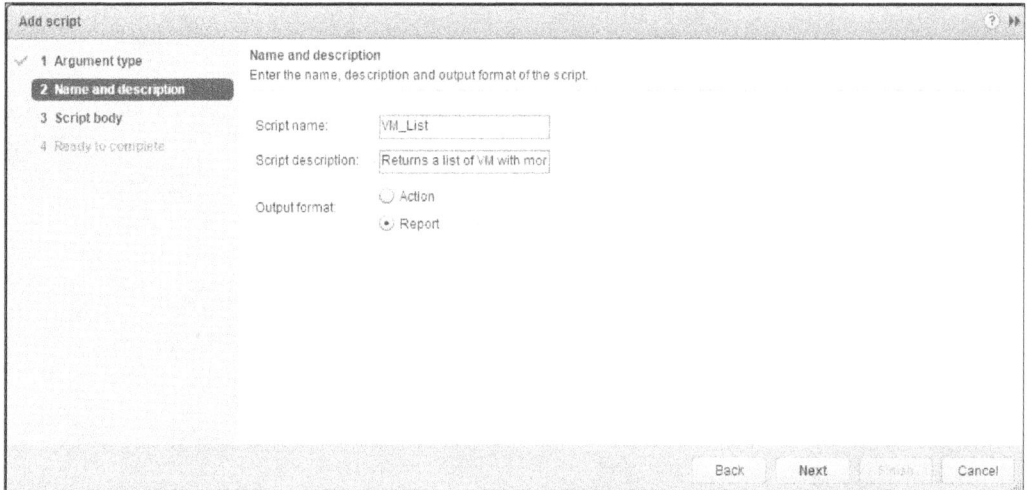

In the next screen, we need to provide the script. Note the default $vParam parameter. By default it will return the entity on which we right click and run the script. For example, if I selected and right clicked on a Cluster in Web Client to run the script against the cluster then $vParam variable will hold the Cluster entity. This value can be used later in the script. In this example, I am trying to get a list of all the VMs in the environment with more than 1 GB memory:

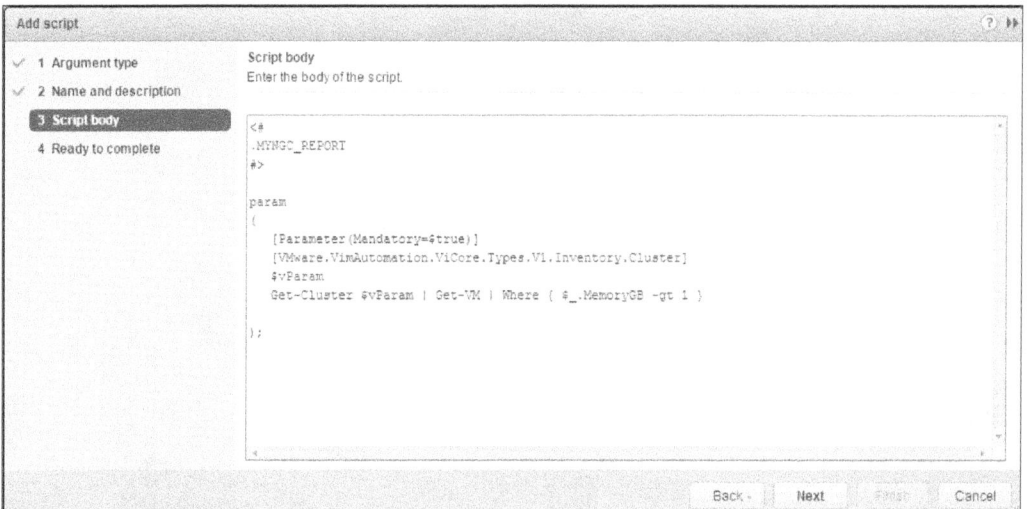

The next screen shows the **Ready to complete** page. In this page, we can check all the information and click on **Finish** to create the script:

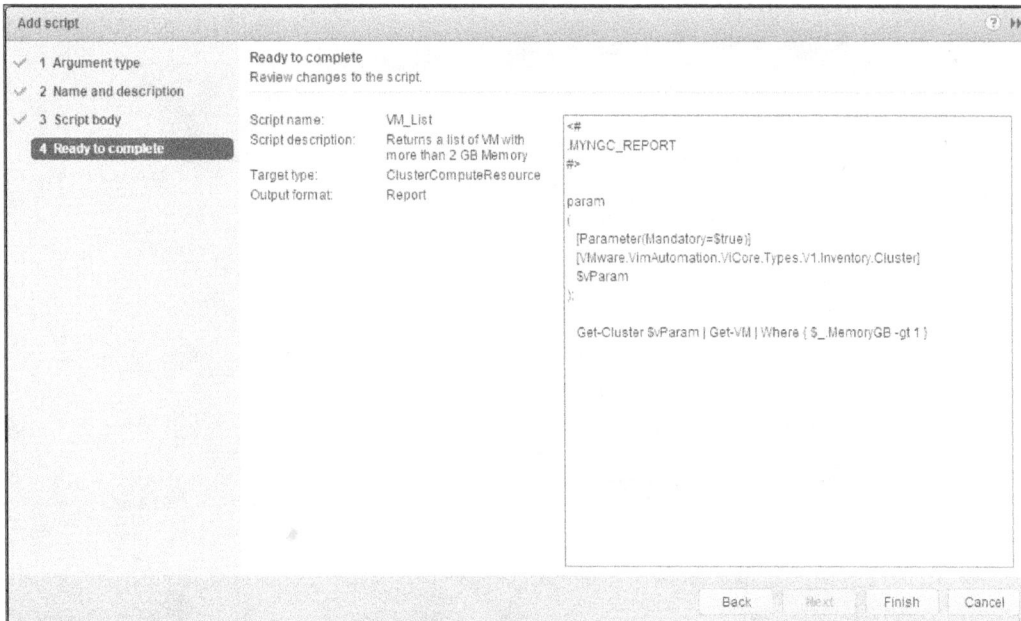

We can click on the **PowerCLI Scripts** button and get a list of all the scripts available in the environment:

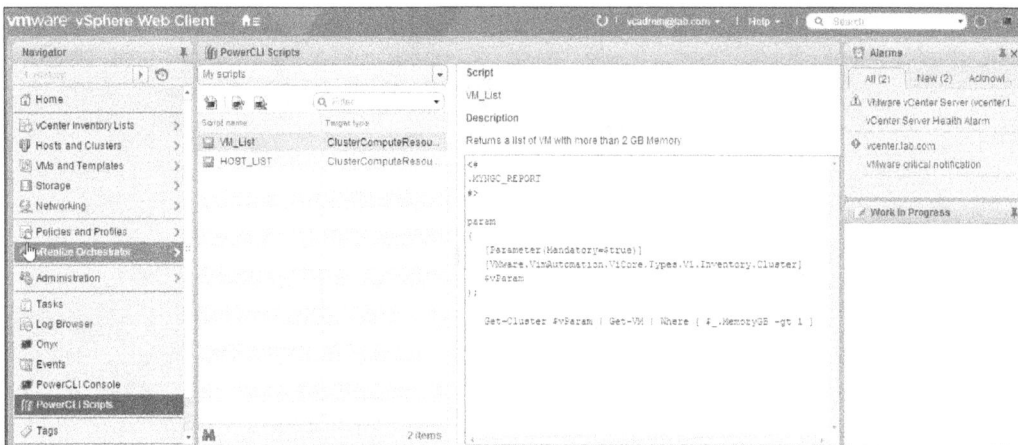

To run a script, we simply select the entity from vSphere Web client, right-click on it, and we get an option for PowerCLI and two further options for **Execute Script** and **Create Script**. This is shown in the following screenshot:

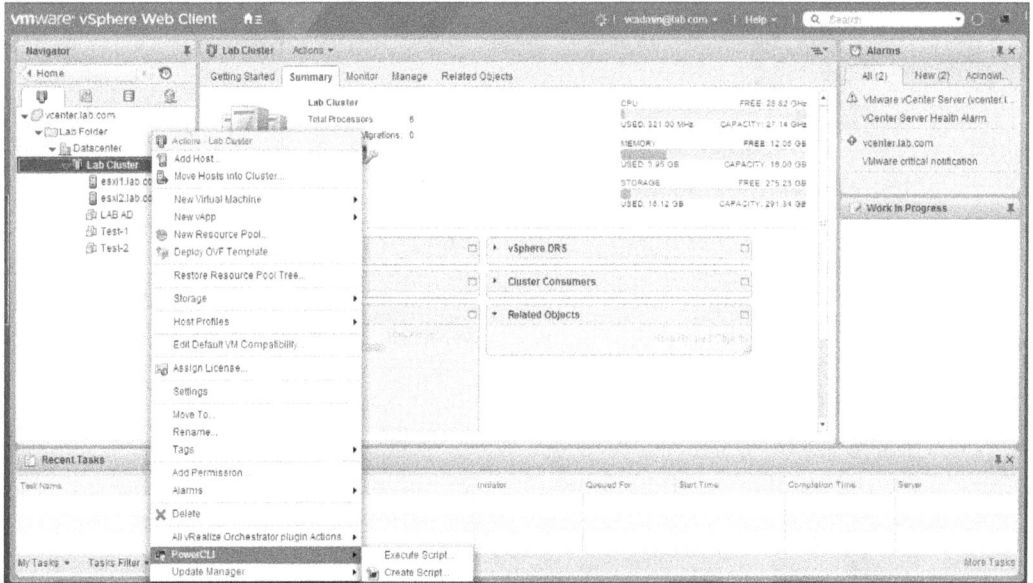

Since we want to execute a script against the Cluster entity (I had written to script to return all the VMs in that Cluster with more than 1 GB memory), we need to select the script from the pop-up window:

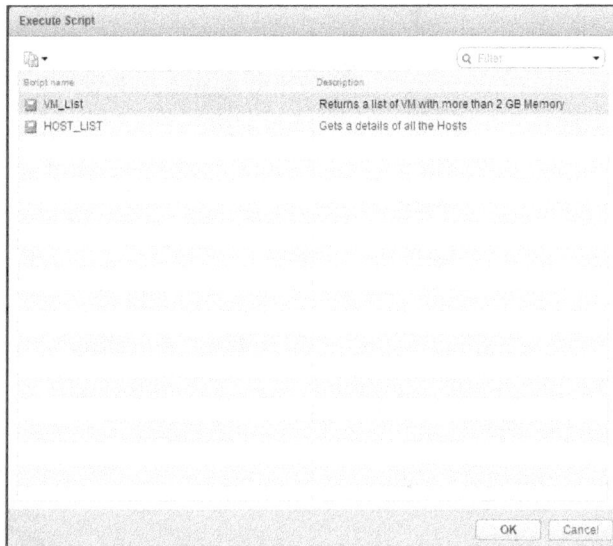

To run the script, select the script and click on **OK**. This will run the script and generate the report in a window:

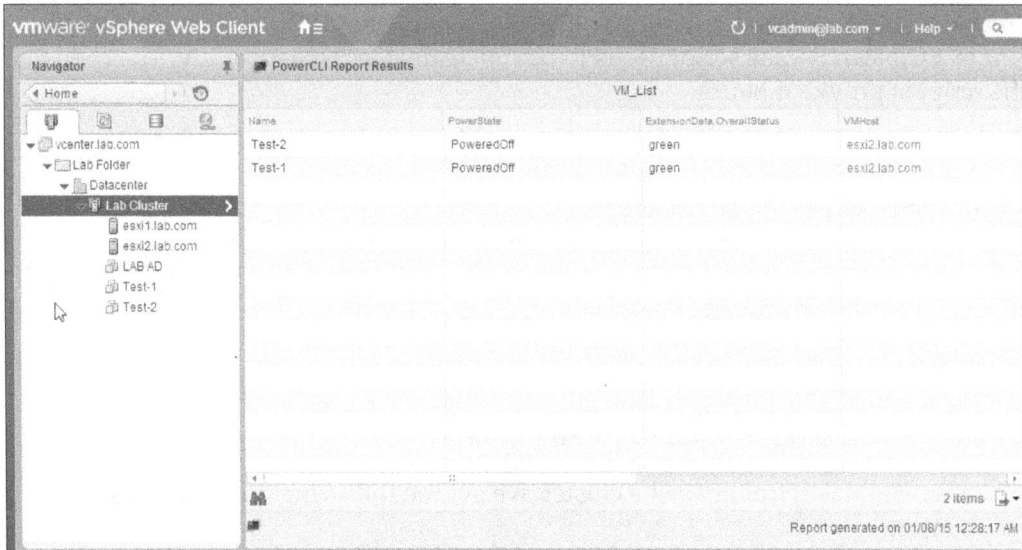

In the following example, I used an action script to increase the resources for the LAB AD VM.

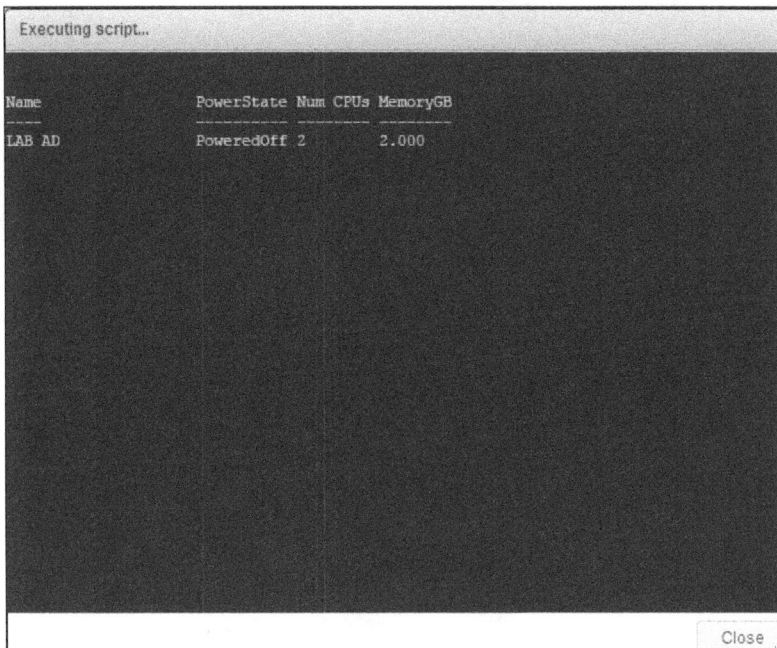

If we are running any Action task and if an input is needed, a popup is shown to provide the input and finally we get a window with the output of the script. After checking the output, we need to close the window to continue. For example, I have created a script `Create-VM`, which will ask for a name for a VM and then create the VM in a Cluster. So, the script needs to be run against a `Cluster` entity. The code for the script is provided here:

```
param
(
    [Parameter(Mandatory=$true)]
    [VMware.VimAutomation.ViCore.Types.V1.Inventory.Cluster]
    $vParam,
    [Parameter(Mandatory=$true)]
    [String]
    $name
);
New-VM -Name $name -ResourcePool -vParam
```

When we run this script against a cluster, we get the following popup that asks for an input:

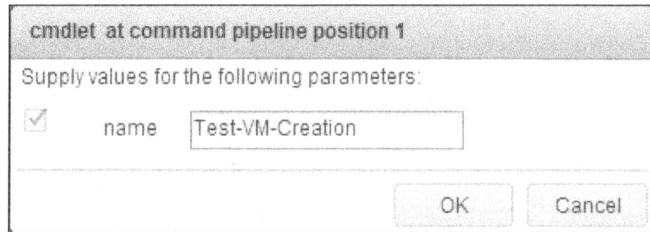

cmdlet at command pipeline position 1
Supply values for the following parameters:
☑   name   Test-VM-Creation
OK   Cancel

The final output is shown in a separate screen:

This is a great tool that lets you automate your daily tasks very easily from the Web Client itself. Your imagination is the limit and you can utilize the feature in so many different ways. Again, Brian Graf has an amazing blog post on this topic at http://blogs.vmware.com/PowerCLI/2015/06/good-news-poweractions-now-available-vsphere-6-0-web-client.html.

Summary

In this chapter, we discussed vSphere APIs and how we can utilize those APIs through PowerCLI to achieve tasks for which there are no direct cmdlets. It is an amazing tool and needs further exploration to achieve tasks which are not possible in the normal way.

In the next chapter, we will discuss REST APIs and how we can utilize them to achieve different tasks in the VMware environment, specifically in vRealize Automation environments.

10
Using REST APIs

In the previous chapter, we discussed how to manage vSphere APIs using PowerCLI. In this chapter, we are going to cover another interesting and helpful topic, REST APIs. In the first part of this chapter, we are going to discuss REST APIs in brief and see how we can manage them using PowerShell. In the next part, we are going to discuss how to manage the vRealize Automation Center by utilizing REST APIs through PowerShell.

We are going to cover the following topics in this chapter:

- Introducing REST APIs
- Introduction to JSON
- The `Invoke-RestMethod` cmdlet
- vRealize Automation REST APIs
- Authenticating and getting a vRealize Automation token
- Managing tenants
- Manage machines
- Managing approvals
- Managing provisioned resources
- Managing network profiles

So let's start our discussion on REST APIs and find out more about them.

Introducing REST APIs

Representational State Transfer (**REST** or **ReST**) is a software architecture style for building scalable Web services. It relies on a stateless, client-server, and cacheable communications protocol. REST is a simple way to manage communication between independent systems. It is inspired by HTTP and HTTP is used in virtually all cases (though it is not limited to HTTP only). Actually, the four most common actions, view, create, edit, and delete, map directly to the HTTP verbs that are already implemented: GET, POST, PUT, and DELETE. So in the case of REST APIs, we use these verbs a lot.

Before we go ahead and talk about the verbs, let's discuss a bit more about REST APIs. The term REST was coined by Roy T. Fielding in his PhD thesis (you can have a look at the thesis at `http://www.ics.uci.edu/~fielding/pubs/dissertation/top.htm`). The primary idea behind REST is to have one standard interface for any service. Instead of exposing an interface with methods, we expose a few methods that are very basic. In this way, the interface is standardized. With any service that supports REST APIs, you know how to access them or which methods to use to access the information. You no longer need to dig into the documentation to find out which method does what, or which method you need to use to get the desired result. Pretty simple, right? You use only a few methods/verbs to do everything.

Coming to the next part, where do we use these verbs? In REST, everything has an ID (uniform resource identifier or URI). Instead of using methods, we give them URIs. In REST, we identity everything with an URI. To get information about that URI, we use **Uniform Resource Locators** (**URLs**). For example, a student Student1 in the 9th grade can be expressed as follows:

```
https://lab.com/Classes/Class-9/Students/Student1
```

The difference between URI and URL is that if URI is an object identifier, then URL is the description by which we can get the URI. For example, if URI is a person's name then URL is the street address where the person lives. For more information, visit `https://en.wikipedia.org/wiki/Uniform_resource_identifier`.

Any such objects are known as Resources in REST. So, we work on the resources and to do so we use those basic verbs.

The advantage is that no matter what the resource or interface is, if it supports REST, we can simply use those predefined verbs only. The resources change, but the action items do not change and remain the same. This simplifies the whole idea of accessing resources and doing something with them.

In REST, using the HTTP protocol we get two points: one is the URL of the resource and another is the method that will be used on this resource. The resource may be a collection resource or collection URI and an Element resource or Element URI.

In the preceding example, `https://lab.com/Classes/Class-9/Students` is an URL representing a collection resource `Students`, whereas `https://lab.com/Classes/Class-9/Student1` is an URL representing an element resource `Student1`.

The most basic tasks that we can do are given by the `CRUD` format. CRUD is short for Create, Read, Update, and Delete operations. The commonly used HTTP methods that we use in RESTful services and their equivalent CRUD format is given in the following table:

HTTP verb	CRUD format	Meaning
POST	Create	To create and object
GET	Read	Get the details of the object
PUT	Update	Update the object
DELETE	Delete	Delete the object

Technically, there are other methods as well: `OPTIONS`, `HEAD`, `TRACE`, and `CONNECT`. Among these, `OPTIONS` and `HEAD` are used most frequently.

Another aspect of REST is getting and using the correct HTTP status codes for the type of request that was made. Here's a list of the codes. Typically, there are four different levels of return codes:

- `2xx`: Success
- `3xx`: Redirect
- `4xx`: User error
- `5xx`: Server error

In all these levels of return codes, the most important ones are as follows:

- **Success codes:**
    - `200`: OK
    - `201`: Created the object
    - `202`: Accepted (in most cases, it's used to denote that the delete operation is accepted)

- **User error codes:**
    - ° 400: Bad Request (generic user error or bad data from user end or client side)
    - ° 401: Unauthorized (to access this particular object, authorization is required)
    - ° 404: Not Found (bad URL)
    - ° 405: Method Not Allowed (wrong HTTP method is used)
    - ° 409: Conflict (typically there is a duplicate resource)

Note that REST is not a protocol; it is an architectural type. So how do you ensure what format the data is returned in? You can request the data in a particular format by putting a request to the server for a particular format, but it entirely depends on the server to reply in a format that was requested from it.

Here's an example of a REST call: GET `https://vmware.com`.

In the next section, we are going to talk about this data format.

Introducing JSON

So far, we talked about REST APIs, the resources that we manage through REST APIs, and the verbs using which we typically manage the resources. But the point is whenever we talk to a resource, we either gather some information about it or do something on it by passing some information to the handling method. Obviously, data passing between a client and server is the main objective. We discussed how we can pass data between client and server, but how do we ensure that the client and server understand each other, the data returned by server is in the same format that the client is expecting, or vice versa? As mentioned earlier, different types of data format are supported since REST is not a protocol. It depends on the protocol that you are using. If the protocol supports a data format, REST can work with it. Two of the frequently used formats are JSON and XML. Because of its simplicity, JSON has become very popular as the format of choice in RESTful services.

JSON (short for **JavaScript Object Notation**) is an open standard format that uses human-readable text to transmit data objects between client and server (typically, a Web application and a server). The data format is in attribute-value pairs. It is used as an alternative to XML.

Though JSON is derived from JavaScript, it is a language-independent data format. Support for parsing data in JSON is in-built in many programming languages.

The major differences between JSON and XML are as follows:

- XML is more verbose than JSON, which means you need to write more in order to use XML. Though this gives more flexibility to XML, JSON becomes easier to write and faster too as you will have to write less.

- XML is used for structured data and does not support arrays, whereas JSON supports arrays.

- Typically, XML parsing is slower than JSON.

- JavaScript directly supports JSON. For that matter, PowerShell also supports direct JSON format.

Note that the following example consists of same data represented in two formats.

The following code is an example of data represented in JSON format:

```
{
  "people": [
    {
      "name": "Sajal Debnath",
      "gender": "male"
    },
    {
      "name": "A. Ray",
      "gender": "female"
    },
    {
      "name": "R. Kanan",
      "gender": "female"
    }
  ]
}
```

The following code is an example of data represented in XML format:

```
<persons>
  <person>
    <name>Sajal Debnath</name>
    <gender>male</gender>
  </person>
  <person>
    <name>A. Ray</name>
    <gender>female</gender>
  </person>
  <person>
    <name>R. Kanan</name>
    <gender>female</gender>
  </person>
</persons>
```

We are going to talk about JSON now, as we will be using JSON for the majority of our tasks. So let's start the discussion with the syntax for JSON. The JSON syntax follows the following rules:

Syntax rules

The syntax rules are as follows:

- Data is a name/value or attribute/value pair
- A name/value pair consists of a filename or attribute name in double quotes, followed by a colon and followed by the value
- Multiple data must be separated by commas
- Objects are defined by curly braces
- Arrays are defined by square brackets

Values

The permitted JSON values are as follows:

- An integer or floating point number
- A string (within double quotes)
- A Boolean value (true or false)
- An array (encompassed by square braces)
- An object (encompassed by curly braces)
- Null

Here's an example of a JSON object:

```
{
"firstName":"Sajal",
"lastName":"Debnath"
}
```

Here's an example of a JSON array; like JavaScript, an array in JSON may contain multiple objects:

```
"Students":[
    {"firstName":"Sajal", "lastName":"Debnath"},
    {"firstName":"Naresh", "lastName":"Purohit"}
]
```

In the preceding example, Students is the array containing two objects (information about two students) and each object in turn contains two attribute/value pairs.

Here's an example of the JSON representation of employee data:

```json
{
  "firstName": "Sajal",
  "lastName": "Debnath",
  "isWorking": true,
  "age": 35,
  "address": {
    "streetAddress": "2435 A.B.C Road",
    "city": "New Delhi",
    "state": "Karnataka",
    "postalCode": "123456"
  },
  "contactNumbers": [
    {
      "type": "home",
      "number": "1234567897"
    },
    {
      "type": "office",
      "number": "123456789876"
    }
  ],
  "children": [],
  "spouse": null
}
```

Finally, the file type in JSON is .json. To mark a file as a JSON type file, we need to save the file with the .json extension.

The MIME type for JSON is application/json. We will discuss where we need to use the MIME type declaration in further sections.

The Invoke-RestMethod cmdlet

The `Invoke-RestMethod` is the PowerShell cmdlet using which we can send an HTTP or HTTPS request to a RESTful Web service. This is the single most important cmdlet for this chapter, as we are going to manage the REST APIs of vRealize Automation using this cmdlet. The syntax for the cmdlet is as follows:

```
Invoke-RestMethod [-Uri] <Uri> [-Body <Object>] [-Certificate
<X509Certificate>] [-CertificateThumbprint <String>] [-ContentType
<String>] [-Credential <PSCredential>] [-DisableKeepAlive] [-Headers
<IDictionary>] [-InFile <String>] [-MaximumRedirection <Int32>] [-
Method <WebRequestMethod>] [-OutFile <String>] [-PassThru] [-Proxy
<Uri>] [-ProxyCredential <PSCredential>] [-
ProxyUseDefaultCredentials] [-SessionVariable <String>] [-TimeoutSec
<Int32>] [-TransferEncoding <String>] [-UseDefaultCredentials]    [-
UserAgent <String>] [-WebSession <WebRequestSession>]
[<CommonParameters>]
```

PowerShell automatically formats the response depending on the returned data type. For an RSS or ATOM feed, the item or Entry XML nodes are returned. For data returned in JSON or XML format, PowerShell converts them to PowerShell Objects.

Let's examine a few of the cmdlet parameters in detail so that we can build and supply values to this cmdlet:

- `-Body <Object>`: The first parameter in the list is `Body`. This specifies the body of the request. This is the content of the request following the headers. This parameter can be used to specify a list of query parameters or the content of response. When this parameter is used with a `GET` request and the body is an `IDictionary` (a key value pair, typically a hash table or JSON string), the body is added to the URI as a query parameter. In other cases (for example, `POST`), the body is set as the value of the request body in the standard `name=value` format. This parameter is optional.

- `-ContentType <String>`: This parameter specifies the content type of the Web request. In case of the `POST` method, if this parameter is omitted, then the content type is set to `application/x-www-form-urlencoded` by default. Otherwise, the content type is not specified in the call. This parameter is optional.

- `-Headers <IDictionary>`: This parameter specifies the headers of the Web request. We need to provide a hash table of dictionary. This parameter is optional.

- `-InFile <String>`: This parameter gets the content of the Web request from a file. This parameter is optional.

- `-Method<WebRequestMethod>`: This parameter specifies the method used for the Web request. The valid values are `Default`, `Delete`, `Get`, `Head`, `Merge`, `Options`, `Patch`, `Post`, `Put`, and `Trace`. This parameter is optional.

- `-Outfile <String>`: This parameter saves the response body in the specified output file. This parameter is optional.

- `-Uri <URI>`: This parameter specifies the URI of the Internet resource to which the Web request is sent. The supported parameters are the `HTTP`, `HTTPS`, `FTP`, and `FILE` values. This parameter is required.

Another cmdlet that we can use is `Invoke-WebRequest`. We can use this cmdlet to get a Web page on the Internet. Another interesting point to note is that this particular cmdlet has an alias: `curl`, the command that is typically used for working with RESTful services:

```
PS C:\> Get-Alias curl

CommandType     Name                                               Version    Source
-----------     ----                                               -------    ------
Alias           curl -> Invoke-WebRequest
```

Before we move on to other topics, we will discuss two important cmdlets in PowerShell: `ConvertTo-Json` and `ConvertFrom-Json`.

The first, `ConvertTo-Json`, converts a PowerShell object to a JSON-formatted string. We will use this cmdlet extensively in PowerShell to build our input data strings later in this chapter. For example, check the following output screenshot:

```
PS C:\> $info = @{username="administrator@vsphere.local"; password="Password";tenant="vsphere.local"}

PS C:\> $info

Name                           Value
----                           -----
username                       administrator@vsphere.local
tenant                         vsphere.local
password                       Password


PS C:\> $json = $info | ConvertTo-Json

PS C:\> $json
{
    "username":  "administrator@vsphere.local",
    "tenant":  "vsphere.local",
    "password":  "Password"
}
```

In the preceding example, we created a variable $info that holds a hash table with the information of a user. Next, we converted the hash table information into a JSON-formatted string and stored it in the variable $json.

The ConvertFrom-Json cmdlet is the opposite of the previous cmdlet. This cmdlet converts a JSON-formatted string to a custom PowerShell object. In the following example, we converted the newly created JSON string stored in the $json variable into a PowerShell object:

```
PS C:\> $object_json = $json | ConvertFrom-Json


PS C:\> $object_json


username                      tenant          password
--------                      ------          --------
administrator@vsphere.local vsphere.local Password
```

Note the type of the object:

```
PS C:\> $object_json.GetType()


IsPublic IsSerial    Name            BaseType
-------- --------    ----            --------
True     False       PSCustomObject  System.Object
```

Also, note that the name/value set of the original hash table is automatically set as properties of the custom object:

```
PS C:\> $object_json | Get-Member


    TypeName: System.Management.Automation.PSCustomObject

Name        MemberType    Definition
----        ----------    ----------
Equals      Method        bool Equals(System.Object obj)
GetHashCode Method        int GetHashCode()
GetType     Method        type GetType()
ToString    Method        string ToString()
password    NoteProperty  string password=Password
tenant      NoteProperty  string tenant=vsphere.local
username    NoteProperty  string username=administrator@vsphere.local
```

vRealize Automation REST APIs

So far, we talked about REST APIs and how we can work with them in PowerShell. In this section, we are going to talk about **vRealize Automation (vRA)** REST APIs as well as how and where we can access them.

There are two documents that are related to vRA REST APIs and they will be very helpful to us: *Programming Guide* and *REST API Reference*. They can be found at `https://www.vmware.com/support/pubs/vcac-pubs.html`. From the link, you can either download the PDF version or explore them in the browser. While the second document provides the reference to all the available REST API in vRA, the first one provides a programming guide to using these REST APIs to manage the vRA environment. While exploring the RESTful services for vRA, we can see that the vRA REST API provides consumer-level, administrator-level, and provider-level access to the service catalog of the same services that are available from the user interface. Whenever a service request is done with a resource URL, the first part of the URL identifies the service and the last part identifies the resource. Here's a list of the REST API services provided by vRA:

Service	Description
Advanced Designer Service	Manage forms, endpoints, service blueprints, tenants, vRealize Orchestrator imports, workflows, and workitems through the Advanced Designer Service.
Approval Service	Retrieve, create, update, and delete approval policies, policy types, policy instances, and policy requests.
Branding Service	Change the background and text colors, company logo, company name, product name, tenant name, and other resources in the console.
Catalog Service	Retrieve global catalog items, entitled catalog items, and entitlements for a catalog item and its service so that the current user can review them. A consumer can retrieve, edit, and submit a request form for a catalog item. A provider can retrieve, register, update, and delete catalog items. Provision and manage systems.
Catalog Registry	Access services from a single location.
EventLog Service	Query system events recorded by other services.
Files Service	Unused.
Identity Service	Manage tenants, business groups, SSO and custom groups, users, and identity stores.
Licensing Service	Retrieve permissions and post serial keys.

Service	Description
Management Service	Retrieve workitem forms, callbacks, and tasks. Manage endpoint details including tenant, password, username, and endpoint URL. Retrieve performance metrics. Retrieve and cancel reclamation requests.
Notification Service	Configure and send notifications for several types of events such as the successful completion of a catalog request or a required approval.
Plug-in Service	Retrieve, create, update, and delete a resource. Retrieve an extension and license notifications.
Portal Service	Retrieve, create, update, and delete a portal resource.
Reservation Service	Retrieve, create, update, and delete a reservation or reservation policy.
vCO Service	Manage vRealize Orchestrator actions, tasks, packages, and workflows. Browse system and plug-in inventories.
WorkItem Service	Retrieve, create, update, complete, cancel, and delete a workitem. Retrieve form data, metadata, detail forms, and submission forms from service providers.

Source: `http://pubs.vmware.com/vra-62/index.jsp#com.vmware.vra.programming.doc/GUID-FBF2B82A-F5F3-43DC-A2FA-66BCF3C79EC3.html`

To explore the REST APIs, we can use the `REST API Reference` document. For example, if we want to manage `Catalog Services`, we would go to the `Catalog Services` portion in the reference document. We can see that in the Introduction it is mentioned that this particular REST API is designed for managing the Service Catalog. In the consumer API section, it is mentioned that these resources will be used by the consumer; that is, any user who wants to request a catalog item will be a consumer of this API. The base URI of this API is as follows:

```
Base URI : /api/consumer
```

Next, we have a table where the resources are listed along with the respective Resource URI. Also, notes are provided with the resource to clarify the point. For example, the URI for the API related to catalog items is `/catalogitems`. So the URI will be `/api/consumer/catalogitems` and the respective URL will be `https://<host>/component-registry/api/consumer/catalogitems`.

It is evident that if we do a GET method on this URL with the required information, then we will get a list of catalog items in the environment.

Similarly, details of the `Catalog Service Provider API` and `Catalog Admin API` are provided on the same page.

In the next section, links to the details of all the REST Resources related to Catalog services are provided. For example, the list starts with the details of the resource `CatalogItem`.

The last section of the page provides a link to the details of all the data elements used in these resources.

Coming back to the preceding example, we want to find out the details of the `CatalogItem` resource. So, we will follow the link to the details page. In the details page, we can see the details of all the related resources and the methods that can be used on them. We can see that as per our original intention of getting a list of catalog items, we need to use the `GET` method on the `/api/catalogitems` URI. The list also provides details of `Parameters` and information about `Response Body`.

We can see that the `Response Body` element is a `Page of CatalogItem`. If we again follow the `CatalogItem` link, it will take us to the details of that `CatalogItem` element. In this details page an example JSON format of the `CatalogItem` is also given. We can directly check the `CatalogItem` element through the `Data` elements browser as well.

Similarly, we can browse the REST API reference document to get details of the resources and the required parameters to use them. From now onwards, we will utilize these resources to achieve our goal.

Authenticating and getting a vRA token

To manage the vRA environment through REST API, we will need HTTP bearer tokens in request headers for the authentication of requests. So we get a bearer token and use that instead of supplying a user ID and password each and every time we want to connect to vRA. Once we get a bearer token, we can use it until it expires or we purposefully delete it. By default, a bearer token is valid for 24 hours. If for some reason you need to change the default duration, follow the instructions provided in the following Web page: `http://pubs.vmware.com/vra-62/index.jsp#com.vmware.vra.programming.doc/GUID-FDB47B40-F651-4FBD-8D1E-AC6FC8FA7A96.html`.

For example, if for security purposes, you want to change the default validity time to a smaller number of hours.

To get a bearer token, we need to POST a request to `https://<vRA>/identity/api/tokens`. Since we would use the HTTP protocol, we need to build `Header` and the `Body`. We need to pass two parameters in `Header`: `Accept: application/json` and `Content-Type: application/json`. Most times, we will need to use these to build a header so the details of these two parameters are provided here:

- **Accept**: This header field specifies which media types are acceptable as the response of the request
- **Content-Type**: This field specifies the media type of the entire-body sent to the recipient

While checking the REST API documentation, you can see that each and every resource provides the details of the `Request Body` and `Response Body` format.

If you need more information, you can check the vRA REST API Programming Guide at `http://pubs.vmware.com/vra-62/index.jsp#com.vmware.vra.programming.doc/GUID-A83C30BB-3EDD-439B-B369-A92B4992EEDD.html`.

So, let's start building the blocks. First, we will start with the header:

```
$headers = New-Object
"System.Collections.Generic.Dictionary[[String],[String]]"
$headers.Add('Accept', 'application/json')
$headers.Add('Content-Type', 'application/json')
```

Next, we will build the body of the request and convert it to JSON format:

```
$body = @{username="administrator@vsphere.local";
password="Vmware1!";tenant="vsphere.local"}
$json =$body | ConvertTo-Json
```

Next, we will invoke the actual request:

```
Invoke-RestMethod -Method Post -Uri
"https://vra.lab.com/identity/api/tokens" -Headers $headers -Body
$json
```

Putting everything together:

```
PS C:\> $headers = New-Object "System.Collections.Generic.Dictionary[[String],[String]]"
PS C:\> $headers.Add('Accept', 'application/json')
PS C:\> $headers.Add('Content-Type', 'application/json')
PS C:\> $headers
Key              Value
---              -----
Accept           application/json
Content-Type     application/json

PS C:\> $body = @{username="administrator@vsphere.local"; password="Vmware1!";tenant="vsphere.local"}
PS C:\> $json =$body | ConvertTo-Json
PS C:\> $json
{
    "username":  "administrator@vsphere.local",
    "tenant":  "vsphere.local",
    "password":  "Vmware1!"
}
PS C:\> Invoke-RestMethod -Method Post -Uri "https://vra.lab.com/identity/api/tokens" -Headers $headers -Body $json
expires                   id
-------                   --
2015-08-09T16:54:19.338Z  MTQzOTA1Mjg1OTM2ODozY2M0Y2Z8TOTF-iNTgUNAUSMzRmMTp0ZW5hbnQ6dnNwaGVyZS5sb2NhbHVzZXJuYW1lOmFkbWluaXN0cmF0b3JAdnNwaGVyZS5sb2NhbDpmOTdkMGUxMDZhN2E5Zj11MGFkYTk5Njc1NjAyMGU4MTc4N...
```

Note the ID of the returned information. This is the token. We need to store this token in a variable and use it for authentication. We can directly save the token in a variable by running the following command:

```
PS C:\> $token = (Invoke-RestMethod -Method Post -Uri
"https://vra.lab.com/identity/api/tokens" -Headers $headers -Body
$json).id
```

```
PS C:\> $token
MTQzOTA1MzEyMDQ3MTpjNTczMzU0YzgzYTRkYmJkZThhZTp0ZW5hbnQ6dnNwaGVyZS5sb
2NhbHVzZXJuYW1lOmFkbWluaXN0cmF0b3JAdnNwaGVyZS5sb2NhbDpmOTdkMGUxMDZhN2
E5ZjllMGFkYTk5NjclNjAyMGU4MTc4N
TVhM2VmNmQ5NjhiZGExNzExYmY3MWU3ODQyZWM2YTcxYmVhMjRmZWI1NmEzNGYzMWM0Nj
RjMDUzNzkyOTVhOTZmNDNkMjg4YTFiNmJhOTE1OThkZTYyYjc4ZjU4NA==
```

Managing tenants

Since we have the token, we can start exploring the vRA environment. We will start by managing the tenants. First, let's get a list of existing tenants. From now onwards, we need to provide authorization for working with the resources. Since we already have a token, we need to pass the authorization as a parameter in the header itself. We will use the following format:

```
Authorization: Bearer $token
```

Here, $token holds the authorization token. For this, we will build out the header. So, define a new object:

```
PS C:\>$headers = New-Object
"System.Collections.Generic.Dictionary[[String],[String]]"
```

Next, add the components of the header:

```
PS C:\> $headers.Add('Accept', 'application/json')
PS C:\> $headers.Add('Authorization', "Bearer $token")
```

Note the Authorization parameter; there needs to be a space between bearer and token. Next, get the information:

```
PS C:\> Invoke-RestMethod -Method Get -Uri
"https://vra.lab.com/identity/api/tenants" -Headers $headers | FL
```

Putting everything together:

Creating a tenant

Next, let's create a tenant. For this, the input JSON file format is provided here:

```
{
    "@type" : "Tenant",
    "id" : "$tenantId",
    "urlName" : "$tenantURL",
    "name" : "$tenantName",
    "description" : "$description",
    "contactEmail" : "$emailAddress",
    "defaultTenant" : false
}
```

We can use a JSON file for this or build the parameters in runtime. First, we will build the header. We will need to mention `Content-Type` and `Authorization`:

```
PS C:\ $headers = New-Object
"System.Collections.Generic.Dictionary[[String],[String]]"
PS C:\ $headers.Add('Content-Type', 'application/json')
PS C:\ $headers.Add('Authorization', "Bearer $token")
```

Next, we will build the body in line with the parameter needed and convert it to the JSON format:

```
PS C:\ $body = @{"@type"="Tenant";"password"="";
id="tenant2";urlName="tenant2";name="tenant2";description="This
Tenant 2";contactEmail="vcadmin@lab.com";defaultTenant="false"}
PS C:\ $json =$body | ConvertTo-Json
```

Finally, we will invoke the `Put` method to create the tenant:

```
PS C:\> Invoke-RestMethod -Method Put -Uri
"https://vra.lab.com/identity/api/tenants/tenant2" -Headers $headers
-Body $json
```

The preceding command will create a tenant named `tenant2`.

Putting everything together:

```
PS C:\> $headers = New-Object "System.Collections.Generic.Dictionary[[String],[String]]"
PS C:\> $headers.Add('Content-Type', 'application/json')
PS C:\> $headers.Add('Authorization', "Bearer $token")
PS C:\> $body = @{"@type"="Tenant";"password"=""; id="tenant2";urlName="tenant2";
name="tenant2";description="This Tenant 2";contactEmail="vcadmin@lab.com";defaultTenant="false"}
PS C:\> $json =$body | ConvertTo-Json
PS C:\> Invoke-RestMethod -Method Put -Uri "https://vra.lab.com/identity/api/tenants/tenant2" -Headers $headers -Body $json

id            : tenant2
urlName       : tenant2
name          : tenant2
description   : This Tenant 2
contactEmail  : vcadmin@lab.com
password      :
defaultTenant : False
```

Listing identity stores for a tenant

To get a list of all the identity stores for a particular tenant, we need to query the directories resource of a tenant. We can get a list of identity stores by using the following method:

```
PS C:\> $headers = New-Object
"System.Collections.Generic.Dictionary[[String],[String]]"


PS C:\> $headers.Add('Accept', 'application/json')


PS C:\> $headers.Add('Content-Type', 'application/json')


PS C:\> $headers.Add('Authorization', "Bearer $token")


PS C:\> (Invoke-RestMethod -Method Get -Uri
"https://vra.lab.com/identity/api/tenants/Test/directories" -Headers
$headers).content
```

Putting everything together:

```
PS C:\> $headers = New-Object "System.Collections.Generic.Dictionary[[String],[String]]"
PS C:\> $headers.Add('Accept', 'application/json')
PS C:\> $headers.Add('Content-Type', 'application/json')
PS C:\> $headers.Add('Authorization', "Bearer $token")
PS C:\> (Invoke-RestMethod -Method Get -Uri "https://vra.lab.com/identity/api/tenants/Test/directories" -Headers $headers).content

@type            : IdentityStore
domain           : lab.com
name             : Lab AD
description      :
alias            :
type             : AD
userNameDn       : CN=Administrator,CN=Users,DC=lab,DC=com
password         :
url              : ldap://lab-ad.lab.com:389
groupBaseSearchDn : CN=Users,DC=lab,DC=com
userBaseSearchDn  : CN=Users,DC=lab,DC=com
new              : False
```

Linking an identity store to a tenant

Next, let's try to add an identity store to a tenant. Remember that we did not add an identity store when we created the tenant tenant2. So let's add a store now. For this, we need to pass the information in the following JSON format:

```
{
    "alias": "$domainAlias",
    "domain": "$domainName",
    "groupBaseSearchDn": "$grpBaseSearchDn",
```

```
    "name": "$identityStoreName",
    "password": "$password",
    "type": "$identityStoreType",
    "url": "$identityServerUrl",
    "userBaseSearchDn": "$usrBaseSearchDn",
    "userNameDn": "$usrNameDn"
}
```

So let's begin the header preparation. We use the following process to build the header:

```
$headers = New-Object
"System.Collections.Generic.Dictionary[[String],[String]]"
$headers.Add('Content-Type', 'application/json')
$headers.Add('Authorization', "Bearer $token")
```

Next, we will build the body and convert it to JSON format:

```
$body =
@{"alias"="lab.com";"domain"="lab.com";"groupBaseSearchDn"="ou=demo,
dc=lab,dc=com";`
"name"="LAB-
AD";"password"="Vmware1!";"type"="LDAP";"url"="ldap://lab.com:389";`
"userBaseSearchDn"="ou=demo,dc=lab,dc=com";"userNameDn"="cn=Administr
ator,ou=Users,dc=lab,dc=com"}


$json = $body | ConvertTo-Json
```

Finally, we will call out the method to add the store.

```
Invoke-RestMethod -Method Put -Uri
"https://vra.lab.com/identity/api/tenants/tenant2/directories/lab.com
" -Headers $headers -Body $json
```

Putting everything together:

We can see from the following screenshot that the identity store has been added:

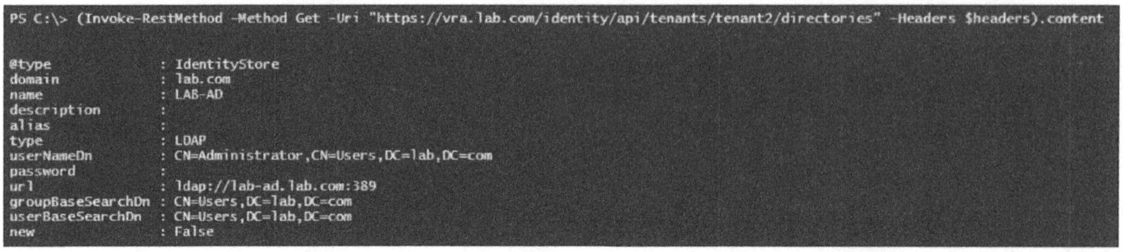

```
PS C:\> (Invoke-RestMethod -Method Get -Uri "https://vra.lab.com/identity/api/tenants/tenant2/directories" -Headers $headers).content

@type              : IdentityStore
domain             : lab.com
name               : LAB-AD
description        :
alias              :
type               : LDAP
userNameDn         : CN=Administrator,CN=Users,DC=lab,DC=com
password           :
url                : ldap://lab-ad.lab.com:389
groupBaseSearchDn  : CN=Users,DC=lab,DC=com
userBaseSearchDn   : CN=Users,DC=lab,DC=com
new                : False
```

Similar to the preceding examples, you can do other tasks related to tenants by using the REST APIs.

Managing machines

Now, we will look at ways to manage the machines in a tenant. For this, we will start by checking a list of all available catalog items.

Listing shared and private catalog items

To get a list of catalog items, first build the header:

```
$headers = New-Object "System.Collections.Generic.
Dictionary[[String],[String]]"

$headers.Add('Content-Type', 'application/json')

$headers.Add('Authorization', "Bearer $token")
```

Next, simply query the resources:

```
PS C:\> (Invoke-RestMethod -Method Get -Uri

"https://vra.lab.com/catalog-

service/api/consumer/entitledCatalogItems" -Headers

$headers).Content.catalogItem[0] | ConvertTo-Json
```

We get a list of items. For readability and easy understanding, we will select only one output. Since the output is a PowerShell object (in this case, it is an array of objects), we are just selecting the first element and then converting it to JSON format:

```
[
    {
        "id":  "bda84bcb-d3f6-4332-8781-89d146ef5e28",
        "version":  2,
        "name":  "Cloud-Test",
        "description":  "",
        "status":  "PUBLISHED",
        "statusName":  "Published",
        "organization":  {
                            "tenantRef":  "vsphere.local",
                            "tenantLabel":  "vsphere.local",
                            "subtenantRef":  null,
                            "subtenantLabel":  null
                         },
        "providerBinding":  {
                            "bindingId":
                            "8fe864f7-cff6-47e1-b04a-
                              9413917290ba",
                            "providerRef":  "@{id=e70b620a-
                            c254-4c0a-87ad-2c4a61cfefd1;
                            label=iaas-service}"
                         },
        "forms":  null,
        "callbacks":  null,
        "isNoteworthy":  true,
        "dateCreated":  "2015-08-07T18:38:54.728Z",
        "lastUpdatedDate":  "2015-08-10T14:47:22.853Z",
        "iconId":  "bda84bcb-d3f6-4332-8781-89d146ef5e28",
        "catalogItemTypeRef":  {
                            "id": "Infrastructure.Virtual",
                            "label":  "Virtual Machine"
                         },
        "serviceRef":  {
                            "id":
                            "1c03d1c3-6b6e-44c6-ad2c-cecb3a58c27d",
                            "label":  "IaaS"
                         },
```

```
                  "outputResourceTypeRef":   {
                                          "id":
                                          "Infrastructure.Virtual",
                                          "label":   "Virtual Machine"
                                      }
            },
```

Following is an example output:

```
id                  : bda84bcb-d3f6-4332-8781-89d146ef5e28
version             : 1
name                : Cloud-Test
description         :
status              : PUBLISHED
statusName          : Published
organization        : @{tenantRef=vsphere.local; tenantLabel=vsphere.local; subtenantRef=; subtenantLabel=}
providerBinding     : @{bindingId=8fe864f7-cff6-47e1-b04a-9413917290ba; providerRef=}
forms               :
callbacks           :
isNoteworthy        : True
dateCreated         : 2015-08-07T18:38:54.728Z
lastUpdatedDate     : 2015-08-07T18:40:03.907Z
iconId              : cafe_default_icon_genericCatalogItem
catalogItemTypeRef  : @{id=Infrastructure.Virtual; label=Virtual Machine}
serviceRef          : @{id=1c03d1c3-6b6e-44c6-ad2c-cecb3a58c27d; label=IaaS}
outputResourceTypeRef : @{id=Infrastructure.Virtual; label=Virtual Machine}
```

From the preceding list, we can see that one catalog item is available with the name
`Cloud-Test`.

Next, we will request a VM from this catalog item. To request a VM, we need to
create a JSON file in the format given in the following link. Because it is a large file,
I have not shown it here. But it is easy to build and understand, so please visit the
Web page and build the JSON file: `http://pubs.vmware.com/vra-62/index.`
`jsp#com.vmware.vra.programming.doc/GUID-6478E29E-F7FC-4F16-8E54-`
`3E5444626DC7.html`.

We need to fill the following parameters in this file: `catalogItemRef`, `tenantRef`,
`subtenantRef`, `provider-blueprintID`, and `provider-provisioningGroupId`.

We can get most of this information from the catalog item list. Note that
`provider-provisioningGroupId` is the same as `subtenantRef`. To build
the previous JSON file, we need to get `subtenantRef`, which can be obtained
by running the following command:

```
PS C:\> (Invoke-RestMethod -Method Get -Uri
"https://vra.lab.com/identity/api/tenants/vsphere.local/subtenants
" -Headers $headers).content | ConvertTo-Json
{
    "@type":  "Subtenant",
    "id":  "5c91a267-581a-4e00-9895-cf6e9c6b313a",
    "name":  "Test",
    "description":  "VMPS",
    "subtenantRoles":  null,
```

```json
    "extensionData":  {
                            "entries":  [

                            ]
                        },
        "tenant":   "vsphere.local"
}
```

By putting everything together, we can build the required JSON file as follows (part of the file is provided here):

```json
{
    "@type": "CatalogItemRequest",
    "catalogItemRef": {
        "id": "bda84bcb-d3f6-4332-8781-89d146ef5e28"
    },
    "organization": {
        "tenantRef": "vsphere.local",
        "subtenantRef": "5c91a267-581a-4e00-9895-cf6e9c6b313a"
    },
    "requestedFor": "vradmin@lab.com",
    "state": "SUBMITTED",
    "requestNumber": 0,
    "requestData": {
        "entries": [{
            "key": "provider-blueprintId",
            "value": {
                "type": "string",
                "value": "8fe864f7-cff6-47e1-b04a-9413917290ba"
            }
        },
        {
            "key": "provider-provisioningGroupId",
            "value": {
                "type": "string",
                "value": "5c91a267-581a-4e00-9895-cf6e9c6b313a"
            }
        },
        {
            "key": "requestedFor",
            "value": {
                "type": "string",
                "value": "vradmin@lab.com"
            }
        },
```

With the input file ready, I saved it as a VM-Input.JSON file and ran the following command to raise the request:

```
PS C:\> Invoke-RestMethod -Method Post -Uri
"https://vra.lab.com/catalog-service/api/consumer/requests" -Headers
$headers -InFile "E:\VM-Input.JSON"
```

This simply raises the request. You can use the same process to raise requests for catalog items.

Managing approvals

In this section, we will discuss how to manage approvals in the vRA environment. First, let's see a list of workitems that are available. In the following command, I am just getting a list of the content:

```
PS C:\> (Invoke-RestMethod -Method Get -Uri
"https://vra.lab.com/workitem-service/api/workitems" -Headers $headers).
content | ConvertTo-Json
```

Part of the output is provided here:

```
{
    "@type":  "WorkItem",
    "id":  "2a11c987-dd8f-4a2d-a15a-b048ca64d729",
    "version":  1,
    "workItemNumber":  2,
    "assignees":  [
                {
                    "principalId":  "vradmin@lab.com",
                    "principalType":  "USER"
                }
            ],
    "subTenantId":  "5c91a267-581a-4e00-9895-cf6e9c6b313a",
    "tenantId":  "vsphere.local",
    "callbackEntityId":  "2a11c987-dd8f-4a2d-a15a-b048ca64d729",
    "workItemType":  {
            "id":  "com.vmware.csp.core.approval.workitem.request",
                    "name":  "Approval",
                    "pluralizedName":  "Approvals",
                    "description":  "Type registered by the
                     Approval Service.",
                    "serviceTypeId":
                    "com.vmware.csp.core.cafe.approvals",
                    "actions":  [
```

```
                        "@{id=com.vmware.csp.core.approval.
                        action.approve; name=Approve;
                        stateName=Approved; icon=;
                        stateNameId={com.vmware.csp.
                        core.cafe.approvals@action.
                        approve.state}}",
                        "@{id=com.vmware.csp.core.
                        approval.action.reject;
                        name=Reject; stateName=Rejected;
                        icon=; stateNameId={com.vmware.
                        csp.core.cafe.approvals@action.
                        reject.state}}"
                        ],
               "completeByEmail":  true,
               "commentsField":
               "businessJustification",
```

From the preceding list, we can get the ID of each workitem. Now, we will get details of a particular workitem. To do so, we will simply extend the query to the workitem in the following format. Note that the `availableActions` option has only two options, `Approve` and `Reject`. The command is as follows:

```
PS C:\> Invoke-RestMethod -Method Get -Uri
"https://vra.lab.com/workitem-service/api/workitems/2a11c987-dd8f-
4a2d-a15a-b048ca64d729" -Headers $headers | ConvertTo-Json
```

Part of the output is provided here:

```
{
    "id":  "2a11c987-dd8f-4a2d-a15a-b048ca64d729",
    "version":  1,
    "workItemNumber":  2,
    .
    .
    .
    .


"availableActions":   [
                     {
                        "id":
                "com.vmware.csp.core.approval.action.approve",
                     "name":  "Approve",
                        "stateName":  "Approved",
```

```
                        "icon":  "@{id=f55ef724-7633-49fc-9889-
                        ed55ce5c93cd; name=approved.png;
                        contentType=image/png; image=}",
                        "stateNameId":
                        "{com.vmware.csp.core.cafe.approvals
                        @action.approve.state}"
                                    },
                                    {
                        "id": "com.vmware.csp.core.
                        approval.action.reject",
                         "name":  "Reject",
                        "stateName":  "Rejected",
                        "icon":  "@{id=388d2935-5050-402b-
                        a71c-9ed9836f2a8d; name=rejected.png;
                        contentType=image/png; image=}",
                        "stateNameId":
                        "{com.vmware.csp.core.cafe.
                        approvals@action.reject.state}"
                                    }
                        ]
    }
```

To approve a request, we need to again build the response JSON file. The format and information for the file are provided here:

```
{
    "formData": {
        "entries": [
            {
                "key": "source-source-provider-
                 Cafe.Shim.VirtualMachine.NumberOfInstances",
                "value": {
                    "type": "integer",
                    "value": 1
                }
            },
            {
                "key": "source-source-provider-
                 VirtualMachine.Memory.Size",
                "value": {
                    "type": "integer",
                    "value": 1024
                }
```

```
        },
        {
            "key": "source-source-provider-
            VirtualMachine.CPU.Count",
            "value": {
                "type": "integer",
                "value": 1
            }
        },
        {

            "key": "source-businessJustification",
            "value": {
                "type": "string",
                "value": "Approved the request"
            }
        },
        {

            "key": "source-source-provider-
            VirtualMachine.LeaseDays",
            "value": {
                "type": "integer",
                "value": 0
            }
        }
    ]
    },
    "workItemId": "2a11c987-dd8f-4a2d-a15a-b048ca64d729",
    "workItemActionId": "com.vmware.csp.core.approval.action.approve"
}
```

We can build the JSON file from the information that we received earlier. Since we got the JSON file, I saved it as a file called `approval.JSON`. We will now use this JSON file to approve the request.

Note that the `workItemActionId` is also obtained from the workitem detailed output. The detailed output actually shows you what action items are available for this workitem.

Now, we approve the request:

```
PS C:\> Invoke-RestMethod -Method Post -Uri
"https://vra.lab.com/workitem-service/api/workitems/2a11c987-dd8f-
4a2d-a15a-b048ca64d729/actions/com.vmware.csp.core.approval.
action.approve" -Headers $headers -InFile "E:\approval.JSON"
```

```
id                        : 2a11c987-dd8f-4a2d-a15a-b048ca64d729
version                   : 2
workItemNumber            : 2
assignees                 : {@{principalId=vradmin@lab.com;
principalType=USER}}
subTenantId               : 5c91a267-581a-4e00-9895-cf6e9c6b313a
tenantId                  : vsphere.local
callbackEntityId          : 2a11c987-dd8f-4a2d-a15a-b048ca64d729
workItemType              :
@{id=com.vmware.csp.core.approval.workitem.request; name=Approval;
pluralizedName=Approvals; description=Type registered by the Approval
Service.; serviceTypeId=com.vmware.csp.core.cafe.approvals;
actions=System.Object[];
                            completeByEmail=True;
commentsField=businessJustification; listView=; version=0; forms=}
completedDate             : 2015-08-10T17:45:36.339Z
assignedDate              : 2015-08-10T16:12:10.475Z
createdDate               : 2015-08-10T16:12:10.475Z
assignedOrCompletedDate   : 2015-08-10T17:45:36.339Z
serviceId                 : 4442cd1b-69fb-4c76-85bd-f7224ea8103e
workItemRequest           : @{itemId=2a11c987-dd8f-4a2d-a15a-
b048ca64d729; itemName=Cloud-Test; itemDescription=;
itemRequestor=vradmin@lab.com; itemCost=0.0; itemData=}
status                    : Approved
completedBy               : vradmin@lab.com
availableActions          :
```

From the UI, we can check whether the request has been approved.

Managing provisioned resources

In this section, we will discuss how to manage provisioned resources. To get a list of all provisioned resources, we can use the following command. Note the page number and limit parameter, and change them according to your requirements:

```
PS C:\> (Invoke-RestMethod -Method Get -Uri
"https://vra.lab.com/catalog-
service/api/consumer/resources/?page=1&limit=20" -Headers
$headers).Content | ConvertTo-Json
```

Part of the output is provided here:

```
{
    "@type":  "CatalogResource",
    "id":  "4998df9f-1ada-4cdb-843c-a7d61a256e94",
    "iconId":  "bda84bcb-d3f6-4332-8781-89d146ef5e28",
    "resourceTypeRef":  {
                        "id":  "Infrastructure.Virtual",
                        "label":  "Virtual Machine"
                   },
    "name":  "vc-01",
    "description":  "TEST machine",
    "status":  "ACTIVE",
    "catalogItem":  {
                    "id":  "bda84bcb-d3f6-4332-8781-
                    89d146ef5e28",
                    "label":  "Cloud-Test"
                },
    "requestId":  "93f010cb-6846-467b-9503-867aaf0d3f57",
    "providerBinding":  {
                    "bindingId":  "cb0a2bc4-79a9-4f21-
                    9514-3016c9a99780",
                    "providerRef":  {
                    "id":  "e70b620a-c254-4c0a-87ad-
                    2c4a61cfefd1",
                    "label":  "iaas-service"
                                }
                },
    "owners":  [
                {
                    "tenantName":  "vsphere.local",
                    "ref":  "vradmin@lab.com",
                    "type":  "USER",
```

```
                              "value":  "vradmin"
                     }
             ],
      "organization": {
                       "tenantRef":  "vsphere.local",
                       "tenantLabel":  "vsphere.local",
                       "subtenantRef":  "5c91a267-581a-4e00-
                       9895-cf6e9c6b313a",
                       "subtenantLabel":  "Test"
              },
```

You can view the details of a particular resource by using the resource ID in the query:

```
PS C:\> Invoke-RestMethod -Method Get -Uri
"https://vra.lab.com/catalog-service/api/consumer/resources/4998df9f-
1ada-4cdb-843c-a7d61a256e94" -Headers $headers | ConvertTo-Json
```

Managing network profiles

Let's see how to manage network profiles in the vRA environment. We will start this discussion with the procedure on how to get a list of network profiles.

For this, we need to query the https://$host/iaas-proxy-provider/api/network/profiles URL and the method we need to use is Get. We can bring everything together and get the information by running the following command.

```
PS C:\> Invoke-RestMethod -Method Get -Uri "https://vra.lab.com/iaas-
proxy-provider/api/network/profiles" -Headers $headers | ConvertTo-
Json
{
    "links":  [

             ],
    "content":  [
                 {
                     "@type":  "ExternalNetworkProfile",
                     "id":  "be64956f-52d3-4eb7-9a9e-
                     29a7db7372b0",
                     "name":  "Cloud-External",
                     "description":  "",
```

```
                        "createdDate":   "2015-08-07T12:58:16.000Z",
                        "lastModifiedDate":   "2015-08-
                        07T12:58:16.000Z",
                        "isHidden":  false,
                        "definedRanges":   "",
                        "profileType":   "EXTERNAL",
                        "subnetMask":   "255.255.255.0",
                        "gatewayAddress":   "192.168.1.1",
                        "primaryDnsAddress":   "192.168.1.39",
                        "secondaryDnsAddress":   "",
                        "dnsSuffix":   "lab.com",
                        "dnsSearchSuffix":   "",
                        "primaryWinsAddress":   "",
                        "secondaryWinsAddress":   ""
                    }
                ],
    "metadata":  {
                    "size":  0,
                    "totalElements":  1,
                    "totalPages":  1,
                    "number":  1,
                    "offset":  0
                }
}
```

Next, we will create a network profile. To create a network profile, we need to create an input JSON file. The syntax for the JSON file and a sample output are provided here:

```
{
"@type": "ExternalNetworkProfile",
"name": "Test_External",
"description": "Test external network",
"isHidden": false,
"definedRanges": [
{
"name": "range",
"description": "",
"beginIPv4Address": "10.10.18.220",
```

```
"endIPv4Address": "10.10.18.240",
"state": "UNALLOCATED"
}
],
"profileType": "EXTERNAL",
"subnetMask": "255.255.255.0",
"gatewayAddress": "10.10.18.253",
"primaryDnsAddress": "10.10.18.45",
"secondaryDnsAddress": "",
"dnsSuffix": "lab.com",
"dnsSearchSuffix": "",
"primaryWinsAddress": "10.0.0.1",
"secondaryWinsAddress": ""
}
```

Next, we will save this to a JSON file called `Network-Profile.JSON` and use the `https://vra.lab.com/iaas-proxy-provider/api/network/profiles` URL with the POST method to create the network. The command is as follows:

```
PS C:\> Invoke-RestMethod -Method Post -Uri
"https://vra.lab.com/iaas-proxy-provider/api/network/profiles" -
Headers $headers -InFile "E:\Network-Profile.JSON"
```

As you can see in the following screenshot, the profile has been created:

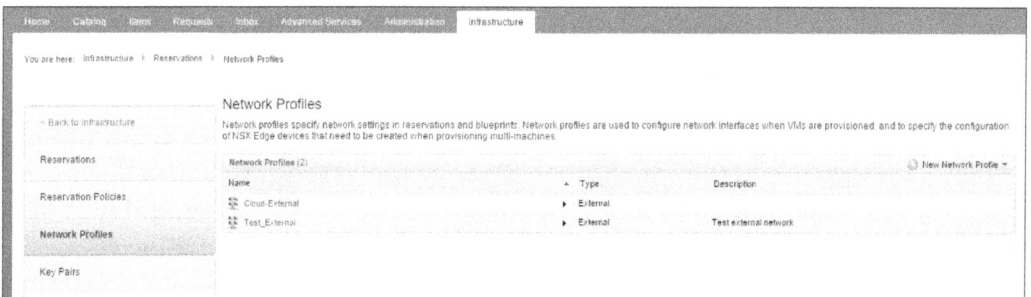

Similarly, to query a network profile, we need to run a `Get` method against the URL `https://$host/iaas-proxy-provider/api/network/profiles/$id`. Here, `$id` is the ID of the Network Profile.

To delete a network profile, all we need to do is run the `Delete` method against the URL `https://$host/iaas-proxy-provider/api/network/profiles/$id`.

Summary

In this chapter, we provided a short conceptual discussion on REST API and how we can use PowerShell to manage RESTful services. Next, we discussed how to manage a vRA environment using the PowerShell and REST APIs.

In the next chapter, we are going to talk about building a Windows GUI, and how we can utilize PowerShell to build a frontend GUI for our backend scripts.

11
Creating Windows GUI

So far, we have discussed all aspects of the VMware environment. In the previous two chapters, we discussed how to utilize the vSphere APIs and REST APIs. In this chapter, we are going to see how to build a Windows GUI and create a frontend for your scripts. Yes, I know it seems strange—if you are creating a script, then why would you create a GUI for that. This is particularly useful for building interactive tasks and is a cool feature to have. It can be very useful in other situations also; for example, I worked for an organization where we frequently received a lot of requests to increase the disk size of Linux VMs. The front line support team was not well versed with LVM, so I had to write a GUI tool for them where they could increase the disks without knowing about the backend commands.

We are going to discuss three different ways to build a GUI using PowerShell and cover the following topics:

- Different ways to create a Windows GUI
- GUI using Windows Forms
- Using SAPIEN PowerShell Studio
- GUI using WPF

In the first topic, we are going to discuss the different ways in which we can build a Windows GUI and their main differences.

Different ways to create a Windows GUI

To build a graphical interface in the Windows environment, we can take two approaches: the simpler one is using Windows Forms and the more complex one is using **Windows Presentation Foundation (WPF)**.

The main difference between these two is as follows:

- **Windows Forms**: Windows Forms is the name given to the GUI class library included in Microsoft .NET Framework. This is the platform that we can use to build the interface tier for a multi-tier client application. Moreover, an application using Windows Forms is typically an event-driven application supported by the .NET Framework, which spends most of its time waiting for end user inputs in some format. It is basically a graphical API that provides access to native Microsoft Windows interface elements.

- **Windows Presentation Foundation**: WPF is a graphical subsystem for rendering user interfaces in Windows-based applications. WPF employs XAML, an XML-based language to define the UI elements and the relationships between other UI elements. Applications based on WPF can be run as a separate standalone desktop application. WPF unifies a number of UI elements and these then can be linked and worked upon based on various events, user interactions, and data bindings.

From the feature perspective, WPF is the modern solution and provides a greater range of options. But it is more complex to implement. Windows Forms is the older technology with limited options, but it is easier to implement.

From building-the-GUI perspective, when we use Windows Forms, we have two options. Either we code everything by hand or use third-party tools such as PowerShell Studio (we will discuss this later in the chapter).

For WPF, we will typically use the Visual Studio suite to build the GUI specifications part. We will discuss more about these in further sections.

Building a GUI using Windows Forms

The first option that we will discuss is Windows Forms. To utilize Windows Forms, we first need to load the respective assemblies. We can load the assemblies by using the following techniques:

```
[void][System.Reflection.Assembly]::LoadWithPartialName
("System.Drawing")
[void][System.Reflection.Assembly]::LoadWithPartialName
("System.Windows.Forms")
```

Alternatively, we can use the following technique:

```
Add-Type -AssemblyNameSystem.Windows.Forms
Add-Type -AssemblyNameSystem.Drawing
```

Once the assemblies are loaded, we need to load the visual styles method as well. We can load the module by using the following method:

```
[void] [System.Windows.Forms.Application]::EnableVisualStyles()
```

I prefer using `[void]` to add the assemblies because it would suppress unnecessary text output. For the rest of the examples, we will use the following three lines to load the assemblies and the method:

```
[void] [System.Reflection.Assembly]::LoadWithPartialName
("System.Drawing")
[void] [System.Reflection.Assembly]::LoadWithPartialName
("System.Windows.Forms")
[void] [System.Windows.Forms.Application]::EnableVisualStyles()
```

Everything in Windows Forms is considered as forms or windows. Each window in the application, be it a dialog box or output screen or something else, is considered as a form. Each item in a form is considered a control; it may be a button or label or textbox.

Each form and control in Windows Forms has a range of properties or attributes that define their characteristics or behavior. For example, the controls are much like PowerShell objects. They have properties that define the controls and they have methods or events that define what we can do on the control object. We typically attach PowerShell cmdlets to these events as event handlers so that when this event occurs, WinForms executes these event handlers. For example, define a button as a control and define some PowerShell cmdlets as the event handler for the click event on this button. When the button is clicked, WinForms executes the PowerShell event handler for this event. This is how we build interactive tasks in WinForms.

Since we have already loaded the modules, we now need to build a form. We can define a Form by using the following method:

```
$TestForm = New-Object system.Windows.Forms.Form
```

We have defined a form, but how do we show it? To show the window, we can use the following method:

```
$TestForm.ShowDialog()
```

Alternatively, we can use the following method:

```
$TestForm.Show()
```

The difference between the two is that Show() will show the new form, but it will let us go back and click on the parent form as well (if it is there). ShowDialog() will show only the current form and will not let us go back to click on the parent form while there is an existing child form.

Putting everything together:

```
[void] [System.Reflection.Assembly]::LoadWithPartialName("System.
Drawing")
[void] [System.Reflection.Assembly]::LoadWithPartialName("System.
Windows.Forms")
[void] [System.Windows.Forms.Application]::EnableVisualStyles()
$TestForm = New-Object system.Windows.Forms.Form
$TestForm.Show()
```

The output of the preceding command is as follows:

```
PS C:\> [void] [System.Reflection.Assembly]::LoadWithPartialName("System.Drawing")
PS C:\> [void] [System.Reflection.Assembly]::LoadWithPartialName("System.Windows.Forms")
PS C:\> [void] [System.Windows.Forms.Application]::EnableVisualStyles()
PS C:\> $TestForm = New-Object system.Windows.Forms.Form
PS C:\> $TestForm.Show()
```

Once we run the code, we get a simple blank window:

Note [void] at the beginning of the assembly load line. The [void] declaration ensures that no information is written back to the PowerShell console.

To get a list of all the tasks that can be done or the properties of the form, we can use the following method:

```
PS C:\> $TestForm | Get-Member
```

This will provide a list of all the available events, methods, and properties associated with the form object. These are all very self-explanatory and extremely useful for controlling the form. I strongly recommend going through the list for more information.

While customizing the form, let's first check the size of the form. We can mention a custom form size and use AutoSize. With the custom size, the Form will start with the size that we have mentioned. With AutoSize on, the form will size to fit the contents in the window. With the GrowAndShrink property and the AutoSize property, the window will grow or shrink as per the data in the window:

```
$TestForm.Size = New-Object System.Drawing.Size(400,200)
$TestForm.AutoSize = $True
$TestForm.AutoSizeMode = "GrowAndShrink"
```

To show a window name, we can use the Text property:

```
$TestForm.Text = "Test Window"
```

Next, we will create a Label or text inside the window. For this, we will use the Label class:

```
$TestLabel = New-Object System.Windows.Forms.Label
$TestLabel.AutoSize = $true
$LabelFont = New-Object System.Drawing.Font("Arial",25,[System.
Drawing.FontStyle]::Bold)
$TestForm.Font = $LabelFont
$TestLabel.Text = "This is a Test Window"
```

So, we have defined the Label. Next, we need to add this $TestLabel control object to the Form $TestForm. We can do this in the following way:

```
$TestForm.Controls.Add($TestLabel)
```

We can check the result by running the ShowDialog() method:

```
$TestForm.ShowDialog()
```

The output can be seen in the following screenshot:

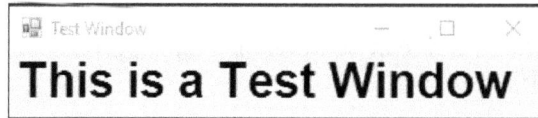

Creating a button

Next, we will create a button in the form and change the default icon in the window. To create a button, we will use the `Button` class by defining a new object of type `System.Windows.Forms.Button`:

```
$TestButton = New-Object System.Windows.Forms.Button
```

Next, we will define the location and size of the button:

```
$TestButton.Location = New-Object System.Drawing.Size(125,50)
$TestButton.Size = New-Object System.Drawing.Size(100,50)
```

Then, we will add text to the button and associate an action (event) to it:

```
$TestButton.Text = "CLOSE"
$TestButton.Add_Click({$TestForm.Close()})
```

In the preceding line, we are adding an `Add_Click` event to the `$TestButton` object, and the event will close the `$TestForm` object window.

Finally, we will add the button to the form:

```
$TestForm.Controls.Add($TestButton)
```

Putting everything together:

```
[void] [System.Reflection.Assembly]::LoadWithPartialName("System.
Drawing")
[void] [System.Reflection.Assembly]::LoadWithPartialName("System.
Windows.Forms")
[void][System.Windows.Forms.Application]::EnableVisualStyles()
$TestForm = New-Object system.Windows.Forms.Form
$TestForm.Size = New-Object System.Drawing.Size(400,200)
$TestForm.AutoSizeMode = "GrowAndShrink"
$TestForm.Text = "Test Window"
```

```
$TestLabel = New-Object System.Windows.Forms.Label
$TestLabel.AutoSize = $true
$LabelFont = New-Object System.Drawing.Font("Arial",18,[System.
Drawing.FontStyle]::Bold)
$TestForm.Font = $LabelFont
$TestLabel.Text = "This is a Test Window"
$TestForm.Controls.Add($TestLabel)
$TestButton = New-Object System.Windows.Forms.Button
$TestButton.Location = New-Object System.Drawing.Size(125,50)
$TestButton.Size = New-Object System.Drawing.Size(150,50)
$TestButton.Text = "CLOSE"
$TestButton.Add_Click({$TestForm.Close()})
$TestForm.Controls.Add($TestButton)
$TestForm.ShowDialog()
```

Once we run the preceding code, we will see the following output window:

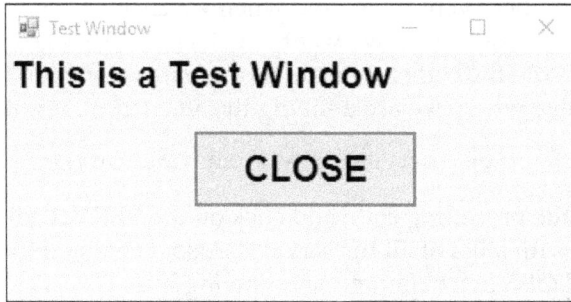

Note that the icon in the window is still a default one. We can change the icon using the following methods:

```
$TestIcon = New-Object system.drawing.icon ("$env:USERPROFILE\desktop\
Window-1.ico")
$TestForm.Icon = $TestIcon
```

I have downloaded an icon from the Internet and saved it as Window-1.ico on the desktop in my computer. For your example, you can use any icon file. Just change the location of the file.

Here, we are simply defining an ICON object and setting the Icon parameter of the form to it. By adding the preceding lines in the code, we get the following output:

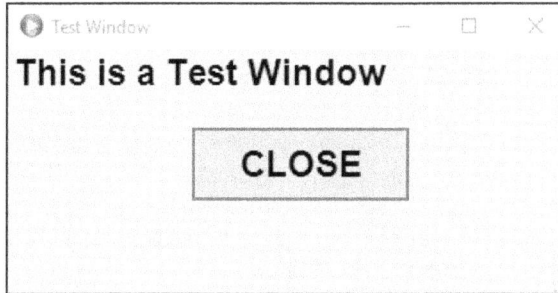

Note that the ICON object at the top-left corner has changed to the icon that I set. Now if I click on the **CLOSE** button, the window will close.

If we want to add another event to be fired when we click on the button, then we can define that as well. For example, if we want to get a list of services when we click on the button, we can write the code inline or use a separate function for that. We can simply replace the line where we are defining the Add_Click event value:

```
$TestButton.Add_Click({Get-Service | Out-Gridview})
```

Now when we run the preceding code and click on the **SERVICES** button, we get a separate window with a list of all the services. Also, I changed the button name to **SERVICES** from **CLOSE** by changing the following line:

```
$TestButton.Text = "CLOSE"
```

Following are the screen shots of the Windows that we get:

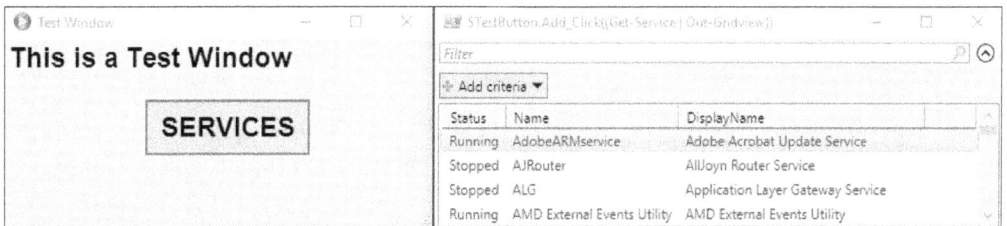

We changed the name of the button and the action related to it.

From this point onwards, we will build a GUI tool to achieve the following:

When the script is run, a window will open and ask the user to provide vCenter Server username and password by using `TextBox` in GUI. Then, depending on the input, it will show a `ListBox`, providing a list of ESXi hosts in the environment. The user will be able to select an ESXi host from the list and also check for the VM list and datastore list using `CheckBox`. Once the user provides the input, based on that information another `ListBox` will be open showing the required information.

We will achieve the preceding tasks in parts and at the end, stitch everything together to build a complete script. In this way, you'll learn how to create different ways to interact with a GUI Form.

We will start with `TextBox` creation.

Creating a TextBox

Out first task is to create multiple textboxes in a form and use the input provided in the textbox for our use. To do this, again we will start by loading the required assemblies:

```
# TextBox Creation

[void] [System.Reflection.Assembly]::LoadWithPartialName("System.
Drawing")
[void] [System.Reflection.Assembly]::LoadWithPartialName("System.
Windows.Forms")
[void] [System.Windows.Forms.Application]::EnableVisualStyles()
```

Next, we will define a function to show the Hosts list:

```
functionHosts_List($vc, $user, $pass)
{
  Connect-VIserver -Server $vc -User $user -Password $pass| Out-Null
    Get-VMHost | Out-GridView
}
```

We are going to call this function when the final **OK** button is clicked or *Enter* is pressed, so the final display will be shown and the form will be closed.

> Since the main aim of these examples is to showcase how to successfully build a GUI, extensive error checking is not done in these examples. For example, no check has been done for wrong credentials or no connectivity to vCenter Server. When implementing this in real life, please take care of these error situations.

Next, we will declare the main form:

```
# Declaring the Main Form

$MainForm = New-Object System.Windows.Forms.Form
$MainForm.Text = "Host List"
$MainForm.Size = New-Object System.Drawing.Size(455,265)
$MainForm.StartPosition = "CenterScreen"
```

Note the `StartPosition` property. This will ensure that the form will start in the center of the screen.

Next, we will define and change the default icon of the `MainForm` form:

```
# Defining an icon
$Icon = New-Object System.Drawing.Icon ' ("$env:USERPROFILE\desktop\
Window-1.ico")
# Changing the default icon in the main form
$MainForm.Icon = $Icon
```

Next, we will define the **OK** button and add it to the main form:

```
# Defining the "OK" Button

$OKButton = New-Object System.Windows.Forms.Button
$OKButton.Location = New-Object System.Drawing.Size(120,185)
$OKButton.Size = New-Object System.Drawing.Size(75,23)
$OKButton.Text = "OK"
$OKButton.Add_Click({Hosts_List -vc $TextBox1.Text -user $TextBox2.
Text -pass $TextBox3.Text})

# Adding the Button to the Main Form
$MainForm.Controls.Add($OKButton)
```

Note the way `Location`, `Size`, and `Text` for the button are defined. Similarly, we will define the `Cancel Button` and add it to the main form:

```
# Defining the "Cancel" Button

$CancelButton = New-Object System.Windows.Forms.Button
```

```
$CancelButton.Location = New-Object System.Drawing.Size(195,185)
$CancelButton.Size = New-Object System.Drawing.Size(75,23)
$CancelButton.Text = "Cancel"
$CancelButton.Add_Click({$MainForm.Close()})

# Adding the Button to the Main Form
$MainForm.Controls.Add($CancelButton)
```

In the next section we will add five Labels for three different textboxes. We will divide the form into two parts. The first part will take information about vCenter and the second part will take the username and password. Let's start with the first label which defines the content for the first part:

```
# Define the First Label

$FontBold = new-object System.Drawing.Font("Arial",8,[Drawing.
FontStyle]'Bold' )

$Label1 = New-Object System.Windows.Forms.Label
$Label1.Location = New-Object System.Drawing.Size(10,20)
$Label1.Size = New-Object System.Drawing.Size(425,20)
$Label1.Font = $fontBold
$Label1.text = "Please enter vCenter Server Name"

# Adding the Label to the Main Form
$MainForm.Controls.Add($Label1)
```

In the second label, we provide the label for the first textbox. This textbox will take the vCenter Server Name. The code is as follows:

```
# Define the Second Label
$Label2 = New-Object System.Windows.Forms.Label
$Label2.Location = New-Object System.Drawing.Size(30,47)
$Label2.Size = New-Object System.Drawing.Size(60,20)
$Label2.Text = "vCenter:"

# Adding the Label to the Main Form
$MainForm.Controls.Add($Label2)
```

In the third label, we provide the label for the second part of the form. This part will take the username and password for the environment. The code is as follows:

```
# Define the Third Label
$Label3 = New-Object System.Windows.Forms.Label
$Label3.Location = New-Object System.Drawing.Size(10,80)
```

```
$Label3.Size = New-Object System.Drawing.Size(425,20)
$Label3.Font = $fontBold
$Label3.Text = "Please enter the User Name and Password"

# Adding the Label to the Main Form
$MainForm.Controls.Add($Label3)
```

In the fourth label, we provide the label for the second textbox. This textbox will take the username:

```
# Define the Fourth Label
$Label4 = New-Object System.Windows.Forms.Label
$Label4.Location = New-Object System.Drawing.Size(30,108)
$Label4.Size = New-Object System.Drawing.Size(60,20)
$Label4.Text = "User:"

# Adding the Label to the Main Form
$MainForm.Controls.Add($Label4)
```

In the fifth label, we provide the label for the third textbox. This textbox will take the password. The code is as follows:

```
# Define the Fifth Label
$Label5 = New-Object System.Windows.Forms.Label
$Label5.Location = New-Object System.Drawing.Size(30,138)
$Label5.Size = New-Object System.Drawing.Size(60,20)
$Label5.Text = "Password:"

# Adding the Label to the Main Form
$MainForm.Controls.Add($Label5)
```

Now that the labels are defined and added to the MainForm form, we will add the actual textboxes. We will add the first and second textboxes that take the inputs for vCenter and username. The position of these boxes needs to be carefully calculated so that the final GUI will look good. The code is as follows:

```
# Define the First Text Box
$TextBox1 = New-Object System.Windows.Forms.TextBox
$TextBox1.Location = New-Object System.Drawing.Size(95,45)
$TextBox1.Size = New-Object System.Drawing.Size(260,20)

# Adding the TextBox to the Main Form
```

```
$MainForm.Controls.Add($TextBox1)

# Define the Second Text Box
$TextBox2 = New-Object System.Windows.Forms.TextBox
$TextBox2.Location = New-Object System.Drawing.Size(95,108)
$TextBox2.Size = New-Object System.Drawing.Size(260,20)

# Adding the TextBox to the Main Form
$MainForm.Controls.Add($TextBox2)
```

Next, we need to add the third textbox for taking the input for password. But this being a password textbox, we cannot simply show the input characters. So, we will use a special parameter `PasswordChar`. Using this parameter masks the input with * and this is very useful for taking passwords as inputs. The code is as follows:

```
# Define the Third Text Box
$TextBox3 = New-Object System.Windows.Forms.TextBox
$TextBox3.Location = New-Object System.Drawing.Size(95,138)
# Masking the Password Character
$TextBox3.PasswordChar = '*'
$TextBox3.Size = New-Object System.Drawing.Size(260,20)

# Adding the TextBox to the Main Form
$MainForm.Controls.Add($TextBox3)
```

Next, we need to decide whether the resulting Form will always be on top. Here, I decided it to be `False` so that when I will finally show the host list, the host list will always be on top. The code is as follows:

```
# Deciding whether the form will always be at top
$MainForm.Topmost = $False
```

We define a handler so that by default the first textbox will be selected. The active control is given to `TextBox1`. The code is as follows:

```
$Handler = {$MainForm.ActiveControl = $TextBox1}

$MainForm.add_Load($Handler)
$MainForm.Add_Shown({$MainForm.Activate()})
# Showing the Main Form
[Void] $MainForm.ShowDialog()
```

When we run the code, we get the following set of outputs. The first screen asks for the inputs:

After providing the required inputs and clicking on the **OK** button, we get the final output:

To come out of the form, we need to either click on the **Cancel** button or click on the **Close** button.

The code is provided in the `TextBox_WinForms.ps1` script.

Creating ListBox

Now, we will extend out code a bit and include a List Box. Instead of providing the list of the ESXi hostnames in Out-GridView, we will show the output in a ListBox and let the users select any one of the ESXi hosts. Once the user selects the ESXi host and clicks on **OK** or presses *Enter*, the list of the VMs running on that hosts will be shown in another `ListBox` window.

To achieve this, we will continue from the preceding example. The only difference is that, instead of simply showing the Hosts list, we will store the Hosts list in a global variable $Hosts. So after the Assembly load, we will define the global variable and the function, as shown here:

```
# Define the Global Variables

$Global:Hosts = $NULL
$Global:HostName = $NULL

functionHosts_List($vc, $user, $pass)
{
    Connect-VIserver -Server $vc -User $user -Password $pass   | Out-
Null
    Get-VMHost
    $MainForm.Close()
}
```

Here, we want that once the hosts list is obtained the first form will be closed.

Another change will be to store this host list in the global variable. To do this, we will define the Click event on the **OK** button on the first form:

```
$OKButton.Add_Click({$Global:Hosts = Hosts_List -vc $TextBox1.Text
-user $TextBox2.Text -pass $TextBox3.Text})
```

Next, we will define a new form with ListBox in it. So, we will define a new form and set the icon on the form:

```
# List Hosts in a new List Box

$ListForm = New-Object System.Windows.Forms.Form
$ListForm.Text = "Select a Host"
$ListForm.Size = New-Object System.Drawing.Size(300,270)
$ListForm.StartPosition = "CenterScreen"

# Defining an icon
$Icon = New-Object System.Drawing.Icon ("$env:USERPROFILE\desktop\
Window-1.ico")
# Changing the default icon in the main form
$ListForm.Icon = $Icon
```

Next, we will define the appropriate tasks for the *Enter* key press or *Escape* key press. Pressing the *Enter* key will be equivalent to clicking on the **OK** button, whereas an *Escape* key press will equate clicking on the **Close** button. We define these parameters in the next section. The code is as follows:

```
# If Enter Key is entered or Escape key is entered.
# Run the task accordingly
$ListForm.KeyPreview = $True
$ListForm.Add_KeyDown({if ($_.KeyCode -eq "Enter")
{ $Global:HostName = $ListBox.SelectedItem}})
$ListForm.Add_KeyDown({if ($_.KeyCode -eq "Escape")
    {$ListForm.Close()}})
```

Next, we will define the **OK** button and related task. Also, we will add the button in the Form. The code is as follows:

```
# Define OK Button and attach the event
$OKButton = New-Object System.Windows.Forms.Button
$OKButton.Location = New-Object System.Drawing.Size(25,175)
$OKButton.Size = New-Object System.Drawing.Size(75,23)
$OKButton.Text = "OK"
$OKButton.Add_Click({$Global:HostName = $ListBox.
SelectedItem;$ListForm.Close() })
$ListForm.Controls.Add($OKButton)
```

When the **OK** button is clicked, the selected item is stored in the global variable $HostName. We will use the content of this variable later to show the VM List. Next, we will define the Label for the Box. The code is as follows:

```
# Define the Label
$ListLabel = New-Object System.Windows.Forms.Label
$ListLabel.Location = New-Object System.Drawing.Size(10,20)
$ListLabel.Size = New-Object System.Drawing.Size(280,20)
$ListLabel.Font = $fontBold
$ListLabel.Text = "Please select a Host:"
$ListForm.Controls.Add($ListLabel)
```

Next, we will create the actual ListBox. To do this, we will create a ListBox object and define parameters for it. The code is as follows:

```
# Create the ListBox
$ListBox = New-Object System.Windows.Forms.ListBox
$ListBox.Location = New-Object System.Drawing.Size(10,40)
$ListBox.Size = New-Object System.Drawing.Size(260,20)
```

```
$ListBox.Height = 80

$ListBox.SelectionMode = [System.Windows.Forms.
SelectionMode]::MultiSimple
$ListBox.Sorted = $true
```

Also, note that we kept the ListBox sorted. Next, we will add the contents in the ListBox, add the ListBox in the Form and show the box. The code is as follows:

```
# Add the contents in the List Box
$Global:Hosts  | %{ [void] $ListBox.Items.Add($_.Name) }

# Add the List Box in the Form
$ListForm.Controls.Add($ListBox)

$ListForm.Topmost = $True

# Show the Box
$ListForm.Add_Shown({$ListForm.Activate()})
[void] $ListForm.ShowDialog()
```

At last, we will create another list box and show the VM list for the selected Host in the earlier form in this ListBox. The code is as follows:

```
# List VMs in another New List Box
    $VmForm = New-Object System.Windows.Forms.Form
    $VmForm.Text = "List of VM's "
    $VmForm.Size = New-Object System.Drawing.Size(300,200)
    $VmForm.StartPosition = "CenterScreen"

    # Defining an icon
    $Icon = New-Object System.Drawing.Icon ("$env:USERPROFILE\desktop\
Window-1.ico")
    # Changing the default icon in the main form
    $VmForm.Icon = $Icon

# Defining the OK Button
    $OKButton = New-Object System.Windows.Forms.Button
    $OKButton.Location = New-Object System.Drawing.Size(75,120)
    $OKButton.Size = New-Object System.Drawing.Size(75,23)
    $OKButton.Text = "OK"
    $OKButton.Add_Click({$VmForm.Close()})
    $VmForm.Controls.Add($OKButton)
```

```
# Creating another List Box to Show the VM List
    $VmListBox = New-Object System.Windows.Forms.ListBox
    $VmListBox.Location = New-Object System.Drawing.Size(10,40)
    $VmListBox.Size = New-Object System.Drawing.Size(260,20)
    $VmListBox.Height = 80
    $VmListBox.Sorted = $true


# Adding the contents of the List Box
    Get-VMHost -Name "$Global:HostName" | Get-VM  | %{ [void]
$VmListBox.Items.Add($_.Name) }


    $VmForm.Controls.Add($VmListBox)


    $VmForm.Topmost = $True


# Showing the list box
    $VmForm.Add_Shown({$VmForm.Activate()})
    [void] $VmForm.ShowDialog()
```

When the preceding code is run, we get the following set of windows. The first
screen asks for inputs:

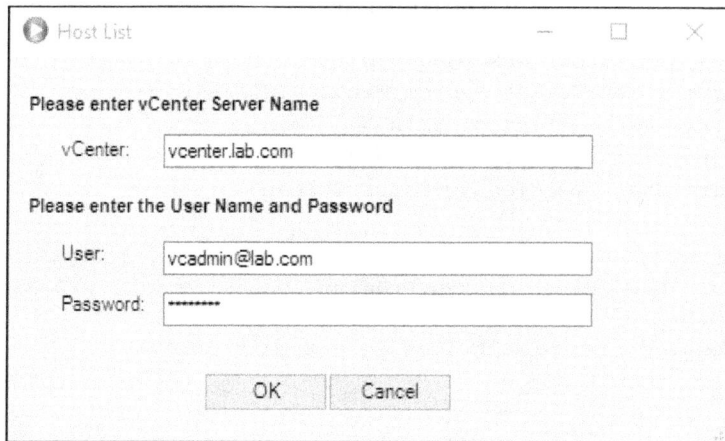

In the next window, the list of ESXi hosts in the environment is shown:

Depending on the selected host, a third window is shown with the list of VMs in the Host:

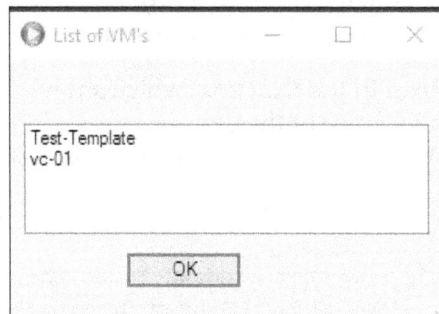

The complete code is available in the `ListBox_WinForms.ps1` script.

Creating CheckBox

Next, we will see how we can add checkboxes in a Windows Form. Here, we will add two checkboxes in the Hosts `ListBox` so that at the time of selecting the Host, end users need also choose whether they want to see a VM List, Datastore List, or both for the selected Host. Depending on the selection, the last `ListBox` will show the required information.

To achieve this, we will extend the preceding code. First, we will define two more global variables:

```
$Global:vmSelect = $false
$Global:dataSelect = $false
```

These variables will be used to store the decision in checkbox selection, whether VM and datastore checkboxes are selected or not. Next, we will define another function that will actually check whether the checkboxes are selected or not. The code is as follows:

```
# Checking whether checkbox has been checked or not
functionCheckBox-Changed($object){

If($object.Checked ){
     Return $True
   }
}
```

When we define a checkbox object, it has a Checked property to see whether it is checked or not. In this function, we check that property of the object and return the Boolean value $True to set the variable to a proper value.

Next, we will add checkboxes in the ListBox, which shows the ESXi hosts list. All we need to do is define an instance of the System.Windows.Forms.CheckBox class and set the properties of the object instance. The code is as follows:

```
# Define and add the first check box

$CheckBox1 = New-Object System.Windows.Forms.CheckBox
$CheckBox1.Location = New-Object System.Drawing.Point(10, 112)
$CheckBox1.size = New-Object System.Drawing.Size(141, 24)
$CheckBox1.Text = "VM List"
$CheckBox1.add_CheckedChanged({$Global:vmSelect = (CheckBox-Changed
$CheckBox1 )})

$ListForm.Controls.Add($CheckBox1)

# Define and add the Second check box
$CheckBox2 = New-Object System.Windows.Forms.CheckBox
$CheckBox2.Location = New-Object System.Drawing.Point(10, 140)
$CheckBox2.Size = New-Object System.Drawing.Size(141, 24)
$CheckBox2.Text = "Datastore List"
```

```
$CheckBox2.add_CheckedChanged({$Global:dataSelect = (CheckBox-Changed
$CheckBox2)})
```

```
$ListForm.Controls.Add($CheckBox2)
```

We defined two checkboxes, one for VM List and another for Datastore List.

We are setting the value of the global variables `$Global:vmSelect` and `$Global:dataSelect` by the value returned from the function call. If the checkboxes are selected, then the variable value is set to `$True`, which we will use to decide which list is to be shown.

The next part is to show the actual list. But before that, we need to decide whether the user wants to see the list of VMs or datastores or both. For this, we will use the `If{} ElseIf{}Else{}` decision mechanism. The first part shows information for both the VM and datastore. The code is as follows:

```
# Showing the required information based on the input
# Showing both the VM and Datastore list
if ($Global:vmSelect -and $Global:dataSelect ) {

# Defining the Main List Form

    $DataVmForm = New-Object System.Windows.Forms.Form
    $DataVmForm.Text = "List of VM's and Datastores"
    $DataVmForm.Size = New-Object System.Drawing.Size(300,300)
    $DataVmForm.StartPosition = "CenterScreen"

    # Defining an icon
    $Icon = New-Object System.Drawing.Icon ("$env:USERPROFILE\desktop\
Window-1.ico")
    # Changing the default icon in the main form
    $DataVmForm.Icon = $Icon

    $OKButton = New-Object System.Windows.Forms.Button
    $OKButton.Location = New-Object System.Drawing.Size(75,230)
    $OKButton.Size = New-Object System.Drawing.Size(75,23)
    $OKButton.Text = "OK"
    $OKButton.Add_Click({$DataVmForm.Close()})
    $DataVmForm.Controls.Add($OKButton)

    $FontBold = new-object System.Drawing.Font("Arial",8,[Drawing.
FontStyle]'Bold' )
```

In the preceding code, we defined only a single form because we want to show information for both VM and datastore in a single window only. So, the windows have two list boxes—one for each type. Next, we create labels for each `ListBox` to inform the user about what information is shown in the `ListBox`. The code is as follows:

```
# Showing label for VM listbox
    $Label1 = New-Object System.Windows.Forms.Label
    $Label1.Location = New-Object System.Drawing.Size(10,20)
    $Label1.Size = New-Object System.Drawing.Size(425,20)
    $Label1.Font = $FontBold
    $Label1.text = "VM's List"
    $DataVmForm.Controls.Add($Label1)


# Adding the VM List Box

    $VmListBox = New-Object System.Windows.Forms.ListBox
    $VmListBox.Location = New-Object System.Drawing.Size(10,40)
    $VmListBox.Size = New-Object System.Drawing.Size(260,30)
    $VmListBox.Height = 80

    Get-VMHost -Name "$Global:HostName" | Get-VM | %{ [void]
$VmListBox.Items.Add($_.Name) }


    $DataVmForm.Controls.Add($VmListBox)
```

Similar to the VM listbox, we are adding another label for `DatastoreListBox` to inform the user that the following information is for datastore. The code is as follows:

```
# Adding label for Datastorelistbox
    $Label2 = New-Object System.Windows.Forms.Label
    $Label2.Location = New-Object System.Drawing.Size(10,120)
    $Label2.Size = New-Object System.Drawing.Size(425,20)
    $Label2.Font = $FontBold
    $Label2.text = "Datastore List"
    $DataVmForm.Controls.Add($Label2)
```

Next, we are actually defining the ListBox and adding values to the ListBox. Also, we are adding the ListBox to the main form. The code is as follows:

```
# Adding the DatastoreListBox
    $DataListBox = New-Object System.Windows.Forms.ListBox
    $DataListBox.Location = New-Object System.Drawing.Size(10,140)
    $DataListBox.Size = New-Object System.Drawing.Size(260,60)
```

```
    $DataListBox.Height = 80
    $DataListBox.Sorted = $true

    Get-VMHost -Name "$Global:HostName" | Get-Datastore  | %{ [void]
$DataListBox.Items.Add($_.Name) }


    $DataVmForm.Controls.Add($DataListBox)

    $DataVmForm.Topmost = $True

    $DataVmForm.Add_Shown({$DataVmForm.Activate()})
    [void] $DataVmForm.ShowDialog()
}
```

The next portion of the code shows the information if only VM list is selected. So, it is the same code but shows information related to VMs only:

```
ElseIf($Global:vmSelect){

# List VMs in another New List Box

    $VmForm = New-Object System.Windows.Forms.Form
    $VmForm.Text = "List of VM's "
    $VmForm.Size = New-Object System.Drawing.Size(300,200)
    $VmForm.StartPosition = "CenterScreen"

    # Defining an icon
    $Icon = New-Object System.Drawing.Icon ("$env:USERPROFILE\desktop\
Window-1.ico")
    # Changing the default icon in the main form
    $VmForm.Icon = $Icon

# Defining the OK Button
    $OKButton = New-Object System.Windows.Forms.Button
    $OKButton.Location = New-Object System.Drawing.Size(75,120)
    $OKButton.Size = New-Object System.Drawing.Size(75,23)
    $OKButton.Text = "OK"
    $OKButton.Add_Click({$VmForm.Close()})
    $VmForm.Controls.Add($OKButton)

# Creating another List Box to Show the VM List
```

```
$VmListBox = New-Object System.Windows.Forms.ListBox
$VmListBox.Location = New-Object System.Drawing.Size(10,40)
$VmListBox.Size = New-Object System.Drawing.Size(260,20)
$VmListBox.Height = 80
$VmListBox.Sorted = $true


# Adding the contents of the List Box
    Get-VMHost -Name "$Global:HostName" | Get-VM  | %{ [void]
$VmListBox.Items.Add($_.Name) }


    $VmForm.Controls.Add($VmListBox)


    $VmForm.Topmost = $True


# Showing the list box
    $VmForm.Add_Shown({$VmForm.Activate()})
    [void] $VmForm.ShowDialog()


}
```

The next portion of the code shows datastore data only, if the user selects only the Datastore List checkbox:

```
ElseIf($Global:dataSelect){

# List Datastores in another New List Box

    $DataForm = New-Object System.Windows.Forms.Form
    $DataForm.Text = "List of Datastores "
    $DataForm.Size = New-Object System.Drawing.Size(300,200)
    $DataForm.StartPosition = "CenterScreen"

    # Defining an icon
    $Icon = New-Object System.Drawing.Icon ("$env:USERPROFILE\desktop\
Window-1.ico")
    # Changing the default icon in the main form
    $DataForm.Icon = $Icon

# Definign the OK Button
    $OKButton = New-Object System.Windows.Forms.Button
    $OKButton.Location = New-Object System.Drawing.Size(75,120)
    $OKButton.Size = New-Object System.Drawing.Size(75,23)
    $OKButton.Text = "OK"
```

```
    $OKButton.Add_Click({$DataForm.Close()})
    $DataForm.Controls.Add($OKButton)

# Adding the Datastore List box
    $DataListBox = New-Object System.Windows.Forms.ListBox
    $DataListBox.Location = New-Object System.Drawing.Size(10,40)
    $DataListBox.Size = New-Object System.Drawing.Size(260,20)
    $DataListBox.Height = 80
    $DataListBox.Sorted = $true

    Get-VMHost -Name "$Global:HostName" | Get-Datastore   | %{ [void]
$DataListBox.Items.Add($_.Name) }

    $DataForm.Controls.Add($DataListBox)

    $DataForm.Topmost = $True

    $DataForm.Add_Shown({$DataForm.Activate()})
    [void] $DataForm.ShowDialog()

}
```

The last portion of the code shows a new window with error labels in it. It is shown if the user does not select any of the checkboxes. The code is as follows:

```
Else {

# Showing Error

    $ErrorForm = New-Object System.Windows.Forms.Form
    $ErrorForm.Text = "Selection Error"
    $ErrorForm.Size = New-Object System.Drawing.Size(300,200)
    $ErrorForm.StartPosition = "CenterScreen"

    # Defining an icon
    $Icon = New-Object System.Drawing.Icon ("$env:USERPROFILE\desktop\
Window-1.ico")
    # Changing the default icon in the main form
    $ErrorForm.Icon = $Icon

# Definign the OK Button
```

```
    $OKButton = New-Object System.Windows.Forms.Button
    $OKButton.Location = New-Object System.Drawing.Size(75,120)
    $OKButton.Size = New-Object System.Drawing.Size(75,23)
    $OKButton.Text = "OK"
    $OKButton.Add_Click({$ErrorForm.Close()})
    $ErrorForm.Controls.Add($OKButton)

# Showing label for VM listbox
    $Label = New-Object System.Windows.Forms.Label
    $Label.Location = New-Object System.Drawing.Size(10,20)
    $Label.Size = New-Object System.Drawing.Size(425,20)
    $Label.Font = $fontBold
    $Label.text = "Please select Something"
    $ErrorForm.Controls.Add($Label)

    $ErrorForm.Topmost = $True

    $ErrorForm.Add_Shown({$ErrorForm.Activate()})
    [void] $ErrorForm.ShowDialog()
}
```

The screenshots from running the script are provided here. When the script is run, the first screen asks for the details:

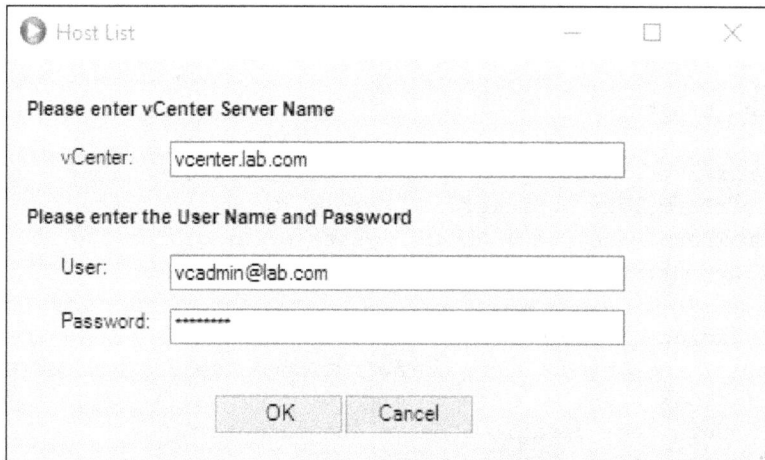

The second screen shows the ESXi hosts list in the environment and also shows the checkboxes:

For simplicity, I will select both the options and get the following output:

The entire code is available in the WinForms-Tool.ps1 script. Due to space and time constraints, I am not showing all the use cases (selecting individual options or not selecting anything at all) and leave it up to you to test them.

In the examples, I have not chosen to beautify the Windows. This is because we have a lot of options to beautify them, and these methods or events are easily available with the `Get-Method` cmdlet. I leave it up to you to further explore these options and many other different options available with Windows Forms. WinForms is a subject by itself and needs to be explored in depth to utilize it according to your requirements. Hopefully, I have given you enough insight into the subject to get you started on it.

Using SAPIEN PowerShell Studio

In the previous section, we discussed how we can utilize WinForms to give a frontend to our scripts. But doing it manually is really painful. To build a simple tool such as the one we have built, we had to write 421 lines of code. We can simplify all these with the use of PowerShell Studio 2015 by SAPIEN. SAPIEN earlier had a free community edition Primal Forms, which has since been discontinued. PowerShell Studio 2015 is a paid version, but if you create a lot of GUIs using WinForms in PowerShell, then this is an invaluable tool for you. It comes with a 45-day trial period so that you can try it before making the final decision. Without wasting much time, let's start the discussion about building a GUI using this tool.

We will start by creating a **New Form Project**:

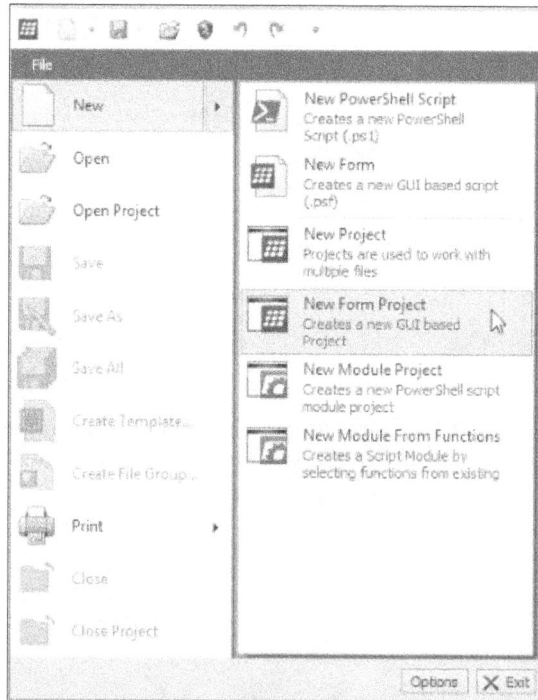

We give it the name `TextBox_PStudio`:

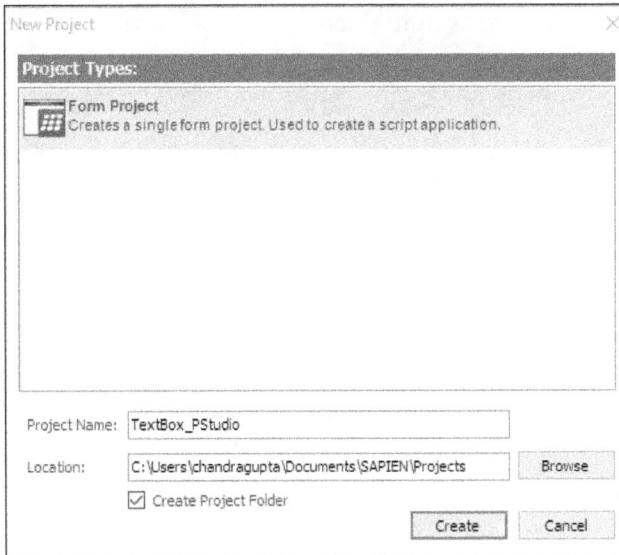

This gives us a blank form:

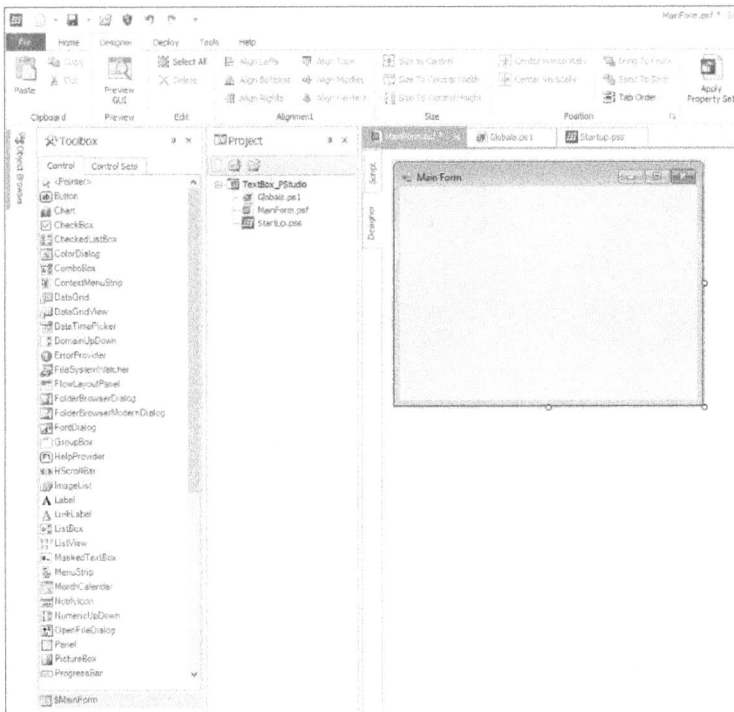

On the left-hand side, we can see that there is a **Toolbox** option. There are all kinds of control and control sets available in **Toolbox**. We can simply click and drag items from the available control items in the **Toolbox** to the form:

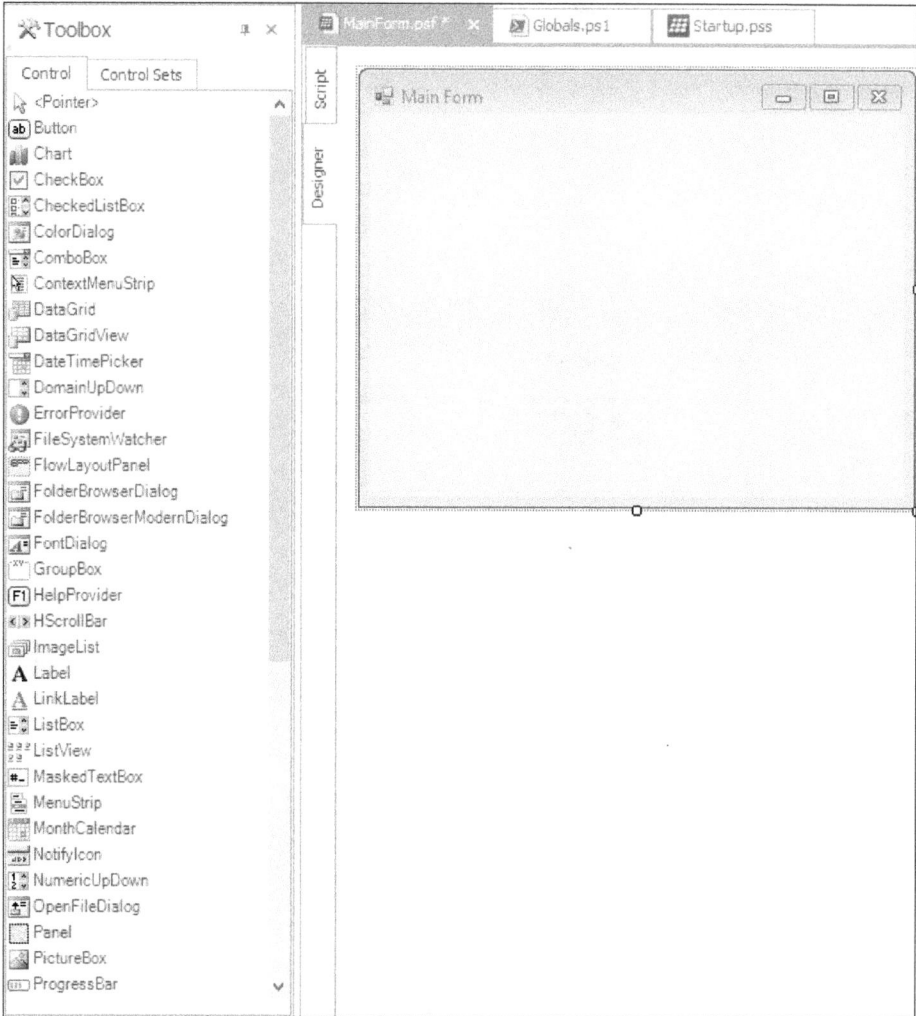

If we select the form, we will be able to see the details related to the form on the right hand-side **Properties** box. We will use these properties to change the characteristics of the form:

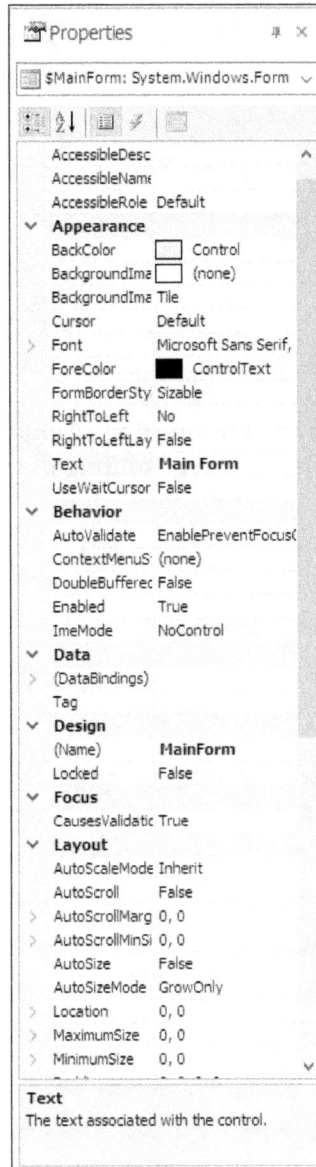

We will start by changing the name of the form to vCenter Details. We can do this by changing the **Text** property for the form:

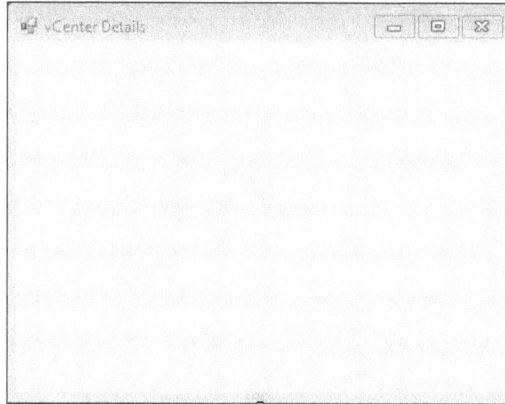

Next, we will insert two labels: one for inserting vCenter information and other for the username and password. Here, we are building the same form that we created by manual coding:

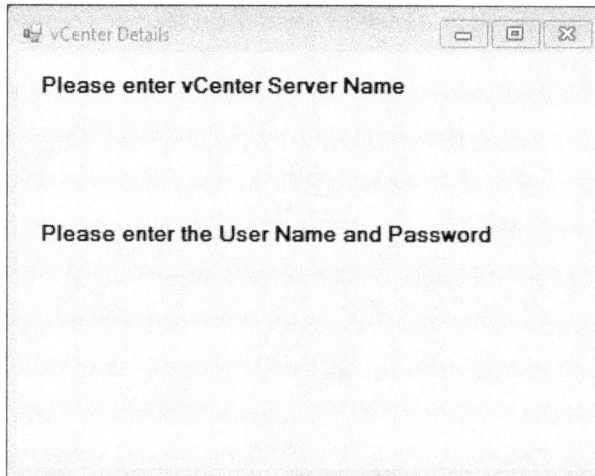

Next, we will insert two textboxes for the user to enter the information and related labels for them:

Note here we used 3D boxes for the Labels. Next we will insert two buttons, **OK** and **CANCEL**, for use in the form:

This completes the initial form. So far, we did not write a single line of code but were able to build the entire form using GUI elements. Now, it is the time for us to export the code into script form. To do this, we will use the **Export to File** option under the **Deploy** option in the main menu:

Note the different **Build** options, one that will build an executable file from this script and another which will create a MSI file from this script. For this example, we will export the form code in a `TextBox_PStudio.ps1` file and examine the code.

At the beginning of the code, the following assemblies are loaded:

```
#----------------------------------------------
#region Import Assemblies
#----------------------------------------------
[void][Reflection.Assembly]::Load('mscorlib, Version=4.0.0.0,
Culture=neutral, PublicKeyToken=b77a5c561934e089')
[void][Reflection.Assembly]::Load('System, Version=2.0.0.0,
Culture=neutral, PublicKeyToken=b77a5c561934e089')
[void][Reflection.Assembly]::Load('System.Windows.Forms,
Version=2.0.0.0, Culture=neutral, PublicKeyToken=b77a5c561934e089')
[void][Reflection.Assembly]::Load('System.Data, Version=2.0.0.0,
Culture=neutral, PublicKeyToken=b77a5c561934e089')
[void][Reflection.Assembly]::Load('System.Drawing, Version=2.0.0.0,
Culture=neutral, PublicKeyToken=b03f5f7f11d50a3a')
[void][Reflection.Assembly]::Load('System.Xml, Version=2.0.0.0,
Culture=neutral, PublicKeyToken=b77a5c561934e089')
[void][Reflection.Assembly]::Load('System.DirectoryServices,
Version=2.0.0.0, Culture=neutral, PublicKeyToken=b03f5f7f11d50a3a')
[void][Reflection.Assembly]::Load('System.Core, Version=3.5.0.0,
Culture=neutral, PublicKeyToken=b77a5c561934e089')
```

```
[void] [Reflection.Assembly]::Load('System.ServiceProcess,
Version=2.0.0.0, Culture=neutral, PublicKeyToken=b03f5f7f11d50a3a')
#endregion Import Assemblies
```

```
#-
#region Import Assemblies
#-
[void][Reflection.Assembly]::Load('mscorlib, Version=4.0.0.0, Culture=neutral, PublicKeyToken=b77a5c561934e089')
[void][Reflection.Assembly]::Load('System, Version=2.0.0.0, Culture=neutral, PublicKeyToken=b77a5c561934e089')
[void][Reflection.Assembly]::Load('System.Windows.Forms, Version=2.0.0.0, Culture=neutral, PublicKeyToken=b77a5c561934e089')
[void][Reflection.Assembly]::Load('System.Data, Version=2.0.0.0, Culture=neutral, PublicKeyToken=b77a5c561934e089')
[void][Reflection.Assembly]::Load('System.Drawing, Version=2.0.0.0, Culture=neutral, PublicKeyToken=b03f5f7f11d50a3a')
[void][Reflection.Assembly]::Load('System.Xml, Version=2.0.0.0, Culture=neutral, PublicKeyToken=b77a5c561934e089')
[void][Reflection.Assembly]::Load('System.DirectoryServices, Version=2.0.0.0, Culture=neutral, PublicKeyToken=b03f5f7f11d50a3a')
[void][Reflection.Assembly]::Load('System.Core, Version=3.5.0.0, Culture=neutral, PublicKeyToken=b77a5c561934e089')
[void][Reflection.Assembly]::Load('System.ServiceProcess, Version=2.0.0.0, Culture=neutral, PublicKeyToken=b03f5f7f11d50a3a')
#endregion Import Assemblies
```

Next, we have the main function definition. The main function starts the project application. The `Call_MainForm_psf` function is defined. Inside the function, first the assemblies are loaded and then all the objects are declared. The code is as follows:

```
#-----------------------------------------------
#region Generated Form Objects
#-----------------------------------------------
[System.Windows.Forms.Application]::EnableVisualStyles()
$MainForm = New-Object 'System.Windows.Forms.Form'
$buttonCANCEL = New-Object 'System.Windows.Forms.Button'
$buttonOK = New-Object 'System.Windows.Forms.Button'
$labelPassword = New-Object 'System.Windows.Forms.Label'
$labelUser = New-Object 'System.Windows.Forms.Label'
$labelVCenter = New-Object 'System.Windows.Forms.Label'
$textbox3 = New-Object 'System.Windows.Forms.TextBox'
$textbox2 = New-Object 'System.Windows.Forms.TextBox'
$textbox1 = New-Object 'System.Windows.Forms.TextBox'
$labelPleaseEnterTheUserNa = New-Object
'System.Windows.Forms.Label'
$labelPleaseEnterVCenterSe = New-Object
'System.Windows.Forms.Label'
$InitialFormWindowState = New-Object
'System.Windows.Forms.FormWindowState'
#endregion Generated Form Objects
```

Near the end of the code, we get the details of the objects:

```
#
# MainForm
#
$MainForm.Controls.Add($buttonCANCEL)
$MainForm.Controls.Add($buttonOK)
$MainForm.Controls.Add($labelPassword)
$MainForm.Controls.Add($labelUser)
$MainForm.Controls.Add($labelVCenter)
$MainForm.Controls.Add($textbox3)
$MainForm.Controls.Add($textbox2)
$MainForm.Controls.Add($textbox1)
$MainForm.Controls.Add($labelPleaseEnterTheUserNa)
$MainForm.Controls.Add($labelPleaseEnterVCenterSe)
$MainForm.ClientSize = '381, 266'
$MainForm.Font = 'Microsoft Sans Serif, 9.75pt, style=Bold'
$MainForm.Name = 'MainForm'
$MainForm.StartPosition = 'CenterScreen'
$MainForm.Text = 'vCenter Details'
$MainForm.add_FormClosed($jobTracker_FormClosed)
$MainForm.add_Load($MainForm_Load)
#
# buttonCANCEL
#
$buttonCANCEL.Location = '214, 231'
$buttonCANCEL.Name = 'buttonCANCEL'
$buttonCANCEL.Size = '75, 23'
$buttonCANCEL.TabIndex = 9
$buttonCANCEL.Text = 'CANCEL'
$buttonCANCEL.UseVisualStyleBackColor = $True
```

To define an event to the **OK** Button, we need to double-click on it and a function is started for the button. We inserted the following code in that function:

```
$buttonOK_Click={
  #TODO: Place custom script here
  Hosts_List -vc $textbox1.Text -user $textbox2.Text -pass $textbox3.
Text
}
```

For the **CANCEL** button, we will define the following action.

We inserted the previously created function `Hosts_List`, which provides the host list. If we run the script now, it will simply produce the same form and output as shown here:

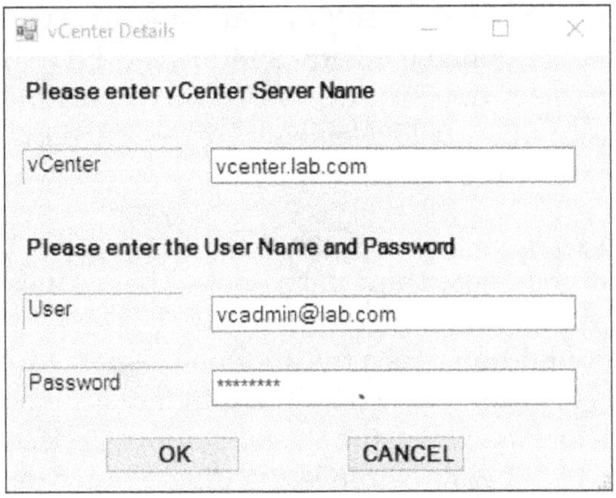

The output is in the new window (using **Out-GridView**).

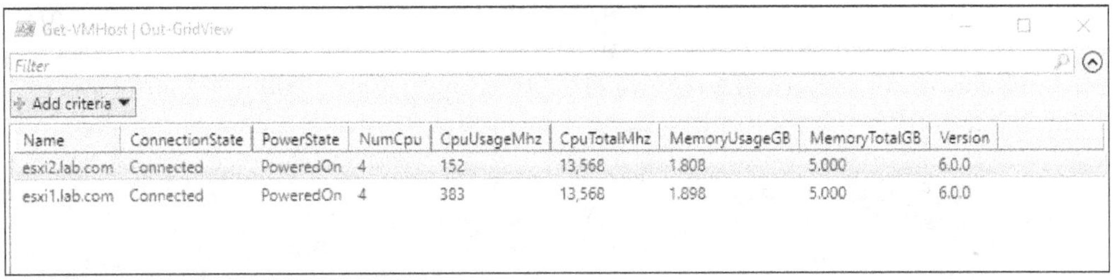

If we build an `.exe` file from this script, once the exe file is run, it simply provides the same form and runs the same tasks for us. We do not need to run the script separately.

As you can see, if we really need to build a GUI-based application using PowerShell, we can use PowerShell Studio 2015 to our advantage. It makes our life a lot easier, and with minimal effort we can build really good applications or extensive GUI applications. I leave it up to you to use PowerShell Studio and build the rest of the form that we built earlier using hand coding. For your reference, the script that was generated by PowerShell Studio 2015 for this example is given in the `TextBox_PStudio.ps1` file.

Building GUI using WPF

In this section, we are going to discuss how to build a windows GUI using WPF and PowerShell. WPF is more modern and provides a lot more flexibility and advanced options than WinForm. Like WinForm, building a GUI in WPF is also an event-driven approach. We define the Form and then add the controls in the form, after we define the events for the Controls so that we can control the behavior of the Form. The difference is in the way UI elements are designed in WPF. Here, we use XAML-based definitions for the UI elements.

There are two ways in which we can build a WPF-based application, either we hand code the XAML definitions or use third-party tools. The most easily available one is Visual Studio 2015, and it provides a great interface. For our use, I will use Visual Studio 2015 Community Edition (it is a free tool). In Visual Studio, we have two options: the first one is to use the Visual Studio interface and the second option is to use Blend for Visual Studio. Using the Visual Studio interface will require more coding, whereas using Blend will require less coding. For a detailed difference, refer to the documentation by Microsoft at `https://msdn.microsoft.com/en-us/library/dn904477(v=vs.110).aspx`.

Since we only want to generate the XAML code for the UI, we will use the easy-to-use Blend for Visual Studio for our example. Blend provides a dark interface so that you can focus on the window that you are working on. Once you open and start up Blend, the default screen looks like this:

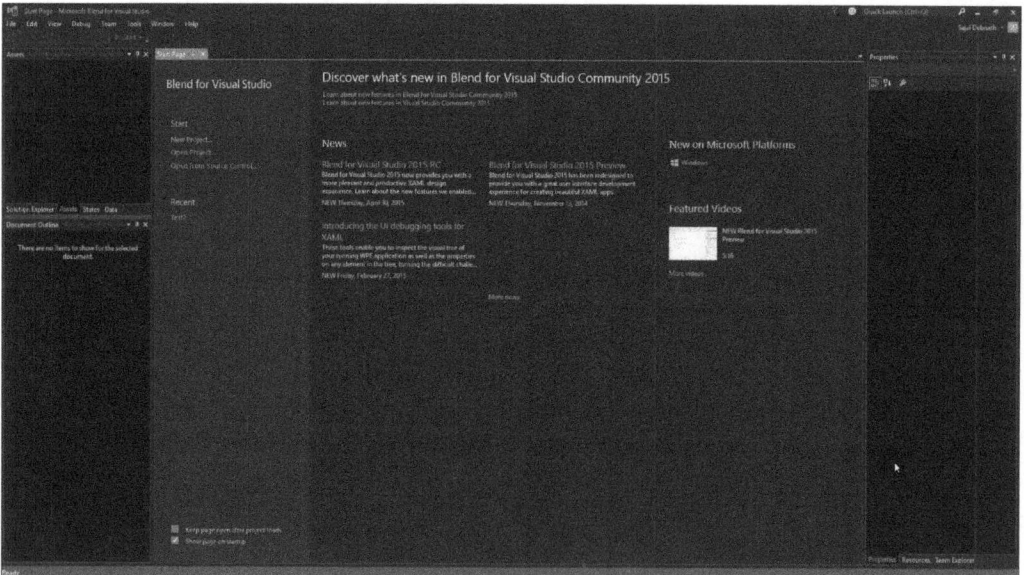

Next, we will start by creating a project `TextBox_WPF` of type **WPF Application**:

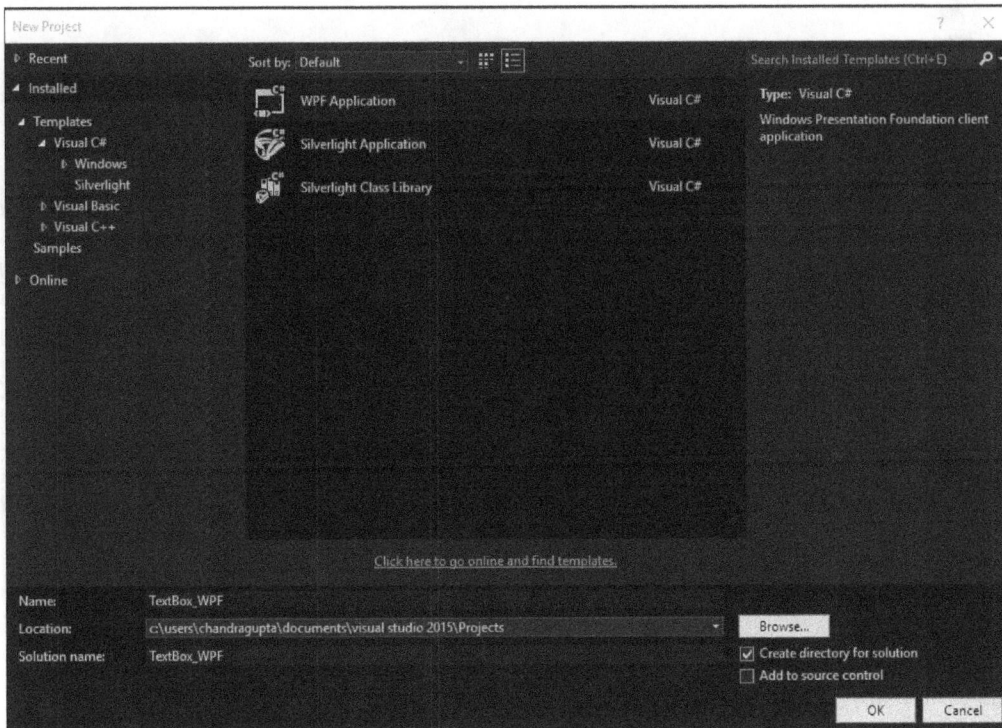

This gives us a blank window. As you can see in the following screenshot, on the left-hand side we get a list of available assets and the middle part shows the window. On the right-hand side, we can see the properties for the selected item in the window.

Also, the most important part for us — the related XAML code — is shown at the bottom of the screen:

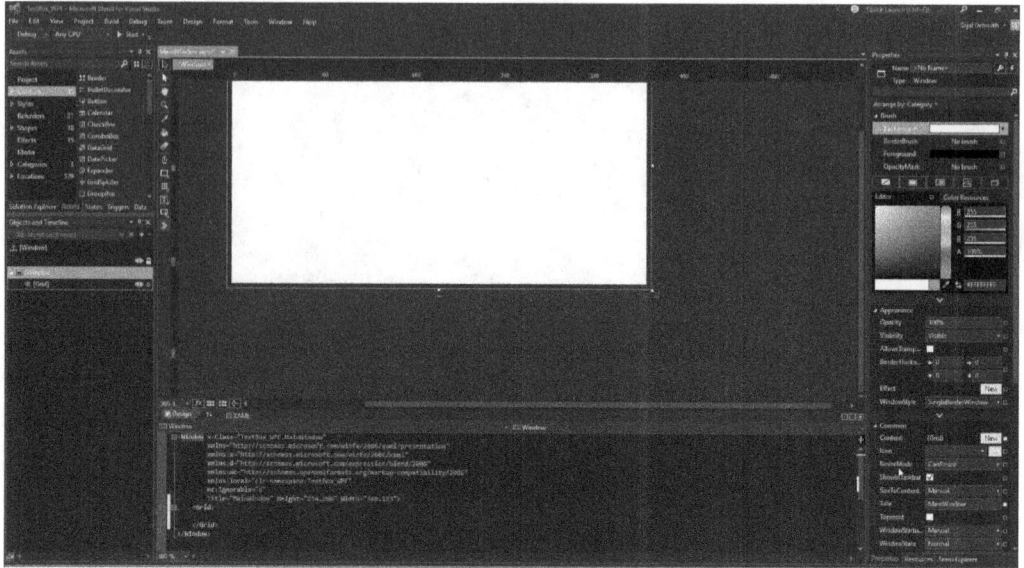

We start building the same TextBox window that we created by hand coding, but this time using Blend. Similar to what we did in PowerShell Studio, in Blend we can simply drag and drop the required control items from the left-hand side and modify the parameters related to the respective control items or elements.

Using the process we have just explained, we created a window similar to the one that we created earlier (shown in the following screenshot). One major difference is that we created `PasswordBox` instead of `TextBox` for the password field. This will mask the input given in the password box by default:

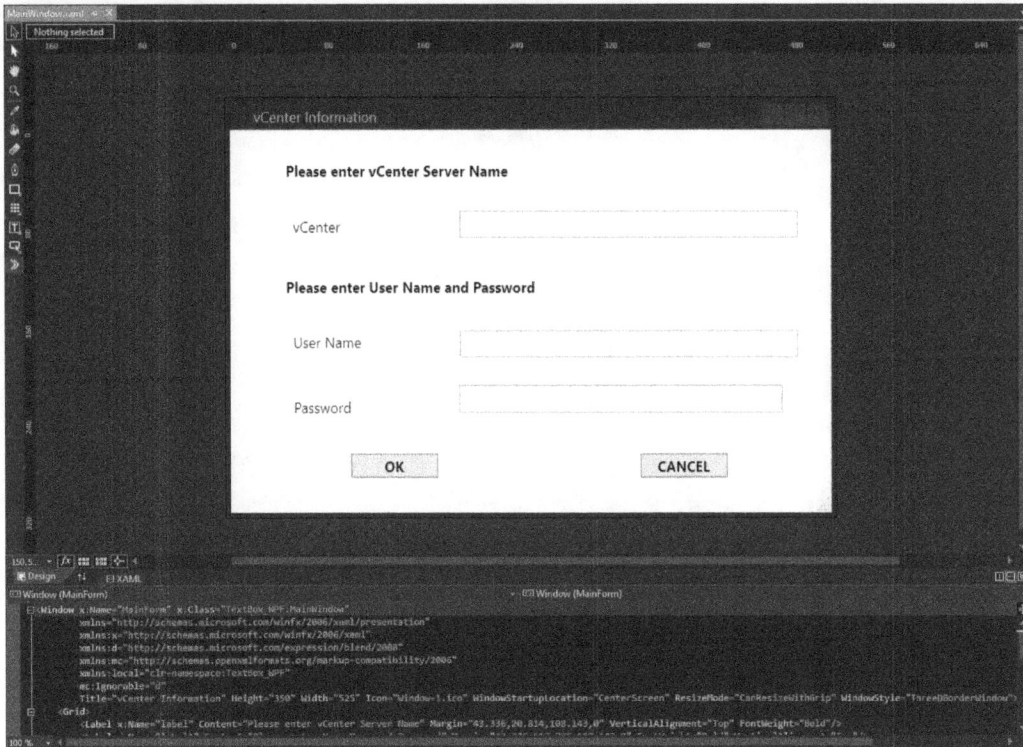

To test whether everything works fine, we can click on the **Start** button at the top-left hand corner of the window. It will run the code and generate the window for us. You should use this process to fine tune your window and make necessary corrections if the result is not satisfactory. For our use, we get the following window:

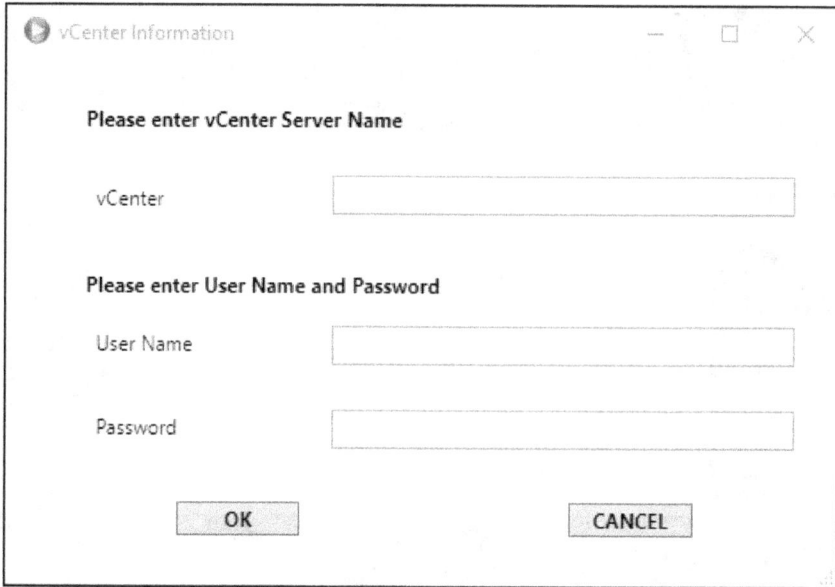

The preceding window looks fine to me. So the easy part is done. Now comes the complex part. We will open an editor and copy and paste the XAML code that is generated for us (available at the bottom-most window in Blend).

For your reference, the code is provided here:

```
<Window x:Name="MainForm" x:Class="TextBox_WPF.MainWindow"
        xmlns="http://schemas.microsoft.com/winfx/2006/xaml/
presentation"
xmlns:x="http://schemas.microsoft.com/winfx/2006/xaml"
xmlns:d="http://schemas.microsoft.com/expression/blend/2008"
        xmlns:mc="http://schemas.openxmlformats.org/markup-
compatibility/2006"
xmlns:local="clr-namespace:TextBox_WPF"
mc:Ignorable="d"
        Title="vCenter Information" Height="350" Width="525"
Icon="Window-1.ico" WindowStartupLocation="CenterScreen"
ResizeMode="CanResizeWithGrip" WindowStyle="ThreeDBorderWindow">
```

```xml
<Grid>
<Label x:Name="label" Content="Please enter vCenter Server
Name" Margin="43.336,20.814,108.143,0" VerticalAlignment="Top"
FontWeight="Bold"/>
<Label x:Name="label1" Content="Please enter User Name and
Password" Margin="43.336,117.876,108.143,0" FontWeight="Bold"
VerticalAlignment="Top"/>
<Label x:Name="label2" Content="vCenter" HorizontalAlignment="Left"
Margin="49.551,67.194,0,0" VerticalAlignment="Top" Width="97.283"/>
<Label x:Name="label3" Content="User Name" HorizontalAlignment="Left"
Margin="49.551,0,0,129.24" Width="97.283" VerticalAlignment="Bottom"/>
<Label x:Name="label4" Content="Password" HorizontalAlignment="Left"
Margin="50,0,0,75" VerticalAlignment="Bottom" Width="97"/>
<TextBox x:Name="textBox" Height="23" Margin="198.255,67.194,29.005,0"
TextWrapping="Wrap" VerticalAlignment="Top"/>
<TextBox x:Name="textBox1" Height="23"
Margin="198.255,0,29.005,129.254" TextWrapping="Wrap"
VerticalAlignment="Bottom"/>
<PasswordBox x:Name="passwordBox" HorizontalAlignment="Left"
Margin="198,213,0,0" VerticalAlignment="Top" Width="276" Height="23"/>
<Button x:Name="button" Content="OK" HorizontalAlignment="Left"
Margin="104.06,0,0,29.113" VerticalAlignment="Bottom" Width="75"
FontWeight="Bold"/>
<Button x:Name="button1" Content="CANCEL" HorizontalAlignment="Right"
Margin="0,0,90.263,29.113" VerticalAlignment="Bottom" Width="75"
FontWeight="Bold"/>
</Grid>
</Window>
```

Next, we need to remove the `x:Class="TextBox_WPF.MainWindow"` class definition from the first line and the following three lines:

```xml
xmlns:d="http://schemas.microsoft.com/expression/blend/2008"
xmlns:mc="http://schemas.openxmlformats.org/markup-compatibility/2006"
mc:Ignorable="d"
```

These are the fourth, fifth, and seventh lines.

Also, we need to remove all instances of x: and replace them with nothing; otherwise, PowerShell will not be able to interpret them properly. Once we do that, the XAML code should look like this:

```
<Window Name="MainForm"
        xmlns="http://schemas.microsoft.com/winfx/2006/xaml/
presentation"
xmlns:x="http://schemas.microsoft.com/winfx/2006/xaml"
xmlns:local="clr-namespace:TextBox_WPF"
        Title="vCenter Information" Height="350" Width="525" WindowSta
rtupLocation="CenterScreen" ResizeMode="CanResizeWithGrip" WindowStyle
="ThreeDBorderWindow">
<Grid>
<Label Name="label" Content="Please enter vCenter Server
Name" Margin="43.336,20.814,108.143,0" VerticalAlignment="Top"
FontWeight="Bold"/>
<Label Name="label1" Content="Please enter User Name and
Password" Margin="43.336,117.876,108.143,0" FontWeight="Bold"
VerticalAlignment="Top"/>
<Label Name="label2" Content="vCenter" HorizontalAlignment="Left"
Margin="49.551,67.194,0,0" VerticalAlignment="Top" Width="97.283"/>
<Label Name="label3" Content="User Name" HorizontalAlignment="Left"
Margin="49.551,0,0,129.24" Width="97.283" VerticalAlignment="Bottom"/>
<Label Name="label4" Content="Password" HorizontalAlignment="Left"
Margin="50,0,0,75" VerticalAlignment="Bottom" Width="97"/>
<TextBox Name="textBox" Height="23" Margin="198.255,67.194,29.005,0"
TextWrapping="Wrap" VerticalAlignment="Top"/>
<TextBox Name="textBox1" Height="23" Margin="198.255,0,29.005,129.254"
TextWrapping="Wrap" VerticalAlignment="Bottom"/>
<PasswordBox Name="passwordBox" HorizontalAlignment="Left"
Margin="198,213,0,0" VerticalAlignment="Top" Width="276" Height="23"/>
<Button Name="button" Content="OK" HorizontalAlignment="Left"
Margin="104.06,0,0,29.113" VerticalAlignment="Bottom" Width="75"
FontWeight="Bold"/>
<Button Name="button1" Content="CANCEL" HorizontalAlignment="Right"
Margin="0,0,90.263,29.113" VerticalAlignment="Bottom" Width="75"
FontWeight="Bold"/>
</Grid>
</Window>
```

For better understanding, a screenshot is provided here:

```
<Window Name="MainForm"
    xmlns="http://schemas.microsoft.com/winfx/2006/xaml/presentation"
    xmlns:x="http://schemas.microsoft.com/winfx/2006/xaml"
    xmlns:local="clr-namespace:TextBox_WPF"
    Title="vCenter Information" Height="350" Width="525" WindowStartupLocation="CenterScreen" ResizeMode="CanResizeWithGrip" WindowStyle="ThreeDBorderWindow">
    <Grid>
        <Label Name="label" Content="Please enter vCenter Server Name" Margin="43.336,20.814,108.143,0" VerticalAlignment="Top" FontWeight="Bold"/>
        <Label Name="label1" Content="Please enter User Name and Password" Margin="43.336,117.876,108.143,0" FontWeight="Bold" VerticalAlignment="Top"/>
        <Label Name="label2" Content="vCenter" HorizontalAlignment="Left" Margin="49.551,67.194,0,0" VerticalAlignment="Top" Width="97.283"/>
        <Label Name="label3" Content="User Name" HorizontalAlignment="Left" Margin="49.551,0,0,129.24" Width="97.283" VerticalAlignment="Bottom"/>
        <Label Name="label4" Content="Password" HorizontalAlignment="Left" Margin="49.551,0,0,80.481" VerticalAlignment="Bottom" Width="97.283"/>
        <TextBox Name="textBox" Height="23" Margin="198.255,67.194,29.005,0" TextWrapping="Wrap" VerticalAlignment="Top"/>
        <TextBox Name="textBox1" Height="23" Margin="198.255,0,29.005,129.254" TextWrapping="Wrap" VerticalAlignment="Bottom"/>
        <TextBox Name="textBox2" Height="23" Margin="198.255,0,29.005,80.482" TextWrapping="Wrap" VerticalAlignment="Bottom"/>
        <Button Name="button" Content="OK" HorizontalAlignment="Left" Margin="104.06,0,0,29.113" VerticalAlignment="Bottom" Width="75" FontWeight="Bold"/>
        <Button Name="button1" Content="CANCEL" HorizontalAlignment="Right" Margin="0,0,90.263,29.113" VerticalAlignment="Bottom" Width="75" FontWeight="Bold"/>
    </Grid>
</Window>
```

By default, PowerShell does not understand XML code in the command line. We have our window defined in the XAML format, but how do we make PowerShell understand it? So, we need to load the assemblies for WPF and WinForm from the .NET framework. We need to start the script with the assembly load:

```
# Load the Assemblies

[void] [System.Reflection.Assembly]::LoadWithPartialName('Presentation
Core')
[void] [System.Reflection.Assembly]::LoadWithPartialName('Presentation
Framework')
[void] [System.Reflection.Assembly]::LoadWithPartialName('WindowsBase')
[void] [System.Reflection.Assembly]::LoadWithPartialName('system.
windows.forms')
```

```
# Load the Assemblies

[void][System.Reflection.Assembly]::LoadWithPartialName('PresentationCore')
[void][System.Reflection.Assembly]::LoadWithPartialName('PresentationFramework')
[void][System.Reflection.Assembly]::LoadWithPartialName('WindowsBase')
[void][System.Reflection.Assembly]::LoadWithPartialName('system.windows.forms')
```

Next, we will define an XML-type PowerShell object $xmlWindow and assign the XAML code to it. For this, we will use the HERE string in PowerShell (for details on HERE strings, visit https://technet.microsoft.com/en-us/library/ee692792.aspx).

So the format will be:

```
[xml] $xmlWindow = @'


'@
```

After putting the XAML code inside the HERE string, the variable will look like this:

```
# Define the XML object and store the XAML code into it

[xml]$xmlWindow = @'
<Window Name="MainForm"
        xmlns="http://schemas.microsoft.com/winfx/2006/xaml/
presentation"
xmlns:x="http://schemas.microsoft.com/winfx/2006/xaml"
xmlns:local="clr-namespace:TextBox_WPF"
        Title="vCenter Information" Height="350" Width="525" WindowSta
rtupLocation="CenterScreen" ResizeMode="CanResizeWithGrip" WindowStyle
="ThreeDBorderWindow">
<Grid>
<Label Name="label" Content="Please enter vCenter Server
Name" Margin="43.336,20.814,108.143,0" VerticalAlignment="Top"
FontWeight="Bold"/>
<Label Name="label1" Content="Please enter User Name and
Password" Margin="43.336,117.876,108.143,0" FontWeight="Bold"
VerticalAlignment="Top"/>
<Label Name="label2" Content="vCenter" HorizontalAlignment="Left"
Margin="49.551,67.194,0,0" VerticalAlignment="Top" Width="97.283"/>
<Label Name="label3" Content="User Name" HorizontalAlignment="Left"
Margin="49.551,0,0,129.24" Width="97.283" VerticalAlignment="Bottom"/>
<Label Name="label4" Content="Password" HorizontalAlignment="Left"
Margin="50,0,0,75" VerticalAlignment="Bottom" Width="97"/>
<TextBox Name="textBox" Height="23" Margin="198.255,67.194,29.005,0"
TextWrapping="Wrap" VerticalAlignment="Top"/>
<TextBox Name="textBox1" Height="23" Margin="198.255,0,29.005,129.254"
TextWrapping="Wrap" VerticalAlignment="Bottom"/>
<PasswordBox Name="passwordBox" HorizontalAlignment="Left"
Margin="198,213,0,0" VerticalAlignment="Top" Width="276" Height="23"/>
<Button Name="button" Content="OK" HorizontalAlignment="Left"
Margin="104.06,0,0,29.113" VerticalAlignment="Bottom" Width="75"
FontWeight="Bold"/>
<Button Name="button1" Content="CANCEL" HorizontalAlignment="Right"
Margin="0,0,90.263,29.113" VerticalAlignment="Bottom" Width="75"
FontWeight="Bold"/>
</Grid>
</Window>
'@
```

```
####################################################
# Define the XML object and store the XAML code into it
####################################################
[xml]$xamlWindow = @'
<Window Name="MainForm"
    xmlns="http://schemas.microsoft.com/winfx/2006/xaml/presentation"
    xmlns:x="http://schemas.microsoft.com/winfx/2006/xaml"
    xmlns:local="clr-namespace:TextBox_WPF"
    Title="vCenter Information" Height="350" Width="525" WindowStartupLocation="CenterScreen" ResizeMode="CanResizeWithGrip" WindowStyle="ThreeDBorderWindow">
    <Grid>
        <Label Name="label" Content="Please enter vCenter Server Name" Margin="43.336,20.814,108.143,0" VerticalAlignment="Top" FontWeight="Bold"/>
        <Label Name="label1" Content="Please enter User Name and Password" Margin="43.336,117.876,108.143,0" FontWeight="Bold" VerticalAlignment="Top"/>
        <Label Name="label2" Content="vCenter" HorizontalAlignment="Left" Margin="49.551,67.194,0,0" VerticalAlignment="Top" Width="97.283"/>
        <Label Name="label3" Content="User Name" HorizontalAlignment="Left" Margin="49.551,0,0,129.24" Width="97.283" VerticalAlignment="Bottom"/>
        <Label Name="label4" Content="Password" HorizontalAlignment="Left" Margin="50,0,0,75" VerticalAlignment="Bottom" Width="97"/>
        <TextBox Name="textBox" Height="23" Margin="198.255,67.194,29.005,0" TextWrapping="Wrap" VerticalAlignment="Top"/>
        <TextBox Name="textBox1" Height="23" Margin="198.255,0,29.005,129.254" TextWrapping="Wrap" VerticalAlignment="Bottom"/>
        <PasswordBox Name="passwordBox" HorizontalAlignment="Left" Margin="198,213,0,0" VerticalAlignment="Top" Width="276" Height="23"/>
        <Button Name="button" Content="OK" HorizontalAlignment="Left" Margin="104.06,0,0,29.113" VerticalAlignment="Bottom" Width="75" FontWeight="Bold"/>
        <Button Name="button1" Content="CANCEL" HorizontalAlignment="Right" Margin="0,0,90.263,29.113" VerticalAlignment="Bottom" Width="75" FontWeight="Bold"/>
    </Grid>
</Window>
'@
```

Next we need to read the all the elements in the $xamlWindow variable and store the names of the named elements in PowerShell. For this, we need to do the following:

```
####################################
# Read the XAML information and
####################################

$xamlReader = New-Object System.Xml.XmlNodeReader $xamlWindow

try{
    $MainForm= [Windows.Markup.XamlReader]::Load( $xamlReader )
}catch{
Write-Host "Unable to load Windows.Markup.XamlReader. Some problem is
there. Please check the XAML code entered."
exit
}
```

Note we defined an object of the System.Xml.XmlNodeReader class and read the XAML code stored in the $xmlWindow variable. Next we defined a variable $MainForm and set the value of this variable according to the ones defined in the XAML format:

```
#=====================================================================
=======
# Store Form Objects In PowerShell
#=====================================================================
=======

$xamlWindow.SelectNodes("//*[@Name]") | %{Set-Variable -Name ($_.Name)
-Value $MainForm.FindName($_.Name)}
```

```
#=======================================================================
=======
# Shows the form
#=======================================================================
=======
$MainForm.ShowDialog() | out-null
```

If we run this script, it will show the form and it requires only 58 lines of code, including all the comments and blank lines. Much smarter, right? But we have not done anything on it yet. We need to define an event on the **OK** and **CANCEL** button so that when we click on the **OK** button, it will show the Hosts list in the environment. Clicking on **CANCEL** should close the form.

In the XAML definition portion, all the controls have names: label, label1, label2, label3, and label4 for the labels and textbox, textBox1, and passwordBox for the textboxes. For the buttons, we have button and button1. We can actually access the properties of these control items from the environment. We will use these to carry out the tasks.

We can access the values that the user has entered into the textboxes. For textbox, it is $textBox.Text; for textBox1, it is $textBox1.Text; and so on.

If we want to get the password for the password box, then we need to access the Password property. So, the password will be accessible from $passwordBox.Password.

As we did earlier, we will declare a function to get a list of the hosts in the vCenter environment. I used the same Hosts_List function we discussed earlier:

```
###############################################################
# Define the Functions
###############################################################

functionHosts_List($vc, $user, $pass)
{
    Add-PSSnapinVMware.VimAutomation.Core
    Connect-VIserver -Server $vc -User $user -Password $pass | Out-
Null
    Get-VMHost | Out-GridView
}
```

Next, we need to define events for the `Click` action for the **OK** and **CANCEL** buttons. We did that in the following way (exactly similar to the earlier examples):

```
# Defining on Click events for the buttons

$button.add_Click({Hosts_List -vc $textBox.Text -user $textBox1.Text
-pass $passwordBox.Password })

$button1.add_Click({Disconnect-VIServer $textBox.Text -Confirm:$False;
$MainForm.Close()})
```

The last line of the script shows the form:

```
#======================================================================
=======
# Shows the form
#======================================================================
=======
$MainForm.ShowDialog() | out-null
```

The following screenshot shows the output of running the completed script:

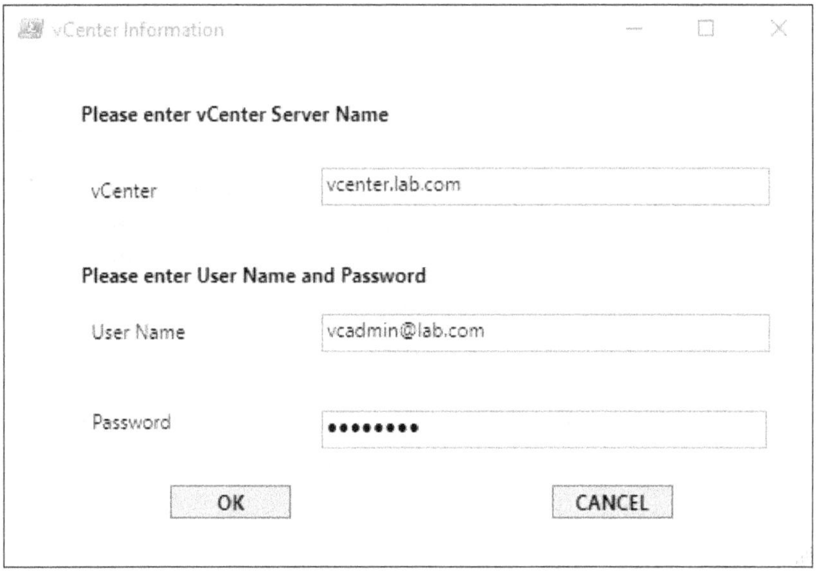

Similar to earlier examples, the first screen is the information gathering screen. Once we provide the required information and click on the **OK** button, the following information is shown. Clicking on the **CANCEL** button closes the form:

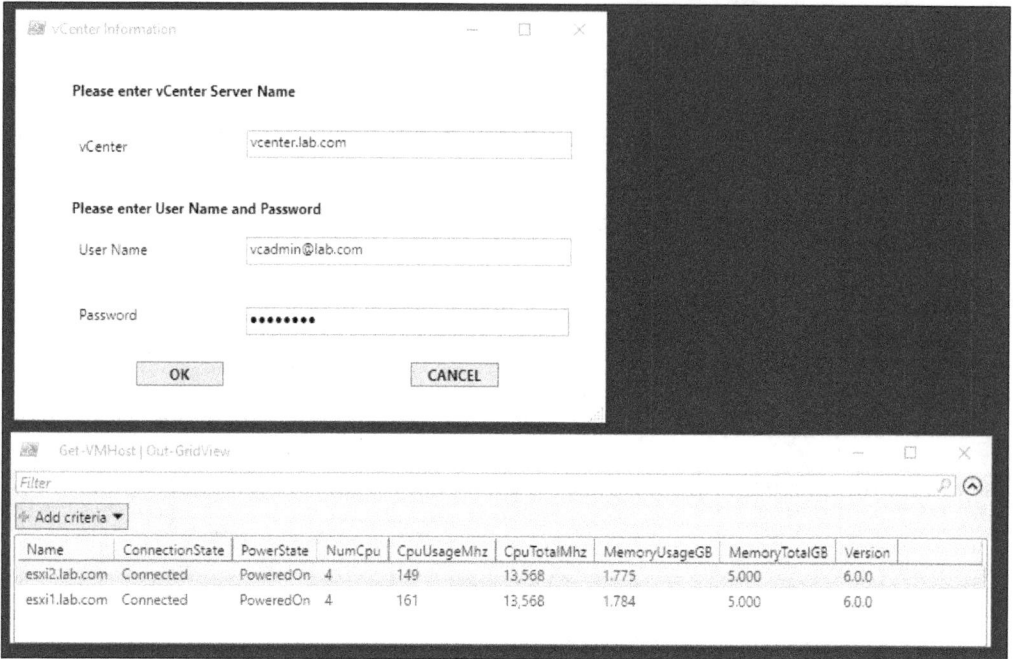

In the end, the event definition and other functions around the form remain same; the difference between all the three approaches is how you build the form. Evidently, using the WPF gives a lot of flexibility and requires comparative less lines of code as well.

This was a very simple example showing the working of WPF and how we can leverage it. You can work out the different options and properties in Blend and create beautiful forms. I find this is a much easier way of creating the form.

Initially, WPF seems to be a bit more complex but once you get the feel of it, it is actually much simpler. The event portion of it remains same for all the three described processes, but in WPF the code required to manage the form is actually pretty less. Besides, WPF is more modern and provides more flexibility.

Hopefully you will be able to build on these examples and complete the rest of the forms. I leave it up to you to complete the task as homework.

Summary

In this chapter, we discussed how to build a Windows GUI using different methods and give a frontend to our scripts. We saw how we can take help of third-party tools to build our own executable file, which when run will show the form and execute the workflows that we define.

This concludes all the topics that I wanted to cover in the book. In the next chapter, we will talk about PowerShell scripting best practices and discuss some sample scripts.

12
Best Practices and Sample Scripts

So far, we have discussed all the topics that we intended to cover. This has been a long journey and I thank you for staying with me this far. This is going to be the last chapter of this book. In this chapter, we are going to talk about various best practices and three sample scripts. We will start with a discussion on general best practices to be followed while writing PowerShell scripts. In the subsequent sections, we will discuss three sample scripts. In general, this chapter will cover the following topics.

- Best practices
- Security hardening script
- Capacity check report
- Using a proper editor

So without wasting much time, let's start our first topic of discussion.

Best practices

We have covered many aspects of PowerShell scripting in the preceding chapters, and while doing so we wrote many examples. The majority of these examples were a few lines or blocks of script, but the main aim of these examples was to showcase the feature or functionality that I was explaining. So I tried to use very simple examples without much fuss about best practices. These scripts probably did not conform to the guidelines, but that was intentional as I wanted you to focus on the example, script, and cmdlet itself and not get distracted by the other best practices. In this section, we are going to talk about the best practices that you should follow while writing scripts for yourself or for others.

If you want to script like a pro, then it is necessary to follow these best practices. Many do not consider scripting to be serious coding, but believe it or not scripting is a serious business. You can achieve the same results as applications written in professional programming language with scripting as well. At times, scripting can do it in a far easier way. With an advanced scripting language like PowerShell, you can do wonders, so you must learn the best practices and conform to them in your daily life. Here are the best practices and their explanations:

- **Make it simple**: The first point to note and perhaps the most important point is to write and create simple scripts. In the world of programming, a task can be achieved in many ways. There is no right or wrong about them, but you should try to find out the easiest way to do a task. Remember this saying by Bill Gates *"I will always choose a lazy person to do a hard job. Because a lazy person will find an easy way to do it."* I know the temptation is to create something really complex and show it to others. But think about the person coming after you and looking at the code. How easy will it be for the person to follow and understand the code? Give it a couple of years and it would be complex enough for you as well. So take this to heart: *simple is elegant.*

- **Use –NoProfile for launching script**: While launching a script externally as a scheduled task, always use -NoProfile. For example, while launching a scheduled task in Windows Scheduler, we typically tend to use the following format:

```
powershell.exe -File c:\test\test1.ps1
```

This is potentially dangerous and inefficient because if there is any profile script present in the environment, then PowerShell will execute all the profile scripts and then it will execute the script that you want to execute. So, you should use the following command:

```
powershell.exe -NoProfile -File c:\test\test1.ps1
```

This will directly execute your script in an untouched environment.

- **Do not use aliases in scripts**: Never use aliases in scripts. Aliases are supposed to be used with interactive PowerShell sessions, not in scripts. Say you used aliases in your scripts and then distribute this script, and someone else uses this script. You can never predict what aliases they set in their computer and because of that your script will be broken or yield unexpected result.

If you check, you can see that there are a total of 155 aliases defined in PowerShell 5. Think about aliases such as `rwmi, shcm, spjb, sujb, spsv,` and so on. How difficult is it for someone else to find out what exactly it does? So the golden rule is: never use aliases in your script.

- **Use single quotes by default**: By default, try to use single quotes. The usage of single quote ensures that the text that you want to use does not get changed by PowerShell. It stays as it was intended to be.

  Double quotes enable PowerShell to make changes in the text in between the quotes. There are situations where you would use double quotes, for example, if you want to expand a variable or use an escape character. So, use double quotes where you absolutely mean to use them. Otherwise, avoid using double quotes and use single quotes.

  I am not going to expand on the difference between single and double quotes, but see the following example:

  ```
  PS C:\>cls
  PS C:\>"This mistake is going to cost me $$$"
  This mistake is going to cost me cls$
  ```

  Not something we were expecting, right? If I use single quotes, I get the following result:

  ```
  PS C:\> 'This mistake is going to cost me $$$'
  This mistake is going to cost me $$$
  ```

  This was something we were expecting. So, use single quotes by default and use double quotes only when you mean it.

- **Use Parameter Block**: There are two ways that we can define parameters in a function. Here's the first way:

  ```
  function Test-Function ($Parameter1, $Parameter2)
  {

      "Entered Parameters: '$Parameter1' and '$Parameter2'"
  }
  ```

This was the simplest way of defining parameters in function. The better way of doing it is like this:

```
function Test-Function
{
param
    (
       $Parameter1,

       $Parameter2
    )
   " Entered Parameters: '$Parameter1' and '$Parameter2'"
}
```

While both declarations are technically right, the second one is more consistent. We can simply use the parameter definitions in normal scripts by removing the function portion. For example, the following portion is perfectly fine:

```
param
    (
       $Parameter1,

       $Parameter2
    )
   " Entered Parameters: '$Parameter1' and '$Parameter2'"
```

So, always try to define parameters in this way:

- **Use named parameters instead of positional or partial parameters:** Positional parameters are more difficult to read and remember, especially with cmdlets with multiple parameters. With newer versions of PowerShell, there is no guarantee that these positional parameters will keep their format or not change their position. In that case, a script using only positional parameters will fail or provide the wrong output. So, it is always better to use the named parameters. For example, consider the following code:

```
# Using Positional parameter
Copy-Item C:\Test1.txt E:\Test1.txt
```

In this example, we can easily get confused about the source and destination path. However, consider the following code:

```
# Using Partial Parameter Name
Copy-Item -Pat C:\Test1.txt -Des E:\Test1.txt
```

In this case, the partial parameter name is not very clear. Consider the following code:

```
# Using Named parameter
Copy-Item -Path C:\Test1.txt -Destination E:\Test1.txt
```

In the preceding case, it is very clear which is the source path and which one is the destination. There is no confusion and no chance of error.

- **Avoid excessive use of comments**: I know it is always suggested to use inline comments as much as possible so that we can understand what we are doing at a later stage. But look at the following code:

```
#######################
##### Start Script #####
#######################


##############################################################
#This script is used to the list of hosts and virtual machines
##############################################################


#######################################################
#### A list of hosts is collected first  ###
#######################################################


# Get the list of hosts
$hosts = Get-VMHost


#######################################################
# We are going to get the list of virtual machines ####
#######################################################


# Get the list of VM's
$vms = Get-VM

Write-Output -InputObject 'End of Script'


#######################
##### End Script #######
#######################
```

Is that a really good script? So, use inline comments as per requirement. Don't make the script overcrowded with comments.

- I suggest that you use `Write-Verbose` and `Write-Debug` for the comments. If you write plain inline comments, then only a person reading the code will benefit from them. But if you use `Write-Verbose` and `Write-Debug`, then normal users can also benefit from these comments. Also, these can be simply turned on or off by using the `-Verbose` or `-Debug` switch. So, maintain a balance between all these three. For example, we can write the same script like this:

```
# Start Script
# This script is used to get list of hosts and virtual machines

Write-Verbose 'Get the list of hosts'
$hosts = Get-VMHost

Write-Verbose 'Get the list of VM's'
$vms = Get-VM

Write-Output -InputObject 'End of Script'
```

- **Use approved list of verbs in names**: While writing scripts, functions, or advance functions, always use verb-singular noun format naming. Also, choose the verb names from the list of the Microsoft-approved names. To get a list of the approved verbs, use the `Get-Verb` cmdlet. Currently, there are 98 approved verbs. Also, use singular form of the noun in the second part. This is because by default PowerShell-approved cmdlets are in verb-noun format.

- **Use –WhatIf and –Confirm parameters**: Try and use the `-WhatIf` and `-Confirm` parameters as much as possible. It is good to use these parameters as this gives the end users the option to see what happens if the function or the script is run. Also, the `-Confirm` parameter gives the users the option to choose or cancel before taking an actual step. For example, before deleting something, users will get the option to choose whether to delete it or not.

- **Use the same parameter name as the native ones**: Always try to use the same parameter names as that of the native parameter. For example, `-Computername` is a parameter that is used natively in PowerShell, so instead of using that if we use `-PC` or `-Desktop`, that sounds unfamiliar and is not easy to remember.

- **Use proper indentation**: I cannot tell you enough how important it is to use consistent indentation. It increases the readability of the code and will be easier to follow. For example, look at the following code:

```
function Hosts_List($vc, $user, $pass){
Connect-VIserver -Server $vc -User $user -Password $pass| Out-Null
Get-VMHost
$MainForm.Close()}


function CheckBox-Changed($object){
If($object.Checked ){
Return $True}}


$MainForm = New-Object System.Windows.Forms.Form
$MainForm.Text = "Host List"
$MainForm.Size = New-Object System.Drawing.Size(455,265)
$MainForm.StartPosition = "CenterScreen"
```

Do you find the code readable? Now, check the following code:

```
function Hosts_List($vc, $user, $pass)
{
        Connect-VIserver -Server $vc -User $user -Password $pass|
Out-Null
    Get-VMHost
    $MainForm.Close()
}
function CheckBox-Changed($object){

If($object.Checked ){
        Return $True
    }
}


$MainForm = New-Object System.Windows.Forms.Form
$MainForm.Text = "Host List"
$MainForm.Size = New-Object System.Drawing.Size(455,265)
$MainForm.StartPosition = "CenterScreen"
```

Which one is more readable? The problem further increases with multiple level of nested logic. So, use whatever indentation style you want to follow, but use indentation for sure.

- **Do not globally set ErrorAction**: Most often, you would see this line in a script:

```
$ErrorActionPreference = 'SilentlyContinue'
```

This globally suppresses ErrorActionPreference and if there is any error, the script continues silently. This essentially overlooks all the errors. So use it per line. For example, in the following line, I want to delete a previously existing log file. If the file does not exist, I really do not care about it and want to continue the execution of the script. The command is as follows:

```
Delete -Path $logfile -ErrorAction 'SilentlyContinue'
```

Use the -ErrorAction parameter with the cmdlet where you want to supress the error.

- **Place user-defined variables at the top**: Try and to put all the user-defined variables at the top. Then, someone looking at your script will not have to search through the entire script to find out the variable declaration. It is a much easier way to manage and, if required, change them.

- **Avoid using Write-Host**: Always try to use the Write-Output cmdlet to provide the output. The Write-Host cmdlet just sends the output to screen and does not return any object. It is not possible to export or convert to other formats and is pretty limited. But there are times when you want to use this, especially if you want to format the color of the output in the output screen then it is useful. Otherwise, stick to Write-Output.

- **Use Set-StrictMode**: There are times when an undeclared variable leads to unexpected results. So, it is advisable to use Set-StrictMode so that it will be checked whether a variable is declared or not.

- **Avoid Out-Null**: It is recommended to avoid using Out-Null. Instead, use [void] or $null. The reason is Out-Null is slower than using [void] or $null.

- **Specify the extension for external applications**: Always specify the extensions of an external application. It is easier to read and understand. Also, if there is a function with the same name as the application, the function takes precedence.

- **Do not write functions simply because they are cool**: Do not write functions simply because they look cool. Writing a function will incur a performance hit. It will always be slower than inline code. But it has its own advantages too. So use it judiciously. Here's the thumb rule: if you are repeatedly using a portion of code multiple times or want to reuse the code, then write a function. Otherwise, stick to simple inline code. Also, do not write advanced functions simply because you can. If it requires a simple function, go ahead and write a simple function. No need for the fancy one.

- **Maintain linearity**: Try to maintain linearity in your code. When you have a big script, it becomes really hard to follow the code and search for where you have written a particular function. So try to write the function and code as per logical linearity so that readers of the code will not have to search here and there for the required information.

Security Hardening Script

Although we discussed it in *Chapter 8, Managing vSphere Security, SRM, vCloud Air and vROps* let's revisit the security checking in vSphere environment. I am going to show a script here that will perform a security audit of the entire vSphere environment. This is the first version of the script and it only checks for the security parameters; it does not set the security parameters. In future, I will create another script that will set the respective parameters as well to make the environment secure. So you will have two scripts, one to check the environment and another to patch the environment as per the VMware security best practices. For these settings, I have used the security guidelines by VMware vSphere_6_0_Hardening_Guide_GA_15_ Jun_2015.xls which can be found easily via Google.

So, I am not going to explain the security checking portion, but we're going to discuss the structure of the script and what each portion does. Remember this is a first cut of the script and by no means finished. Actually, I am planning to keep it open. It will be hosted in my blog http://vlearner.blogspot.com and I would welcome comments and suggestions from my readers. So, I am going to collaborate with you to make it more flexible and useful. Also, I already have a to-do list in my mind for the script that I am going to elaborate on later (once I finish explaining the script).

What better way to start the explanation than to show the output?:

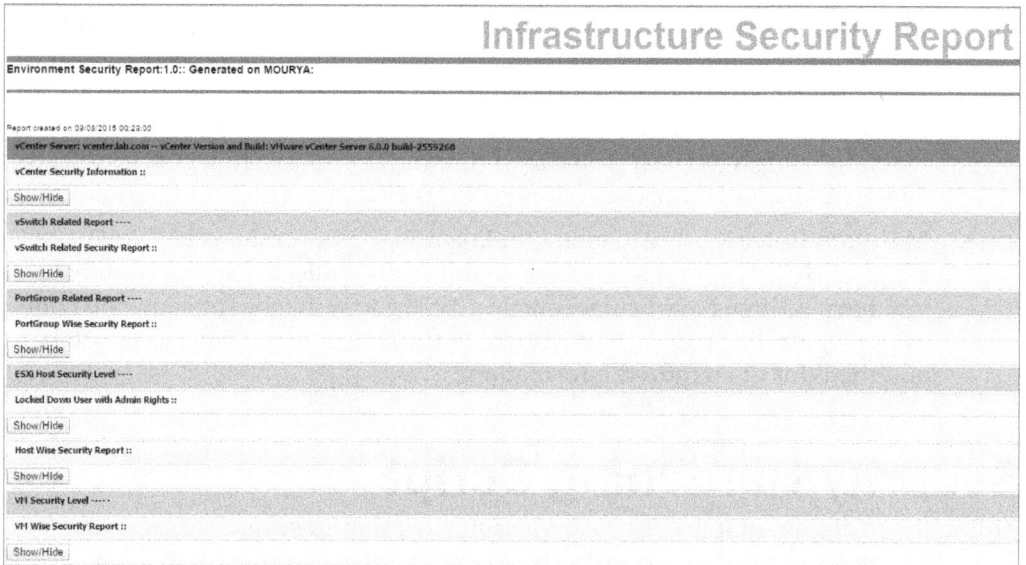

As you can see in the preceding screenshot, by default when you see the HTML report, it only shows the main headings about which the report is generated. Since there is a lot of information, I prefer to start with a hide option. If you click on the **Show/Hide** button of the respective area, it will show the information pertaining to that area only. For example, I want to see only vSwitch-related security information, so I click on the respective **Show/Hide** button. I get the following screen:

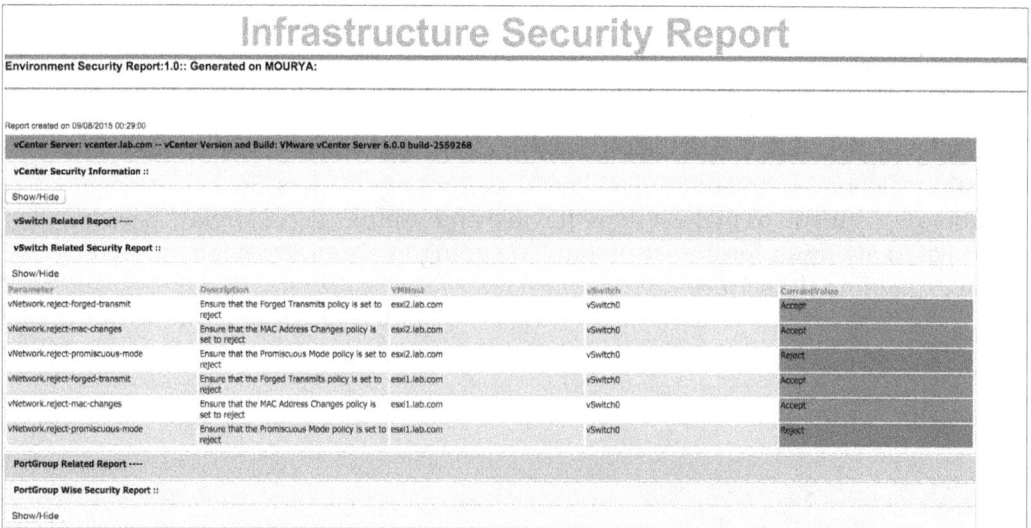

For readability, I have selected alternate rows to be colored; the cells that have the security best practices values are automatically marked in green and the concern areas are automatically marked in red. This is very useful to find out the errors at a glance.

The script is available as `Get-Security.ps1` and the related functions file is `SecurityFunctions.ps1`. These are not completed scripts or the most elegant ones, but they do the work and will be refined further.

So let's start exploring the interesting areas of the script. The most important portion of the script is in the `SecurityFunctions.ps1` script.

The functions can be divided into three main categories. The first category is the one (`Get-Custom*`) that generate the HTML reports, the second one (`Write-Log`) is the one that generates the logs, and the third one (`Get-SecurityFunction`) is the main one that actually does the audit.

So, let's analyze them. The HTML generation reports were actually taken from an old vCheck script written by Alan Renouf. I took them and modified them according to my requirements. There are many tutorials and examples of how to create custom HTML using PowerShell, but these functions are the easiest ones that do the job. Since I have been using them for reporting for a long time now, I am somewhat addicted to them.

If you use the `ConvertTo-HTML` cmdlet, it actually converts your data and if you use the `-Fragment` switch along with it, you can easily build the HTML without these fancy functions as well.

For example, I have a variable with six objects in it:

```
Parameter                        Description                                            VMHost         vSwitch  CurrentValue
---------                        -----------                                            ------         -------  ------------
vNetwork.reject-forged-transmit  Ensure that the Forged Transmits policy is set to reject   esxi2.lab.com  vSwitch0 RED Accept
vNetwork.reject-mac-changes      Ensure that the MAC Address Changes policy is set to reject esxi2.lab.com  vSwitch0 RED Accept
vNetwork.reject-promiscuous-mode Ensure that the Promiscuous Mode policy is set to reject   esxi2.lab.com  vSwitch0 Green Reject
vNetwork.reject-forged-transmit  Ensure that the Forged Transmits policy is set to reject   esxi1.lab.com  vSwitch0 RED Accept
vNetwork.reject-mac-changes      Ensure that the MAC Address Changes policy is set to reject esxi1.lab.com  vSwitch0 RED Accept
vNetwork.reject-promiscuous-mode Ensure that the Promiscuous Mode policy is set to reject   esxi1.lab.com  vSwitch0 Green Reject
```

Next, I want to convert this data into an HTML file:

```
PS E:\> $data1 | ConvertTo-Html
<!DOCTYPE html PUBLIC "-//W3C//DTD XHTML 1.0 Strict//EN"  "http://www.
w3.org/TR/xhtml1/DTD/xhtml1-strict.dtd">
<html xmlns="http://www.w3.org/1999/xhtml">
<head>
```

```
<title>HTML TABLE</title>
</head><body>
<table>
<colgroup><col/><col/><col/><col/><col/></colgroup>
<tr><th>Parameter</th><th>Description</th><th>VMHost</th><th>vSwitch</
th><th>CurrentValue</th></tr>
<tr><td>vNetwork.reject-forged-transmit</td><td>Ensure that the
Forged Transmits policy is set to reject</td><td>esxi2.lab.com</
td><td>vSwitch0</td><td>RED Accept</td></tr>
<tr><td>vNetwork.reject-mac-changes</td><td>Ensure that the MAC
Address Changes policy is set to reject</td><td>esxi2.lab.com</
td><td>vSwitch0</td><td>RED Accept</td></tr>
<tr><td>vNetwork.reject-promiscuous-mode</td><td>Ensure that the
Promiscuous Mode policy is set to reject</td><td>esxi2.lab.com</
td><td>vSwitch0</td><td>Green Reject</td></tr>
<tr><td>vNetwork.reject-forged-transmit</td><td>Ensure that the
Forged Transmits policy is set to reject</td><td>esxi1.lab.com</
td><td>vSwitch0</td><td>RED Accept</td></tr>
<tr><td>vNetwork.reject-mac-changes</td><td>Ensure that the MAC
Address Changes policy is set to reject</td><td>esxi1.lab.com</
td><td>vSwitch0</td><td>RED Accept</td></tr>
<tr><td>vNetwork.reject-promiscuous-mode</td><td>Ensure that the
Promiscuous Mode policy is set to reject</td><td>esxi1.lab.com</
td><td>vSwitch0</td><td>Green Reject</td></tr>
</table>
</body></html>
```

Plain conversion provides the HTML header information. Now, we want this information to be part of a bigger HTML document, so we will convert it as a Fragment. The code is as follows:

```
PS E:\Google Drive\Mastering PowerCLI\Chapters\Chapter 12> $data1 |
ConvertTo-Html -Fragment
<table>
<colgroup><col/><col/><col/><col/><col/></colgroup>
<tr><th>Parameter</th><th>Description</th><th>VMHost</th><th>vSwitch</
th><th>CurrentValue</th></tr>
```

```
<tr><td>vNetwork.reject-forged-transmit</td><td>Ensure that the
Forged Transmits policy is set to reject</td><td>esxi2.lab.com</
td><td>vSwitch0</td><td>RED Accept</td></tr>
```

```
<tr><td>vNetwork.reject-mac-changes</td><td>Ensure that the MAC
Address Changes policy is set to reject</td><td>esxi2.lab.com</
td><td>vSwitch0</td><td>RED Accept</td></tr>
```

```
<tr><td>vNetwork.reject-promiscuous-mode</td><td>Ensure that the
Promiscuous Mode policy is set to reject</td><td>esxi2.lab.com</
td><td>vSwitch0</td><td>Green Reject</td></tr>
```

```
<tr><td>vNetwork.reject-forged-transmit</td><td>Ensure that the
Forged Transmits policy is set to reject</td><td>esxi1.lab.com</
td><td>vSwitch0</td><td>RED Accept</td></tr>
```

```
<tr><td>vNetwork.reject-mac-changes</td><td>Ensure that the MAC
Address Changes policy is set to reject</td><td>esxi1.lab.com</
td><td>vSwitch0</td><td>RED Accept</td></tr>
```

```
<tr><td>vNetwork.reject-promiscuous-mode</td><td>Ensure that the
Promiscuous Mode policy is set to reject</td><td>esxi1.lab.com</
td><td>vSwitch0</td><td>Green Reject</td></tr>
</table>
```

I will further explore HTML creation and customization in my blog.

The `Get-CustomHTML()` function creates the main header portion, defines a different style in CSS format, and a small JavaScript function to hide and unhide the portion of the document as per button click. The rest of the functions are to format the output of the HTML, for example, provide different colors to different types of headings and so on. In this main function, two points are important:

```
tr:nth-child(odd) {
                        background-color:#d3d3d3;
            }
tr:nth-child(even) {
background-color:white;
}
```

The `tr` portion is used to specify the parameters for the table row information. I am using this to color the alternate rows in gray.

The next important function is the `Get-HTMLTable` function:

```
function Get-HTMLTable {
param([array]$Content)
    $HTMLTable = $Content | ConvertTo-Html -Fragment
    $HTMLTable = $HTMLTable -replace '>RED ', ' bgcolor="RED">'
    $HTMLTable = $HTMLTable -replace '>Green ', ' bgcolor="Green">'
    return $HTMLTable
}
```

We are using this function to generate the tabular format of our data. Since all information in HTML is typically a table, the first line converts the input data into a HTML table. Consider these two lines:

```
$HTMLTable = $HTMLTable -replace '>RED ', ' bgcolor="RED">'
    $HTMLTable = $HTMLTable -replace '>Green ', ' bgcolor="Green">'
```

Remember, our main aim was to change the color of the cells according to their information. If the information is as expected (security best practice is implemented), then the cell is colored in green, and no change needs to be made to this parameter. Whereas a red color indicates that action needs to be taken on this parameter. To achieve this, while making the output, I marked the information as either RED or Green. In this function, I am checking all the information of the table and wherever RED is mentioned. This means that a particular cell color should be RED. So, we are simply replacing that text RED with `bgcolor="RED"` so that the cell format will change from `<td>RED Accept</td>` to `<tdbgcolor="RED">Accept</td>`.

Now, we have the original intended information and the format for making the cell color to RED. A similar change happens for green color as well. So, while generating the value at runtime, I am passing formatting information to my HTML table creation function and using this information to build the cell as per my requirement. We could use a similar approach to change other aspects as well. For example, instead of changing the color of the cell, changing the color of the entire row.

The next important function is the `Write-Log` function. This is a very useful function that can be leveraged to create logging. There are multiple functions like this available on the Internet, or I could write a custom one. But instead of reinventing the wheel, I have used the one written by Jason Wasser, which is available at `https://gallery.technet.microsoft.com/scriptcenter/Write-Log-PowerShell-999c32d0`. I strongly suggest you visit the site and check the details there.

I am yet to fully integrate this logging functionality into my overall script.

The third function, `Get-SecurityFunction`, is the main function that checks the environment and then generates the report. The function is a typical advanced function with defined `BEGIN{}`, `PROCESS{}`, and `END{}` sections. In the first part, I am adding the snapin and importing the `VMware.VimAutomation.Vds` module.

I am not checking whether the modules are successfully loaded or not. There should be a check for this. Also, I am assuming that the PowerCLI package was installed in the default location; if it is located in another location, then this particular module will not be loaded and the script will fail to produce results in some places. So, a more elaborate method needs to be used to find out the location of the modules and load them.

Next, we are disconnecting from any connected sessions and then connecting to the vCenter server using the `try{}catch{}` method. If the connection fails, we will get an error and exit the script. In the Begin section, we are declaring the variables that will store further data.

In the process section, we are actually finding out the different security parameters as defined in the VMware best practices. The only interesting point to note is the addition of the Red or Green text as part of the `$Value` variable. We will use this later to decide the color of the cell.

Throughout the script, I have used the `If()` `{}Else{}` statement to decide the color. Since I am using it in so many places, it is better to use a separate function for this decision. Then, I wouldn't have to write the same format so many times. This is not a good use of scripting skills. In future versions, it will be changed.

The important point about functions is where to use them and where to avoid using them. Calling a script stores all the current running variables in a stack and then calls out to the function. So, calling functions will be slower than the inline code, but the benefit is cleaner, reusable code. Avoid using a function inside a nested loop that will run multiple times; this can quickly consume memory. Ultimately, you need to decide between benefit and cost. So, use your best judgement.

In the END portion, we are building the HTML report from the information that we got in the PROCESS section.

At the end, we are storing the data in an HTML file and opening it in the default browser.

Capacity check report

The capacity check report script checks the capacity of the vSphere environment and provides a report in HTML format. The details of the script are provided here.

The report is divided into four major parts:

- Entire Infrastructure Capacity Report
- Infrastructure Capacity at Cluster Level (Cluster Wise Capacity Report)
- Infrastructure Capacity at ESXi Host Level (Host Wise Capacity Report)
- Infrastructure Capacity at Datastore Level (Datastore Wise Capacity Report)

The relation between the major report parts is shown in the following figure:

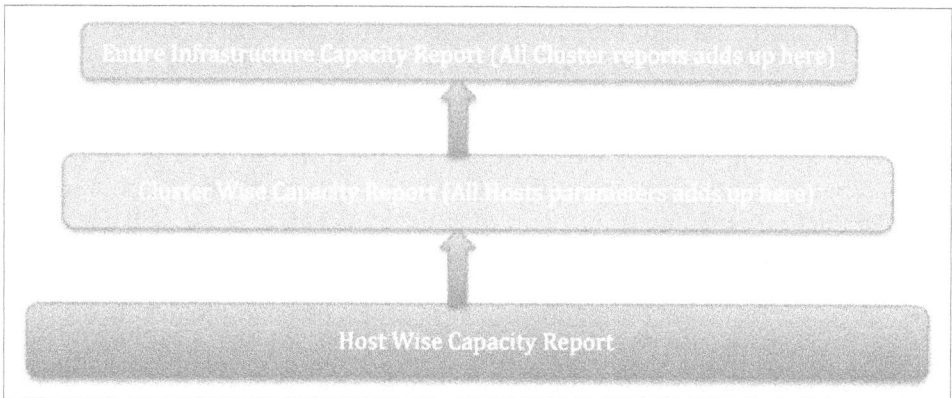

We'll discuss the parameter description for all the parts in the next section.

Note that all the information is calculated at individual ESXi host level. At the Cluster level, all the individual ESXi parameters are summed up and then divided by the number of hosts in that cluster so that we get an average value for this cluster. For example, if there are two ESXi hosts in a cluster with CPU utilization of 10 percent and 15 percent, then the average CPU utilization of that Cluster will be *(10+15)/2= 12.5%*. Also if there are a total of 4 clusters in an environment and the CPU utilization of those clusters are 10 percent, 20 percent, 30 percent, 20 percent, respectively, then the average CPU utilization of the total environment is *(10 + 20 + 30 + 20) / 4 = 20*. This same process is followed for all the parameters.

Parameter descriptions

This is the portion where the capacitive and utilization report for the Entire Infrastructure is provided. The value seen here is a summation of all the reports from Cluster Level Report. The parameters are explained here:

- **Physical core**: This is the available physical core under the entire infrastructure. This is the summation of all available physical CPU capacity of all the ESXi hosts.

- **Allo. vCPU**: This is the total allocated vCPU in all the VMs in the entire environment.

- **Used vCPU**: This is the actual usage of the physical servers converted in vCPU. For example, if the total actual usage in all the ESXi hosts in the environment is 6 GHz and a single physical CPU core is 2 GHz, then the total used vCPU is $(6/2) = 3$. This is to easily relate how much CPU capacity of a vCPU equivalent is used.

- **vCPU remaining**: This is the actual vCPU remaining, considering the actual usage and overcommit value. For example, if you have a total of 12 physical cores in your environment and you decide to calculate a CPU overcommit value of 3 (1:3 ratio), then the total available vCPU in the environment is 36 vCPU. Now, consider the actual equivalent usage as 6 vCPU, then the vCPU remaining is $(36 - 6) = 30$.

- **Host usage %**: This is the actual CPU usage percent of the host averaged for the entire environment.

- **Physical Mem**: This is the summation of all the available memory in all the ESXi hosts.

- **Allo. MEM**: This is the allocated memory in all the virtual machines. It is in GB.

- **Used Mem**: This is the actual used memory in all the physical hosts. It is in GB.

- **Aval MEM**: This is the available memory after the used memory.

- **Used Mem %**: This is the average of used memory percentage in the cluster.

- **Total VM**: This is the total number of deployed VMs in the environment.

The preceding parameters are also defined under Cluster and ESXi. The parameters defined in the datastore are self-explanatory. The output of the report is shown in the following screenshot:

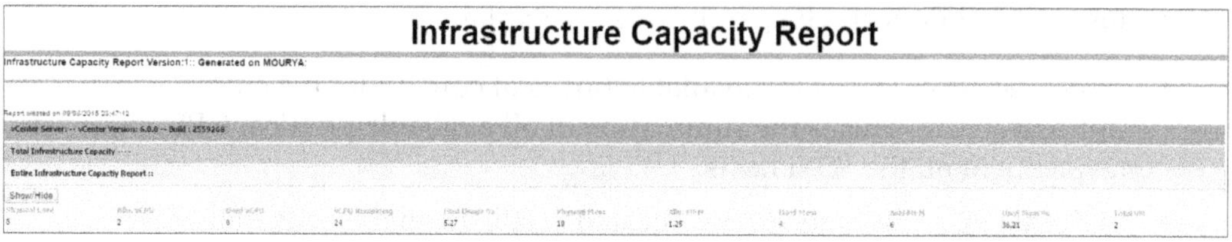

Here's the next part of the screenshot:

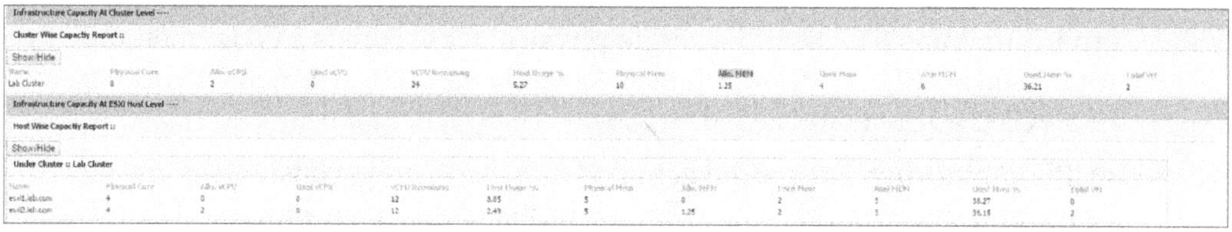

Here's the datastore section:

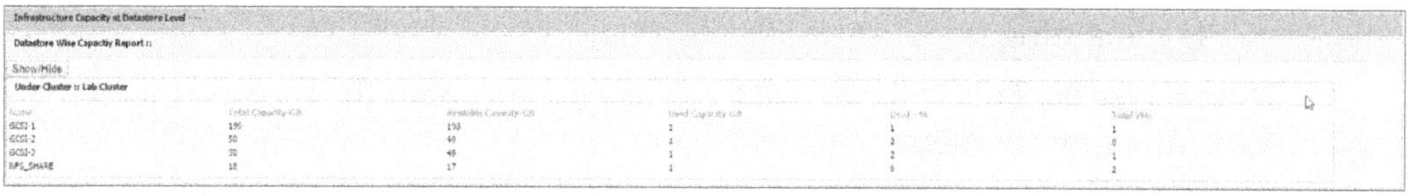

There are no advanced functions in this script; it is pretty straightforward. The first part of the script has the same functions defined as the scripts used for reporting HTML and logs. The important part of the script is where we actually calculate the utilizations:

```
# Calculating usage history of the host for the last 7 days

$stats = Get-Stat -Entity $host1 -start (get-date).
AddDays(-7) -Finish (Get-Date) -MaxSamples 10000 -stat "cpu.usagemhz.
average","cpu.usage.average","mem.consumed.average","mem.usage.
average"
```

The stat variable stores the statistics of the ESXi host. I am getting the value for the past seven days and the number of samples is also mentioned. I am pointing out the actual parameters that I need. I am using the following parameters:

- `Cpu.usagemhz.average`
- `Cpu.usage.average`
- `Mem.consumed.average`
- `Mem.usage.average`

For a list of available statistics, you can run the following command and find out the values:

```
Get-Stat -Entity $esxihost
```

Next, we use this statistic to further calculate average, maximum, and minimum values:

```
$stats | Group-Object -Property Entity | %{
    $cpu = $_.Group | where {$_.MetricId -eq "cpu.usagemhz.
average"} | Measure-Object -Property value -Average -Maximum -Minimum
        $acpu = $_.Group | where {$_.MetricId -eq "cpu.usage.average"}
 | Measure-Object -Property value -Average -Maximum -Minimum
        $mem = $_.Group | where {$_.MetricId -eq "mem.consumed.
average"} | Measure-Object -Property value -Average -Maximum -Minimum
        $amem = $_.Group | where {$_.MetricId -eq "mem.usage.average"}
 | Measure-Object -Property value -Average -Maximum -Minimum
        }
```

The last part actually builds the HTML file and shows the information. The To Do list for this script is to create functions out of the script portions.

Using a proper editor

The last topic of this chapter is about an editor. An editor is the proper tool for any script writer. Depending on the editor that you use, your actual scripting time may lessen. So I have decided to discuss my favorite editors here.

Sublime Text

In Mac, I use Sublime Text as my PowerShell editor. It is probably one of the most useful editors in a Mac environment. It does what it is supposed to do: work as an editor. By default, it does not support PowerShell formatting but you can add the PowerShell support by using the required packaging. Follow the instructions provided in these links and you are good to go.

First, follow the steps in this link to install the Package Control: `https://packagecontrol.io/installation`.

Then, install the package for PowerShell using the information provided at `https://github.com/SublimeText/PowerShell`.

This is what the editor looks like once the PowerShell support is added to it:

In my environment, I use Sublime Text 3. One of the best blogs describing the features of Sublime Text 3 is by Chris Sevilleja. You can read more about it at `https://scotch.io/bar-talk/best-of-sublime-text-3-features-plugins-and-settings`.

ISESteroids

I have come to know about ISESteroids recently and it has quickly become my favorite editor. It is by far the most useful one that I have used until now. It was developed by Dr. Tobias Weltner. I learned PowerShell from his book, so I was delighted when he responded back to my mail and provided me details of this editor.

The name says a lot about the editor, and yes it is the default ISE Editor on Steroids.

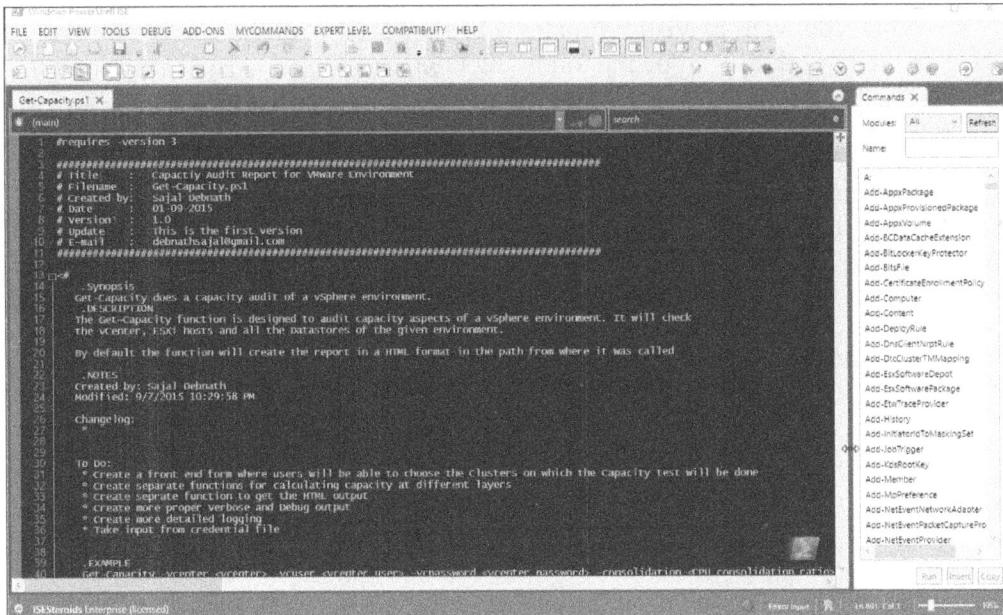

There are many handy features in the editor. The first one is the command console. You can simply toggle between the script console and command console by clicking on the icon at the bottom right corner of the screen. If you are like me, then you can simply pop out of the command console altogether.

Other major points to note are as follows:

Whenever you type something and it turns a particular color, press *Tab* to insert a snippet. Note that snippets support enclosures too. Suppose you have code like this:

```
Write-Host "Error follows"
```

If you want to wrap it into an error handler, select the code and press *Ctrl + J* to open the snippet selector. Type `try` to quickly find the try…catch handler, and press *Enter*. It replaces the code inside a `try{}catch{}` handler:

- Press *Tab* for code completion. For example, write `Get-Process` then write `for`. This turns the color of `For` and next press *Tab* and it inserts the code into the line.

```
Get-Process | ForEach-Object { $_. }
```

- When you want to write a function, you can start with the syntax you are after. For example, type the following line:

```
Test-Function [-Name] <string> [[-ID] <int>] -Force
```

- Next, select the line, right-click, and choose **Create Function** from **Syntax**. This creates the following function snippet for you:

```
function Test-Function
{
    [CmdletBinding()]
param
    (
        [Parameter(Position=0, Mandatory=$true)]
        [string]
        $Name,

        [Parameter(Position=1, Mandatory=$false)]
        [int]
        $ID,

        [Parameter(Mandatory=$false)]
        [switch]
        $Force
    )

    # TODO: place your function code here
    # this code gets executed when the function is called
    # and all parameters have been processed
}
```

Pretty cool, right?

- Press *Ctrl + Q* multiple times until the code you are after is selected. The status bar shows what you are selecting. Once you have selected something with *Ctrl + Q*, you can type a delimiter such as a brace or quote to enclose it. While writing the code, it actually shows you the best practices. For example, if you use double quotes for a simple string, it suggests you to change it to single quotes. So you can be sure to adhere to best practices.

A detailed list of the features is available at `http://www.powertheshell.com/isesteroids2/feature-overview/`.

All of the features are pretty useful and worth the try. I am pretty impressed with this editor and fully recommend it to users.

The only downside that I see for now is that sometimes it is bit sluggish, especially while saving or opening the scripts. But I am pretty sure with time these will be taken care of. For now, I am in love with this editor and working on it.

I wholly recommend this editor, especially if you are a regular and serious scripter. You can go ahead and get the editor from `http://www.powertheshell.com/isesteroids/`.

Summary

In this chapter, we discussed the general best practices for PowerShell. We also discussed two sample scripts. The scripts that I used were not the final ones; they contain some portions that do not adhere to the best practices. I discussed those points and mentioned them here. It is intentional as I want you to work on it and give suggestions so that we can rectify this script. It is a task and challenge for you.

In the entire book, I have not given any tasks for practice. These two scripts are the practice scripts for you. Visit my blog and comment there so that we can take it forward. These scripts might not be useful to you in their current state, but they were provided as a starting point to help sharpen your skills.

I plan to host two more scripts in the blog. The first one is `Set-Security`, which will set the security of the entire vSphere environment as per VMware best practices (it will be the logical next step of `Get-Security`). The next one will be for elaborate reporting for a vSPhere and vCloud Air environment in a single location. In this way, we will be able to practice further and sharpen our skills. Also, a collaborative environment gives way to more ideas and I welcome all ideas from my readers. I will be able to directly communicate with you all in this way.

The aim of this book was to give you enough knowledge on PowerShell and PowerCLI so that you can build on that knowledge to become as master of the subject. Hope fully I was successful in doing so. You can contact me at `debnathsajal@gmail.com` or visit my blog `http://vlearner.blogspot.com/`.

Index

Symbols

L

logical operators 9

M

machines
  managing 304
MoRef (Managed Object Reference) 249

N

Netflow
  configuring 120, 121
  URL 120
Netflow, disabling
  URL 121
network adapters
  cmdlets, defining 190
Network Addressing Authority (NAA) 129
networking
  managing, for ESXi 108, 109
network profiles
  managing 314-316
New-Datastore cmdlet
  URL 134
New-VM cmdlet
  URL 185
NFS storage
  configuring 135, 136
NIC Teaming 110

O

Object categories
  data object types 251
  enumerated data types 251
  fault type 251
  managed object types 251
Onyx
  about 265
  reference 265
  URL 265
  used, for generating PowerCLI
    code 265-271
options, CmdletBinding()
  defining 49

options, parameter attributes
  Alias 54
  Mandatory argument 51
  Position argument 51
  ValueFromPipeline 52
OS customization specifications
  managing 196-198

P

Package Control
  URL 390
parameter attributes
  specifying 51-54
  URL 57
parameters, capacity check report
  defining 387
parameters, PowerShell function
  dynamic 50
  static 50
parameters, vRA
  Accept 298
  Content-Type 298
parameter validation attributes
  AllowNull / AllowEmptyString 55
  using 55-57
  ValidateCount 56
  ValidateLength 56
  ValidatePattern 57
permissible types, ViewType parameter
  defining 240, 241
Pester
  about 35
  URL 36
  used, for testing scripts 34-42
port blocking
  cmdlets, defining 123
port group management
  cmdlets 114
port groups
  managing 113-115
ports
  cmdlets, defining 121
  port blocking, configuring 123
  security policy, configuring 123
  teaming policy, configuring 124

[PACKT] enterprise ✕
PUBLISHING   professional expertise distilled

Thank you for buying
Mastering PowerCLI

About Packt Publishing

Packt, pronounced 'packed', published its first book, *Mastering phpMyAdmin for Effective MySQL Management*, in April 2004, and subsequently continued to specialize in publishing highly focused books on specific technologies and solutions.

Our books and publications share the experiences of your fellow IT professionals in adapting and customizing today's systems, applications, and frameworks. Our solution-based books give you the knowledge and power to customize the software and technologies you're using to get the job done. Packt books are more specific and less general than the IT books you have seen in the past. Our unique business model allows us to bring you more focused information, giving you more of what you need to know, and less of what you don't.

Packt is a modern yet unique publishing company that focuses on producing quality, cutting-edge books for communities of developers, administrators, and newbies alike. For more information, please visit our website at www.packtpub.com.

About Packt Enterprise

In 2010, Packt launched two new brands, Packt Enterprise and Packt Open Source, in order to continue its focus on specialization. This book is part of the Packt Enterprise brand, home to books published on enterprise software – software created by major vendors, including (but not limited to) IBM, Microsoft, and Oracle, often for use in other corporations. Its titles will offer information relevant to a range of users of this software, including administrators, developers, architects, and end users.

Writing for Packt

We welcome all inquiries from people who are interested in authoring. Book proposals should be sent to author@packtpub.com. If your book idea is still at an early stage and you would like to discuss it first before writing a formal book proposal, then please contact us; one of our commissioning editors will get in touch with you.

We're not just looking for published authors; if you have strong technical skills but no writing experience, our experienced editors can help you develop a writing career, or simply get some additional reward for your expertise.

[PACKT] enterprise

PUBLISHING

professional expertise distilled

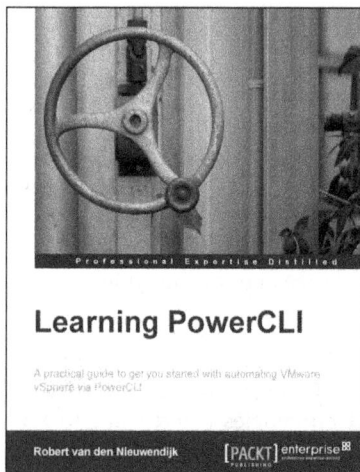

Learning PowerCLI

ISBN: 978-1-78217-016-7   Paperback: 374 pages

A practical guide to get you started with automating VMware vSphere via PowerCLI

1. Automate your VMware vSphere environment including hosts, clusters, storage, and vCenter Server virtual machines and networks.

2. Create good-looking, clean reports in no time, increasing your efficiency.

3. Get to grips with PowerCLI to automate routine tasks using practical examples.

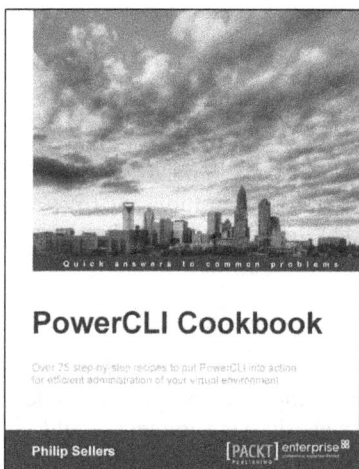

PowerCLI Cookbook

ISBN: 978-1-78439-372-4   Paperback: 274 pages

Over 75 step-by-step recipes to put PowerCLI into action for efficient administration of your virtual environment

1. Solve complex problems in vSphere by creating custom PowerCLI routines that can be accessed with simple native commands.

2. Explore specific use cases for PowerCLI that illustrate methods that can apply to other situations and problems encountered in vSphere.

3. Step-by-step instructions to create scripts to automate repetitive tasks in vSphere using predefined PowerCLI commands.

Please check **www.PacktPub.com** for information on our titles

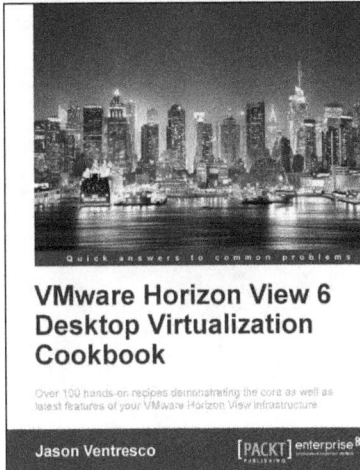

VMware Horizon View 6 Desktop Virtualization Cookbook

ISBN: 978-1-78217-164-5   Paperback: 332 pages

Over 100 hands-on recipes demonstrating the core as well as latest features of your VMware Horizon View infrastructure

1. Gain a detailed insight into the configuration and administration of core features of VMware Horizon View.

2. Learn how to deploy the newest features of the VMware Horizon View 6.0 such as Cloud Pod Architecture, VSAN integration, and more.

3. Benefit from practical examples that provide a greater level of detail than the VMware Horizon View documentation.

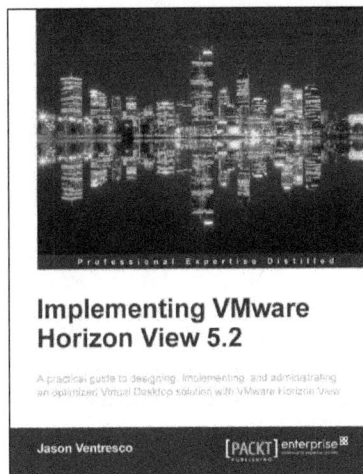

VMware Horizon View 6 Desktop Virtualization Cookbook

Over 100 hands-on recipes demonstrating the core as well as latest features of your VMware Horizon View infrastructure

Jason Ventresco   [PACKT] enterprise ⌗

Implementing VMware Horizon View 5.2

ISBN: 978-1-84968-796-6   Paperback: 390 pages

A practical guide to designing, implementing, and administrating an optimized Virtual Desktop solution with VMware Horizon View

1. Detailed description of the deployment and administration of the VMware Horizon View suite.

2. Learn how to determine the resources your virtual desktops will require.

3. Design your desktop solution to avoid potential problems, and ensure minimal loss of time in the later stages.

Implementing VMware Horizon View 5.2

A practical guide to designing, implementing, and administrating an optimized Virtual Desktop solution with VMware Horizon View

Jason Ventresco   [PACKT] enterprise ⌗

Please check **www.PacktPub.com** for information on our titles